TO ELIZABETH

Bolingbroke

Bolingbroke in his parliamentary robes
by Godfrey Kneller

BOLINGBROKE

H. T. Dickinson

Constable   London

First published in 1970 by
Constable & Company Ltd.
10 Orange Street, London WC2
Copyright © 1970 by H. T. Dickinson

ISBN 0 09 455690 3

Printed in Great Britain by
The Anchor Press Ltd, and bound
by Wm. Brendon & Son Ltd, both of Tiptree, Essex

Contents

Illustrations

Preface

Henry St John, Viscount Bolingbroke, engendered so much affection and hostility in his own lifetime that he has always attracted the kind of biographer who is stimulated by the problems posed by a brilliant but wayward genius. However, he was involved in so many major controversies, and he was in contact with such important ideas and so many prominent historical characters, that his career presents a challenge to every historian of the period. He played many roles – Secretary at War during Marlborough's great victories, Secretary of State during the making of the Treaty of Utrecht, the would-be leader of the Tory party during the Succession crisis of 1714–15, the Pretender's Secretary of State during the 1715 rebellion, and the greatest opponent of Sir Robert Walpole. He was involved in most of the ideological battles of the day – in the bitter conflict between the landed and the moneyed interests, in the opposition to the political system developed by the Whig oligarchy, in the rise of Deism and the challenge to orthodox Christianity, and in the development of the Enlightenment. His career and his ideas impinged on the lives of many of the great men of his day – on Marlborough, Robert Harley, Robert Walpole, Jonathan Swift, Alexander Pope and Voltaire. Nevertheless, despite the inherent attractions of his character and personality, there has been no full-scale biography of him, claiming to use all the available material, since the two-volume work by Walter Sichel in 1901–2.

Sichel was not a professional historian and his study is heavily biased in Bolingbroke's favour, but there are more positive reasons for attempting a new full-scale biography of Bolingbroke than the weaknesses which have always been apparent in this particular work. In the first place, a vast amount of new evidence has come to light over the last seventy years. Collections of Bolingbroke letters, never before used by any biographer, have been unearthed in record offices, libraries and private homes throughout Britain and in libraries in France and the U.S.A. Major manuscript collections, such as the Stowe MSS. in the Huntington Library, the Harley papers in Loan 29 in the British Museum, the Marlborough papers at Blenheim Palace, and the diplomatic papers in the national archives of France, Hanover, Prussia and the Netherlands, have all significantly altered our understanding of the political world in which Bolingbroke operated for fifty years. It is not merely a question of new evidence, however voluminous this has proved to be. Our concept of eighteenth-century politics has been revolutionised since the appearance of Sichel's biography. Sir Lewis Namier and his disciples changed our views of mid-eighteenth-century politics and, more recently, Geoffrey Holmes and Professor J. H. Plumb have led the way in performing the same task, though with different results, on the period before 1715. To this research into political history we need to add the researches of economic historians, such as H. J. Habakkuk, G. E. Mingay and P. G. M. Dickson, whose work has deepened our appreciation of the realities underpinning the political conflicts of the first half of the eighteenth century. Finally, in the last few years there has been a rapidly developing interest in the study of the political ideology of this period, in the political ideas, arguments and assumptions of the men engaged in the struggles of Whig and Tory, Court and Country. Much of this interest has concentrated on the works of Bolingbroke and there have been important recent contributions to this debate by Jeffrey Hart, Sydney Wayne Jackman, Kurt Kluxen, Isaac Kramnick, Harvey C. Mansfield, George Nadel, J. G. A. Pocock and Caroline Robbins.

This new biography of Bolingbroke is an attempt both to utilise all this new manuscript and printed source material and to integrate all the recent research into political history, economic history and the history of ideas in order to understand the background to Bolingbroke's career. When this is done, it is easier to understand the twists and turns in Bolingbroke's career and to reconcile some of the apparent inconsistencies in his conduct and his character. Since this work attempts to grapple with the challenging aspects of Bolingbroke's personality and career, to analyse his behaviour and his writings, and to assess his contribution to several major debates and controversies, it does not make claims to be a straight narrative biography. Bolingbroke's whole life is examined and the biographical details of his private life, for example, are not ignored, but this study is an attempt to answer questions and to explain a remarkable career rather than an account of what Bolingbroke did from his birth to his death. Thus, while the chronological narrative is retained throughout much of this book, there are sections – for example, chapters 11 and 15 and parts of chapters

1, 9, 10 and 14 – which concentrate on digesting the evidence rather than recounting the facts.

In a work of this nature, which has required years of research, I have naturally incurred many debts which I cannot hope to repay, but which I must acknowledge here. My work has been greatly assisted by the kindness of my professors and colleagues in the History Departments at Newcastle and Edinburgh Universities and by research and travel grants from both these universities. In this general academic category my greatest debt is owed to the late Professor W. L. Burn, without whose support I would never have embarked on an academic career. For nine years he assisted me at every turn. Only those who knew him can fully appreciate how kind and helpful he was to me. During the last two years of this period, 1964–66, I was privileged to hold an Earl Grey Fellowship at the University of Newcastle. While I held this position I did much of the research for my Ph.D. thesis and ultimately for this book.

While I was gathering material for this book, I was greatly assisted by numerous librarians, archivists and private owners, who were unfailingly helpful. Since several hundred people answered my queries and nearly one hundred allowed me to consult their manuscript collections or sent me microfilm, xerox or photo-copies, it is impossible to thank them all individually. I am grateful to them all, but I would like to acknowledge the help of the owners and custodians of those collections which have made this particular book possible and which are listed in the bibliography. Jean Preston at the Huntington Library, Jean McNiece of the New York Public Library, Edwin Welch of Churchill College Library, and the librarians and archivists at the British Museum, the Public Record Office, the Scottish Record Office, the Quai d'Orsay, Berkshire Record Office, the Bodleian Library, the Pierpont Morgan Library, Harvard College Library and Yale University Library have been particularly helpful and have allowed me to quote from the manuscript collections in their care. Several private owners have also allowed me to consult and quote from their manuscript collections. In this respect I wish to acknowledge my obligations to the Duke of Marlborough, the Duke of Portland, the Marquess of Downshire, Earl Bathurst, the Earl of Egremont, Mrs O. R. Bagot and the late Admiral Sir Reginald Plunkett-Ernle-Erle-Drax. In searching for suitable illustrations I have been assisted by Frank T. Smallwood, D. A. Hartley Russell, the Rev. Michael O. West, Mrs J. Prescott, D. Murray John, D. Beatrice Harris, Lucien Barbereau of Orleans, and the staff of the National Portrait Gallery, the Scottish

National Portrait Gallery, the Radio Times Hulton Picture Library and the Departments of Maps and of Prints and Drawings in the British Museum. I would also like to thank the editor of the *Journal of British Studies* for allowing me to incorporate in chapter 1 parts of my article published in that journal in May 1968.

For permission to quote from contemporary letters printed in modern works I would like to thank the following publishers: The Clarendon Press, the publishers of Swift's *Journal to Stella* (ed. Harold Williams), Richard Steele's *The Englishman* (ed. Rae Blanchard), *The Correspondence of Alexander Pope* (ed. George Sherburn) and *The Complete Letters of Lady Mary Wortley Montagu* (ed. Robert Halsband); Eyre and Spottiswoode, the publishers of *The Letters of Philip Dormer Stanhope, Fourth Earl of Chesterfield* (ed. Bonamy Dobrée) and *Some Materials Towards Memoirs of the Reign of King George II, by John, Lord Hervey* (ed. Romney Sedgwick); George Bell and Sons, the publishers of *The Correspondence of Jonathan Swift* (ed. F. Elrington Ball); Basil Blackwell, the publishers of *The Prose Works of Jonathan Swift* (ed. Herbert Davis); Frank Cass, the publishers of the 1967 edition of *The Works of Lord Bolingbroke*; Centaur Press, the publishers of the 1964 edition of *Anecdotes, Observations and Characters of Books and Men collected from the conversation of Mr Pope and other eminent persons of his time by the Reverend Joseph Spence* (ed. S. W. Singer); George G. Harrap, the publishers of W. S. Churchill, *Marlborough: His Life and Times*; and Yale University Press, the publishers of *The Correspondence of Horace Walpole* (ed. W. S. Lewis).

During my work on the political background to this book, I have enjoyed and profited from the advice of several fellow-researchers in the field. Dr W. A. Speck supervised my research for my Ph.D., guided me in the paths of scholarship and set me an example in rigorous and analytical historical research. Geoffrey Holmes gave me the benefit of his unrivalled knowledge of late Stuart politics, lent me valuable material and microfilms, and frequently advised me on the most complex historical problems. I have also learned a great deal from discussions with my colleague, John M. Simpson, who also read several of the chapters and made very helpful comments on them. On Bolingbroke's career, particularly on the personal details of his early life and his relations with his father, I have benefited enormously from the constant advice, stretching over several years, of Frank T. Smallwood, who has devoted a lifetime of research to the St John family. George H. Nadel, Giles Barber and Dennis Fletcher also gave me valuable advice on Bolingbroke, while Professor J. R. Jones, Michele

Levenbook, Richard Wood and Angus McInnes have all helped me on various general points. Frances Dow read an early draft of the whole book with the greatest care and the closest attention. Her valuable comments prevented me from being obscure and ambiguous on many points. The faults which remain are my own responsibility and not that of any of those who have assisted me. My final, much-amended draft was typed with speed and accuracy by Anna Campbell and Margaret Walgate.

Last, but by no means least, are the heavy personal debts I owe to my wife and my parents for their encouragement over many years. My wife has assisted me at every stage in the production of this study. She has discussed with me the evidence, the historical problems, the organisation and the presentation. She has influenced every aspect of this work and the final product bears her imprint as well as mine. This book is dedicated to her with love and gratitude.

HARRY DICKINSON
Edinburgh University, December 1969

CHAPTER I

Henry St John and the Tory Party

THE enigmatic Henry St John, later Viscount Bolingbroke, dazzled, provoked and exasperated his contemporaries. The inconsistencies in his character and the twists and turns in his career have also dazzled his biographers[1] to such an extent that they, in their turn, have provoked and exasperated many of their readers. It is not only that they have misunderstood Henry St John and his career, but they have succeeded in passing on factual errors from one to another.[2] There is, for example, surprisingly little known about Henry St John's early life, but this has not prevented these biographers from making quite definite, and frequently erroneous, statements about his childhood and education.

What can be tentatively pieced together, however,[3] suggests that St John had an unusual background and education, a fact which might go far to explain his lack of fixed principles and the suspicion with which he was regarded by many people. In his early years he clearly lacked a stable, integrated family background and was subjected to conflicting pressures. The St John family had been divided by the Civil War, though two of the junior branches had reunited on the marriage of his paternal grandparents. Sir Walter St John of Lydiard Tregoze, Wiltshire, of the Cavalier branch, married Johanna St John of Bletsoe, daughter of Oliver Cromwell's Lord Chief Justice. The marriage alliance may have helped Sir Walter to change his political allegiance, but it did not end the religious disagreements. Sir Walter was always a conforming member of the Church of England and endowed the grammar school at Battersea, which still bears his name. He was prepared to accept Charles II's return, in 1660, though he did not become a staunch royalist. Lady Johanna apparently retained her Puritan sympathies and was reputed to be a patroness of the Dissenting ministers, Daniel Burgess and Dr Thomas Manton. Little is known of their son, Henry St John senior, who appears to have been a typical Restoration rake, at least in his earlier years. He killed Sir William Estcourt in a tavern brawl and was sentenced to death, but managed to secure

Charles II's pardon by means of a large bribe. He never managed to get on amicable terms with his eldest son and they showed neither love nor respect for each other. This son, Henry St John the younger, had the further misfortune to lose his mother, Mary Rich, a daughter of the third Earl of Warwick, shortly after his birth.[4] Being deprived of a mother, having an unreliable father, and being born into a family with divided religious, moral and political principles, may explain the fundamental instability which St John exhibited throughout his career.

Henry St John was born on 16 September 1678, and not on 1 October as nearly all his biographers have asserted. It also seems likely that he was born at Lydiard Tregoze, the family seat in Wiltshire, where his mother was buried on 2 October, though he was later christened at Battersea, the home of his paternal grandparents.[5] He probably remained in their house at Battersea until his father remarried in 1687. Old Sir Walter St John took immense pride in the ancient lineage of the St John family which, he believed, could trace its ancestry back to the Conquest. He longed to see the revival of the family fortunes and he pinned his hopes on young Henry, who for several years was his only grandson. Henry, in fact, was always a sickly child and two serious illnesses caused his grandfather considerable alarm.[6] His grandmother is always reckoned to have taken a great interest in his education and for this purpose to have employed the two Dissenting ministers, Daniel Burgess and Thomas Manton. Certainly, in later years Bolingbroke claimed that he had been compelled to spend many weary hours studying the latter's works. In a letter to Swift, he wrote: 'I resolve . . . to make my letter at least as long as one of your sermons; and, if you do not mend, my next shall be as long as one of Dr Manton's, who taught my youth to yawn, and prepared me to be a High-Churchman, that I might never hear him read, nor read him more.'[7] However, Dr Manton had died in 1677, a year before St John's birth, and could not have been his tutor, but his sermons might well have been prescribed reading in the St John household. Nor is it certain that Burgess was ever employed to teach young Henry, though, as a Wiltshire man, he may have been connected with the St John family.[8] It has also been a fairly common practice to assert that Henry St John was educated at Eton and Christ Church, Oxford. There is precious little evidence to support either claim. His name does not appear on any list or register at Eton. The evidence of Horace Walpole, that St John and Robert Walpole 'had set out rivals at Eton',[9] is unreliable. Not only was Horace Walpole prejudiced and writing much later than the event, but Robert Walpole was two years older than Henry

St John, and unlikely to have been his schoolboy rival. It has sometimes been claimed that St John himself acknowledged that he had been educated at Eton. In 1717 he wrote to his father:

> Your sending the eldest of your two sons to Eaton makes me hope that his health is mended. It is late for him to go thither unless he has been instructed according to the method of that school. I remember the pain it cost me to fall into that method, and to overtake those in points of form, who were behind me in the knowledge of the Latin tongue.[10]

This, however, refers to the Eton 'method' of teaching Latin, which differed from that used at Winchester. Other schools normally adopted one or other of these approaches and St John had evidently experienced the difficulty of transferring from one method to the other.

There is no evidence whatsoever that St John went to Christ Church, Oxford. Not only is he not listed on any register there, but the only evidence that has been cited is a single remark, in a letter to the Duke of Shrewsbury, on 3 December 1713, that 'as to Dr Freind, I have known him long, and cannot be without some partiality for him, since he was of Christ Church'.[11] This can be explained by the fact that in August 1702 St John had had an honorary degree conferred on him at Christ Church, no doubt because of his services to the Tory party. Rather than such a High Church education at Eton and Oxford, it is possible that St John went instead to a Dissenting Academy. His grandmother, Lady Johanna, may well have employed a Dissenting tutor, if not Burgess. Moreover, when St John's father remarried in 1687 he may have reassumed his parental responsibilities and taken his son away from Battersea to his house in Berkeley Street, in the west end of London. St John certainly became devoted in later life to his half-sister, Henrietta, and, it is interesting to note, his stepmother, Angelica Magdalena Wharton, née Pellissary, came from a French-Swiss Huguenot family.[12] It is possible that he went to Eton for a very short period, just before his father's remarriage, but was then sent to a Dissenting Academy at the desire of his stepmother, who retained her strong links with the Huguenots in London. On the authority of the manuscript account in Dr Williams's Library, Joshua Toulmin listed St John as one of the pupils at Sheriffhales Academy, though unfortunately the accuracy of this manuscript is open to question.[13] On his Grand Tour, St John did visit Geneva, where many of the products of Sheriffhales completed their studies, and he always showed an interest in languages, civil law and science, which he was more likely to have imbibed

at Sheriffhales than at Eton. It has also been suggested that when Lord
Wharton opposed the Schism Bill in 1714, saying that 'he could not but
wonder, that persons who had been educated in dissenting academies,
whom he could point at, and whose tutors he could name, should appear
the most forward in suppressing them',[14] one of those he had in mind was
Henry St John, who had inspired this bill.[15] Though the evidence is not
conclusive, there are grounds for believing that Henry St John, who in
1714 tried to destroy Dissenting Academies by the Schism Act, was, in
fact, educated at one of them.

The evidence for St John's early life does not become substantial until
1698, when he toured Europe, in the course of which he visited France,
Switzerland and Italy before 1700. During this tour he showed those
inconsistencies of character and principle which were probably the result
of his family and educational upbringing. He made friends with young
Whigs such as James Stanhope and Edward Hopkins,[16] yet corresponded
with the experienced, moderate Tory, Sir William Trumbull, who had
once been Secretary of State to William III.[17] Though he enjoyed the
pleasures of a young rake, his letters show that he spent some time studying
and that he took a great interest in politics and religion. He expressed his
dislike of the absolutism of Louis XIV's government and considered that
only the tyranny of the clergy was worse.[18] Trumbull encouraged him to
believe that liberty 'is the salt of life and gives a taste to everything'. In a
passage which presaged St John's own writings on the spirit of patriotism
nearly forty years later, he wrote to his young protégé: 'There appears
indeed amongst us [in England] a strong disposition to liberty, but neither
honesty nor virtue enough to support it.'[19] St John himself noted the
threatening situation in Europe, where the problem of the Spanish
succession aroused considerable speculation and where it was strongly
believed that the French were preparing for war.[20] On his return to
England he succeeded his father as one of the members for the family
parliamentary seat at Wootton Bassett, Wiltshire, for which he was elected
in February 1701. His father, with whom he disagreed in politics, had
only sat in the Commons for the previous, very short parliament. He may
have offered the seat to his son, in return for his consent to marry Frances
Winchcombe, an heiress with estates in Berkshire.[21]

In the early years of his public career Henry St John gave evidence of
those qualities and defects of character and ability which were to surround
his name with controversy, both during his lifetime and ever since. More
than his talents or his achievements, it was St John's personality which

impressed contemporaries and his character which has intrigued historians. A handsome man, with graceful manners and a ready wit, St John also had the quickness of perception, the vividness of imagination, and the clarity and force of expression to captivate some of the finest minds and most discerning critics of his age. Jonathan Swift, who appreciated the skill and moderation of Robert Harley, and who was alarmed at some of St John's qualities, was still fascinated by the latter. In 1712 he wrote:

> The Secretary [of State] is much the greatest Commoner in England, and turns the whole Parliament, who can do nothing without him, and if he lives and has his health, will I believe be one day at the Head of Affairs. I have told him sometimes, that if I were a dozen years younger, I would cultivate his Favour, and trust my Fortune with his.[22]

These sentiments were echoed, many years later, by other friends of St John. Alexander Pope, Voltaire and Chesterfield were all seduced, at least for a time, by the force and charms of his personality. Even St John's severest critics, anxious to reveal all his faults, could not help acknowledging some of his personal qualities, though they labelled them superficial and specious. Richard Steele wrote of him:

> They who know him well, will tell you, that he is in himself a Person of as great Consequence as a man can be, who has neither Wisdom nor Virtue . . . but in the room of them he has Wit and Eloquence, a Graceful Person, Good Nature, and Good Breeding. His Conceptions are very superficial; but he expresses those Conceptions with much Grace and Address. Tho' he has not Judgment to chuse the right part, he can either Speak, Write, or Debate upon what he does pursue, or take into his Thoughts, with a most specious Force and Energy. Thus, tho' it was the most painful Thing imaginable to a wise Man to hear him Harangue, there was little Help against him, for he charmed all who had not deep Discerning.[23]

Later writers, while not accepting all of Steele's strictures, have gained a similar impression of the striking contrast between St John's virtues and his vices. Indeed, St John himself seems to have been aware of his own psychological make-up. His professed models were Alcibiades and Petronius, while, even during his early career, he earned and accepted such nicknames as 'Man of Mercury' or 'Mercurialis', the 'Captain', and the 'Thracian';[24] suggesting a mixture of instability and vitality.

The aspect of St John's character that attracted most contemporary comment was his flagrant debauchery. We need not be deterred by Walter

Sichel's comment that there is little evidence for his life of pleasure or that he was no more of a libertine than most of his contemporaries.[25] Some of the stories about St John were the figments of vivid imaginations, including that of Voltaire,[26] but St John justifies some of the legends himself. To his fellow-rakes, Thomas Coke and Thomas Erle, he wrote:

> ... as to whores, dear friend, I am very unable to help thee. I have heard of a certain housemaid that is very handsome: if she can be got ready against your arrival, she shall serve for your first meal.

> I got to Town last night early, writ my Letters, lay with my Mistress, and after nine hours continued sleep, find myself in perfect health, so that I discover with great joy in your humble servant a Constitution fit for one that is Secretary to so many Rakes.[27]

St John appeared to take a positive delight in displaying that he could live a life of pleasure, while also excelling in public affairs. He wished to excel in every sphere, even in taking his liquor, and craved admiration for every facet of his character and ability. This often led to accusations of affectation, in the most obvious form. Gallas, the Austrian envoy, who was a hostile critic, reported of St John:

> He is given to the bottle and debauchery to the point of almost making a virtue out of his open affectation that public affairs are a bagatelle to him, and that his capacity is on so high a level that he has no need to give up his pleasures in the slightest degree for any cause.[28]

Even Swift, a friendly witness, admitted: 'His only fault is talking to his friends in way of complaint of too great a load of business, which looks a little like affectation; and he endeavours too much to mix the fine gentleman, and man of pleasure with the man of business.'[29] St John never abandoned his image of a man of pleasure, even when he had abandoned the practice. In 1735 he advised Charles Wyndham on how to treat a Parisian actress who had attracted him:

> With all ladys, with those particularly, good Engineers proceed by assaults, not sappes. If you have enjoyed [her], stick to her close, work yourself hard, she will like you the more and you will like her the less. Whilst I loved much, I never loved long, but was inconstant to them all for the sake of all.[30]

A frequent charge levelled against St John is that his immorality extended to a readiness to betray his friends, to serve his own ambition and passion.

There is, of course, some justification for this view. Particularly repre-
hensible was his treatment of his first wife, Frances Winchcombe. Though
it was a marriage of convenience, his wife was attractive in her person and
her character, and she remained faithful and devoted to him, even in his
worst days in 1715. St John, however, showed her little, if any, consideration. His conduct so offended the sensibilities of Queen Anne that, too
late, St John tried to assume a devotion to his wife, so as 'to answer
objections in the world, and that somebody may with a better grace
confide in him'.[31] St John has also been accused of similar baseness in the
manner in which he repaid the affection of Marlborough, Robert Harley
and Alexander Pope. In these instances, as this study will show, there can
be some defence. St John was never the first to seek to break with his
former friends. Moreover, if these examples are to be cited to his dis-
advantage, it is only fair to look at the other side of the coin. St John had
attractive qualities, which made him a stimulating and convivial com-
panion. Among his circle of rakes, and perhaps rogues, were many whom
he genuinely liked. These included Thomas Coke, Thomas Erle, James
Brydges and Arthur Moore. He even managed to remain on friendly,
first-name terms with James Stanhope, the Whig soldier and statesman,
despite their differences in politics. It should also be remembered to his
credit that he formed lifelong attachments to Sir William Wyndham,
Lord Bathurst and Jonathan Swift; that for many years he was on excellent
terms with scholars such as Brook Taylor, the mathematician, and
politicians such as Lord Chesterfield and George Lyttelton; and that he
showed considerable devotion to his second wife. Clearly, he could hold
friends as well as lose them.

More striking was St John's early capacity for hero-worship. Though he
himself was anxious to excel in all things, he was frank and generous
enough to recognise talent in others. His first hero and model was Sir
William Trumbull, the former Tory Secretary of State. In 1698 he declared to him:

> Having chose you for my pattern, and being resolved to draw as good a copy
> as I can after so excellent an original, I apply myself to that study in which you
> became so perfect a master; and tho' I despair of arriving to the same pitch,
> I am resolv'd it shall be my misfortune and not my fault.[32]

By 1702 he was addressing Trumbull as 'Dear Patron, Master and Friend',
and he continued to write to him during his years in parliament.[33]
When he was Secretary at War, from 1704 to 1708, St John had ample

opportunity to witness the splendid talents of the Duke of Marlborough
and he was ever ready to applaud them. This was so, even after his resignation. In 1709, after he had become convinced of the damaging effects of
the War of the Spanish Succession, he could admit: 'I should not be so
merry upon so grave a Subject had I not a faith, which comes near to
Superstition, in my Lord Duke.'[34] Many years later he wrote: 'I take with
pleasure this opportunity of doing justice to that great man, whose faults
I knew, whose virtues I admired; and whose memory, as the greatest
general, and as the greatest minister, that our country or perhaps any other
has produced, I honour.'[35] The third great influence on the young
politician was Robert Harley, despite their eventual rivalry. In the early
years of Anne's reign St John was under the spell of Harley's superior
political gifts, and his letters to him concluded with such sentiments as:
'Adieu, make haste to town where the public as well as your friends
wants you. No man is more entirely, dear Master, yours, than H.'[36]
It is interesting to note that in later life St John tended to reverse these roles
and expected others to hero-worship him. Though he was probably too
patronising, especially towards Alexander Pope, there was an attractive
side to this aspect of his character. He took a great interest in the
proper education of the young, particularly the sons of his political
friends.

    As with his role of a man of business and of pleasure, so in the frequent
declarations of his love of learning and of study, St John has been accused
of striking a flattering pose. Contemporaries were suspicious of the
ambitious politician who, bitterly frustrated by his failure to obtain a seat
at the 1708 general election, could still declare: 'If I continue in the
country, the sports of the field and the pleasures of my study will take up
all my thoughts, and serve to amuse me as long as I live.'[37] It is certainly
true that in his later career Bolingbroke pursued his various studies most
assiduously, when he was debarred from an active political career. Yet it
must also be accepted that St John was genuinely attracted by learning and
literary pursuits throughout his life. His early letters to Sir William
Trumbull contain frequent references to his study of civil law and the
Latin classics. Either from his stepmother or during his European tour, he
acquired such a mastery of French that, in the peace negotiations leading
to the Treaty of Utrecht, he surprised and impressed Torcy and the French
Court. Yet at that time he had not been abroad for ten years; which
argues either a phenomenal memory or continued study. As a young man
he contributed a poem to the preface of Dryden's translation of the works

of Virgil. This was followed by other attempts at verse: *Almahide – an ode, To Miss Clara A———s*, and the prologues to George Granville's play, *Heroick Love*, and Charles Boyle's revision of *The General*.[38] Though these are poor efforts, far better forgotten, St John never abandoned his taste for writing. Even during his strenuous labours as a minister, he could contemplate the needs and attractions of scholarship. In February 1707, while engaged in the complicated preparations for a new campaign in Flanders and Spain, and busy in the Commons, he could still write to his friend, General Erle, who was on service in Spain: 'Remember to keep any material papers that fall into your hands. I collect in every part, as well as I can, those things which may hereafter be useful in writing the history of this memorable war, of which perhaps there is no part so much hitherto in the dark as Spain.'[39] In 1710 St John took up his pen to write *A Letter to the Examiner*, which was virtually that newspaper's manifesto, and he also appears to have helped Swift with his great pamphlet, *The Conduct of the Allies*.[40] He discovered a genuine talent for political journalism, an ability which was to blossom forth in his contributions to *The Craftsman* from 1727 to 1736. Throughout his life St John was at the centre of a literary coterie and he delighted in the company of Swift, Pope, Gay, Voltaire and others. When he formed the Brothers' Club, in 1711, he wrote to Lord Orrery: 'We shall begin to meet in a small number, and that will be composed of some who have wit and learning to recommend them; . . . The improvement of friendship, and the encouragement of letters are to be the two great ends of our society.'[41] Though in all this there was a degree of affectation, a wish to excel, and a desire to be admired by men of talent, it remains possible to accept St John's later claim that 'this love and this desire [of study] I have felt all my life, and I am not quite a stranger to this industry and application . . . Reflection had often its turn, and the love of study and the desire of knowledge have never quite abandoned me.'[42]

Affectation is a harmless enough flaw, but in St John's case it seemed rooted in a condition of temperamental instability. In his early career he gave evidence of his lifelong conflict: a struggle between his mind and his temperament, a clash between his intellect and his passions. He had a cool, rational intelligence and a fierce, unbridled nature. While he always aspired to display the former, he was more often betrayed by the latter. Tense, sensitive, highly strung, he reacted violently to criticism and came near to panic in a crisis. He was resentful when he believed his talents and his political services were not sufficiently valued, and he could hardly bear criticism. In severe crises, as when Guiscard attempted to assassinate Robert Harley, or when Queen Anne died and the Whigs spoke of revenge against her late Tory ministers, he clearly lost his nerve. At times St John could recognise his emotional moods: 'I have no very great stock of philosophy, and am far from being a Stoic. Pain to me is pain, and pleasure pleasure.'[43] Yet, despite his restless ambition and the fluctuations of his moods, he could still claim, and probably believe: 'Whether it is owing to a constitution or to Philosophy I can't tell, but certain it is, that I can make myself easy in any sort of life.'[44] His attempts at philosophic indifference were numerous, but never carried conviction. There was always a sharp contrast, indeed a struggle, between what he hoped to feel and how he actually felt. Though he was often frank in confessing the flaws in his character and the errors of his conduct, he was also a compulsive defender of his actions, even when, the more he protested, the more he attracted attention and damaged his own case. He was a strange, paradoxical mixture of hypocrisy and candour.

As in his character, so in his political ability St John revealed a stark contrast between his transcendent gifts and grave defects. His talents evoked considerable admiration, even from a man of Swift's temperament: 'I think Mr St John the greatest young man I ever knew; wit, capacity, beauty, quickness of apprehension, good learning, and an excellent taste; the best orator in the house of commons, admirable conversation, good nature, and good manners, generous and a despiser of money.'[45] Of all his gifts, it was his oratory which commanded most attention. Though he attacked the superficiality of his arguments, Richard Steele admitted the force of their impact on the Commons. Lord Chesterfield, though more favourably disposed towards St John, came to a similar conclusion: 'I am old enough to have heard him speak in Parliament. And I remember that though prejudiced against him by party, I felt all the force and charm of his eloquence. Like Belial in Milton, "he made the worse appear the better cause".'[46] Unfortunately, no drafts of St John's speeches have survived. A few short speeches have been recorded, but there is no proof that these are verbatim reports. In 1714 he delivered some of the Queen's speeches to parliament, but these were not necessarily his own compositions. His impact was only considerable when he was putting forward his own ideas. After one debate a commentator reported 'that Mr St John outdid himself they say in speaking and my cousin's character of him is that when he speaks his own thoughts no one speaks better, and no one worse, others'.[47] Moreover, even if his speeches had survived, only

contemporary testimony could describe the impact which he was able to
make on his listeners.

More substantial qualities for the career of a minister of the crown were
St John's application to business and his capacity for high administrative
duties. Immediately upon his entry into parliament he made his mark.
Though this was due to some extent to his eloquence and extreme
partisanship, a cursory examination of the *Commons Journals* illustrates his
immense energy and the recognition he was gaining among his fellow-
backbenchers. He was appointed to committees dealing with a diversity of
topics: the piracies of Captain Kidd, the discharging of seamen without
pay, the establishing of the Cottonian Library, the dealing with the poor
of Halifax, the abuses of wire-drawers, the distilling of unwholesome
brandies in London, and the encouraging of Greenwich Hospital.[48]
As Secretary at War, and then as Secretary of State, his industry cannot be
questioned by anyone who has consulted his letters in manuscript and his
published correspondence. Beautifully composed, both in English and
French, they show a minister with remarkable skill in instructing his
agents and spies, in obeying the instructions of his superiors, in informing
his colleagues and subordinates, and in negotiating with both his allies
and his opponents. They support the praise lavished on St John's talents
from all quarters. Swift declared:

> He had been early bred to Business, was a most Artfull Negotiator, and
> perfectly understood foreign Affairs. But what I have often wondered at in a
> Man of his Temper, was his prodigious Application whenever he thought it
> necessary; For he would plod whole Days and Nights like the lowest Clerk
> in an Office.[49]

In 1711 the Duke of Marlborough, long acquainted with all the Tory
ministers, informed Robethon, the Hanoverian minister: 'Only the
Secretary of State, St John, applies himself to business and, being a man of
talent, will soon learn how to deal with it. You in Hanover would do well
to look after him. He speaks more boldly to the Queen in council than
anyone else.'[50] Even Count Gallas, the hostile Austrian envoy in London,
had to admit: 'To talk to Dartmouth is like talking to a brick-wall. St
John is just the opposite. He investigates everything, takes everything
in, and can always be relied upon to make a formal statement.'[51]

St John displayed not only a considerable capacity for office, but a
positive relish for political power, almost a prerequisite for the successful
politician. With some justice it can be claimed that political ambition

was the motivating force of his entire life. It does much to explain his first years in parliament, as a young man in a hurry, anxious to carve out a career for himself. Though there were other reasons, it was his ambition which was the principal cause of the final breach with Robert Harley and of the personal antagonism towards Robert Walpole. All his life, even after his disastrous flight to France in 1715, he remained fascinated by politics and yearned to return to power. His later claims that he had never been interested in power for its own sake fail to carry conviction. Thus, in 1738, he maintained, after forty years of seeking office:

> I have been fond of power, and as they were necessary to that, desirous but not fond of riches . . . [But] I have never valued power any further than I retained the liberty of applying it to those purposes to which my opinion and my sentiments led me to apply it. There has not been these thirty years a point of time where the greatest degree of power, and the highest elevation in honour and dignity in an administration whose conduct I disapproved, or despised, and could not hope to alter, would have tempted me.[52]

While far from blind to the real issues of principle at stake during his political career, St John did have a much firmer grasp of public opinion and a greater interest in wielding political power. He was always aware of the trend of political developments and ready to re-adjust his sail, though not to change his course completely, to suit the prevailing political wind.

These political talents were accompanied by corresponding defects. St John's chief failing was his inability to manage men, other than his personal friends and adherents. He lacked the tact and conciliatory skill of which Harley and Walpole were such masters. His imperious spirit could show the Tory squires game to hunt and his eloquence could sway the backbenchers, but he found it difficult to negotiate support by personal contact and shrewd bargaining. He could offer a bold lead, but he could not ensure a large following. He was probably too much of the patrician to stoop to mere management. Another fatal flaw was his inability to plan his long-term political strategy. He reacted to immediate or recent developments, but, unlike Harley or Walpole, he never appears to have planned a forward strategy or to have decided on his political priorities. His declarations of principle never carried real conviction. Only the pressure of adverse circumstances forced him to develop a coherent political philosophy, by which time it was too late to convince men of his sincerity. In addition, his personal integrity was always suspect, which made it difficult for him to secure unquestioning loyalty. In this respect his affectation was of less account than his financial dishonesty. Throughout his life he was dependent upon his father or his wives for much of his wealth. His father survived until 1742, and a man of St John's temperament and ambition resented this financial dependence. He was always trying to free himself from such irksome restrictions. At the outset of his career he confessed to Sir William Trumbull:

> You know me enough, I believe, to find that I have some spirit, and indeed I have too much to sit easily down under a strait fortune, and though in time if I live my estate will be very considerable, yet for a great while I must expect to be in low circumstances unless I raise 'em myself, and that is what, to you I make nothing a secret, I long to do.[53]

Even when in office, the normal remuneration did not satisfy his needs and he attempted to augment it. Marlborough secured him extra perquisites while he was Secretary at War, though Harley was more reluctant to advance him half a year's secret service money when St John was Secretary of State.[54]

Moreover, there is evidence that St John was quite willing to appropriate public money by less direct and open means. He was accused of promoting the Quebec expedition of 1711 in order to make money out of the contracts for supplying clothes for the troops,[55] and the accusation was probably well founded. Certainly, he was intimately connected with Arthur Moore and James Brydges, two experts in purloining government money. When, in April 1711, the Tories began pressing home their attacks on the financial record of the late Whig ministry, they were astonished to find St John coming to the defence of Brydges, who as Paymaster-General was one of their main targets.[56] St John, in fact, had a great deal to hide and could ill afford a close examination of Brydges, who, with the connivance of St John and Arthur Moore, had supplied inferior equipment to the troops in Spain.[57] In the summer of 1714 a similar, though more famous, instance occurred, when St John rushed to the defence of Arthur Moore, who was accused of defrauding the South Sea Company. It was confidently believed that the Lords would implicate St John and so he persuaded the Queen to prorogue parliament.[58] During his opposition to Walpole he unwisely accepted a pension from the French Court. Though this was not revealed to all, it did become a subject for rumours and damaging innuendoes. With such a record of debauchery and dishonesty, it was not surprising that St John could never gain the trust of his sovereign or of the independent backbenchers, however much his talents were admired.

It cannot be denied that St John was bold, determined to secure political power, and none too scrupulous in his personal or public behaviour. His ambition and the many real (and apparent) inconsistencies of his actions have led to frequent accusations, both during his life and ever since, that he was devoid of any political principles. His family background and education were probably more Whig than Tory. His father was certainly reckoned to be a Whig by contemporary observers,[59] and the elder Henry St John was given a peerage in 1716, at a time when his son was in exile and an attainted traitor. It was certainly claimed, at the time, that the younger Henry St John only joined the Tory party because he could force himself to the forefront more easily from its less talented ranks. Edward Hopkins, a Whig who had travelled with St John in Europe, was shocked when he allied himself with the Tories: 'The Chief of the Party opposite to the Court by buoying up his Vanity, of which he was very susceptible, had gained him to that side . . . his whole actions now in publick matters were diametrically opposite to the principles he profess'd with vehemence when abroad.'[60] Nevertheless, it is not true, as has so often been maintained, that in his early career he was merely a factious, partisan Tory, without any genuine principles. Nor were his later writings, in which he attacked party labels, merely political expedients or a complete rebuttal of all his active career in parliament. Whatever the mixture of motives St John had for becoming a Tory, it cannot be said that he failed to serve the party of his choice nor that he deserted all the principles for which it stood. His early career, from 1701 to 1715, shows that he never supported the Whig party nor Whig policies, though he did not always associate with the more extreme Tories. His later career, which he spent in opposition to the Whig supremacy, reveals him trying to break free from the concept of a Whig-Tory political dichotomy, because it burdened all the Tories with the guilt of Jacobitism and entrenched the Whigs, who were clearly loyal to the Hanoverian dynasty, in power. It was to his political advantage to purge the Tories of the taint of Jacobitism and to stress that they were opposed to corrupt ministers and not to the House of Hanover. However, while he was anxious not to revive the party rivalry between Whig and Tory, he had not abandoned all the principles of the old Tory party. He believed that, once he had cut the Tories free from Jacobitism, they would be able to uphold their other principles and vested interests more effectively. Thus, it can be shown that, throughout both his political careers, St John was not entirely devoid of genuine political principles, but was constantly attached to men who labelled themselves 'Tories'. An examination of the nature of the Tory party at the outset of St John's career can do much to explain his subsequent actions and to reveal a certain consistency in his behaviour. There was a vein of principle running through St John's whole career that indicates his permanent attachment to some of the ideals of the Tory squirearchy.

Henry St John's very first year in parliament, 1701–2, witnessed the strong revival of Toryism, which had suffered so traumatically at the Revolution of 1688. Before the Revolution the Tories had been distinguished from the Whigs by some sharp differences of principle. The Tories had stood for divine right, hereditary succession and non-resistance, in opposition to the Whig theory of monarchy, which was based on consent and which allowed the people to resist an arbitrary sovereign. While the Tories exalted the royal prerogative, the Whigs deferred to the ultimate sovereignty of the people. Most of the Tories connected their attitude to the crown with their loyalty to the privileges of the Church of England, whereas the Whigs stood for freedom of worship for Protestant Dissenters. The policies of James II confirmed the Whigs in their opinions, but they caused the Tories much heart-searching and ultimately divided them. They had to stand back and see the privileges of their cherished Anglican Church whittled away by the Catholic James II, or resist his policies and abandon their theory of divine right and their submission to the royal prerogative. The majority of Tories chose to defend their Church, though some of them refused to renounce their allegiance to James II and became Jacobites. Though most of the Tories accepted the accession of William III, they did so with extreme reluctance. The fact that William was a Dutchman and a Calvinist, and that he had no direct hereditary claim to the throne, made him unpopular with the Tories, who began to criticise the policies of the Court and the exercise of William's royal prerogative. They could not stomach many of the consequences of the Revolution and most of them drifted into sullen opposition. While the new King sought to conciliate and employ leading Tories, like the Earl of Nottingham, the Tory rank and file expressed their hostility to the King's expensive foreign policy, to the scale of the concessions to the Dissenters, to the expansion of the central administration and to the creation of the National Debt and the system of public credit, associated with the newly-formed Bank of England. Unable to uphold their former principles of divine right and hereditary succession, the Tories claimed, instead, that they were defending the interests of the whole nation, the 'Country', in opposition to the dangerous policies of the Court. Seriously divided on questions of principle, without adequate leadership, and reluctant to support the present sovereign, the Tories were chiefly distinguished for their 'Country' attitude in the 1690s, for their distrust and dislike of the measures of the government.

Nor had the Whigs weathered the Revolution unscathed. Admittedly, they had achieved their basic aims, but their leaders found that William III was not willing to let them monopolise office and dictate policy, while some of the rank and file distrusted the use to which William put his royal prerogative. William was not quite the Whig king they had expected. Thus, during the early years of William's reign, the Whig-Tory alignment broke down and the sharp conflict of their opinions was blunted. The more obvious division in politics was between those who were prepared to support the Court and the government of the day, and those who claimed to be defending the national or 'Country' interest. In these years, administrations were coalitions of former Whigs and Tories, while the opposition, the 'Country', also saw Whigs and Tories joined in common action. Not surprisingly, the Whig elements soon predominated at Court and the Tories became the backbone of the Country party. While this tended to keep Whigs and Tories apart, it did not divide them so much on questions of principle as on their attitude to the specific policies of William III, in other words on Court-Country lines. By the time Henry St John entered parliament, however, party rivalry was being renewed and men were beginning to divide once more on Whig-Tory principles.

The primary reason for the revival of the positive aspects of Toryism was the change in the succession problem. The death of James II, the doubts about the legitimacy of his son, the recognition of this Pretender by Louis XIV of France, despite treaty obligations to the contrary, and the knowledge that Princess Anne, a daughter of James II, would succeed the childless William III; all helped to salve the Tory conscience, which had been so troubled by the events of 1688. The Tory split, over whether to desert James II and accept William III, could be forgotten by all but the most devoted Jacobites. Old wounds could be bound up and the divergent strands of the Tory party could come together on more than an opposition or 'Country' platform. The Tory supporters of the Country party enjoyed their greatest triumph with the Act of Settlement of 1701. While they were forced to safeguard the Protestant succession by recognising the

Lydiard Tregoze

Henry St John
aged 16

Frances, 1st wife of
Henry St John

Hanoverians as the heirs of Princess Anne, should she die childless, they were more concerned with the clauses which would limit the royal prerogative of this new royal family. The Hanoverians would not be allowed the same freedom as William III. In many ways, however, this was the last great fling of the Tory-dominated Country party. With the accession of Queen Anne, the Tories could begin to abandon their preoccupation with the negative policies of a Country opposition. Anne had the strongest hereditary claim to the throne if the Pretender were disqualified, and she was devoted to the Church of England. For the Tories, there was the enticing prospect of being able, once more, to rally to the cause of the throne and altar. The undisguised relief and joy of the Tories at the accession of Anne left them singularly free of Jacobite tendencies at this time. Despite the Act of Settlement, however, they were not all committed to the Hanoverian succession as were their Whig opponents. With a new reign dawning, the Tories shied away from the problem of the succession to Anne, though it was eventually to confront and divide them. From the beginning of the reign their equivocal attitude was in sharp contrast to the Whigs' devotion to the principle of the Hanoverian succession.

Another reason for the clearer Whig-Tory distinctions under Anne was the renewal of the war with France. Though Louis XIV's provocative actions in recognising the Pretender and in seeking to control the policies of his grandson, the new King of Spain, united both Whigs and Tories behind the declaration of war, there were differences between the Whigs and Tories on the precise role England should play in this new European conflict. The war helped to redefine their policies, not only with regard to strategy, but in their attitudes towards the economic repercussions of the war, towards the great European powers, and even towards foreigners in general. The Whigs accepted the need to defeat France on land, an expensive form of warfare, in order to secure an adequate peace settlement, but most Tories favoured a naval war, which might result in profitable gains in trade and colonies. While the Whigs, therefore, accepted a system of continental alliances and worked for closer relations with the Dutch and Austrian allies, the Tories resented these ties and many of them grew to distrust all foreigners. At the bottom of the Tories' opposition to the scale and strategy of the war against France were their objection to the way the burden of taxation fell on the squires, through the land tax, and their conviction that the Whig moneyed men and the Whig army officers were enriching themselves in this war.

B

Besides this new major ideological issue, which divided Whig and Tory, there was a revival of some of the traditional differences between the two parties. With Anne's accession some of the Tories could appeal once more to the doctrines of hereditary succession and non-resistance. With the prospect of enjoying Anne's favour, there was a renewed emphasis on the royal prerogative. Even the theory of divine right enjoyed a minor revival. William III could now be depicted as God's instrument of punishment and salvation and his accession explained away as the divine right of providence. In general, however, the Tories avoided laying too much stress on such principles, because of the danger of being labelled Jacobites or of dividing among themselves on the vexed problem of the Hanoverian succession. In order to paper over the fissures in their own ranks, but also because of their long-standing devotion to the Church of England, the Tories emphasised their religious principles. Indeed, after their decision, in 1688, to safeguard their Church at the expense of their king, they can be quite accurately described as the Church Party, a label many of them frequently adopted. They had regarded both William III and the Whigs as too partial to the Dissenters and too ready to reduce the privileges of the Church of England. During the last years of William III, and throughout the reign of Anne, the Tories skilfully used the cry of 'the Church in danger' as a means of rallying support to themselves and of damaging their opponents. Tory propaganda of this nature reached its peak over the impeachment of the high-Church Dr Henry Sacheverell, in 1710, and it had a considerable effect on the party's electoral fortunes later that year.

The Tories also began to regard themselves as the defenders of the landed interest, which they believed was threatened by those financial innovations associated with the Revolution – the foundation of the Bank of England, the new system of public credit, which created the National Debt, and the considerable expansion of the Treasury's activities. The operation of the new finance market, the development of joint-stock companies and the mysterious, and apparently nefarious, dealings of the stockjobbers confused and alarmed the Tory squires. They attributed all these unwelcome developments to their Whig opponents, who seemed to them to be ready, even anxious, to corrupt the government and subvert the constitution. Their conviction that the Whig-inspired financial revolution threatened their own position in society and politics seemed to be confirmed by the vast fortunes apparently made on the money market, at a time when the nation was burdened by a major war and the squires were hard-pressed by a heavy land tax of four shillings in the pound and encumbered by mortgages. Landed estates appeared to be slipping out of the hands of smaller squires, while the great aristocrats were able to buy up more land from the fruits of office and royal favour and the financiers made their fortunes in the City. Thus, the social background of the Tories – the great majority of them were landed gentlemen with little contact with the new money market – and their experience in the Country opposition to William III added a new ideological dimension to the party conflict of Anne's reign. The prejudices and genuine, if exaggerated, fears of the landed interest, as embodied in and represented by the Tory squires, became a major element in the political controversies of this period.

The revival and development of a Tory ideology did not, however, lead to a united Tory party. The Tories, though they enjoyed the favour of Queen Anne and the support of the majority of the nation, suffered from several inherent weaknesses, which were ultimately to prove fatal. Their greatest handicap was the fundamental contradictions in their political philosophy. In 1688 it had proved impossible to maintain their loyalty to the crown and their devotion to the Church of England. While they had reluctantly decided in favour of the latter, many of them had refused to abandon such doctrines as hereditary succession and non-resistance, or their sympathy for the Jacobite cause. In a similar manner, their objections to a land war in Europe and their well-known dislike of foreigners conflicted with their apparent recognition of the Hanoverian succession, for this German family was in favour of the continental strategy. There was, therefore, a strong tendency for the Tories to divide three ways on the succession, into Jacobites, Hanoverians and those who sat obstinately on the fence. The succession question could be temporarily ignored by the Tories, because they hoped Anne would produce her own Stuart heir. Besides, the war was the more pressing political problem and it absorbed the attentions of both Whigs and Tories. As Anne grew older, without an heir of her own body, the succession problem loomed larger on the horizon. Once the war was concluded, the question of who would succeed Anne became the principal political issue and it found the Tories still unable to face it as a united body.

These divisions on fundamental principles were exacerbated by the lack of a vigorous, unified leadership in the Tory party. Prominent Tories differed as much as the rank and file on which issues the party should support. William Bromley and the Earl of Nottingham were staunch supporters of the Church of England, while Robert Harley was much more tolerant of the Dissenters and Henry St John lacked deep-rooted religious convictions. Nottingham and the Earl of Rochester disliked the military strategy of the Duke of Marlborough, but Harley and St John were prepared to give it a chance of succeeding. When the succession problem loomed large, Nottingham and Sir Thomas Hanmer committed themselves to the Hanoverian cause, whereas both Harley and St John dabbled in Jacobite intrigues. There was even a generation gap between those leaders such as Nottingham, Rochester and Sir Edward Seymour, who were still embarrassed and encumbered by their role in the events of 1688, and the younger leaders like Robert Harley, William Bromley and Henry St John, who were endeavouring to form a new Toryism, which would accept the Revolution, if not all its conse-quences. The problem of leading the Tory party was also due to its social composition, which made it difficult for the leaders to mobilise their rank and file. The Tory squires were reluctant to concert measures in London before the parliamentary session began, and they often drifted back to their estates before all the business was completed

The problems faced by the Tory party were not always insuperable, for they enjoyed a majority in parliament more often than the Whigs, in the period 1700–14. They did, in fact, develop an organisation which allowed them to poll effectively in general elections and to raise large votes in parliament on crucial issues. Yet the Tories never solved their basic weaknesses. They were much more prone to internal disputes and open dissension. In addition to the rifts within the party on questions of fundamental principle and over the major issues of the day, the Tories also showed a distressing tendency to split on their attitude towards government and power. What can be described as the Court group, which included the party leaders, the ambitious backbenchers, and placemen-courtiers, such as St John's friends, James Brydges and Thomas Coke, was ready to make some compromises and practical adjustments of their principles, in order to wield power and decide government policy. The Country element, which included a high proportion of the Tory backbenchers, either instinctively distrusted any government, because they believed that office tainted and that power corrupted, or were immune to the allure of place or pension, because it might restrict their independence or lead them to betray their principles. The Tories were predominantly squires, they disliked many of the consequences of the Revolution, which were still with them, and they were divided in crucial issues, such as the succession problem, so that it was easier for most of the

rank and file to cooperate on negative, anti-government policies. The
Country Tories, the major element in the party, were hostile to the new
financial world of stockjobbers and paper credit, to the expense of the
war and the standing army, to the expanding administration and the
growing number of pensioners and placemen, and to the encroachments
on the privileges of the Church of England and the growth of religious
toleration. There was a grave danger that the Tory party would develop a
purely negative, reactive ideology. Only the war against France, and the
accession of Anne, gave the Tory party the chance to develop its Court
philosophy once more and to make a determined bid for power. In
contrast, the Whigs, who were numerically inferior, were a much more
united party and eager to control government policy. They profited from
a coherent political platform – a firm commitment to Revolution
principles, which involved an acceptance of the financial innovations of
the 1690s, toleration for the Dissenters, the defeat of the pretensions of
Louis XIV and the recognition of the Hanoverian succession. In the
famous Whig Junto of Somers, Halifax, Wharton, Sunderland and
Orford, and in a formidable group of young Whigs, including James
Stanhope, Robert Walpole, Nicholas Lechmere and Sir Joseph Jekyll,
they had a united, able leadership in both Houses of parliament. The
Whigs had their Country element too, but it was less significant, especially
in its ability to control the party's policies. The Whig party was not so
dominated by one particular social group, but included a wide spectrum.
The squires were a much smaller element in the Whig party than in the
Tory party. On major issues, such as the war and the Hanoverian succession, they were usually prepared to follow the positive policies of the
Whig leaders.[61]

In view of the divisive tendencies within the Tory party, Henry St
John could never be typically or consistently Tory in all his attitudes and
actions. Nevertheless, he can be identified with many of those prejudices
and principles which are recognisably Tory. Though he opposed the
doctrine of divine right, he remained a firm supporter of the royal
prerogative.[62] He never challenged the sovereign's right to choose his or
her own ministers and to have a considerable say in the making of policy.
Even in his later career, when he was seeking every opportunity to oust
Walpole, he did not deny that the King had the right to appoint him. In
The Idea of a Patriot King, he expected the king to save the nation, when
honest politicians had failed to defeat wicked ministers, but he never
claimed that parliament or any political group could force such honest

men upon him. The doctrine of hereditary succession, however, only appealed to him in so far as it could avoid continual disputes after the death of every monarch. He was never a Jacobite as a matter of principle. At the outset of his career he even contemplated visiting the Hanoverian Court, to declare his loyalty to the Protestant succession.[63] His later refusal to endorse the Hanoverian succession unequivocally was because he feared to alienate too many Tory backbenchers, when he was bidding for the leadership of the party. In his religious opinions St John was never a pious Anglican, like William Bromley or the Earl of Nottingham. According to Jonathan Swift, he only took communion occasionally in order to qualify for office.[64] In later life he could best be described as a Deist. His private religious views, however, never prevented him from loyally supporting the Church of England as the principal institution for the encouragement of both private and public morality, and political harmony. He once declared to Sir William Trumbull: 'I have resolved to neglect nothing in my power which may contribute towards making the Church interest the prevailing one in our country.'[65] And for many years he pursued this policy. He attacked the Dissenters, whom he despised as a factious element and as the allies of the Whigs, during the debates on the Occasional Conformity bills of 1702 and 1703, and in 1714 he introduced the Schism Act to destroy the educational system of the Dissenters. When he became involved in tentative Jacobite negotiations, he insisted that the Pretender should conform to the Church of England. Later, as the Pretender's Secretary of State, he tried to persuade him to guarantee the Church of England's privileges. During his opposition to Walpole, though he avoided alienating the Dissenters, he never suggested that the special status of the Anglican Church should be altered.

In the disputes over the conduct of the War of the Spanish Succession, St John did not adopt an intransigent Tory line. During the early years of the war, and in the final peace negotiations, he showed a degree of responsibility for the balance of power in Europe, though he also came to share the alarm of the Tory backbenchers at the enormous cost of the war and at the gradual, and unwarranted, extension of the war aims of Britain and her allies. The political conviction most deeply rooted in St John was his belief that the landed gentry were the backbone of the nation. This stemmed from his immense pride in the ancient lineage of his family, but he also fully shared – indeed, he encouraged – the Tory prejudice against the upstart financiers and stockjobbers, who were corrupting the government, warping the constitution, and ousting the men of landed property from their position as the natural leaders in politics and society. With eloquence and persistence, he resisted the economic and political encroachments of the new rich. While he was one of the new generation of Tories, who accepted the Revolution and the balance between crown and parliament, he shared the widespread Tory hostility to the other consequences of 1688–89. Even in small matters St John shared Tory views. He loved the countryside, rural sports and the life of a country gentleman, and he shared the Tory prejudice of foreigners, in his case chiefly the Dutch and the Austrians, though, again like most Tories, he had a sneaking regard for the French. In 1717 St John gave an accurate and honest appraisal of the Tory principles, which he upheld all his life:

> We [the Tory majority of 1710] looked on the political principles which had generally prevailed in our government from the revolution in one thousand six hundred and eighty-eight to be destructive of our true interest, to have mingled us too much in the affairs of the continent, to tend to the impoverishing [of] our people, and to the loosening [of] the bands of our constitution in church and state. We supposed the tory party to be the bulk of the landed interest, and to have no contrary influence blended into its composition. We supposed the whigs to be the remains of a party . . . still so weak as to lean for support on the presbyterians and other sectaries, on the bank and the other corporations, on the Dutch and the other allies. From hence we judged it to follow, that they had been forced and must continue, so to render the national interest subservient to the interest of those who lent them an additional strength, without which they could never be the prevalent party.[66]

Sir Keith Feiling recognised these strands of Tory principle in St John, for he wrote: 'It is, we believe, a demonstrable and vital truth, that a certain thin continuity of idea runs all through St John's political life.'[67]

St John never had a firm or consistent allegiance to either the Court or Country wing of the Tory party. He shared the deepest prejudices of the Country Tories, their hostility to the unwelcome developments associated with the financial revolution and their desire to protect the interests of the landed classes, but his overweening ambition led him to crave office. Thus, even in his early political career, he oscillated between the Court and Country Tories, according to the circumstances of the day and the power he desired. At times he led the backbenchers in order to make himself so troublesome that he could lever himself into office or even seize the leadership of the Tory party. In other circumstances he sought the assistance of the Country Tories to carry through specific policies, such as the Treaty of Utrecht and the Schism Act. Only during his years of opposition to Walpole, a period when the Court wing of the Tories had ceased to exist, did he attach himself wholeheartedly to the Country Tories. Then, however, he strove to convert the Tory backbenchers into *the* Country Party, the embodiment of the landed interest and the representatives of the nation at large. His real problem was not dissimilar from that of the Tory leaders in the reign of Anne; to give the Country Party a positive dimension to its ideology, so that it would not only negatively oppose the government's policies but seek to implement its own programme.

CHAPTER 2

A Leader in the Making

HENRY St John first entered parliament in February 1701 and he was soon engaged in those fierce political disputes which were such a feature of the last years of William III. In this parliamentary battle he ranged himself alongside the Tory backbenchers, who were a majority in the Commons and who were just beginning to cease being exclusively 'Country' in their ideas and policies. St John shared some of their principles and misgivings, but no doubt he was not slow to see the opportunity of rapidly making a name for himself as the eloquent spokesman of the inarticulate and frustrated Tory squires. He may also have reckoned that the Whig party represented only a minority of the nation and that it was in considerable disarray at this time. With the accession of Anne in the offing, the immediate future appeared to lie with the Tories. Whatever his motives for joining the Tories, St John's undoubted ability soon made him a leading figure on the backbenches.

One of the first issues which came before the new parliament was the question of the succession, a problem made acute by the death of the Duke of Gloucester, Princess Anne's last surviving child. The solution devised by parliament was to recognise the Hanoverian family as the successors to Princess Anne, should she fail to produce another heir. This arrangement was embodied in the Act of Settlement, to which the Tories added several clauses indicting the conduct of William III and preventing any future Hanoverian sovereign from following a similar course of action. For example, the Hanoverians were not to leave England without parliamentary consent nor involve her in war for their territories abroad, as William III had done. Despite these reflections on foreign rulers the Tories made no opposition to the main terms of the act. It has often been asserted that St John was among those who helped to introduce the bill into the House of Commons.[1] In fact, there is no evidence to prove that St John supported the Act of Settlement, and historians have probably been misled by the reference to St John bringing in 'a Bill for a security of his

Majesty's Person, and the Succession of the Crown in the Protestant Line; and extinguishing the Hopes of the pretended Prince of Wales'.[2] This was not the Act of Settlement, but a much less important bill. Moreover, St John was ordered to prepare this measure in January 1702 after a general election had intervened between this decision and the Act of Settlement of the previous year.

St John, however, was very active in all the Tory onslaughts against the Whig Junto and especially in the attacks on the Partition treaties. He was on the committee appointed, on 21 March 1701, to draw up an address against these diplomatic negotiations by which the King and his Whig ministers had attempted to solve the intractable problem of the succession to the Spanish dominions, but which the Tories feared would involve the country in continental alliances and an expensive war. Three weeks later, when the Commons voted to address the King to remove Lord Somers, one of the Whig Junto, for his complicity in these negotiations, Henry St John acted as one of the tellers for the Tory majority. When the Whigs sought in vain to amend the address, because of its unsettling effect on the European situation, St John was again a teller for the Tories. The Whigs then appealed to public opinion outside parliament and stage-managed the Kentish Petition of 8 May 1701, which criticised the Commons for their misguided attacks on the Partition treaties. The Tories replied to this with an address, which St John helped to compose, against those raising 'tumults and seditions'. When the enraged Commons contemplated impeaching Lord Somers and other Whig ministers, the House of Lords, where there was a Whig majority, tried to indemnify them before their conduct could be condemned. On 20 June 1701 a specific motion in the Commons attacked this manœuvre as likely to cause a breach between the two chambers. Once again St John was one of those whipping up the Tory majority.[3] He claimed that his recent attacks on the Whig leaders were dictated by the necessity of forcing the King to change his dangerous policies, which might embroil the country in an unnecessary war, and by a desire to safeguard the constitution.

> The design of that party for whom you and I have so great respect [wrote St John to Sir William Trumbull] is to widen the breach to that degree that they may be able to persuade the King it will be impossible for this House of Commons to meet the Lords in another session with any success. But if I take it aright, my Lord Somers and his partizans have managed their affairs so very wisely that it is no longer the cause of this particular impeachment, but of all that ever may happen in the course of time. It is whether the Commons

shall suffer the Lords to break through all the rules of reason, all the constitution of Parliament, that my Lord Somers may by undergoing a sham trial evade that justice which he deserves; it is in short the cause of my Lord Somers against all the gentlemen of England.[4]

The Whig leaders were impeached by the Commons, but they were found not guilty by their peers. When the Tories refused to give an undertaking that they would not revive the constitutional feud over the impeachments, the King dissolved parliament.

In his first and very short parliament St John had acted with Tory extremists of long standing, such as Sir Edward Seymour and Sir Christopher Musgrave, and with those rising young Tories, William Bromley and Simon Harcourt. He was also on good terms with Robert Harley, later the apostle of political moderation, though at this time equally hostile to the Whig leaders. St John had clearly made a considerable impact in his first months in the Commons, but he was not entirely satisfied. His straitened financial circumstances made him anxious to secure a good position at Court and not merely on the backbenches of the House of Commons. With the possibility that the King still might turn to the Whigs for support, St John considered setting out for Hanover to seek his political fortune there. He expressed his doubts and uncertainties to his experienced friend and adviser, Sir William Trumbull:

> I might venture to go to Hanover, where I should propose serving my country by being near those that are like to wear the crown of England, and laying the foundation of a future fortune to myself; but if the Parliament should address the King to invite the Princess Sophia into England, which he will hardly do of himself, then my ends would be lost, and I by consequence should not desire the employment. And then on the other side if the old rogues return again into play, it will be, I fear, impossible for me to keep a Place at Court and in St. Stephen's Chapel [the Commons]. Something I should be glad to do.[5]

This was an honest and candid appraisal of St John's position at this early stage in his political career. He was ambitious for power, he desired a place, he sought to promote his own fortune, but he sided with the Tories and he hoped that they might still come to power. While there was no hint of Jacobite sympathies, he regarded the Whigs as rogues. 'I shall, I believe,' he confessed to Trumbull,

> have more grounds to desire an employment than I can tell you in this letter else in these times I should not be ambitious of pushing myself into business.

It would vex a man to learn with pain and trouble how to serve his country, and yet not be able to do it, and this, I fear, is the case among those few that are honest in public station.[6]

The Tories were indignant at the King's decision to dissolve parliament so soon after a general election. St John was particularly incensed at the royal proclamation, which asked the electors to return good Englishmen and Protestants. He regarded this as a libel against the Tory majority in the last parliament.[7] The Whigs circulated their own blacklist of members of the late parliament, who, they claimed, ought to be opposed by all those who wished 'to save their Native Country from being made a Province of France'. They named 167 Tory M.P.s, including most of the future leaders of the party: Robert Harley, William Bromley, Simon Harcourt and Henry St John.[8] The Whig propaganda and the diplomatic crisis in Europe caused a swing of opinion away from the Tories, though St John secured his re-election at Wootton Bassett without difficulty. The result of the elections as a whole was very uncertain and the choice of the Speaker was regarded as the first indication of the strength of the two parties in the new parliament. St John took a leading part in assisting Robert Harley to victory by a mere four votes over the King's candidate, Sir Thomas Littleton.[9] In this new parliament St John was again prominent in the disputes between the two parties. The Tories had not forgotten their failure in the last parliament, and on 26 February 1702 St John tried to bring in a motion to protest that the Commons 'had not right done them in the matter of the [late] impeachments'. The attempt was narrowly thwarted in a very full House.[10]

When William III died St John was one of those Tories chosen to present an address of condolence and congratulation to Queen Anne.[11] Her accession had a spectacular effect on the fortunes of the Tory party, which could scarcely contain its jubilation. Tories such as Nottingham, Rochester, Seymour and Harcourt were all found places in the new administration, while Somers, Halifax and Orford, all members of the Whig Junto, were struck off the Privy Council. These changes had been anticipated in the Commons. Within days of the King's death, the Lower House had elected Commissioners of Accounts to investigate alleged mismanagement in the previous reign. All seven Commissioners were Tories; one of them being Henry St John.[12] This post brought with it a salary of £500 per annum, which was most welcome to him. Now that the administration was being put on a Tory footing, St John's political future and his fortune seemed assured. In June he visited the fleet in the company of Prince George, the Queen's husband, who had been made Lord High Admiral, and he began to have ambitions to play the courtier.[13] Two months later he accompanied the Queen to Oxford University, where he was awarded an honorary doctorate at Christ Church.

The numerous changes in favour of the Tories did not entirely satisfy St John, who feared that the Whigs would still be formidable after the new general election, which was required by law because of the accession of the Queen. He told Sir William Trumbull that there were too many Whig Lords Lieutenant left unmolested and therefore capable of influencing elections in their party's favour. If more care were not taken the new reign would be as tumultuous as the last and the Queen would be exposed to the uneasiness created by two contending parties.[14] Despite these fears that some of those at Court might not like to see a great Tory majority returned at the general election, St John was soon able to report that the Tories had, in fact, achieved a considerable majority. He now believed that the Tories, the true representatives of the nation in his estimation, could restore political harmony to the nation: 'If we are wise we shall have it in our power to heal the wounds our constitution has suffered of late years, and to confound and condemn those we have so long exclaimed against in the most factual manner, that is by doing well ourselves.'[15] In order to end old disputes within the Tory party, he supported a bill, in February 1703, which gave the Jacobites and non-jurors, who had never accepted William III, more time to abjure the Pretender and acknowledge Anne as the legitimate sovereign. Unfortunately for the unity of the Tory party, the Lords passed three amendments to this bill, which would bind those who took the oath more firmly to the Hanoverian succession. This faced the Tories with a choice of opposing these amendments, and thus appearing lukewarm in the Hanoverian interest, or abandoning the attempt to conciliate the Jacobite minority. St John joined his Tory colleagues in an attempt to defeat the first amendment, which failed by a single vote.[16] Resistance was then abandoned, though St John was to be reminded in later years of his apparent sympathy with the Jacobites on this occasion. This Tory policy of conciliation was not extended to their Whig opponents. On the contrary, in the first two years of the new reign, many of the Tories wasted their energies and exhausted much of their store of goodwill at Court, by a sterile policy of insulting the late King's policies and persecuting those Whigs who had supported them. The older Tory leaders, notably the Earl of Rochester and Sir Edward Seymour, encouraged this factious and partisan spirit. The Queen's chief advisers, the triumvirate of Marlborough, Godolphin and Harley, who would all have preferred to associate with moderate Tories rather than with the Whigs, struggled to maintain domestic harmony, while they endeavoured to prosecute the war in Europe. Marlborough, a general with great potential, was heavily committed to a land campaign against France, which was opposed by many Tories, both within the ministry and on the back-benches. The main concern of Godolphin, the Lord Treasurer, was to find the necessary supplies for the war. They both began to despair of the factious conduct of the Tories, who regularly obstructed vital parlia-mentary business. Not only did they decide that it would be unwise to dis-miss those moderate Whigs who still held minor offices and places; they even contemplated relying more heavily on the Whigs. As a minority in the Commons, the Whigs were naturally on the defensive and they had no desire to see the continuation of the disputes between the two parties. These quarrels, after all, chiefly revolved around the conduct of the Whigs in the previous reign. Moreover, the Whigs supported Marl-borough's strategy. They wanted to see a reduction of the exorbitant power of Louis XIV, and their experience in William's reign had con-vinced them that only a major land war could accomplish this. For them the war also involved the Protestant succession. Louis XIV supported the Pretender, who held court in France, and would install him in England, if ever he had the power to do so. The Elector of Hanover, on the other hand, was fighting against France and he was a staunch supporter of the Austrian claim to the throne of Spain.

An accommodation between the ministry and the Whigs might have been accomplished quite early in Anne's reign, but for the opposition of the third member of the triumvirate, Robert Harley. Not only was Harley the Speaker of the House of Commons, a vital political position, in which he could influence both debates and the order of business; he was also the most able political manager in parliament. Marlborough and Godolphin relied heavily upon him to control the Commons and get the necessary bills of supply voted. Harley wished to avoid a situation in which the ministry was dominated by the leaders of either party. He hoped that the chief posts in the administration could be monopolised by non-party or moderate party men, while the more committed party members held the minor offices and places, which would prevent them from dictating actual policy. As a political realist, he knew that the ministry could not survive without the support of the dedicated party men, who were a substantial majority of the Commons. What the ministry had to decide was which party it should accommodate. While he fully recognised the problem of handling the Tory high-flyers, Harley believed that there were so many Tories that he might procure a majority, without putting the ministry in the hands of the extremists. The Whigs, on the other hand, were both more united and numerically inferior. If the ministry turned to them it would have to come to terms with the experienced Whig leaders, especially the Junto lords, who would not be content to be lobby fodder. Once in a position to do so, they would want to control government policy. Less personally committed to the war than Marlborough and Godolphin, Harley saw every reason to continue negotiations with the Tories, rather than turn prematurely and disastrously to the Whigs. He therefore made strenuous efforts to cool the temper of some of the warm Tories. Henry St John was one of those backbenchers who, at first, joined in the most factious attacks on the Whigs, but who was eventually persuaded to support the ministry and the war. His conversion, among others, helped to halt, albeit temporarily, the drift to the Whigs by Marlborough and Godolphin.

At first, however, St John took a leading part in the attacks on the Whigs and in the most bitter party disputes. When the new parliament met, on 20 October 1702, the Queen spoke of the 'just and necessary war' which had been declared against France in the previous May. The Commons planned an address to Marlborough for having, by his first military operations, 'signally retrieved the ancient honour and glory of the English nation'.[17] The Whigs recognised this as a reflection on William III's military shortcomings and wished to substitute 'maintained' for 'retrieved'. At this suggestion, 'Mr St Johns stood up and own'd it was a reflexion, and for that reason he desir'd it should be in, but not so much upon the late King as his Ministers, who, he said, were the worst any Prince ever had.'[18] The amendment was defeated. The Tories were emboldened by this success and began a series of vindictive attacks on their Whig opponents. In December they also showed that they were capable of flouting the express wishes of the Queen, who proposed to grant Marlborough a pension of £5000 per annum from the Post Office funds, as a reward for his military services in the first campaign of the war. The Commons refused to endorse the grant after the strong criticisms which had been levelled so often at the exorbitant grants made by William III. St John was chairman of the committee which rejected the Queen's suggestion, but he was among the minority which was in favour of allowing the grant. He and his friend, George Granville, followed Robert Harley's lead on this issue and differed with their high-Tory associates, Seymour and Bromley.[19] St John was to continue to vote with the Tory extremists on most issues over the next year or more, but this was probably his first signal to the Court that he was not intractable and might be open to offers of preferment.

The Tories had always believed that the Whigs had lined their pockets out of exchequer funds in William's reign, and in this new parliament they again elected Commissioners of Accounts to investigate their suspicions. Once more, Henry St John was among those chosen. He had envisaged, even planned, this examination as early as August 1702. Then, he had written to Sir William Trumbull of efforts 'to bring some few of those deeds of darkness, which have long been the great grievances of this deluded nation, and which have been either covered or defended with so much art and industry, to light'. He hoped all these labours would not go unrewarded.[20] There was no need for him to worry about the reaction of the Tory backbenchers. The investigations appealed to all their deep-rooted prejudices. By February the Commissioners had brought serious charges of financial irregularity against the Earl of Ranelagh, an Irish peer sitting in the Commons, who had served as Paymaster-General under William III. After the unfortunate Earl had been expelled from the Commons, St John and his fellow Commissioners began to prepare a detailed charge against the Earl of Halifax, who had been First Lord of the Treasury under William and who was one of the members of the Whig Junto. In the Lords, the Whig majority rushed to clear Halifax of what were, in any case, only minor, technical offences. The Tories in the Commons were incensed and claimed that they were not being allowed time to formulate all their accusations. The result was a serious clash between the two Houses, which was only cut short by the prorogation of parliament, on 28 February 1703, but which was to be resumed in the next session.

St John also played a prominent role in the religious disputes, which the Tories instigated early in Anne's reign and which proved to be the most serious embarrassment to the Marlborough-Godolphin ministry. One source of controversy centred on the divisions within Convocation, where the bishops of the Upper House and the clergy of the Lower House mirrored the party disputes between the Lords and the Commons in parliament. Their arguments took on a political as well as a religious complexion, for the bishops tended to be moderate churchmen and

Whiggish in politics and the ordinary clergy were predominantly high-Church and Tory. In parliament the Tories objected violently to the practice of occasional conformity, whereby Dissenters qualified for office, by obtaining a certificate of attendance at the sacrament in an Anglican church, but continued to frequent their own meeting-houses. The Tories disliked this on both religious and political grounds. They wished to uphold the privileges of the Church of England in both religious and secular life, and to exclude some of their opponents from office. Henry St John supported their efforts to abolish the practice of occasional conformity, largely on political grounds. On 4 November 1702 he was ordered by the Commons to assist William Bromley and Arthur Annesley in preparing a bill to end this practice. The bill which he helped to produce included severe penalties, among them a fine of £100, which was to be paid to the informer who betrayed any infringement of the law. This first Occasional Conformity bill rapidly passed through all its stages in the Commons, but ran into difficulties in the Lords, where it was severely amended by the Whig majority. In an attempt to resolve the differences, both Houses appointed a committee of five to meet in conference. Henry St John was one of the five Tories chosen by the Commons, whereas the Lords chose five Whigs. Among these was Gilbert Burnet, Bishop of Salisbury, who observed during the conference that some of the strongest supporters of the bill were descended from Dissenting families. While he said this he apparently stared fixedly at Henry St John, who remained unabashed.[21] The conference proved abortive, neither side being prepared to moderate its position, and the bill was lost.

Despite this setback, the Tory backbenchers in the Commons did not readily abandon their cherished bill. The Court and the ministry used all the influence at their command to prevent its re-introduction in the next session, but to no avail. During the summer recess it had been rumoured that the Court might be able to buy off St John, by including him in the entourage of Archduke Charles of Austria,[22] who was about to sail for Spain in an attempt to seize the throne from Philip V. It was more than likely that St John believed that his ability and his nuisance value merited a greater reward than a place in a foreign Court. In November 1703 he was one of the foremost speakers in favour of bringing in another Occasional Conformity bill[23] and, once again, he was ordered to assist Bromley and Annesley in preparing it. The new bill was substantially the same as the first, though the penalties were reduced. It passed the Commons with majorities of over seventy. In the Lords it met with stiff resistance now that it was clear that the ministry disliked it and that even the Queen, staunch Anglican though she was, regarded it as inopportune. This time it was defeated by twelve votes on the first reading. Henry St John's support for it was his last action in conjunction with Bromley and the high-flying Tories for several years. He was about to make the transition from the backbenches to the role of a Court-Tory.

St John's conversion owed much to his desire to hold office. He had made the occasional signal to the Court that he was prepared to trim his sails and moderate his conduct, but he was not prepared to be bought off lightly. To show his value to the ministers, he showed them how dangerous he could be when leading the Tory extremists. His ambiguous conduct naturally led to speculation. His friend, Sir William Trumbull, was told: 'I was assured positively yesterday that while St John pretends to be of the Duke of Marlborough's party, he is his determined enemy, and that his seeming to be his friend does great hurt by deceiving many who else would not join with him; you may guess better than I, but my Author was good, and no doubt he holds himself at a very high price.'[24] This last remark was probably the key to St John's actions in the 1703–4 session. Nevertheless, though his desire for office might reveal him as a political adventurer, at least he wanted to serve an administration which was still ostensibly Tory. His decision also speaks well for his political judgement. He had accurately gauged the drift of support away from the high-Church Tories and towards the ministry. Robert Harley had been the ministry's principal agent in managing the Commons. He had kept in touch with St John and he had either learned his price or had helped to convert him to more moderate policies.[25]

St John's decision to abandon the partisan measures of the Tory back-benchers was not based solely on serving his own narrow ends. He came to respect Robert Harley's political judgement, that there must be enough moderate Tories to support the ministry or else it would of necessity drift towards the Whigs. The Tories must not be controlled by their Country element or they would hand over power to their opponents. This conviction grew as he observed the developments of the war, which was, of necessity, the principal preoccupation of the ministry. St John had his own views on how the war should be conducted. He shared the Tory preference for a naval war and he waxed indignant at the Whig criticisms of the failure of the attack on Cadiz. Yet, while he thought more might be done in other theatres, such as Italy, he never attacked Marlborough's conduct of the war in Flanders. The responsibility for the disappointments there, in 1702 and 1703, he laid squarely at the door of the Dutch, who had hampered all Marlborough's manœuvres.[26] He was, in fact, already demonstrating his capacity for hero-worshipping the great commander: 'My great dependence is on his admirable good . . . He has the most glorious field to range in that ever subject had, and it lyes in his power to make himself the darling of good men and a terror of others.'[27] In contrast, many of his Tory friends were not only opposed to Marlborough's conduct of the war, but were prepared to obstruct operations by any conceivable means. They continually harassed the government over the conduct of the Dutch, which was already a sufficient headache, and hindered the supply of extra troops and money. St John refused to cooperate in such obstructive tactics. He was convinced that the war had to be waged in order to reduce the exorbitant power of France and he believed that Marlborough was the man most likely to ensure victory. In January 1704 he finally broke with his high-flying colleagues over their attempt to delay a vital money bill, merely out of pique at the Lords' defeat of the second Occasional Conformity bill. With other former, and more experienced, Tory stalwarts, such as Sir Christopher Musgrave and Jack Howe, he helped to defeat such a short-sighted factious motion.[28]

Having once taken the plunge, St John began to break his ties with the Tory extremists, though he did not abandon all his Tory principles nor all his Tory colleagues. In this same month, January 1704, the celebrated Aylesbury election case came to a head and again embroiled the Lords and Commons in a lengthy disagreement. The Lords upheld the Whig accusation of unfair electoral practices by the Tories at Aylesbury, but the Commons complained that this was an infringement of their privilege to decide election disputes. The Tories were particularly warm in their support of the rights of the Commons. St John agreed with their general argument, but his moderate speech contrasted with their wilder assertions:

> Sir, I do not rise up to trouble you long, but to speak to one point that was mentioned by a noble lord over the way. I shall be as tender as any man alive, of doing anything against the liberty of the people; but I am for this; because I take it to be the greatest security for their liberty. The noble lord was pleased to take notice, that, in the consequence, the Crown would have a great influence on those that are to return the members of the House of Commons; and when they were in, they might vote for one another. I cannot think that the liberties of the people of England are safer in any hands below, or that the influence of the Crown will be stronger here than in other Courts.[29]

St John's contribution to this debate did nothing to prevent the case dragging on, but much more significant was his *volte-face* over the new investigations into the alleged financial misdemeanours of William III's reign. When, in February 1704, the Commons again chose seven Tory Commissioners of Accounts, St John was not of their number. He had specifically declined the honour.[30] It was a wise move because, once more, the issue brought a clash between Lords and Commons and further exasperated the Court and the more moderate ministers.

St John's transition from the backbenches to ministerial office coincided with his involvement in the disputes between Lords and Commons, over the Scotch Plot and the conduct of the Earl of Nottingham. The Earl, a high-Church Tory, had disagreed with the conduct of the war and had gone to great lengths to support the Occasional Conformity bills, despite his ministerial position as one of the Secretaries of State. It was in his ministerial capacity, through his investigations of a Jacobite plot in Scotland, that he came under fire from the Whig majority in the House of Lords. The peers appointed a committee of seven Whigs to examine the Scottish prisoners. The Tory majority in the Commons resented this implied criticism of Nottingham's examination of these prisoners and claimed that the Lords were infringing the royal prerogative, by carrying out a separate investigation. They therefore appointed a committee, on 20 December 1703, to draw up an address to the Queen. Henry St John was appointed to the committee and he was given the honour of reporting the address next day. At this time he was still putting pressure on the Court, so that his value would be clearly recognised, but there was no doubt that he also disliked the way the Whigs were hounding the most upright high-Church Tory in the Lords. The address, which he helped to draw up, was both a criticism of the Lords and a defence of Nottingham's conduct. When the Lords replied to this address St John was again one of eleven Tory members charged by the Commons to search for any precedents for their lordships' action. When yet another address in reply to the Lords was ordered, on 3 February 1704, St John was once more selected to put forward the case of the Tory majority.[31] Though he was at this time abandoning the more factious policies of the Tory high-flyers, he was not prepared to abandon individual Tories or the party as a whole to the equally partisan attacks of the Whig peers.

Ironically, despite his loyalty to Nottingham on this occasion, the Scotch Plot was to pave the way to the Earl's downfall and to St John's promotion to ministerial rank. Nottingham was so embittered by the attempts to censure his conduct that, in revenge, he demanded that all those Whigs still in office should be turned out. The continual disputes, between the two parties and the two chambers, also convinced Marlborough and Godolphin that alterations would have to be made in the ministry. The changes which they envisaged, however, were not those that Nottingham had recommended. On the contrary, they regarded the high-flying Tories as responsible for most of the ministry's difficulties. This did not mean that they were prepared to rush into the arms of the Whigs, for they believed that they could win over enough Tories to sustain a policy of moderation. Henry St John had been one of those Tory backbenchers signalling to the Court that they had grown tired of factious policies and were prepared to come to an accommodation with the Marlborough-Godolphin leadership, on a moderate Tory basis. In April 1704 the Queen finally accepted Nottingham's resignation, instead of his ultimatum. Several Tories, including Sir Edward Seymour and Lord Jersey, were also removed. The replacements were mainly Tories, but they were men who had shown a willingness to moderate their conduct to bring it more into line with the policies and priorities of the Court. Robert Harley reluctantly agreed to become Secretary of State, and his friend Thomas Mansell, a moderate Tory, replaced Seymour. Henry St John's friends, George Granville, Thomas Coke, Arthur Moore and Brigadier John Webb, all moved over to the Court. He himself was made Secretary at War. To some extent he owed his elevation to the good offices of Harley and the great influence of Marlborough. St John had been associated with Harley for some years and he had evidently become convinced of the need for moderation in parliament, in view of the pressing military and financial problems facing the government. He had several connections with Marlborough. The general's father, Sir Winston Churchill, had once lived at Wootton Bassett, St John's constituency and the ancestral home of the St John family. One of Marlborough's favourite generals was Lord Cutts, a kinsman of St John. The new Secretary at War may also have owed much to his old patron, Sir William Trumbull, who was on good terms with the Duchess of Marlborough. Some time later St John attributed his promotion to Trumbull's influence with Marlborough: 'I am chiefly engaged to you, who first gave him impressions that he has been good enough to retain.'[32] Nevertheless, despite these advantages it is clear that St John owed his new place to his own abilities. In a few years he had won a reputation with the whole House of Commons, not merely with the less talented Tory backbenchers. His decision to take office, moreover, was received with some satisfaction by the ministry; a potentially dangerous opponent had been muzzled, rather than a client rewarded.

Once he had taken office St John was anxious to end his association with the extreme Tories. In a letter to Sir William Trumbull, he accused Lord Jersey of being deeply engaged in a cabal designed to draw the Queen and her ministers into its power. This 'gang' had to be broken and disabled.[33] With some justice, he claimed that the ministerial changes had resulted in a more moderate Tory government and not in any sell-out to the Whigs. Among the Tories admitted to office were Sir Christopher Musgrave, Jack Howe and Sir Simon Harcourt. St John could also point out several of his fellow-rakes, including James Brydges, Arthur Moore and Thomas Coke, who were also holding places under the Crown. Nevertheless, there was more than a trace of special pleading in the explanations he gave to Trumbull. Of course there had been changes, but those excluded, he argued, were not really contending for the Church of England interest, only for their own personal interests: 'There is a good deal of jealousy and dissatisfaction alive among some of our friends, and art and industry have not been wanting to inflame, but when by the whole tenor of the Queen's conduct they see their apprehensions were without foundation, they will discover that the dispute was for persons and not for things.'[34] There was some truth in these remarks, but there was something incongruous about them emanating from Henry St John. He had clearly abandoned the high Tories with a vengeance and he had helped to divide the party as a whole and to deprive the Tory rank and file of some of their best leaders. In another letter, bordering on the hypocritical, he criticised the way that the support for the Occasional Conformity bill had been taken to extreme lengths and he expressed his opposition to any plan to reintroduce it at the present juncture:

> As long as we are in such nice and dangerous circumstances, and that bringing in this bill can only serve for to rally and unite the Whig party, and join with them in the most violent manner the whole herd of fanatics, as long as the ministry must have the odium of our priests for not carrying what is impossible for them to do, why not delay that than confound all to no purpose whatsoever.[35]

St John took office at a most opportune moment. During the summer of 1704 the ministry's popularity was given a tremendous fillip by the great successes won abroad. On the Danube, Marlborough fought a magnificent campaign, which culminated in the great victory at Blenheim. At sea, Admiral Rooke's expedition captured Gibraltar. These achievements transformed the domestic political scene. For a time they made nonsense of the factious Tory opposition to the war. St John rejoiced at Marlborough's victory, but also paid tribute to the Tory admiral and refuted Whig criticisms of his conduct at the battle of Malaga, in defence of Gibraltar.[36] The Tory extremists remained intransigent and were soon making plans to further their aims in the new parliamentary session. In reply, St John cooperated with Robert Harley and the other ministers in stressing the need for moderation. In October 1704 he requested the support of Sir William Trumbull:

> The meeting of Parliament comes on apace and though there is inclination enough to do mischief, and there have been several meetings for this good purpose, I really am sanguine enough to expect the public business will be vigorously carried on, and our private feuds of no consequence. But for God's sake come up yourself and if you will not appear on the stage, advise, like an old actor, those that do. I expect you with impatience.[37]

To his fellow-rake and colleague, Thomas Coke, one of the Tellers of the Exchequer, he wrote in similar terms:

> For God's sake do not at furthest stay longer than Sunday, because it is most certain our patriots design some gallant things to open the session with, and that is what, out of kindness to them, everyone should oppose. Though I believe in a little time all the endeavours of their friends to keep 'em on their legs will prove ineffectual.[38]

In the new session, the high-Church Tories hoped to reassert their hold over the party by introducing a third Occasional Conformity bill, whose more moderate terms might induce former allies, such as Henry St John, to return to the fold. There were suggestions that, if necessary, the bill should be tacked to the land tax, in order to carry it through the Lords. The decision to bring in a bill was carried by only twenty-six votes. The moderate Tories had not all rallied to it. St John may have given it his qualified support, but he clearly expressed the hope that nothing would be done which would delay the voting of the supplies necessary for the war.[39] He would probably have agreed with Godolphin's observation that he could expect no quarter from his old friends if he opposed them now.[40] This naturally made him hesitate to sever all links with his former backbench colleagues. He was, perhaps, prepared to support the introduction of this new Occasional Conformity bill, knowing that the ministry could ensure its defeat, but he was not ready to support the more irresponsible Tories, who insisted on forcing the bill through parliament by tacking it to the land tax. When this policy was resolved upon, St John believed he could abandon his erstwhile colleagues with a clear conscience, though the campaign to spike the guns of the high-flyers was led and master-minded by Robert Harley. St John simply acted as one of his loyal lieutenants. When the extremists resorted to the threatened tack they were heavily defeated by 251 to 134 votes. This was one of the most crucial party votes of the reign. It was on this rock that the flimsy and superficial unity of the Tory party was rudely shattered. It took four years to patch up the breach between the moderate Tories, who were prepared to come to terms with the ministry, such as Harcourt and St John, and the high-Church Tories, such as Bromley, who refused to compromise their principles, even when the country was at war. It took a further two years in opposition before the Tory party returned to power in 1710. On this particular issue of the tack, at least twenty-four Tories renegaded and were castigated as 'sneakers'. They included Robert Harley, Simon Harcourt, Henry St John himself, and his cronies, George Granville, Thomas Coke and Arthur Moore.[41]

By the end of 1704 the position of the high-Church Tories was at its lowest ebb since Queen Anne's accession. The defection of men of the calibre of St John was a crushing blow. Early in the new year the high-flyers tried to regain their hold over the rank-and-file Tories and to boost their own morale, by bringing forward such popular issues as the Aylesbury election case and a bill against placemen sitting in the Commons. Though they made no real progress, and the Tory party went into the 1705 general election hopelessly divided, the results were not disastrous for the party. It could still count upon more support in the Commons than could the Whigs, though the Court and its moderate Tory allies held the balance between the Whigs and the bulk of the Tories. It was a precarious balance, however, because the ministry could not command a majority, without the support of either the Whigs or the Tories. This was a potential source of friction within the ministry, though it took time to appear. Marlborough and Godolphin, because of their overriding commitment to the war, were prepared to negotiate with the Whigs, who could be counted upon to support the campaign in Flanders. Harley and St John continued to hope that the ministry could survive with the backing of an increased number of moderate Tories.

St John, having cut himself off from the high-flyers, now saw his fortune tied to the careers of his two patrons and heroes, Harley and Marlborough. The Secretary at War took a keen interest in those elections which particularly involved the great commander. He kept him informed of Cadogan's election at Woodstock, where Marlborough had a considerable interest, and he proffered his congratulations when some tackers were defeated.[42] To Marlborough, he appeared in the role of the moderate courtier, above party and faction: 'The Tories look on themselves as abandoned, and the Whigs think their reward not proportionable to their merit, thus all party men are dissatisfyed, and ever will be so under a wise administration.'[43] He was no doubt gratified at the general's interest in his own successful campaign at Wootton Bassett. Despite his new attachment to Marlborough, St John did not desert the Tories entirely. Like Harley, he was adamant that the ministry should never become the captive of the Whigs, but must continue to seek an accommodation with elements of the Tory party. When the Court decided on its candidate for the Speakership, and its choice fell on John Smith, a moderate Whig, St John expressed genuine misgivings. 'Her Majesty', he wrote to Marlborough,

> having been pleased to direct her servants to promote all they can Mr. Smith's advancement to the chair of the House of Commons makes it too late for another. It had been happy if that [candidate] could have been found whom the Whigs would have voted for, and who might have reconciled a great many of those people to him, that may cease to be Torys but never can become Whigs.[44]

Among the latter, he would have included himself. The intractable problem which faced him was that the ministry needed the support of one of the two powerful parties in the Commons, but he and Harley were unable to persuade the Tory party to accept those policies which the ministry regarded as essential to the proper conduct of the war.

The morale of the Tories had revived after the general election and they planned a united front in the contest for the Speakership in the new parliament. They put forward a very strong candidate in William Bromley, a popular high-Church Tory of unimpeachable integrity. St John must have been embarrassed by this choice, for he had been a friend and active colleague of Bromley, but, charmed by the fruits of office, he silenced his own doubts and worked to convince some of his Tory friends that the Court was upholding the national interest. He hoped that Marlborough's successes abroad would 'keep down the ferment here, which rises apace, and promises a stormy winter'.[45] Meanwhile, he canvassed his friends to rally to the Court. He urged his friend, James Grahme, a former Jacobite, to hurry down from Westmorland for the beginning of the session.[46] To Thomas Coke, in Derbyshire, he was more explicit:

> I should be glad to know what temper you find gentlemen in: whether they will think it reasonable to support the Queen, who has nothing to ask but what we are undone if we do not grant: and who, if she does make use of hands they do not like, has been forced to it by the indiscretions of our friends. The real foundation of difference between the two parties is removed, and she removes to throw herself on the gentlemen of England, who had much better have her at the head of 'em than any ringleaders of fashion. Unless gentlemen can show that her administration puts the Church or the State in danger, they must own the contest to be about persons: and if it be so, can any honest man hesitate which side to take.[47]

St John's campaigning was cut short by illness. He decided on a fort-night's convalescence on his Berkshire estate, 'to recover my health perfectly before our winter campagne begins, which will be warm, and give us trouble enough though without dispute the publick service will prevail and the Queen will obtain whatever she desires. It would be hard if she should not, when she has nothing to ask but what is our indispensable interest to grant'.[48] Though for a time his life was actually in some danger, his health quickly recovered and he set out to face the new parliament with improved strength and vigour.[49]

He was to need all his energy, vitality and optimism in the new parliament. On the first day, 25 October 1705, John Smith was elected Speaker, by 248 to 205 votes, in a very full House. The successful candidate was proposed and seconded by two Whigs, while all the leading Tories, including Arthur Annesley, Sir Edward Seymour, Sir Thomas Hanmer and Sir Roger Mostyn, spoke up for William Bromley. The voting was, in fact, almost entirely on party lines. Not a single Whig supported Bromley, apart from John Smith's courtesy vote. The only Tories oppos-ing Bromley were those who held office, such as Harley, Harcourt, Mansell and St John, or their close friends and adherents.[50] Clearly, St John had cut himself off from the Tories to a greater degree than he had planned. His position was now uncomfortable and equivocal. He could only hope that he would not be further compromised by the ministry depending more and more upon the Whigs. Much depended upon the skill of Robert Harley in his task of converting more Tories and convincing Marlborough and Godolphin of the folly of rushing into the arms of the Whigs. The new Secretary of State was optimistic. The zeal of the Tory backbenchers, he claimed, was much greater than their knowledge. They had been excited by the false arguments of their leaders, but, with care and application, he expected that some of those who had acted out of ignorance rather than malice might be persuaded to have a better opinion of the Queen's government.[51] Before the end of this parliament, Harley and St John were to confess defeat and to resign, rather than serve in a ministry dominated by the Whigs.

CHAPTER 3

Secretary at War

WITH his appointment as Secretary at War, in April 1704, Henry St John had shown himself more interested in office than in remaining true to his high-Tory principles. He never became a Whig, but his ambition had led him to abandon some of his former colleagues. Having taken the plunge, he set about making sure that he was not a servile courtier but a vigorous and capable administrator, helping the national interest in the war against France.

The Secretaryship at War was a junior appointment and did not admit St John to the inner counsels of the Cabinet, but, with the country engaged in a major war, it was a vital post. As the head of an administrative department, St John was responsible for recruitment, billeting, the supply of clothes and equipment, convoys, transport, the care of sick and wounded troops and a whole complex of logistical details.[1] This gave him a finger in many pies and allowed him to see at first hand some of the most intractable problems thrown up by the war. In particular, it brought home to him the enormous difficulties involved in reinforcing the armies overseas and in organising a military expedition to a distant theatre of war. At least, he learned that the task of conquering Spain was beyond England's capabilities, though he did not learn enough to prevent him planning the abortive Quebec expedition of 1711. As the first politician holding the post of Secretary at War, St John unwittingly inaugurated the era of parliamentary control over the army, though he was quick to seize the opportunity of combining the roles of politician and administrator. Through its ability to call the Secretary at War to account, parliament began to control and guide the armed forces. In parliament, St John's main duty was to pilot the recruiting bills and the army estimates through the Commons. These were major political issues affecting many members, particularly those who were country gentlemen and justices of the peace. As the war progressed and became a greater burden, these issues assumed even greater importance. Thus, in the 1707–8 session, St John bore the brunt of the ministry's attempts to explain the shortage of troops in Spain and Portugal, and the way in which the money which had been voted by the Commons had been spent. The Secretary at War had no control over pay and ordnance, which were under separate offices, but his duties did bring him into regular contact with the Secretaries of State and the Commander-in-Chief. For St John this meant the chance of working closely with his two heroes and patrons, Robert Harley and Marlborough. He also worked directly under Lord Treasurer Godolphin, in such matters as the preparation of warrants, and he frequently had direct access to the Queen. While he had to refer many important matters to the Secretaries of State for a Cabinet decision, he could still exercise considerable initiative, and in many matters his opinions carried as much weight as his superiors. He spoke regularly in the Commons on military matters and in many ways he was the Cabinet's director of army affairs. Thus, St John's new post gave him an excellent opportunity to prove himself in office and to show the world he was a leading minister in the making.

St John was shrewd enough to realise that in wartime the vague responsibilities of his office were capable of extension. He was also sufficiently astute as a politician to know that work meant power. His first task was to master his duties and his officials. To Sir William Trumbull he explained that his dependence upon his clerks would last as long as they knew more about the business of his office than he did, but that he hoped to be out of their guardianship within a month.[2] His private and business letters bear witness to his energy and his industry. St John, of course, was also a man of pleasure, who had no wish to appear as a common clerk, and who liked to suggest that his approach to work was that of the dilettante. It was in this spirit that he wrote to Marlborough, in July 1705: 'I received the honour of your Grace's letter of the 9th instant yesterday at this place [Bucklebury], where I intend to continue all the summer; since the routine of my office, which is all the business I have, requires no more dispatch than I can give it by paying my duty once a week to the Queen at Windsor.'[3] In fact, less than two weeks earlier he had written to his friend, James Grahme, M.P. for Appleby: 'I have been in so great a hurry with country business, elections, the Court, the office, and the lawyers, that I have had hardly the least minute for anything else these six weeks.'[4] St John spent most of the summer at Whitehall, until ill health forced him to retire for a short time to Bucklebury, his Berkshire estate, in October, to regain his strength. Throughout his period in office

Marlborough expressed complete confidence and satisfaction in the way he performed his duties.

St John had long been anxious for office, to offset his personal financial dependence upon his father and upon his wife's estates. His new post brought him an annual allowance of £1000, plus pay of one pound per day. He was also granted £455 a year for the rent of his office at Whitehall and for his clerical staff. There were also the perquisites of one day's pay from every officer he registered on the muster rolls and for every leave of absence granted to a serving officer. St John always insisted on receiving these payments. Nor was he above taking advantage of army contracts to help line his own pockets. Later, as Secretary of State, he was involved in shady deals with his crony, James Brydges, the Paymaster-General of the Forces Abroad, who made a fortune arranging army contracts and payments. As Secretary at War, St John also worked closely with Brydges over the supplies for the expedition to Spain, and some of these contracts were far from satisfactory. Certainly Brydges wished to avoid close inspection of some of those he had arranged with St John.[5] Nonetheless, unlike Brydges, St John never made a fortune, though he did procure Marlborough's support in obtaining additional allowances from the Lord Treasurer. Even before this was finalised St John was thanking the general for his kindness: 'I hope your Grace believes that any accession to me, serves only to increase a fortune that will always be, as it ought to be, at your disposal and that no man living can be more perfectly than myself devoted to your interest.'[6] Years later the Duchess of Marlborough endorsed one of St John's letters to her husband: 'The Duke of Marlborough never was so kind to any man as to him; and I have heard my Lord Godolphin say, that he never had anything to reproach himself of, in the whole time that he served the Queen, but in complying with the Duke of Marlborough in doing unreasonable things, in point of money, for Mr St John, at the Duke of Marlborough's request.'[7]

More important than his industry or the desire to augment his pay was St John's ambition to extend his duties and to increase the jurisdiction of the war office. On two occasions his attempts aroused opposition in other departments; yet this did not effectively restrict his activities. His first venture was to counter-sign commissions for officers, a practice that was officially the prerogative of the Secretaries of State, Sir Charles Hedges and Robert Harley. He then informed Hedges of his actions, as if he had a perfect right to act in this way.[8] This led to a mild rebuff from Harley, the other Secretary of State. St John was quick to apologise,[9] but in fact he retained considerable control over the issuing of commissions and continued to impinge on Hedges' responsibilities, though his relations with Harley were much closer and more harmonious. Hedges was primarily responsible for military affairs in Spain, but he allowed St John to usurp his authority. It was St John who found contractors for Charles III's troops and who established a hospital in Catalonia. On each occasion he merely informed Hedges of his plans and then took them direct to the Cabinet.[10] In his encounter with the Commissioners of Victualling, who were responsible for supplying the provisions required by men on board transport ships, St John was less successful, though he got his own way much of the time. At the end of 1706 St John began short-circuiting the Secretary of State and Prince George's Admiralty Council, and informed the Commissioners himself of the number of troops and the amount of supplies needed for the transports. When he got away with this he began to lecture the Commissioners for delaying the work of embarkation. This led the Commissioners to question his right to issue orders to them at all. He replied by writing to the Admiralty, to have his orders passed on to the Commissioners. The Admiralty insisted that they could only receive instructions from a Secretary of State. The dispute was still unresolved when St John resigned early in 1708.[11]

St John's appetite for power was not satisfied by the Secretaryship at War. He was soon seeking to replace George Clarke, secretary to Prince George, the Lord High Admiral, in addition to retaining his other post. Clarke had voted for Bromley in the contest for the Speakership in 1705 and so he was ripe for dismissal. St John wrote to Harley, suggesting that he should take over Clarke's duties, though he denied that this was merely to increase his income. In this instance his denial was probably genuine. He was more interested in the power than the profit which could be derived from office. The day after Clarke voted for Bromley, St John contacted Harley:

> I should be vexed to be thought greedy after profit, which I despise with all my heart, and serve the Queen on a much better principle. All I can say on this head is, that I will promise to make less of both places than the two gentlemen that had them made of each; and that as I design to make no fortune so I will spend in the Queen's service whatever I get in it. There are some iniquities which do make a noise, that if I do not begin by destroying I will forfeit my character with you for ever willingly.[12]

He soon justified his self-confidence. His petition was successful and he took over the extra duties of Prince George's secretary. This meant that he was now involved in recruiting men for the navy as well as for the army. It also made him the chief aide of a principal source of patronage.[13]

Marlborough was very satisfied with St John's efforts on behalf of his army in Flanders. The Secretary at War improved the supplies sent to the troops and his registration of all officers on the muster rolls proved useful for indicating their seniority and whereabouts. He proved extremely capable at organising the supply and embarkation of troops for distant theatres of war, especially for the expedition to Spain and the planned descent on the French coast in 1706. His chief difficulty, and the one which he laboured strenuously to overcome, was the raising of sufficient recruits for the ever-expanding army. On 10 March 1704 the Commons had agreed to a form of conscription in the counties. The local mayors and justices of the peace were to recruit 'able bodied men as have not any lawful calling or employment'.[14] Once St John took up his duties, he maintained a considerable correspondence with both civil and military authorities, dealing with a vast number and range of individual problems. He forwarded the reports of J.P.s to the Clerk of the Council or to the Secretaries of State, to be laid before the Council, and he completed the whole operation by making arrangements with the Transport Commissioners, the Admiralty, and the regiments themselves, for transportation to Marlborough's army. Each year the routine was the same and St John, on the whole, supplied Marlborough's needs, and before the campaigning season opened. The commander's great victories owed something to St John's energetic work behind the scenes. The system, in fact, only began to break down when England had to contribute large forces to the war in Spain and Portugal. This culminated in the great shortage of troops at the battle of Almanza, in April 1707. The shortage was due principally to the failure to recruit satisfactorily for this service. Yet the collapse of the system was not due to any administrative inefficiency by St John. He was always very active in recruiting for Spain, but he laboured under enormous difficulties, as one of his letters to his friend, Lieutenant-General Erle, makes abundantly clear:

> I expect daily to have directions to prepare for reinforcing and supplying your army, which in my apprehension is the most pressing service imaginable. One difficulty occurs to me, and I cannot answer it to myself. The regiments in Catalonia and Valencia are extremely weak. Those with you will grow so every day. The garrison of Gibraltar is extraordinarily thin. How, in the present emergency, shall this large demand of recruits be answered? Draughts from England or Ireland you know cannot be had, especially when besides

Queen Anne in coronation robes

Sir William Trumbull

John Churchill, 1st Duke of Marlborough

Henry St John in about 1705

the corps which I hope we shall send you, my Lord Marlborough will take over 3 battalions. One thing occurs to me so reasonable as to send over some officers, such as best can be relied upon, fix the number you expect, and send me this account. They shall have my assistance, and not want my exhortations to perform this service with diligence.[15]

The insoluble problem was the general shortage of manpower for an army which now required 12,000 new recruits each year. The government had simply undertaken commitments far in excess of its capabilities. No Secretary at War could have coped with the problem.[16] Godolphin himself had admitted as much: 'We have too many irons in the fire. We can't be in the Mediterranean, in Portugal, upon the coast of France, and in the West Indies all at once.'[17] And he had not even mentioned the two largest bodies of men, those serving under Marlborough and with the Royal Navy.

St John's position as Secretary at War gave him the opportunity to make a reputation in office, to match his fame as a backbench orator. He was fortunate in holding the post when the country was engaged in a major war. Even more fortunate was he to serve the great Duke of Marlborough, for he could bask in some of the reflected glory of Blenheim and Ramillies. To his credit, St John always recognised his personal debt to the general's transcendent military ability and he frequently paid tribute to Marlborough. He wrote effusive letters of congratulation to the commander, while he was acting as his Secretary at War, but he did not spare his praises even when he was neither in office nor in parliament.[18] To his friends he acknowledged how much he owed to Marlborough. After the battle of Ramillies he wrote to Sir William Trumbull: 'The Duke of Marlborough has crowned all his glorious actions. I do indeed take a particular part in all his fortune, ... I have been so happy as to share his good fortune, and I would with pleasure have shared his bad. I never can forget those to whom I owe so much as I do to him and to you.'[19] In 1709, by which time he was convinced that peace was essential, he could still tell James Brydges of his near superstitious faith in Marlborough.[20] Despite his eventual breach with the commander, he never lost his admiration for him.

In addition to his friendly relations with Marlborough, St John was soon on amicable terms with the general's friends and clients, notably William Cadogan, Adam de Cardonnel, James Brydges and Thomas Erle. Of greater importance for the development of his future career were the

C

impressions he gained of the allies and of the conduct of the war in general.
When he later became Secretary of State, and took a leading part in the
peace negotiations, he was accused of betraying England's allies. His poor
opinion of these countries was not assumed simply as an excuse for
leaving them in the lurch by making a separate peace. His impressions
had been gained during his years as Secretary at War, when he frequently
accused them of hindering Marlborough and obstructing the successful
prosecution of the war. He was furious with the Dutch when, in 1705,
they refused to assist Marlborough to continue his offensive operations.
He confessed to Thomas Erle: 'One would run mad if one was to think of
the combination of villainy and stupidity we have to struggle with. I hope
Lord Marlborough will be able to cheat 'em into an engagement and
when they are at the ball they must dance.'[21] St John was even more
hostile towards England's Austrian allies. On one occasion he wrote to
his kinsman, Lord Cutts, of Marlborough's visit to Vienna: 'Pray God
they may be able to do any good at that Court! It is insufferable that
England and Holland must every day take a greater burden upon them,
while the House of Austria – entirely applied to secure the confiscations of
Hungary and procure more – seems rather neuter than a party in the war
against France.'[22] As late as 1707 he was still cursing the conduct of affairs
in Germany, where 'our friends are at their usual rate, backward, unprepared, helpless.'[23]

Whatever personal advantages he acquired from his post as Secretary
at War, St John retained enough of the attributes and prejudices of the
Tory country gentlemen to want a good peace as rapidly as possible.
There is little evidence that he agreed with the Whigs, when they insisted
that there should be 'no peace without Spain', though of course he did
hope that Spain might be wrested from French domination. He was
genuinely disappointed at the failure of Archduke Charles, the Austrian
claimant, to retain his tenuous hold on the throne of Spain in 1706. 'By
our accounts from Spain,' he told his friend, Thomas Erle, who was
then on his way to that theatre of war, 'King Charles seems to have payed
dear for not striking whilst the iron was hot. Great contention arises here
where the blame of all this fatal ill success should be layed. For my part I
am indifferent as to that matter, in comparison of the concern I have to see
this lost game retrieved.' By the end of that year he could still speak hope-
fully of the prospects in the next campaigning season, but this strained
optimism was outweighed by his gloomy account of the state of the
allied army in Spain. He warned Erle:

You will find a King destitute of any one able and honest minister; a Court without order or economy; the Portuguese difficult to be managed and made to do more good than harm; the English and Dutch dispersed, broken in spirit, and reduced in numbers; one general [Galway] tired and overburdened, eager only to get from under the load, which however he is ordered from hence still to continue to bear; the other [Peterborough] (if he is not gone from Spain upon some other project once more) full of pique and cavils at what is passed; accounts and all other matters in the utmost confusion; and to conclude all the Spaniards either animated against you, or at best distrusting your strength and afraid to declare for you.

The crushing defeat at Almanza, in April 1707, convinced him that the allies would never wrest Spain from Philip V, the French claimant. He could only foresee a new war, which would require entirely new measures and more resources than England could command.[24] Before the next campaign, however, he had resigned his post as Secretary at War.

St John did become disillusioned, both with the conduct of the allies and with the prospects of securing Spain for the Austrian claimant, but his resignation was caused by his untenable political position. The election of the Speaker in 1705 had left St John out on a limb with a group of less than thirty moderate Tories, who could be counted upon to support the ministry. The bulk of the Tories were united behind Bromley in the Commons, and behind Nottingham and Rochester in the Lords; but in opposition to the government. St John had assured Tom Coke that the Queen desired to be above party and free of factious disputes, and he had not misrepresented her intentions. Robert Harley, whom St John now regarded as his political mentor, shared his view that the ministry must not alienate the Tories any further by relying too much on the Whigs. He warned Godolphin that the government must avoid alienating the country gentlemen (by this, he meant the Tory backbenchers) and encouraging them to combine against the Queen's service. If the Court turned men out of office, merely because they were not Whigs and not because of any specific action which they had performed, then the Tories would be convinced of the need to combat the dangerous influence of the Whigs. The Queen must convince the gentlemen of England (the Tories) that she would stand aloof from narrow party interests and that her policies, not those of a factious party, would be followed. If this were not done, then he, Harley, could not answer for the actions of the Tory backbenchers.[25] Holding such views, St John and Harley could hardly have been pleased with the appointment of the Whig, William Cowper, as Lord Keeper, on

11 October 1705. Even more alarming was Godolphin's calculation that it was more important to hold on to Whig support than to conciliate the Tories. This decision was born of an awareness of Whig support for the war and of weariness at several years of obstructive tactics by the high Tories. It was confirmed in the first two sessions of the new parliament, as the Tories did their best to embarrass and hinder the policies of the ministry, without putting forward any genuine or practical alternatives.

St John, Harley and their small group of moderate or Court Tories attempted first to arrest, and then to reverse, Marlborough's and Godolphin's drift to the Whig camp. This involved them in opposing the more obstructive tactics of the Tory opposition, because this would only encourage the Lord Treasurer and the commander to rely on the Whigs. In December 1705 St John, Harley and Harcourt spoke against the Tory motion to bring over Princess Sophia of Hanover in order to safeguard the Protestant succession, a move carefully calculated to embarrass the ministry with either Queen Anne or the Hanoverian family. The Queen, never in good health and without a child, was strongly opposed to the idea of a rival Hanoverian Court being established in England during her lifetime. It would smack too much of vultures waiting for her death and it would encourage ambitious politicians to cabal with this other Court. On the other hand, the Hanoverians were very sensitive about their claim to the throne and always feared a Jacobite plot to restore the Pretender on Anne's death. They would have preferred to be safely established in England before Anne's demise in order to safeguard their inheritance. To avoid alienating either Anne or the Hanoverians, St John and his friends supported the Regency Act, a measure which would smooth the transition to the Hanoverians on the death of Anne, by appointing Regents or Lords Justices to administer the country until the new sovereign arrived from Hanover. St John was also active in resisting the opposition's plans to exclude all placemen from parliament in the new reign. Unfortunately, these debates revealed a marked Whig-Tory division, with the ministry overwhelmingly dependent upon Whig support. St John had little more than twenty Tories voting with him. On a Court-Country issue, like the motion to exclude placemen, the vast majority of Tories had been even more reluctant to follow the lead of Harley and St John, and they had opposed the ministry.[26] In the debate on 'the Church in danger', in December 1705, which was very much a Whig-Tory clash, St John was even more at odds with all his old Tory friends, when he helped to reject the motion.[27] A few weeks earlier he had been associated with the drawing up of an address in support of the war,[28] a motion which drew solid backing from the Whigs, but only hostile criticisms from the Tories. Thus, in the three major debates of this session, the ministry had sound majorities. Unfortunately for St John, they were majorities based on Whig support. The efforts to win over the Tories, 'the gentlemen of England', had signally failed. St John began to fear that, if these developments continued, he would not be able to remain in office much longer. In July 1706 he admitted to his friend, James Grahme: 'A peace may be made and more leisure fall to my share, or I may happen to fall on the slippery ground of a Court, and roll down to this quiet place [his estate at Bucklebury], in either case my horses and my dogs will help me pass most of the time which I can spare from the offices of friendship.' A few weeks later he added: 'We stand on slippery ground and thank God I will fall soft whenever it comes to my lot to tumble. I keep you before my eyes, you have been a courtier and are a northern country gentleman.'[29]

When the Whigs began to press the ministry for some tangible rewards for their support in parliament, and suggested that the Earl of Sunderland should replace Sir Charles Hedges, a Court Tory, as Secretary of State, Harley and St John tried to dig in their heels and halt a threatened capitulation to the Whigs. St John feared that events were in danger of getting out of control, as far as he was concerned, and that his position was becoming untenable. He agreed with Harley that they must begin to seek an escape hatch and so safeguard their political future, by resuming contact with the Tory leaders of greatest integrity, particularly William Bromley and Sir Thomas Hanmer. On 5 November he penned a very important letter to Harley, which is worth quoting at some length as an indication of his political thinking at this critical juncture:

Nothing, dear Master, will continue long within its due bounds, but a short-lived inundation may prove a lasting evil. The torrent may make such a havoc and leave such scars in a little time as years will not repair. If you will give me leave to bring the allegory still more close, no husbandman in his right senses ever let that flood violently in to spoil his grounds and destroy his fruits which with care he might have guided in gentle streams to the improvement of both.

I am glad you find the same disposition where you have been as I believe is in other places. It will be one of the greatest pleasures I can have to be instrumental under you in making a proper use of it; in order to this, sure we must have a little more commerce with some gentlemen than has been of late kept up.

I did not believe when I writ last to you that the application made to
Mr B[romley] and Sir T[homas] H[anmer] was the effect of your advice, but
I do imagine in fact there has been some negotiation of that sort.[30]

These negotiations were, at first, rather hesitant and desultory, but they
became more serious when the situation of the Harley-St John group had
indeed become intolerable. The first giant step in this direction was taken
when Sunderland became Harley's fellow-Secretary of State in December
1706.

The enemies of Harley and St John were already convinced that they
could no longer be trusted to support the ministry. The Duchess of
Marlborough warned Godolphin that they were plotting with the Tories
to hinder government business in the 1706–7 session. Bishop Burnet
believed that this situation was avoided only because the Tories resisted the
offers and blandishments of Harley and St John.[31] In fact, though Harley
urged the Queen to resist further concessions to the Whigs, he and St John
loyally supported the ministry during this session. Harley was particularly
influential in pushing through the Act of Union against the Tory opposition in the Commons. St John, though disturbed by the promotion of a
few more Whigs early in 1707, was still hoping to steer a course between
the Scylla of the Junto Whigs and the Charybdis of the high Tories.
His future was delicately balanced on a razor's edge, but he hoped that the
mixed ministry and the ability of Marlborough might yet carry the day.
In July 1707 he wrote to Marlborough: 'I hope in a week or ten days
time to go into the counties where I have some acquaintance and friends,
and at my return will acquaint your Grace as far as I am able to discover in what disposition I find people – I may venture to say in general
that the greatest part have a mind to be quiet, if busy people will suffer
them to be so.'

Ten days later he wrote from Bucklebury: 'All people here are quiet,
and we enjoy the appearance of a perfect calm – a very little will keep it
so, and a very little will ruffle the waters.' Shortly before the opening of
the 1707–8 session St John still appeared willing to support the existing
alignment of ministerial forces:

We have many new characters this sessions to deal with and party seems to be
as restless as ever, tho' a man would be apt to think that one side has had
experience enough to make them sober, and the other countenance enough to
make them satisfied. The greatest part of my time in the country has been
spent in looking after my farms. I find the people I have conversed with poor

but hearty and the landed interest, which is bowed under the burthen of taxes, is still willing to pay them.[32]

In the new session, however, St John's hopes were finally blasted. The Whigs continued their advance, Marlborough and Godolphin succumbed to their embrace, and St John and Harley refused to sever all their links with the Tories.

The Whigs were in no mood to continue bolstering a ministry which refused to dismiss recalcitrant Tory office-holders. They planned to scotch the plans of the Harley-St John group for greater reliance on the Tories, by showing that they held the whip hand in parliament. Schemes were drawn up to harass the ministry on all fronts, until substantial concessions had been wrung from it. Attacks were made on the competence of the Admiralty, the administration of Scotland and the conduct of the war. St John was particularly involved in the debates on recruiting troops for the war and on the state of the army in Spain, issues which came to a head in January 1708. On 12 and 16 January the Commons discussed ways of raising further recruits, especially for Spain, but St John, who had been struggling with the problem for months, had no specific proposals to make. He admitted that 19,000 recruits were needed, though 14,000 might suffice. When, on the 17th, he at last suggested that these recruits might be raised from the parishes and counties, according to their population, his proposal was defeated. It was left to Simon Harcourt to suggest that renewed efforts should be made to recruit all able-bodied men without employment or means of livelihood. When a recruiting bill to this end was ordered St John was not even included among those who were to prepare it. This oversight was not remedied until two days later. On 23 January it was again Harcourt, not St John, who suggested offering additional incentives for raising the necessary recruits. Parish officers should be paid £1 for each new recruit, while every volunteer should be given a £4 bounty.[33] Obviously St John had lost interest in his major task, recruiting men for the war. There were two reasons for this. He was convinced that the country had scraped the barrel pretty thoroughly in the past and he was preoccupied with an even more serious problem, the size of the army in Spain at the time of the battle of Almanza.

The debate on this issue began quietly, on 8 December 1707, when St John was asked for information about the number of English troops in Spain and Portugal at the time of the battle of Almanza, which had been fought in April 1707. St John at once wrote to all those army officers who had served in Spain, but who were now in England, asking for these details; but he was unable to give the Commons any precise information and so the debate was adjourned until January 1708.[34] Despite this breathing-space, St John had considerable difficulty in finding out the truth about the number of troops in Spain in April 1707. During the Christmas recess he confessed to Harley:

> Tho' it may be expected that I should give a more satisfactory account of those matters, I cannot but take notice to you that notwithstanding my early endeavours to procure such information from Spain as might have enabled me to have answered more fully to those several points the correspondence has not only been very uncertain but the accounts that have come to my hands from thence have been very imperfect.[35]

On 12 January 1708 St John was able to lay before the Commons a list of the number of troops in English pay at the battle of Almanza. This totalled a mere 8,660 men.[36] Four days later James Brydges, the Paymaster, presented his accounts for maintaining 29,395 men in Spain and Portugal up to 23 December 1707.[37] These accounts cover two full pages of the *Commons Journals* and the troop figures, split into 20,562 and 8,833, were not given any special prominence. This, and the fact that they were laid before the House four days after St John's list, probably explains why their significance was not immediately grasped. St John himself was probably well aware of the explosive nature of these figures, but he did not bring this to the attention of the House. It was not, in fact, until 29 January that Sir Thomas Hanmer demanded to know why there were only 8,660 troops at the battle of Almanza when parliament had arranged to pay for no less than 29,395 men. St John was unable to present an adequate defence. He made various excuses, that his total of 8,660 men referred only to effective troops and that it did not include officers, prisoners of war, the sick or the four regiments recently sent to Portugal. Hard-pressed by the Tory opposition and undefended by the Whigs, the ministry was pleased to seek an adjournment until 3 February. St John's lame defence, followed soon after by Harley's fall and his own resignation, has led many historians to contend that Harley and St John had deliberately primed the Tory opposition with these explosive figures, in order to destroy the ministry.[38] Harley and St John were certainly unhappy with the state of affairs which these figures revealed, but their breach with the Godolphin ministry was not over this specific issue.[39] There is every reason to believe that these figures alarmed them, but it seems that they were ready to defend them. They were not, however, prepared to defend the wider policies of the ministry, and their opposition to these pre-dated the Almanza debate.

On 3 February 1707 the debate on Spain was resumed and St John produced additional figures to account for the huge discrepancy between the number of effective troops and the number for which parliament had voted funds. His detailed statistics gave a variety of explanations: six regiments had been sent home to recruit before the battle was fought; 2,800 men had been lost on the voyage out to Spain with Earl Rivers, in 1706–7; 2,160 were in Portugal at the time of the battle; 2,000 had been captured before the battle, etc. In this way he reduced the discrepancy to a mere 801 men.[40] Though his figures probably represent an adequate defence,[41] the Tories, roused to great heights of moral indignation, refused to regard them as satisfactory. They were only prepared to add officers and servants to the figure of 8,660 effective troops. The Whigs, now ready to teach the Godolphin ministry a lesson, allowed the Tories to pass an address of protest and a request for a proper explanation of the shortage of troops at Almanza. The ministry now saw that its only hope of survival lay in buying off one of the two parties, with tangible concessions in the form of offices and places. The Almanza debate finally tipped the ministry off the razor's edge, but it was only the culmination of a long struggle within the ministry, to decide which party it should look to for loyal and essential support. It was because they lost this battle, and not because they maliciously planned the Almanza debate, that Harley and St John left the ministry.

Harley and St John believed that the ministry could placate the Tories with fewer concessions and that the Tories could be more easily prevented from dictating to the ministers and the Court. The Whig Junto, on the other hand, would probably insist on shaping policy, once they controlled the chief ministerial posts. Godolphin, however, after the traumatic experience of the tack in 1704, had become convinced that supplies for the war could only be voted with the support of the Whigs, though he still hoped to obtain their votes without losing control of the ministry. The Queen held the key to the situation, and Harley and Godolphin each pressed her to follow his advice. Harley suggested re-shaping the ministry by bringing in more Tories and it was soon rumoured that Rochester, Buckingham, Sir Thomas Hanmer and Bromley were all being considered for office, while St John was to be promoted to the office of Secretary of

State.[42] St John was, of course, privy to all these plans. Swift and Burnet even claimed that they were laid openly before Marlborough and Godolphin,[43] though the latter always accused Harley of treachery and underhand dealing. Whatever they told Godolphin, Harley and St John began quietly approaching the Tories. On 4 February 1708 Sir John Cropley reported that 'Harley has at last secured a good reception with the Tories and his friends Harcourt, St John, and all that crew [are] to stand and fall with him . . . I do believe the Whigs will carry their point but 'tis not yet done. The parties are both so potent and equally determined the Court shall have done with all trimming.'[44] These manœuvres were clearly becoming common knowledge, for James Vernon told the Duke of Shrewsbury of a rumour 'publicly spoken of, that messages have been carried as from the Queen to several leading men among the Tory party, to engage them to stand by her Majesty against the Whigs, whose management she was dissatisfied with, and no less with the influence they had upon her ministers. This is laid to the charge of Mr Attorney [Harcourt] and Mr St John, but more particularly the latter, so that they are looked upon as a triumvirate that were framing a new scheme of administration.'[45] With the support of the new royal favourite, Mrs Masham, who was a distant relative, Harley was prepared to undermine Godolphin's reputation with the Queen. The revelations of the Almanza debate provided him with useful ammunition, though they were not the real cause of the open breach with Godolphin.

There was no corresponding plan to oust Marlborough, who, while the war continued to be waged seriously, was indispensable to any ministry. It was later suggested, not without a grain of truth, that Marlborough feared Whig domination more than Godolphin, and that he had a natural 'inclination to the Tories, and more particularly to St John, Harcourt and Mansell (and at this instant, even to Harley himself)'.[46] Godolphin at last got wind of these intrigues and complained to Marlborough. Harley was denying any hint of treachery as late as 28 January 1708, the day before the Almanza debate exploded in the face of the ministry.[47] On the very day of this debate, when St John and Harley were desperately trying to defend the ministry, Godolphin was complaining to Harley that he was convinced of his treachery: 'I am very far from having deserved it from you. God forgive you.'[48] The debate itself pushed Godolphin into the arms of the Whigs. When it was resumed, on 3 February, the Whigs joined the Tories in opposition, though the Lord Treasurer now had no doubts about which party he should conciliate. Harley played his last card and sent St John to persuade Marlborough to ditch Godolphin and throw in his lot with the Tories. St John was not without hopes of success for, according to Swift, 'the Queen told Mr St John a week ago, that she was resolved to part with Lord Treasurer; and sent him with a letter to the Duke of Marlborough, which she read to him, to that purpose; and she gave St John leave to tell it about the town, which he did without any reserve'.[49] After some thought, Marlborough decided to stand by Godolphin, and together, on 8 February 1708, they offered their resignation rather than serve with Harley. The Secretary of State failed to carry the rest of the Cabinet with him, and the Whigs damaged his reputation by opening an inquiry into the treasonable activities of Harley's clerk, William Greg, with the French. In the Commons the Whigs further demonstrated their mastery by holding up the passage of all the essential money bills. On 11 February the Queen very reluctantly accepted Harley's resignation. St John, Harcourt and Mansell followed him out of office and several Tory placemen were dismissed in the next few months. The ministry had capitulated to the Whigs.

Henry St John has often been accused of being a mere political adventurer, a man only interested in power, a man without political principles. Though there is much to be said for this view, it breaks down as an explanation of his whole career when his resignation in 1708 is examined. He was not forced to resign. Indeed, Marlborough, who held him in high regard, was anxious to persuade him to remain in office. His favourite general, William Cadogan, wrote to James Brydges: 'I am beyond expression concerned and surprised at our friend Harry St John's resigning. I had a letter from him on that subject to justify the resolution he had taken. I am sorry he thought he had reason for it. I am sure the whole army and particularly those that know him will have reason to regret it.'[50] Lord Raby expressed considerable surprise at the news of St John's resignation: 'How comes it that Lord Treasurer and my Lord Duke were so violent against Harley and all his party, for I thought you told me that Harry St Johns and his gang were all entirely my Lord Duke's.'[51] Marlborough and St John did, in fact, remain on good terms, despite his resignation. The Duke continued to regret St John's decision to leave the ministry[52] and St John never lost his personal regard for Marlborough. After the latter's great victory at Oudenarde, St John wrote to him: 'I am preparing to return again to the country, in the midst of which retreat I shall inviolably preserve in my heart that gratitude for all favours, that zeal for your service, and that true unaffected love for your person, which I have never knowingly departed from.'[53]

Clearly St John had not been forced to resign. But why had he chosen to do so? It is possible to take a cynical view and argue that St John saw it was not in his own best interests to remain in office. According to this view, St John had always believed that the Tory party represented the majority of the nation, particularly 'the gentlemen of England', and so it could not be excluded from power for any length of time. Moreover, he must have been aware that Harley was replacing Marlborough and Godolphin as the Queen's most trusted political adviser, while at the same time his ally, Mrs Masham, was displacing the Duchess of Marlborough as the royal favourite. Thus, it could be argued that St John envisaged the eventual triumph of Harley and the Tories, and that he anticipated that he himself would ride back to power on the crest of this wave. Though this situation did eventually materialise, it was to take two and a half years of Tory scheming, and the unexpected failure of the ministry to make a satisfactory peace, to accomplish it. If St John foresaw all this, he had remarkable political judgement, a quality these same critics would deny him. Another possible explanation of St John's resignation in 1708 was his horror at discovering the discrepancy between the number of troops voted by parliament for the service in Spain and Portugal, and the number actually effective at the time of Almanza. His consternation was certainly genuine, as can be seen from his letter to Harley on 14 January 1708:

Have received your letter of yesterday's date, with a copy of the address of the House of Commons to her Majesty for an account of the effective men of the Portuguese troops yearly since the treaty with Portugal, and of the number of them present at the battle of Almanza, or at that time in other parts of Spain or Portugal. Having never received any account, either from her Majesty's ministers or from the general officers serving abroad with these forces, of the condition or strength thereof, I am not able to make any return of what is required, unless I can receive information from any of the officers now in Britain who have served in Portugal and Spain, which I will endeavour to get.[54]

Nevertheless, it was not the conviction that the ministry was mismanaging the war that caused St John to resign. In the first place, he was fully aware of the problem of getting exact statistics of troops serving in a distant theatre of war. After considerable effort, he did explain the discrepancy in the figures, and a recent authority has accepted his explanation and has concluded that all the missing men could be accounted for, without resorting to suggestions of gross mismanagement.[55] The Commons may not have accepted the explanation, but St John's defence was essentially sound and honest. Moreover, he had played a leading role in the recruiting and supplying of troops in Spain and Portugal. If he had believed that there had been gross inefficiency here, then either he would not have resigned voluntarily after giving his explanation to the House or, after he had done so, he would have expressed dissatisfaction with the explanation he had had to give and would have tried to shift the blame for the discrepancy onto his erstwhile colleagues. It seems inconceivable that St John, never a politician to take all the blame for any disaster, would not have exposed the ministry, if he had believed that it had been grossly negligent or was hiding some financial misdemeanour connected with the recruitment of troops for Spain and Portugal. On the other hand, if the fault had lain mostly at his door, then the ministry would not have continued to defend his explanation, but would have rounded upon him. Neither event occurred when the debate on Almanza was resumed, on 24 February, by which time St John was again a free agent on the opposition backbenches. On this occasion, the ministry was now defended by the Whigs, who, having seen the remnants of the Harley-St John Tories pushed out of office, could look forward to rich pickings. The opposition was now composed solely of Tories. When the censure motion came to the vote St John, who had spoken in his own defence, explaining that the figures he had presented to the House accounted for most of the discrepancy, decided to abstain. Harley, who had refrained from any comment during the debate, Harcourt and Mansell voted against the ministry, though the support of the Whigs ensured a comfortable majority for the government.[56]

The most obvious explanation of St John's resignation probably does him too much credit to satisfy his many critics. He resigned because his political principles were affronted by a ministry coming under the domination of the Whigs. He was not prepared to cut himself completely adrift from his former Tory colleagues, whether moderates such as Harley and Harcourt, or high-flyers such as William Bromley. His decision was the product of at least a modicum of political principle. There is a great deal of evidence to support this hypothesis. Since 1704 he had followed Harley's lead in supporting a moderate ministry, relying to some extent on the more reasonable elements of the Tory party. He had voiced misgivings about the choice of John Smith as Speaker in 1705, and he had approved of Harley's tentative negotiations with the main body of the Tories in 1706. When Harley reopened these negotiations, in January 1708, St John strongly supported him and acted as his chief aide in his dealings with Marlborough. Thus, when Harley's schemes failed, St John believed that he had no alternative but to resign. This was the explanation his friend, James Brydges, gave to Cadogan, to explain why St John and Harcourt had resigned:

> The reasons they give are because Mr Harley was turned out, which they looked upon as a full declaration of the ministry's intentions to join entirely with the Whigs, which they thought was inconsistent with the declaration they had made to them, and the assurances which by the authority and permission as also by the Queen's commands they had given the Tories that no such thing should be done.[57]

This seems the best explanation of St John's conduct. It is fully consonant with his previous actions and with the way he subsequently urged Harley to join the main body of the Tories.

Enforced Retirement

WHEN St John and his friends resigned it seemed obvious that there would be a rapid realignment of forces. The ministry, it appeared, would be captured by the Whigs, while St John, Harley, Harcourt, Granville and Mansell would rejoin the Tories. Neither of these eventualities was accomplished without considerable difficulty. The Queen stubbornly resisted a ministerial capitulation to the Whig Junto, and the Tories refused to allow Harley, St John and Harcourt simply to assume the leadership of the party in the Commons. St John, like the others, had to serve a period of probation before he was fully accepted. Thus, the rest of the 1707–8 session saw St John, Harley and Harcourt vying with Bromley and Hanmer in launching attacks on the ministry and the Whigs. Two events further delayed a reconciliation between the leading Tories and played into the hands of their Whig opponents. Harley's clerk, William Greg, was found guilty of treasonable correspondence with France and was duly executed. Harley's reputation as an efficient minister suffered as a consequence. Then, in March 1708, the Pretender led an abortive attempt to raise a Jacobite rebellion in Scotland. This Jacobite scare naturally aroused suspicions about the Tory party's attitude to the Hanoverian succession and strengthened the position of the Whigs. These two fortuitous developments enabled the Whigs to take the offensive during the 1708 general election campaign and, for the only time in the reign, they secured a narrow majority over the Tories in the House of Commons.

The greatest shock in the general election was not the loss of about thirty seats by the Tories, but Henry St John's failure to secure his re-election for Wootton Bassett. This was the result of a rift between him and his father. There were two possible causes of this breach. St John had long fretted at his precarious financial position. He had ambitions to play the great country gentleman, but, as long as his father lived, he could not lay claim to the family estates in Wiltshire nor to the property at Battersea. His wife's property was encumbered by their marriage settlement, leaving St John to some extent financially dependent on his spouse. Another source of friction was the political principles of his father, who was apparently a Whig, though not a politically active one. In April 1708, James Brydges informed General Cadogan: 'Our friend Mr St John will hardly I believe be in Parliament, his father designing to stand at the place he hoped to have been chose for, and hath wrote him word that he supposed he would have that duty for him as not to oppose his coming in.'[1] St John's father may, as Horatio Walpole claimed, have reacted with indignation to his son's decision to resign, rather than serve with the Whigs.[2] When he himself contested the seat he was rejected in a constituency where the St John family had always carried great weight.[3] Clearly, St John could have defeated his father, had he been prepared to defy his express command.

St John was compelled to search, cap-in-hand, for another seat. Though he had only been in parliament for seven years, he had made a considerable reputation both in office and on the backbenches, but he was handicapped by having to begin his search only a month before the general election. Most candidates had been making interest long before this and even family boroughs had to be nursed with great care in an age of frequent elections and bitter party strife. At the beginning of May he told Harley that there was no point in standing at Cricklade, where two candidates had already engaged all but fifty of the votes. Westbury had been suggested to him, but he did not think that he could obtain the support of Lord Arlington, the virtual patron of the borough. He concluded: 'I neither have omitted, nor would omit, any trouble, care or expense in my power since my friends think I might be of some little use to them and to my country, but know not which way to turn myself.'[4] His friends were all engaged in assisting him to find a seat. George Granville tried, unsuccessfully, to nominate him for a Cornish borough, but had to confess his failure: 'Our friend Harry [St John], he seemed pretty confident of succeeding in some place or other, and I own I took it for granted he knew himself secure. I join with you in being under the greatest concern for this disappointment.'[5] Simon Harcourt advised Harley to approach Lord Weymouth, who was in a position to offer a seat to St John. Harley had needed no urging. He had already opened negotiations, but to no avail.[6]

It was quite evident that Harley wished to have St John returned to the Commons, yet St John held him at least partially responsible for his failure to gain re-election. This appears clearly in a letter which St John wrote to James Grahme:

> I take this event to be of very small moment to the publick, and no great misfortune to me. After I had taken the resolution of not appearing at my own Borough I did all I could to get myself elected in some other place, but found it utterly impossible, as I can satisfy you whenever we meet; tho' I hear that some of our friends pretend to affirm the contrary. If I could have been of any great use, that which was impossible for me to compass in my circumstances had been brought about by those whom it is my inclination and my principle to serve and since they have left me out I conclude they do not want me.
>
> I shall now have three years to live to myself which is a blessing I never yet enjoyed, and if I live to another Parliament, I will be elected without an obligation to anybody but the people who choose.[7]

Though St John did Harley less than justice in this instance, their relationship did not recover its former intimacy. Never again was Harley 'master' or St John 'faithful Harry'. When he returned to parliament in 1710 St John was no longer Harley's loyal and tractable lieutenant.[8]

St John remained out of the Commons during this whole parliament, but his political career was only interrupted for two years. During much of this period he lived on his estate at Bucklebury in Berkshire, where he enjoyed the rural life of a country squire and re-established his contacts with grass-roots Toryism. He expressed himself thoroughly content with his retirement. To James Brydges he wrote: 'No Man Loves You better, or can taste more Satisfaction in Your Conversation, and could I Enjoy you and a very few more friends as frequently at this Place as it is Easy [to] do in London, I w[oul]d not only make people believe I intended to Spend the rem[ainde]r of my days here but I would steadily resolve to do so.'[9] Even after a further year of enforced idleness he could still write to Harley: 'In three weeks time I intend to go to Lavington, my hounds and horses are already there, my books will soon follow. In that retreat if I may hear sometimes that you and the few friends which I have in the world are well, all will be well with me.'[10] Though St John could, and did, enjoy the life of a country gentleman, there was a strong element of affectation in his frequent declarations of his love for rural pursuits and his satisfaction with his retirement. Despite his posturing, he was constantly betraying his energetic temperament and his unlimited, unquenchable ambition. In December 1708 he was aroused by the possibilities of returning to the Commons by means of the by-elections to be held at Weobley and Milborne Port,[11] though his expectations were dashed. Even when he wrote of his contented retirement his hopes of a political comeback were clearly discernible. This emerges from a letter which he wrote to James Grahme, as early as September 1708:

> The character you give of the Age and Court is so true, that it serves as another consideration to take off the edge of my Ambition.
>
> After all this, it is no part of my Scheme, whenever the Service of my country, or of any particular friend calls me forth, to sit still. I hope and promise myself that on any such occasion I should exert some vigour and make no despicable figure. But I have done dear James with the implicit past, and for the future, where I have no knowledge of the projection I will have no Share in the execution.[12]

In a letter to another friend, Lord Orrery, he waxed almost lyrical on his life in the country, but acknowledged his readiness to resume his political career at a moment's notice:

> Whether it is owing to constitution or to Philosophy I can't tell, but certain it is, that I can make myself easy in any sort of life . . .
>
> Happiness, I imagine, depends much more on desiring little, than enjoying much; and perhaps the surest road to it is Indifference. If I continue in the country, the sports of the field and the pleasures of my study will take up all my thoughts, and serve to amuse me as long as I live. If any accident should call me again to the pleasure and business of London, I shall be as eager as ever I was in the pursuit of both.[13]

These letters show that St John had not given up his hopes of a quick return to active politics and that, should he be successful, he would act with even more vigour and determination. They also reveal his insatiable interest in public affairs. While he could not remain in the forefront of the Tory party in parliament, he continued to take a great interest in its fortunes. He was particularly outspoken in his efforts to reunite the party and to get Harley, Harcourt and his other friends into a firm alliance with Bromley, Hanmer and the other Tory leaders. From his country retreat, he also detected the drift of public opinion in the country at large. He was soon convinced that the landed interest was unwilling to shoulder any more financial burdens and was vociferous in its demands for a rapid end to the war. St John, however, was restricted to offering advice to his Tory colleagues and to detecting the drift of public opinion, or at least the opinions of the hard-pressed squirearchy. He could not take positive political action. He had to remain on the sidelines, while the changing fortunes of the Tory party and the skilful political machinations of Robert Harley were shaping his political future for him.

The reunion of the Harley-St John group with the main body of the Tories proved very difficult. Men like Bromley and Hanmer, who had led the party in recent years, were not prepared to step down in favour of the Tory renegades of 1704. Nor could they easily absorb such able politicians into their ranks or adjust readily to Harley's brand of Toryism. The process, if accomplished, would mean changes in leadership and policies. The negotiations were, therefore, delicate and protracted. Though both sides were aware of the mutual benefits which would accrue from an accommodation, many personal and political differences had to be reconciled. Henry St John, though he could not profit at once from any reunion in the Commons, pressed Harley to persevere with his negoti-ations with Bromley. He knew that failure would leave him out on a limb, functioning neither at Court nor with either of the two political parties. The only haven open to him was the Tory party. He advised Harley to steer resolutely in that direction:

> There is no hope I am fully convinced but in the Church of England party, nor in that neither on the foot it now stands, and without more confidence than is yet re-established between them and us. Why do you not gain Bromley entirely? The task is not difficult, and by governing him without seeming to do so, you will influence them . . . You broke the party, unite it again, their sufferings have made them wise, and whatever piques or jealousies they may entertain at present, as they feel the success of better conduct these will wear off, and you will have it in your power by reasonable measures to lead them to reasonable ends.[14]

This was a particularly valuable statement of St John's attitude at this juncture. He was anxious to ally with the high-Church Tories, but he was not advocating the adoption of all their policies. He still approved of Harley's endeavours to convert the Tories to more moderate conduct, though he no longer adopted a subservient tone towards Harley. Though generally labelled a Tory extremist, St John had, in fact, loyally supported Harley's strategy for several years. Of course, when he felt that it was in his own interests, and to the advantage of the Tory party as a whole, he was capable of straying from the moderate line of Harley and of occasion-ally advocating the more partisan policies of the high Tories; but he had not yet reverted to his old high-flying tactics of 1701–4. This interpretation of his attitude can be reinforced by another of his letters, which he wrote to Harley, on the subject of coming to terms with Bromley:

> It is impossible either that you should be safe from daily insults, or that the least progress should be made towards those which you purpose, unless a number of gentlemen be satisfied of their danger, unless they can be convinced that to preserve themselves they must follow you, . . . The fiery trial of affliction has made the gentlemen of the Church of England more prepared to form such a party than from their former conduct it might have been expected.[15]

Despite all this exhortation, it took many months to end most of the old feuds and to bring the Harley group and the bulk of the Tories into a political alliance. The reunion was cemented by a common hostility to the Whigs and to the conduct of the reorganised Godolphin ministry. Harley's path was smoothed by the mistakes made by the government. The influx of thousands of poor Palatines from Germany following the General Naturalisation Act of 1709, the failure of the government to make peace when France was almost on her knees, and the decision to impeach Dr Henry Sacheverell, a high-Church divine, for preaching the doctrine of non-resistance, swung public opinion firmly in the direction of the Tory party.

Without a seat in the Commons, St John could not take part in the Tory onslaught on the Whigs. He appears to have played no part in the famous trial of Dr Sacheverell, the high-Churchman, whose impeachment by the Whig ministry for casting doubt on the justifications for the Revolution, provoked an outburst of popular sentiment in favour of the theory of 'the Church in danger' and the Tory cause in general. In his rural retreat, however, he was able to see and to voice another widespread Tory grievance, the growing discontent of the landed interest at the increasing financial burden of the war and at the ministry's failure to secure a satisfactory peace in the negotiations of 1709. The complaints of the Tory landed gentry were not without foundation. They had been paying a land tax of four shillings in the pound for some years and a growing number of them were having to mortgage their estates. In 1709–10 there was something of an economic crisis, particularly in the rural areas. Bad harvests led to a sharp increase in the price of food, a slump in the export of grain and a contraction in the consumption of other goods. The price of grain nearly doubled between 1708 and 1709, and the cost of living was thirty per cent higher in 1710 than it had been in 1700.[16]

St John, who throughout his life was a spokesman for the landed gentry, passionately and eloquently expressed their fears and demands at this time. After the 1708 campaign he was convinced that a good peace could be achieved, if the allies would accept the loss of Spain. When, in November 1708, he declared to Harley, 'For God's sake let us be out of Spain!',[17] he was not only speaking from bitter experience. He showed a better grasp of the realities of the military situation than did the allied powers at the peace negotiations of 1709. Throughout that year his demands for peace became more strident and insistent. In July he wrote to Lord Orrery:

> We have now been twenty years engaged in the two most expensive wars that Europe ever saw. The whole burthen of this charge has lain upon the landed interest during the whole time. The men of estates have generally speaking, neither served in the Fleets nor armies, nor meddled in the public funds and management of the Treasury.
>
> A new interest has been created out of their fortunes, and a sort of property which was not known twenty years ago, is now increased to be almost equal to the terra firma of our island. The consequence of all this is that the landed men are become poor and dispirited. They either abandon all thoughts of the public, turn arrant farmers, and improve the estates they have left: or else to seek to repair their shattered fortunes by listing at court, or under the heads of partys. In the meanwhile those men are become their masters, who formerly would with joy have been their servants.[18]

This was a classic exposition of the prejudices of the landed interest and of their growing alarm at the advance of the moneyed men as a result of the financial revolution which had gathered pace since the Revolution. St John was putting forward the views of the Tory squires, a substantial element in the political nation. Yet he could also justify the need for peace on sound economic grounds. In another letter to Lord Orerry he wrote:

> Tho' the condition of France by evident tokens appears to be miserable, yet their ill Circumstances are certainly exaggerated in our accounts. I doubt we may add that our own state is not much better than our enemy's, and that an unseasonable harvest would reduce our people to the same misery as we triumph over.
>
> Peace is as much our interest as their's. I am so firmly persuaded of this, that I will continue to hope the winter may ripen this glorious fruit, which the summer could not.[19]

In a similar letter he told James Brydges:

Peace is at this time the most desirable publick or private good. If you will not think that I put on too much of the country esquire I'll venture to tell you, that we want it more than perhaps any man out of the country can imagine. Glorious successes and the hopes of a last campaign are sovereign cordials. They elevate the few spirits we have left and we are not seen to pine or languish; but should the distemper continue the strings of life may crack at once.[20]

After the costly victory at Malplaquet, St John could still offer congratulations to Marlborough, but to Brydges he expressed the fervent hope that peace could not now be far off. The true lustre of military glory was the promise of a good peace. As the details of this bloody battle filtered back to England, he claimed that the government was afraid to tell the country how dearly victory had been bought. The renewed confidence of the French, and the efforts to secure even more English recruits, filled him with despair. The war would continue for yet another campaign, when the country was already groaning under the heavy burden.[21]

The cost of war, in both men and money, was rapidly becoming insupportable to a majority of the nation, which felt aggrieved at the allies' failure to negotiate a satisfactory peace. The Sacheverell trial, raising again the cry of 'the Church in danger', completed the swing of political opinion away from the Whigs and towards the Tories, in the early summer of 1710. At the same time the Tories and the supporters of Harley had struck up a close working relationship. Nevertheless, the ministerial revolution of 1710 was achieved neither in parliament nor in the country at large, but at Court and through secret negotiations. It was primarily the achievement of one man, Robert Harley. Having gained the support of the bulk of the Tory party, Harley set to work winning the allegiance of moderate Whigs and the sympathy of the Queen. By dint of assiduous courtship and persuasive political arguments, he enticed several of the Whigs into his camp, including the Duke of Newcastle, Earl Rivers, the Earl of Mar, and the Earl of Peterborough. His most useful convert was the Duke of Shrewsbury, though the Whig Dukes of Somerset and Argyll were spectacular, if temporary, gains. This successful recruitment owed much to Harley's skill in political management and to his reputation as a moderate, who was unwilling to obey the dictates of party extremists.

St John fully approved of this policy of broadening the basis of support by the enlistment of moderate Whigs. After his fall in 1708, he is usually portrayed as immediately reverting to his former high-Tory policies and tactics. Though his personal relations with Harley had suffered a severe blow by his failure to gain re-election in 1708, he could still appreciate the wisdom of trying to persuade influential politicians, such as Somerset and Argyll, to desert the Whigs. A great opportunist, and generally an excellent reader of the political situation, he recognised that only Harley's policies could achieve success in the existing circumstances. In March 1710 he was actively participating in Harley's intrigues: 'I went from you to Court where I met Lord Rochester and the Duke of Argyll; they both told me that Hampden had been this day with the Duke of Somerset to tell him that he was empowered to let his Grace know that, if he was engaged in any measures where their assistance was necessary; he and his friends were ready to follow his directions.'[22] Next day he was expressing the hope that Argyll might even be persuaded to vote with the Tory opposition in the Sacheverell trial.[23] The importance of St John to Harley's schemes was clearly recognised by contemporaries. Brydges warned Cadogan that St John was deeply committed in these intrigues, and he informed John Drummond: 'Matters run very high at Court and the new schemes of administration grow very fast . . . Your friends Mr Harley and Mr St John are very near at the top of it and are likely to be the most considerable in it.'[24] The keystone of the ministerial revolution, however, was undoubtedly Robert Harley, for it was he who gained the ear of the Queen. By the spring of 1710 he had gained so much influence at Court that he could begin to remodel Godolphin's ministry piecemeal and against the Lord Treasurer's advice. He was not prepared simply to lead a Tory ministry back into power, for he feared that the Tories would again seek to dictate policy. His aim was to keep the real power in his own hands and to rely as much as possible on loyal and moderate men. It was Harley's great influence with the Queen that was to prove the principal stumbling block to the creation of a genuine Tory ministry in the last years of the reign. In the last resort it was to thwart St John's challenge for the leadership of the ministry and the party.

By mid-August 1710 Harley had completed the piecemeal destruction of the Godolphin ministry, but had steadfastly refused to create a Tory substitute. His willingness to rely on moderates, even if they were Whigs, alarmed many of his Tory supporters. Henry St John, who had loyally assisted Harley, expected a leading post in the new ministry. He was shocked to learn that Harley's idea of a suitable reward was to appoint him secretary to the Duke of Marlborough. It was made immediately clear to Harley that he expected something better than this: 'I am indifferent what employment is reserved for me, but I must own that to succeed Mr Cardonnel, upon the same foot as Mr Cardonnel was, is not coming into the service a second time with so good a grace as I came in the first; and keeping one's present situation is a good deal better than sinking while one affects to rise.'[25] The post of Treasurer of the Navy was apparently the next offer,[26] but this could hardly be regarded as promotion, since Robert Walpole filled this office, in addition to that of Secretary at War, St John's old position. After two years in the wilderness St John was adamant that he would only serve in a senior position. He was particularly anxious for a Secretaryship of State, but Harley clearly preferred someone more amenable in such a vital office and was reluctant to oblige his thrusting colleague. This almost certainly caused a temporary breach with the ambitious St John.[27] The latter's insistence had the desired effect. By September, Harley had capitulated and St John became Secretary of State for the Northern Department.

St John was no doubt piqued that Harley's estimation of him did not match his own, but he was not entirely opposed to Harley's schemes, though he was not sure that a mixed ministry could long stand the strain of party rivalry. He confided in his old crony, James Brydges: 'The treaty you mention I was not let into the secret of. I can only say that it seems to me very difficult, if not utterly impossible, to carry on with success a negotiation of that kind between parties amongst whom there is not the least confidence remaining.'[28] Nevertheless, while he envisaged greater concessions to the Tories than did Harley, he recognised the need to pursue rather devious means to accomplish certain political ends. He claimed that he had never altered his political principles, but the secrets of the Court and the intrigues of parties necessitated taking a roundabout route to his destination.[29] A letter to Lord Orrery expressed a similar conclusion: 'I begin now to see my way; and though in every respect it will not be possible . . . to play the game just as we would wish to do, or as we at first proposed, yet certainly with common address, and uncommon steadiness, we may be able to build up as well as we have been to pull down.' This letter goes on to show that, though St John wished to build the ministry on a Tory foundation, he did not anticipate, and had no intention of advising, any capitulation to the extremists. He was confident that Harley, though he disagreed with him to some extent, was on the correct tack:

It is incredible to what a degree the Whigs are united in opposition; but their numbers will soon diminish if the Tories can be made to proceed reasonably;

which I do not really much doubt, though I must think that we do take these in with the best grace, and with the greatest advantage to ourselves. Several persons imagine that the new measures of Harley cannot last; these will come over as soon as they see a firm foundation of strength layed. Others are alarmed and expected the utmost violence of a contrary extreme; these will likewise be recovered when they find the Tories kept in order, and the true interest pursued.[30]

When St John returned to office he entered the front rank of politicians for the first time. His two years of enforced retirement had weakened his ties with Harley and had increased his awareness of the strength of Toryism in the country at large. He was beginning to see an opportunity of leading the Tory country gentlemen from his position in the Cabinet, as he had previously done from the backbenches. This led him to favour a dissolution and an immediate general election, to catch the strong Tory tide. Moreover, since he was now a Secretary of State, but not actually in parliament, it was only natural that he should seek a rapid return to the Commons. As early as June 1710 he had been laying plans for his successful return and he had canvassed his old patron and mentor, Sir William Trumbull, for support in Berkshire, where he intended to stand for the Church of England interest. Should the opposition there prove too strong, he was confident that, this time, he could regain his old seat at Wootton Bassett.[31] Presumably his father had also become disenchanted with the Whigs by this time. Robert Harley, however, feared that a general election would result in a massive Tory victory, which would overwhelm his delicately constructed ministry. St John was forced to join the other Tories in counterbalancing the advice of Harley's new Whig friends.[32] Harley finally capitulated and a general election was held in the autumn of 1710.

St John played a notable part in one of the great election issues, the increasing demand for an end to the war. The Whigs, in fact, debated this more thoroughly than the Tories, who concentrated on fanning the prejudices aroused by the Sacheverell trial. It was surprising, in view of the considerable war-weariness of the country, that St John was one of the few Tories to make this a major plank in his election platform. In *A Letter to the Examiner*, published before the elections, he emphasised the changed character of the war: 'We engaged as confederates, but we have been made to proceed as principals; principals in expence of blood and treasure, whilst hardly a second place in respect and dignity is allowed to us.'[33] Even if not fully exploited, the widespread dissatisfaction with the war undoubtedly assisted the Tory cause to a considerable extent.

St John himself was elected for both Berkshire and Wootton Bassett, choosing to sit for the more prestigious county seat. The two seats at Wootton Bassett were filled by his clients and future followers, Edmund Pleydell and Richard Goddard. The new Secretary of State was much less successful in the county election in Bedfordshire, where he unwisely supported a challenger to the Russell interest.[34] This was a very minor blot on what looked to be a golden future. A knight of the shire and a leading minister, and barely thirty-two, he could anticipate playing a great role in the new parliament. Robert Harley was alarmed at the large Tory majority in the new House of Commons, but St John was to find in it a means to bid for the leadership of the party and the administration.

CHAPTER 5

The Breach with Harley

THE supreme political skill and backstairs influence of Robert Harley had engineered the ministerial revolution of 1710, but he had not been able to prevent a large, and potentially unruly, Tory majority from being returned at the general election. Though Harley had the support, if not the absolute allegiance, of several Tory leaders, including Bromley and Rochester, as well as St John and Harcourt, there were other prominent Tories who opposed his moderate, trimming policy. The most important of these was the Earl of Nottingham, whose integrity and high-Church principles commanded widespread respect among the Tory rank and file. Deliberately excluded from the new ministry by Harley, he was an obvious rallying point for those Tories disgruntled with Harley's conduct and policies. Sir Thomas Hanmer, who was assuming a similar prominence in the Commons, had not fully accepted Harley's leadership either. Despite these manifestations of early trouble, Harley pressed on with his plans to reduce faction at home and secure peace abroad. The essential prerequisite was to restore financial confidence, a task much more difficult than his backbench Tory critics ever realised. To secure the support of at least some of the leading financiers, Harley had to be seen to be holding the Tory extremists in check. It was against this background, of unhelpful allies and devious enemies abroad, and of determined Whig opponents and dissatisfied Tory supporters at home, that the struggle for the leadership of the Tory party was contested over the next four years.

The objectives of Henry St John at this early, critical stage have always been interpreted as being diametrically opposite to those of Harley. He has been described as a factious Tory, who returned to parliament in 1710, determined to lead the high-Church Tories in a policy of persecuting the Whigs. It is, in fact, even possible to cite his own confession:

I am afraid that we came to court in the same dispositions as all parties have done; that the principal spring of our actions was to have the government of

75

the state in our hands; that our principal views were the conservation of this power, great employments to ourselves, and great opportunities of rewarding those who had helped to raise us, and of hurting those who stood in opposition to us . . . The view, therefore, of those amongst us, who thought in this manner, was to break the body of the whigs, to render their supports useless to them, and to fill the employments of the kingdom, down to the meanest, with tories.[1]

Though this admission, written in 1717, might have been a true reflection of the views held by St John and many Tory backbenchers early in 1711, it was not an accurate description of their opinions in the autumn of 1710. St John himself was simply not in a position to control government policy at this stage, nor even to make a serious challenge for greater power. He had been peeved at the attempt to palm him off with a junior post, but he had no wish to rock the new and untried boat at this juncture. He had to accept that the new ministry was very much Harley's accomplishment and that for the moment Harley was both skipper and pilot. Harley was, indeed, the effective prime minister, enjoying the confidence of the Queen and his other Cabinet colleagues. It was not until the spring of 1711, when the Tory backbenchers broke out into open revolt and an attempt was made by a French agent to assassinate Robert Harley, that St John could lay claim to the position of deputy leader and even entertain the possibility of replacing Harley.

Nor is there any sign, in the autumn of 1710, that St John had adopted an extreme Tory policy. He was still quite favourably disposed to Harley's brand of moderation, a conviction born of the experiences of 1704–8. With his hopes for a speedy end to the war and with the Tory backbenchers ready, at least during the autumn of 1710, to follow Harley's lead, there was neither reason nor opportunity to challenge Harley's policies. Moreover, St John's personal ties were still with the Harleyites and the more moderate, almost non-party, politicians, such as James Brydges and Arthur Moore. As soon as he was appointed Secretary of State, he tried to re-establish cordial relations with his old friends in the army. He wrote to William Cadogan, a Whig, and offered him his full support, provided it did not conflict with his loyalty to his Tory colleagues. He was particularly anxious to win over Marlborough and to persuade the great commander to cooperate with his new political masters. To conciliate Marlborough, he cooperated with him in sabotaging the working of the Committee of Council at the War Office, which threatened to weaken the General's control over the affairs of the army.[2] In the political sphere, his conduct towards Marlborough was a skilful combination of the carrot and the whip. While St John desperately wanted to end the war, he knew that the pressure would have to be kept on the French for at least one more campaign and so he was anxious to keep Marlborough at the head of the army. He was not, however, prepared to see him combine with the Whigs, to embarrass the government at home, and so he passed on several warnings to him, requesting him to refrain from meddling with domestic politics. At the same time he urged him to return to the Tory fold, where he would find his legitimate pretensions supported.[3] It was not until the spring of 1711 that St John was convinced that Marlborough would obstruct the policies of the new ministry and that the Tory backbenchers would not be content until the scale of the war had been sharply reduced. It was then that he began to abandon Marlborough and to push for a rapid peace settlement.

Thus, during the first months of the new government, St John did not have any serious difference of opinion with Harley. His primary objective was to end the ruinous war with France, and his early letters as Secretary of State were full of hopes for a speedy peace and of criticisms of the allies. Harley, too, wished for peace, but he was not prepared to see St John negotiate it. Since July 1710 the French had made tentative approaches, through Lord Jersey, who was given considerable freedom of manœuvre by Harley. It was not until January 1711 that the French agent Gaultier was sent to Versailles for letters of credence and for clear and direct French propositions.[4] Throughout these preliminary overtures, St John had been quite deliberately kept in ignorance. It was not until Guiscard's murderous assault had laid Harley low, in March 1711, that St John realised just how far and how long he had been ignored. His real grievances with Harley, over policy and strategy, coincided, therefore, with the opportunity to assert himself in the Cabinet. At the same time developments in the Commons, where many Tory backbenchers were growing increasingly exasperated with Harley's policies, convinced St John that he might aspire to lead the Tory party out of Harley's tutelage. It was, therefore, not in the autumn of 1710, but in the spring of 1711, that he really began to eschew Harley's moderate policies. A combination of personal and political differences, of favourable parliamentary developments and of Harley's enforced absence from the Cabinet, made the crisis of March–April 1711 crucial in the relationship between St John and Harley, and in the former's bid for the leadership of the Tory party.

At first the Tory backbenchers were more anxious than St John to

pursue a policy which was frankly partisan, but even they did not demand
the immediate implementation of all their aims. Many were prepared to
give Harley a chance, knowing that he faced difficulties in securing sufficient financial support for his administration and in opening peace
negotiations with the French. Within a few months, however, they had
begun to rebel against Harley's continued moderation towards his
Whig opponents and his refusal to fill all available places with Tories.
Their increasing dissatisfaction with Harley persuaded St John to recon-
sider his own line of action. The more he saw Harley's policy of moderation alienating the Tory rank and file, the more he was tempted to swim
with the tide. He always showed a gambler's streak and a willingness to go
for the quick, easy results; and he always shied away from the long haul.
Harley's enforced withdrawal from active affairs, in March 1711, encouraged the ambitious St John to make a premature bid for the leadership.

Some of the hot-heads among the Tory squires were prepared to reject
Harley's moderation at once. This vocal and active minority soon made its
presence in the Commons felt, and by January 1711 it had sharply increased
its representation on the backbenches. One of their primary objectives
was a strict inquiry into the supposed financial abuses of the late Whig
ministry. Others were the enactment of a Place bill and the repeal of the
General Naturalisation Act of 1709. Harley tried to restrain them on all
fronts. St John's behaviour was much less consistent. In some debates,
those on the Place bill for instance, he supported Harley; but on other
issues he seemed to be encouraging the Tory rebels. In December 1710 he
was active in promoting a popular bill, aimed at determining the qualifications necessary to sit in the Commons. This bill reckoned the qualifications
for parliamentary candidates in terms of land and real estate, as distinct
from money in the forms of funds and stocks. On 20 and 21 December,
St John supported the bill in debate and also managed to get in some sharp
digs at the late Whig ministry. He attacked the opposition for being
critical of the powers of the Crown, when they were not prepared to have
the activities of their own ministers scrutinised.[5] His attack on the moneyed
interest delighted the Tory backwoodsmen:

> Mr. St John's speech was pretty remarkable, for in setting out how necessary
> this bill was to be enacted he gave some touches upon the late management, as
> that we might see a time when the money'd men might bid fair to keep out of
> that house all the landed men and he had heard of Societys of them that
> joint'd Stocks to bring in members, and such a thing might be an Administra-
> tion within an Administration, a juncto.[6]

This was playing upon Tory prejudices with a vengeance, though it is only fair to add that they were prejudices St John always shared. Once the bill had passed through parliament, it enhanced St John's prestige and popularity among the Tory rank and file. It gave him a clear indication of where he could turn for support and how he might aspire to lead the party. It whetted his already growing ambition and it exacerbated his dissatisfaction with Harley's conduct of affairs. His first success with the backbenchers led him to contemplate leading some inquiries into the conduct of the late ministry, after the Christmas recess. He could not see 'how those who are now in the administration, and who have taken such a broken shattered game into their hands can be safe, and avoid bearing the load of other people's guilt, unless they make a plain and obvious discrimination between their own management, and the natural necessary consequences of that which went before'.[7] This shift in St John's attitude, away from a policy of moderation, can be traced in the debates on the conduct of the war in Spain. When a new inquiry opened in the Commons, early in December 1710, St John maintained 'a profound silence'. Since the inquiry concentrated on the operations in Spain in the years 1705–7, when St John himself had been Secretary at War, his inhibitions were understandable. Over the Christmas recess, however, he abandoned his reservations. The news of further reverses in Spain probably convinced him that he should now lead the inevitable Tory onslaught. On 4 January 1711 he strongly supported the criticisms levelled against the previous Whig ministry.[8] Robert Walpole, who had just lost his post as Treasurer of the Navy, criticised the present administration and urged the need to consult the allies before taking any steps towards a peace settlement. St John promptly took him up on this. He accused him of harbouring private resentments and poured scorn on the idea of consulting the allies, who had supported the Whigs during the ministerial changes of 1710: 'Those allies, says he, that were brought in to support, a tottering ministry I won't call them, but a tottering faction.'[9]

St John's dissatisfaction with Harley's measures, and his desire to impress the Tory backbenchers, received a sharp boost with the appearance of the celebrated October Club. For more than two months the Tories had been critical of Harley's refusal to inquire into the gross financial misdemeanours which they were sure had been committed by the previous administration. On 5 February 1711 they took affairs into their own hands and passed several resolutions for inquiries into these suspected financial abuses. Their actions were sufficiently coordinated for contemporaries to

describe the appearance of a new party in the Commons. At first only 70 to
80 members strong, it rapidly doubled in size. The October Club, as this
pressure group described itself, did not only attract the inexperienced and
the rash from among the Tory rank and file, as has often been asserted.
There were men far advanced in years; men such as Ralph Freeman and
Sir John Pakington, who were veterans of the Tory campaigns of 1702–4;
and men of unimpeachable integrity and considerable influence, such as Sir
Justinian Isham, Peter Shakerley and, for a time, Sir Thomas Hanmer
himself. With recruits of this calibre, the October Club was a major threat
to the Harley administration.[10] Indeed, this pressure group soon created
havoc in the Commons and even hindered the voting of supplies. As in
1701–2, it adopted the Tory practice of choosing Commissioners of
Accounts, to investigate the activities of the previous ministry. It
threatened to wreck the whole basis of the Harley administration.

Harley could not even count upon the loyalty of his colleagues. St John
was clearly showing signs of joining the rebellion or at least of helping the
rebels to alter Harley's course. It seems likely that his decision was not
made because of a firm commitment to extremist policies in themselves,
but was dictated by personal ambition and his concern for the welfare and
the future prospects of the Tory party. He was less attached to Harley now,
he was anxious to raise his own standing in the ministry and the party,
and he believed that some concessions must be made to satisfy the Tory
backbenchers or else the Whigs would profit from their divisions.
His only deep-rooted prejudice was his hostility to the moneyed interest,
but his ambition and his assessment of the political situation led him to
support other factious policies in order to conciliate the Tory rank and file.
The longer Harley clung to power and stuck to a policy of moderation,
and the more the Whigs were emboldened by the prospect of the Hanoverian succession and their own return to power, the more St John was
betrayed into frantic efforts to keep the Tories together and in power.
Thus, by early 1711, he was beginning to break with Harley in order to
consolidate his own position and safeguard that of the Tory party.

The clamorous Tory demands for an inquiry into the management of
the Treasury before 1710 won his approval and marked another step away
from Harley's policy of moderation. 'The House of Commons', he wrote,
'are entering on the examination of frauds committed in the victualling,
they will proceed afterwards to some others, and I make no question, but
that the late applauded administration of the Treasury will appear, before
this session concludes, to have been the most loose, the most negligent, the

Bucklebury Manor House

Charles Boyle, 4th Earl of Orrery

Robert Harley, Earl of Oxford

Jonathan Swift

most partial that ever any country suffered by.'[11] The tone of this letter, and the fact that it was written a month before the actual appearance of the October Club, suggests that St John was not merely agreeing with Harley's critics, but was positively inciting them to further action. Harley later claimed that it was in February 1711, when the October Club first made its appearance, that 'there began a separation in the House of Commons, and Mr Secretary St John began listing a party, and set up for governing the House'. To meet this threat, Harley, Rochester, Shrewsbury, Dartmouth and other ministers called upon St John. These ministers were all adherents of Harley. Even Rochester had been won over to his policy of moderation and he 'took much pains' to settle the dispute, but he and his colleagues failed to quash St John or convert him, for 'this was the last time Robert Harley was ever invited to Mr Secretary's House'.[12] Indeed, St John was encouraged to pursue his dangerous course by an attempt to assassinate Harley, that threw the leadership issue wide open.

On 8 March 1711, Antoine de Guiscard, a French refugee, was examined by Harley, St John and four other ministers, for alleged treasonable correspondence with France. Having picked up a penknife, he launched a murderous attack on Harley, stabbing him in the chest. Harley survived the attack, but he was incapacitated for several weeks. The attempted assassination did much to revive Harley's sagging prestige among his Tory critics. St John, who feared that his own influence would, in consequence, diminish, tried to salvage some sympathy and credit for himself. It could be convincingly argued that Guiscard had more reason to hate the Secretary, for St John had ordered his arrest and had conducted the investigation. Guiscard had even attempted, during the inquiry, to speak to him alone, perhaps with the object of assassinating him. These factors enabled St John to embroider accounts for public consumption, in which he appeared as the intended victim. It was a cheap attempt to deprive Harley of the sympathy he had earned and the incident, no doubt, widened the breach between the two ministers.[13] Harley's brother, Edward, even believed that it was from this point that St John 'began to form a party against the Chancellor [of the Exchequer] while he lay ill of his wound. This was carried on under the pretence that some person should be put at the head of the Church party, who would without reserve comply with all their passions.'[14] Harley himself would have dated the breach a month earlier, but clearly the assassination attempt was crucial in the relationship between the two men. It exacerbated their mutual

D

hostility and it gave St John the opportunity to lead the Tories in Harley's absence.

In his first years in parliament St John had shown that his oratorical gifts and his imperious spirit could sway the Tory squires by showing them 'game'. Now, because of the precarious financial situation which still faced the ministry, St John could not afford to kick over the traces and lead an October Club rebellion which would destroy the present administration. Instead, he had to try to emulate Harley's tact and diplomacy in order to secure backbench support for the continuation of relatively moderate policies. In trying to achieve Harley's ends, without Harley's means, he bungled his whole strategy and saw the October Club slip out of his control. These Tory malcontents had been silenced for a couple of weeks by the attack upon Harley's life, but they were soon baying once more for Whig dismissals. On 26 March, William Lowndes, the Secretary to the Treasury, introduced a tax on leather, which, to the ministry's consternation, was opposed by the October men. St John was taken completely by surprise and he was not even in the Commons when the bill was introduced. When he did arrive his speech came too late to retrieve the situation.[15] With some justice, Peter Wentworth commented:

> Several politicians that could not endure Mr. Harley say they see now there's no man the Court employs has address enough to manage the House of Commons but him; if he had been well he would either have had intelligence of what was intended and so have endeavoured to have brought them to the house in a better temper, or at least when there he would have seen how 'twoud have gone and would have put it off for a fitter opportunity.[16]

The ministry had been badly mauled, though naturally Harley's reputation soared. The infuriated and embarrassed St John attempted to salvage something from the disaster. Since the leather tax could not be reintroduced in the same session, and supplies were essential, he resorted to the rather shabby expedient of proposing instead a tax on hides and skins. When this bill was introduced he harangued the Tory backbenchers, warning them that another adverse vote would arouse the resentment of the Queen and the nation. This bill met little opposition.[17]

St John had not, however, succeeded in establishing his control over the Commons. There were other serious blunders. The October Club voted for Commissioners of Accounts to examine the financial actions of the previous administration, and made sure that the seven members who were elected were from among its own members. Another money bill, the

Post Office bill, was mutilated and commissioners to examine the grants of land made by the Crown since 1688 were appointed at the instigation of the rebellious Tory backbenchers. On 24 April 1711 the Commons went on to examine the accounts of the Godolphin administration and came to the astonishing, although erroneous, conclusion that £35 million could not be accounted for.[18] At last there appeared to be some justification for all the wild accusations of the October Club. Following this disclosure St John was quite unable to control the Tory backbenchers. He had been convinced that they would never be able to find proof to support their accusations. Now he was not only embarrassed by the apparent financial abuses brought to light, but alarmed that he might find himself implicated in these charges. Over six of the missing millions were from the accounts of his crony, James Brydges, the Paymaster of the forces abroad. When he had been Secretary at War St John had arranged army contracts through Brydges and he feared that these might not bear close scrutiny. He felt compelled to save his crony, so he had the investigations postponed for a few days. His defence of Brydges, 'which was very desperately spoken, and giving up the whole cause', annoyed his fellow-ministers. They had been irritated at the way he had tried to curry favour with the rebellious backbenchers in February, and were aghast at his failure to control them in March and April. It was even rumoured that St John would be fortunate to survive as Secretary of State. Nor could he rely on the support and loyalty of the October Club, which was dissatisfied with his handling of the inquiry, once it was resumed.[19] He was in danger of cutting himself off from all support, an astonishing fall from grace after the excellent prospects which had faced him when Harley was first incapacitated.

St John was compelled to acknowledge that Harley was irreplaceable and, indeed, absolutely indispensable, for without him the ministry could not be put on a sound financial footing. When he returned to his parliamentary duties Harley was able to delight his Tory critics with his bill to set up the South Sea Company as a rival to the great Whig trading and moneyed corporations. He began to conciliate some of the October men by giving them minor posts, though they were denied the power to shape government policy. When he had to find replacements, in the summer of 1711, for Rochester and Newcastle, who had both died, he was determined to keep Nottingham out of the ministry once again. Instead, he promoted his loyal supporters, especially Lord Poulett, into the important political posts and made only one genuine change, bringing in the moderate John Robinson, Bishop of Bristol, as Lord Privy Seal. To crown his triumph, Harley was appointed Lord Treasurer and elevated to the peerage as Earl of Oxford.

In contrast, St John's fortunes were at their lowest ebb. He had failed to consolidate his position as a potential leader of the Tory backbenchers. He had also irritated Harley, whose own reputation had been enhanced and whose position had been considerably strengthened. His reputation as a man of affairs had suffered a heavy blow. The Secretary's reaction was typical. He put the blame on others. In a letter to his friend, Lord Orrery, he complained of Harley's conduct:

> Mr Harley, since his recovery, has not appeared at the Council or at the Treasury at all, and very seldom in the House of Commons. We, who are reputed to be in his intimacy, have few opportunities of seeing him, and none of talking freely with him. As he is the only true channel through which the Queen's pleasure is conveyed; so there is, and must be a perfect stagnation, till he is pleased to open himself, and set the water flowing.[20]

Nor was St John satisfied with the October men, whom he now accused of being too anxious for office and too willing to offer themselves for sale. His uneasiness seemed to be confirmed by the success Harley was having at drawing the teeth of the October Club with a few minor places. Though he was prepared to admit that Harley deserved his appointment as Lord Treasurer and his elevation to the peerage, he feared that the 'prime minister' might not prove loyal to his colleagues. With some trace of anxiety, he confessed to Lord Orrery: 'The companions of his evil fortune are most likely to be the supporters of his good; and I dare say he makes this a maxim to himself; for though he often wants that grace and openness which engages the affection, yet I must own, I never knew that he wanted either the constancy or the friendship which engages the esteem.'[21]

In addition to these blows to his political career, St John was in the midst of personal problems in the summer of 1711. His marriage was little more than a hollow mockery and his shameless treatment of his wife shocked many contemporaries, notably Oxford and the Queen. In July, William Stratford told young Edward Harley of a visit he had made to Mrs St John, in Berkshire: 'I met nothing there but sorrow and disorder. That unfortunate gentleman is more irregular, if possible, in his private than [his public] capacities. A sad instance to all young gentlemen of quality, how the greatest parts and expectations may be made useless and be disappointed by the folly of vice – the only way in which that unhappy gentleman will ever be of any use in the world.'[22] Such strongly worded criticisms illustrate the decline in St John's friendship with the Harley family. He was also at odds with his old friend, Simon Harcourt, and he was once more quarrelling with his father.[23] As a reaction to this ostracism, St John set up a special club, which included his personal friends, such as Lord Orrery, Jack Hill and Sir William Wyndham, and eminent wits, such as Swift, Prior and Arbuthnot. Significantly, the Lord Treasurer was deliberately excluded, a decision approved by St John.[24] The breach with Oxford was clearly widening.

This dispute with Oxford was exacerbated by the Secretary's efforts to increase his influence over the ministry's foreign policy. As one of the Secretaries of State, St John should have had a considerable influence on foreign affairs, but he had been quite deliberately excluded from the major policy-making decisions. St John's first attempt to display an independent initiative in foreign policy was to plan a bold stroke against French power in Canada. He planned such an expedition and then, in January 1711, he worked hard to convince Harley of the value of an attack on Quebec: 'Pray do me the justice to believe that I am not light nor whimsical in this project. It will certainly succeed if the secret is preserved, and if it succeeds you will have done more service to Britain in half a year, than the ministers who went before you did in all their administration. I hope you will support me in it since I have gone so far.'[25] Harley had not approved of the project, but, while he was incapacitated after the Guiscard affair, St John bulldozed the plan through the Cabinet. On 25 March 1711 the Cabinet had met in Harley's absence and the Queen gave her approval for the expedition. For a time it looked as if Harley and Rochester might still be able to halt the project, but St John strongly backed his brain-child and he ingratiated himself with the Queen and Mrs Masham by suggesting that the latter's brother should command the land forces sent to Canada.[26] The success of the venture largely depended upon secrecy, but the whole design was soon public knowledge. St John, incapable of keeping a secret himself, was not concerned and the expedition continued. In the event, it failed dismally and St John could salvage little from the disaster, which, however, was due more to the timidity of the commanders than to any defects in the overall conception. Oxford was not disconcerted. He later charged St John with planning to enrich himself by the contracts for the clothes and supplies for the expeditionary force.[27]

The breach between Oxford and St John widened substantially when the Secretary discovered that he had been quite deliberately excluded from the ministry's tentative peace negotiations with France. These had been under way since July 1710, but, even as late as March 1711, only an inner group of ministers – Harley, Shrewsbury, Dartmouth and Rochester – were fully apprised of these developments. St John had been kept in ignorance. Already he had shown himself to be the most forceful member of the Cabinet and he had begun to sympathise with some of the demands of the Tory backbenchers. Harley probably feared that peace negotiations in St John's hands would quickly become partisan. There was a danger that he would lead a public campaign against the allies or compete with them to secure the best separate agreement with France.[28] The French Foreign Minister, the Marquis de Torcy, believed that St John came into the peace negotiations only when Harley had temporarily to relinquish the reins, in March 1711.[29] In fact, it was more than a month later before St John learned of the peace negotiations. Shrewsbury had become increasingly ill at ease at the nature of the peace proposals made by the French and he wished to divest himself of responsibility. When these preliminary proposals arrived, on 22 April 1711, Shrewsbury was opposed to keeping the negotiations secret any longer and he suggested that the whole Cabinet should discuss them. Harley and Dartmouth reluctantly gave way. On 25 April the Cabinet considered the French offer and St John learned belatedly of the earlier peace negotiations. He was no doubt incensed that his fellow Secretary of State, Lord Dartmouth, had been considered more important and more trustworthy than himself. His irritation was no doubt aggravated by his failure to dominate the negoti-ations, even after he learned of them. Until the autumn of 1711 he had only a very general grasp of the intricacies of the peace negotiations. Time and again Oxford refused to entrust the finer points of diplomacy to his thrusting Secretary of State, but preferred to conduct all the important discussions himself, with both the allies and the French agents.[30]

St John did not accept this without a struggle. For several months he had been at odds with Oxford on a whole range of major topics, affecting the domestic and foreign policy of the ministry. He had failed to emerge as the leader of the Tories in the Commons, he had seen Oxford's credit soar, and he could only watch the Lord Treasurer's control over the ministry and parliament grow more sure. Now, after the failure of the Quebec expedition, he was determined not to be ignored in the great peace negotiations, which were getting under way between Britain and France. The ministry was heading for its greatest test and St John was determined to play a major role in it. When he and Dartmouth met Mesnager, the French agent, he dominated the discussions and acted as the link between Mesnager and the Cabinet. Yet still he was not allowed a free hand, even when the other ministers could not suggest alternative policies. He became so furious at his failure to dominate ministerial strategy that he insisted that the Whig Duke of Somerset, who opposed these peace negotiations, should be excluded from the Cabinet.[31] Though he won a minor triumph on this issue, he could not combat the stronger influence of Oxford.

The disputes between St John and Oxford, that had been simmering for months, now threatened to disrupt the whole ministry. Swift reported: 'The Whigs whisper, that our new ministry differ among themselves, and they begin to talk out Mr Secretary [St John]: they have some reasons for their whispers, although I thought it was a greater secret. I do not much like the posture of things; I always apprehended, that any falling out would ruin them, and so I have told them several times.'[32] Fortunately for St John, he was not easily replaced. There were not many moderates of ministerial calibre to whom Oxford could turn instead, and, with the Lord Treasurer in the Lords, St John was now the administration's most effective spokesman in the Commons. Nevertheless, Oxford's friends were beginning to believe that there might be no alternative but to dismiss St John and risk the consequences. They traced the source of the dispute to the efforts made by some of the Tory backbenchers, to convince St John that 'he was of capacity enough to stand upon his own legs'. Others suspected St John of secretly negotiating with the Duke of Marlborough, a charge which the Secretary indignantly denied.[33]

St John had clearly renounced his close ties with Oxford's policies and fortunes and had now begun to shift for himself. Though he had won few friends in high places, he knew that he could find at least a refuge with the Tory malcontents. It was not his intention, however, to be a backbench spokesman, but to hold government office and to lead a ministry. His early ventures in this direction, since February 1711, had failed and he had come close to losing all. The experience taught him several lessons. He needed a greater reputation as a minister, he required more widespread political support, and he would have to rival Oxford's influence with the Queen. Though he committed himself to these objectives, his inordinate ambition and his erratic temperament rendered him incapable of making any surreptitious advance. During the rest of the reign he emerged more and more as the open rival and would-be successor to Oxford. His conduct weakened the ministry, obstructed its work, and hindered the Tories coming to terms with the Hanoverian succession. Yet, despite these strictures upon St John, it must be acknowledged that Oxford played no small part in the ultimate disaster. His monopoly of the Queen's confidence, his inveterate secrecy, and his frequent contacts with the Whigs, were bound to create jealousy among his ministerial colleagues. Moreover, he failed to offer a real lead to the Tory party, especially over the dilemma of the succession. At home he continued to resist the Tory demands for a more partisan policy, while abroad he moved towards peace by a most tortuous route. Unwilling or unable to get rid of St John, in August–September 1711, he continually thwarted the Secretary's efforts to give a clearer, though less honourable, lead in domestic and foreign policy.

Disputes over the conduct of the peace negotiations aggravated the strained relations between Oxford and St John. The Lord Treasurer wanted to keep these negotiations on the level of tentative discussions, until he could persuade the allies to take part in a general peace settlement. The initial talks might be secret, but, in his opinion, they should not lead to a partisan or unilateral peace. To avoid being trapped into such an undertaking, an escape route was essential. In fact, his room for manœuvre was continually diminishing. St John realised this and pressed for decisive action. He, at least, clearly recognised that special terms for Britain could only be secured at the expense of the allies and he knew that opposition to the peace was inevitable. While Oxford hesitated St John began to stamp his vigorous presence on the peace negotiations. In two meetings with Gaultier and Mesnager, on 19 and 23 September 1711, he made the running and dominated the discussions. After the first meeting he drew up a report for the benefit of the Queen and reported personally to the Cabinet. In these discussions he tried to raise new subjects of contention between Britain and France, that threatened to obstruct the whole negotiation, but he was forced to climb down on the intervention of the Queen. He was easily persuaded, for he was now intent on peace at nearly any price. Though he failed to obtain clear answers from the French on such major issues as commerce, Dunkirk, Newfoundland and the West Indies, he was quite prepared to join, with Dartmouth and Mesnager, in signing the peace preliminaries, on 27 September 1711.[34]

These preliminaries were open to serious criticism, but St John had no hesitation in defending them and went to greater lengths than Oxford to do so. When James Dayrolle, a British representative at The Hague, criticised these terms St John insisted on his recall.[35] The Secretary of State could not silence his ministerial colleagues quite so easily and some of them were far from happy with the preliminaries. Shrewsbury refused to sign them and the Duke of Buckingham could scarcely believe that the ministry had not secured some other secret, advantageous terms. On the backbenches there was a real threat of a Tory rebellion, led by the Earl of Nottingham in the Lords and Sir Thomas Hanmer in the Commons.[36] As the new parliamentary session approached, St John worked hard to combat the unfavourable reaction to the meagre gains Britain had obtained by the peace preliminaries. He arrested several booksellers and publishers for disseminating hostile Whig pamphlets. As a counterblast, he assisted Swift in the preparation of his celebrated pamphlet, *The Conduct of the Allies*.[37] The publication of this savage attack on the allies was a victory for St John's view that the ministry must use strong measures to counter the complaints of the opposition. This pamphlet accused the allies of failing to bear a fair share of the burden of war, while being prepared to neglect Britain's legitimate interests. It also sought to associate in the public mind the unjustified complaints of the allies with the factious opposition of the Whigs. That the general public readily accepted such arguments was illustrated by the immense sale and considerable impact of this pamphlet.

St John was not only active in the propaganda field, where he hoped to rally the Tories and public opinion in general behind the peace preliminaries. He was also trying to bully the allies into tamely following the ministry's initiative. In order to accomplish both these objectives, the ministry produced two different versions of the preliminaries. The first, which the government hoped to keep secret for the moment, listed the special advantages for Britain, including Gibraltar, Minorca and the Asiento treaty, which accorded Britain favourable trading rights with the Spanish Americas. The second, 'the paper for Holland' as St John called it, outlined the general terms on which the allies were to negotiate, but omitted the special terms already granted to Britain. The Dutch and the Austrians were aghast at the vague terms of this second paper and began to prepare an opposition campaign in conjunction with the Whigs. The ministry replied by publishing the first paper, and St John, in particular, was incensed by the conspiratorial activities of Count Gallas, the Austrian envoy. In a letter to the Queen, he protested: 'Nothing can be more insolent and ungrateful to your Majesty, the great protectress of the Austrian family, more brutal to your servants, nor more villainous in its own nature, in every part.'[38] He succeeded in having Gallas dismissed

from the Court. The Hanoverians needed to be handled more carefully.
Oxford tried to explain Britain's need for peace, while asserting the
ministry's loyalty to the Hanoverian succession. Despite the evident
need for tact, St John left Kreienberg, the Hanoverian resident, in no doubt
that the ministry was determined on peace at any price.[39] He was confident
that the government would secure popular support, either for 'pressing
roundly' on the allies or for a separate peace with France if the allies
proved obstinate.

When the new parliamentary session opened, the administration was
far from confident that it could carry the peace preliminaries through the
two Houses, especially the Lords. These fears were soon realised. On
7 December 1711 the Earl of Nottingham joined the Whigs in opposing
any peace which allowed Spain and the West Indies to remain in the hands
of the Bourbons. Though there was no major Tory rebellion in the Lords,
Nottingham's defection enabled the Whigs to add their motion, to
support no peace without Spain, to the address to the Queen. In the
Commons the opposition was less successful. St John sought to justify
the ministry's conduct by claiming that the Dutch were satisfied with
developments and were in favour of peace. This provoked a major
dispute with Sir Peter King, an able Whig lawyer, in which, according
to the report of the Dutch resident, St John was outpointed.[40] At the
division, however, the opposition amendment was easily defeated, though
there were eleven Tory rebels. This small, but significant, group may have
been the first 'Whimsical' or 'Hanoverian' Tories; the first signs of a
defection which was ultimately to disrupt the Tory party. These rebels
disliked the move towards separate peace negotiations and suspected the
ministry's loyalty to the Hanoverian succession. Thus, peace negotiations
had not united the Tory party, but had reopened the basic divisions
within it ranks.[41]

In the long run the Hanoverian Tories in the Commons were to be a
more serious disruptive force than the defection of Nottingham. Yet, at
the time, the situation in the Lords was much more alarming for the
ministers. There, the opposition's offensive threatened to destroy the
administration and decisive action was clearly needed. St John had always
dreaded that Oxford's moderation would play into the hands of the
opposition in the Lords.[42] He now urged that the ministry must ignore the
opposition to the peace, even when substantial objections to it emanated
from the Court of Hanover, in the form of a memorial presented to the
ministry by Baron Bothmer, the Hanoverian representative. This policy

The Breach with Harley 91

meant depending more wholeheartedly on the Tory majority in the Commons and in the nation at large. In a letter to Lord Strafford he wrote:

> The whole turns on the Queen's resolution; if she has vigour and firmness enough to assert her own dignity, she will unite the bulk of the nation in her interest, and leave the faction nothing but impotent malice, wherewith to torment themselves, but not to hurt her, or those who serve her. It is inconceivable how much mankind is allarmed at Bothmar's memorial, and at his conduct; once more, if she is true to herself, the success of the Whigs in the House of Lords will be their ruin and her salvation.
>
> I hope she will, I believe she will; and by the next post your Excellency will know what has passed, for the crisis has come, and the delay cannot be long.[43]

Despite the clamour of the ministers and their Tory supporters, the Queen and Oxford did not act for three weeks. The Tory backbenchers in the Commons took matters into their own hands by attacking the financial dealings of Marlborough and Robert Walpole, the previous Secretary at War. In the Lords it was the opposition which took the offensive, with motions to concert all peace negotiations with the allies and to safeguard the Hanoverian succession. In the middle of this crisis the Scottish peers rebelled over the Hamilton peerage case, which appeared to prevent Scottish peers from being created peers of Great Britain and sitting in the Lords by virtue of this title.[44] The government was clearly no longer in control of the situation and the ministry's hangers-on, such as Jonathan Swift and Matthew Prior, were considering whether to abandon the sinking ship. These plans were thrown aside when Oxford once more came to the rescue. He had persuaded the Queen to create twelve new Tory peers, to give the government a safe majority in the Lords. St John was considered for promotion to the Lords and there were strong rumours that he would become Earl of Bolingbroke, but at present his ability in the Commons was regarded as indispensable.[45] The Secretary was a little piqued at this decision, especially as all the new peers were personal friends or connections of the Lord Treasurer.

Having confounded the Whigs, Oxford set about conciliating the Tory malcontents. Marlborough was dismissed from his command and his removal was quickly followed by that of Cadogan and the Duke of Somerset. Plans were laid for arraigning both Marlborough and Robert Walpole, on the basis of the report on their financial dealings by the Tory Commissioners of Accounts. The hostility of the October men was further reduced by the offer of a few government places, by the process of infiltrating their ranks with moderate Tories, and by a press campaign explicitly designed to convince them of the need to support the ministry. In *A Letter to the October Club*, published in January 1712, Swift urged its members to remain loyal to Oxford, even though he had not yet turned out every Whig in office. They should remember that his room for manœuvre was limited by the royal prerogative.

Oxford ended the year 1711 on a note of triumph and, indeed, the whole year had enhanced his reputation and strengthened his control of the ministry. He had withstood an assassination attempt, the obstruction of the October Club, the defection of Nottingham and the intrigues of Henry St John. He had solved the ministry's pressing financial problems, he had controlled the early peace negotiations, he had rewarded his friends with offices and peerages, and he had demonstrated his influence at Court. In contrast, Henry St John had suffered several setbacks and had come close to dismissal. His reputation as a man of affairs had been harmed by failures in the Commons and in Canada. The peace negotiations had been started without his knowledge and were still not under his control. The attempts to lead the October Club rebels, or a faction in the ministry, had both floundered. Nevertheless, there were several hopeful signs for St John and a few dark clouds on Oxford's horizon. In foreign affairs, the Lord Treasurer was now committed to making peace with France, even at the expense of bullying or deserting the allies. He had also failed to keep the discussions secret, tentative, or entirely under his own control. St John had at least begun to wrest some measure of influence over these vital negotiations. At home Oxford had retained control of the chief ministerial posts, but he had been compelled to make concessions to the Tory backbenchers. The attacks on Marlborough and Walpole strained the links he had so carefully maintained with the moderate Whigs. This allowed his ambitious rival, Henry St John, to strengthen his own hold over the Tories, upon whom the Lord Treasurer was now more dependent than ever.

CHAPTER 6

Bolingbroke and the Treaty of Utrecht

THE making of the peace was to have a great influence on the rivalry between Oxford and St John and on the whole question of the leadership of the Tory party. The ministerial revolution of 1710, and the Tory triumph in the general election, had owed a great deal to the widespread desire for peace. The ministers and the Tory backbenchers were frequently at odds in the next three years, but their common determination on a peace helped to keep the Tory party together, though relations were often strained. Ironically, once the great peace had been accomplished the party began to disintegrate. In later years St John acknowledged that the most serious problems which the Tories had to face only appeared after the Treaty of Utrecht had been signed: 'The peace had been judged with reason to be the only solid foundation whereupon we could erect a tory system: and yet when it was made we found ourselves at a full stand. Nay the very work, which ought to have been the basis of our strength, was in part demolished before our eyes, and we were stoned with the ruins of it.'[1] The actual peace negotiations themselves, however, were responsible for increasing the tension between Oxford and St John, for the two leading ministers disagreed on how best to end the war. The great Cabinet split, which occurred in September 1712, was not the result of pressure on the ministry from recalcitrant Tory backbenchers, but the consequence of the Secretary's eagerness to take control of the negotiations with France and to make a separate peace. When St John failed to make peace on his own terms he had to continue in uneasy alliance with Oxford. Once peace was finally accomplished the ministry appeared to lose its whole *raison d'être* and its sense of direction. As a consequence, the disputes between the two leading ministers overlapped with the disintegration of the Tory party.

The decision to make peace, despite the opposition of the Whigs and the allies, and Oxford's willingness to make some concessions to the October Club, gave St John the chance to play the role for which he was most suited, that of a partisan leader. Unfortunately, the design of censuring Marlborough, for accepting the perquisites and percentages from the army contracts and the pay of the troops, placed St John in a predicament. He had always been on good terms with Marlborough and even now he had no wish for an irreparable breach. Though he could not ward off this blow entirely, without alienating the Tory backbenchers, he did warn Marlborough to act reasonably and the censure would be made as light as possible. When the Duke decided to defend his conduct St John could do nothing to save him, but he played no part in the censure debate.[2] The Secretary showed a much greater willingness to placate the Tories by hastening the peace. In February 1712 he set about intimidating the Dutch by launching a parliamentary attack on the Barrier Treaty, which the Dutch had arranged with the previous Whig administration. When Bothmer, the Hanoverian envoy, expressed the hope that this would not nullify the clause by which the Dutch guaranteed the Hanoverian succession, St John saw fit to send him 'a peppering answer'.[3] In the debate in the Commons, on 14 February, 'Mr St Johns began to tell the house of what dangerous consequence this treaty was to England, 'twas not only a barrier for the Dutch against the French but against the [English] . . . he expaciated very handsomely upon these subjects and then said other gentlemen that would speak after him would no doubt lay the pernicious consequences more home to them.' This bitter attack was seconded by his personal friends, Arthur Moore and Sir William Wyndham. When a leading Whig, Nicholas Lechmere, suggested that the administration wished to censure the Barrier Treaty, by which Britain had guaranteed the Dutch certain fortresses and trading concessions in the Low Countries, because it prevented the ministers concluding an inglorious and ignominious peace, 'St John told him those that had the honour to be advisers to the Queen abhorred the French and French interest as much as anybody could, but 'twas not this treaty that stood in the way of a good peace, but from her Majesty's factious subjects at home, who writ letters abroad and bid the Dutch stand out.'[4] Two days later the Commons voted the Barrier Treaty destructive to the trade and interest of Britain.

St John made sure that the news of these debates reached The Hague as quickly as possible. Yet it is doubtful whether his campaign in parliament had much success in intimidating the Dutch. He may even have stiffened Dutch resistance to a peace dictated by Britain. Oxford probably had more influence over the Dutch by using persuasion instead of threats.[5] On the home front, however, St John had scored a significant success. He had delighted the Tories with the attack on the Barrier Treaty and with his determination that the Dutch would be forced to play their due role in the war. After his disasters in the previous session he now appeared to have recovered his reputation as a parliamentary manager, as well as having gained popularity with the Tory backbenchers, through his vigorous denunciation of the allies. Swift noted: 'The Secretary is much the greatest Commoner in England, and turns the whole Parliament, who can do nothing without him, and if he lives and has his health, will I believe be one day at the head of affairs.'[6] St John had scored a notable success with the October Club. For one of their evening meetings he had the satisfaction of being elected president. There were many other signs that the October Club was coming to terms with the ministry, for about fifteen of its leading members, including Charles Eversfield, Charles Caesar, Sir William Wyndham, John Hynde Cotton, Sir Simeon Stuart and Sir George Beaumont, all of whom had considerable influence with the rank and file, had accepted minor offices and places.

Nevertheless, despite these successes, it did not take long for St John to learn that it was no easy task to forge and lead a united Tory party. He had hoped that the Tories would tamely follow a vigorous lead, but the divisive nature of the party soon taught him otherwise. His success with the October Club did not unite the disparate Tory elements. Some of its members resented the influence which the ministry had begun to exercise over their colleagues, who they feared had been bought off from their declared principles. At the end of March 1712 this dissident minority broke away to form a new society, the March Club. It soon numbered about 50 members, mainly the Country element, inherently and instinctively hostile to the Court. They were also suspicious of the ministry's peace proposals and its equivocal attitude towards the succession problem. They formed another 'Hanoverian' splinter group. Since they were only a minority, however, they left the bulk of the October Club more than ever under St John's influence. This was underlined when the March Club excluded from their society both Charles Eversfield and Sir Simeon Stuart, two of the most active members of the October Club, for introducing St John into that society. The seven Commissioners of Accounts were also blackballed, as instruments of St John and Oxford.[7]

This new and surprising political development again found St John wanting in the finer arts of parliamentary management. Just when he seemed to have gained control of the Commons, the situation became even more confused. Unfortunately for the Secretary, an incident which involved him personally allowed the March Club to give him a stinging rebuff. The issue arose when a poor family, the Sandes, petitioned the Commons for the recovery of money from Arthur Moore, St John's crony, who sought to defend himself by claiming the special privileges of an M.P. In a committee of the Commons, on 2 April 1712, St John secured a resolution 'that the said petition is frivolous and vexatious'. When this was reported to the whole House a great debate ensued. St John's resolution was supported by his new friends in the October Club, but it was defeated when the March Club joined the Whigs in opposition to it. A month later St John found himself supporting the March Club against the October men. The latter unwisely decided to tack the bill, to appoint commissioners to examine royal grants of land since 1688, to the Lottery bill. Both the ministry and the March Club wished to avoid a clash with the Lords, which would result from such a 'tack'. St John failed to prevent the issue coming to the vote and had to see his own supporters, the October men, crushed.[8] Clearly, the October men were willing to support St John on some partisan issues, but they had demonstrated that they were not his personal followers nor his dependable allies. Without the support of the majority of the Tory backbenchers, St John could not mount a sustained challenge for the leadership of the party nor exert a commanding influence in the Cabinet. Not surprisingly, the Secretary was somewhat disillusioned with the task of trying to manage the dissident Tories. He confessed as much to the Earl of Peterborough:

> In all your experience, I may venture to affirm, you never passed through such a scene of confusion and difficulty, as this winter has afforded us; and though we have kept one point steadily in sight, and worked towards it, yet have been forced to shift our course, and try different measures, almost every day.
>
> Faction can invent nothing more ruinous to the public, the rage of woman nothing more barbarous towards particular men, than some of the intrigues which have been lately carried on.[9]

A week later he was more confident. Successful peace negotiations might yet solve all the political problems he was facing:

> It is certainly true my Lord that our affairs are and have been in great confusion. Those who are most employed feel sufficiently the load and burden of it, but this ought to be the less surprising when it is considered what an entire change has been wrought this winter in the system of the war, and in the measures of all our foreign negociations. I hope we see daylight, and I make

no doubt we shall extricate our country from the difficulties which she groans under.[10]

The fortunes of St John and Oxford depended on the ministry's ability to make a satisfactory peace. This was far from easy when, besides the beginnings of a Hanoverian Tory group and the hostility of recalcitrant Whigs and foreign allies, the two ministers themselves could not see eye to eye on how to conduct the negotiations. The Lord Treasurer confessed to Gaultier, the French agent, that he was unwilling to discuss certain parts of their negotiations with St John.[11] He also kept the Secretary in the dark about his discussions with the allies. When he planned to solve the vexed problem of the succession to the Spanish throne he disclosed his proposals to Shrewsbury instead.[12] With his cruder, but more incisive, diplomatic talents, St John realised that the peace terms would never satisfy all the powers concerned. He was quite prepared to make a separate peace, since he believed the favourable terms which Britain was to receive could never, in any event, be wholly acceptable to the Dutch and the Austrians. The specific terms by which Philip V was to renounce the French crown did not worry him, and, provided Britain's own demands were met, he was quite ready to ditch the allies. If necessary, he would send them an ultimatum. Indeed, he seemed quite pleased with the obstinacy of the Dutch: 'I begin to wish the Dutch may continue still to be dully obstinate over the Assiento, since we do not want them either to make or superintend the peace, and since it will be better settled for England without their concurrence than with it.'[13]

The prospect of an imminent peace persuaded the ministry to send the notorious 'restraining orders' to the Duke of Ormonde, the new commander-in-chief. St John and Dartmouth, the Secretaries of State, issued them:

> It is therefore the Queen's positive command to your Grace, that you avoid engaging in any siege, or hazarding a battle, till you have farther orders from her Majesty. I am at the same time, directed to let your Grace know, that the Queen would have you disguise the receipt of this order; and her Majesty thinks that you cannot want pretences for conducting yourself so as to answer her ends, without owning that which might, at present, have an ill effect, if it was publicly known.[14]

This breach of faith with the allies was bad enough, but, to compound the treachery, the ministers informed Marshal Villars of Ormonde's orders, and the two 'enemy' generals began combining to deceive Britain's allies. This decision to desert the allies smacked of St John's handiwork, though St John always claimed that the orders had emanated from the Lord Treasurer.[15] Oxford had probably been compelled, at last, to make a clear declaration of policy, but he may have thought the risk was worth taking, when peace seemed assured. Despite his later disclaimers, St John applauded the decision and was even prepared to see Villars teach the allies a military lesson.[16]

The Whigs soon suspected that Ormonde had been given orders not to fight and so they renewed their attacks on the ministry's conduct of the peace negotiations. In the Commons St John bore the brunt of the government's defence. He defeated a motion critical of Ormonde's refusal to take offensive action and, in another debate, when an opposition spokesman castigated the trifling peace negotiations, 'Mr. Secretary St John highly piqued at, and resenting that expression, said, "It reflected on her Majesty and her Ministers, and that some had been sent to the Tower for less offences".'[17] On 6 June the Queen was able to present to parliament the terms on which Britain could make peace. These included the acquisition of Gibraltar, Minorca, Newfoundland, Nova Scotia and Hudson Bay, and further trading concessions, in addition to the Asiento, which gave Britain the right to send slaves and one trading ship a year to the Spanish Americas, though these had not been finally settled. Sir John Stonehouse, one of St John's lieutenants, proposed an address of thanks and the Secretary himself skilfully avoided any division which the Whigs might have planned. Taking the offensive, he led the Commons in motions of censure on the Whig Bishop of St Asaph's *Four Sermons* and *A Letter from the States General to the Queen of Great Britain*, which were critical of the ministry and the peace negotiations.[18]

The favourable terms for Britain had enabled the government to recover astonishingly well from the débâcle of December 1711. The debates of 1712 made it clear that there was considerable support for the peace in parliament, and in the country as a whole there was an even greater majority in favour of peace. The peace terms were sufficiently advantageous to Britain for most people to ignore the criticisms of the Whigs, the protests of the allies and even the murmurings of dissatisfaction emanating from Hanover. All this enabled St John to press for an immediate peace, with or without the agreement of the allies. The terms of Philip V's renunciation of the French throne were not such a stumbling block to him as they were to the Lord Treasurer. Though Oxford still kept in touch with all St John's negotiations with Torcy, he could not prevent the Secretary making the running in the summer of 1712. His bold, rash and imperious temperament led St John to drastic and high-handed action against the allies. The subtle, if tortuous, diplomacy of Oxford was replaced by insensitive bullying. Ormonde was ordered to leave the confederate army and to march his troops to Dunkirk, which the French had agreed to hand over as proof of their good faith. Should the Dutch endeavour to withhold supplies during the march, then force was to be used. The representatives of those auxiliary powers with troops in British pay were called to St John's office, on 20 June, and ordered to make sure that their troops obeyed Ormonde's orders, or else Britain would cut off their pay. The threat was not very effective, for, much to the Secretary's annoyance, most of these troops preferred to continue serving under Prince Eugene, the commander of the Austrian forces.[19] Some of the lesser German princes, including the Elector of Hanover, preferred to forego British pay in order to continue to fight for the Austrian cause. The French success at Denain, however, convinced the Dutch, at least, that they must cooperate with Britain. The only alternatives were a new war or even worse peace terms.

  Though the Dutch were now more tractable, not all the ministers were happy with the conduct of the peace negotiations. Oxford, in particular, still tried to restrain St John. Their disputes were just as serious on the home front, where the Lord Treasurer had to respond to Tory pressure by dismissing a number of Whigs still in office. Though Oxford had to promote Tories to these vacancies, he selected, in the main, personal adherents or the more moderate Tories. St John did strengthen his position too, for some of his friends had to be rewarded. Sir William Wyndham became Secretary at War, Charles Eversfield was appointed Treasurer and Paymaster of the Ordnance, and Jack Hill was sent out as Governor of Dunkirk. Henry St John himself was rewarded for his exertions in the Commons, and for his work on the peace negotiations, with his long-awaited peerage. It had generally been expected,[20] not least by St John, that he would obtain an earldom, as the Lord Treasurer had done in 1711. Instead, he was given a viscountcy. This was such a blow to his pride that he even offered to remain in the Commons[21] and he almost decided against the title of Bolingbroke, which, as an earldom, had belonged to the senior branch of his family. He regarded the lesser honour as a blow to his ambition, to his status and to his family's honour. The decision to deny him an earldom may well have been taken by the Queen, as Oxford claimed,[22] but the Secretary was convinced that he could detect the Lord Treasurer's baleful influence behind it. He complained bitterly to Lord Strafford:

> My promotion was a mortification to me. In the House of Commons, I may say, that I was at the head of business, and I must have continued so, whether I had been in court or out of court. There was therefore nothing to flatter my ambition in removing me from thence, but giving me the title which had been many years in my family . . . To make me a peer was no great compliment, when so many others were forced to be made to gain strength in Parliament [in December 1711] . . . Thus far, there seems to be nothing done for my sake, or as a mark of favour to me in particular; . . . I own to you that I felt more indignation than ever in my life I had done; and the only consideration which kept me from running to extremities, was that which should have inclined somebody [Oxford] to use me better. I knew that any appearance of breach between myself and the Lord Treasurer, would give our common enemies spirit, and that if I declined serving at this conjuncture, the home part of the business would, at least for some time, proceed but lamely. To friendship, therefore, and the public good if I may be pardoned so vain an expression, I sacrificed my private resentment, and remain clothed with as little of the Queen's favour as she could contrive to bestow.[23]

Despite this show of self-sacrifice, Bolingbroke never forgot this incident,[24] for it permanently soured his relationship with Oxford. It completed the personal breach between them. In addition to the personal hostility, and the widening differences in political strategy, Bolingbroke was now convinced that his services to the Tory party and to the ministry would never receive adequate recompense, while Oxford remained at the head of both. It spurred him to renewed efforts to safeguard his own political future. After leaving the Commons as the commanding personality, he had no intention of going to the Lords, merely to play second fiddle to Oxford.

Meanwhile, the peace negotiations at Utrecht were progressing very slowly, with several important problems not yet settled. Not only had the terms for the allies still to be arranged, but Britain's commercial interests and her position in North America were unresolved. In order to speed up negotiations, the French pressed Britain to send a responsible minister to Paris, to renew direct consultations. Partly under pressure and partly to soothe Bolingbroke's ruffled pride, Oxford agreed to send the Secretary, though he clearly believed that he should confine himself to discussing the interests of the Duke of Savoy.[25] Certainly, Bolingbroke's instructions carefully avoided any mention of a separate peace. He was 'to have especial care to avoid entangling us in any new engagements' or 'any stipulation which may oblige us to make war, and especially with our old Allies, in order to procure this settlement'.[26] At first Bolingbroke, who was accompanied by Gaultier and Matthew Prior, concentrated on gaining some of the demands for Savoy. He also managed to extend the armistice and he made no difficulty about the form of Philip V's renunciation of the French throne, which needed to be made more watertight after recent deaths in the French royal family.[27] Delighted with his magnificent reception, he spun out his visit for another week. During this period he laid himself open to criticism by attending the opera at the same time as the Pretender, though there is no proof that he met him secretly.[28] More serious was his attempt to give a very different turn to the peace negotiations. With the encouragement of the French ministers, he sought to take a decisive step in the direction of a separate peace. For some time he had been convinced that Britain could not safeguard her own interests, while cooperating fully with the allies. Before he left Paris, he encouraged Louis XIV and Torcy to believe that, as soon as Philip V signed the renunciation of the French crown, peace could be signed by Britain, France and Savoy. The French would then have a free hand to force the Dutch and the Austrians to the conference table. Bolingbroke was prepared to let the French have the fortresses of Condé and Tournai, and he urged the French to make peace now, before the Dutch agreed to come to terms and the ministry was compelled to support their demands on the French.

Though Bolingbroke had clearly exceeded his instructions, he was not, in fact, able to accomplish his designs. Oxford saw to that. The Lord Treasurer had always opposed the idea of a separate peace and he now set about slowing down the pace of the Anglo-French entente, until the Dutch could be persuaded to make peace. He put Dartmouth in control of the correspondence with Torcy and with Matthew Prior, who had been left behind in Paris. Technically, there was nothing unusual about this, for Dartmouth was Secretary of State for the southern department, which included France, but, in view of the extraordinary position Bolingbroke had won for himself in the peace negotiations, it was, in fact, a deliberate rebuff. Torcy was dismayed and he kept up his correspondence with Bolingbroke, but it was some months before Dartmouth's intrusion could be neutralised. Under pressure, Bolingbroke had to remind the English

plenipotentiaries that there would be no separate peace. The Secretary
resented what he regarded as Oxford's obstructive tactics and faint-
hearted policy. During September there was growing friction between
them. Bolingbroke stayed away from his office, though, on a number of
occasions, he visited the Queen and Lady Masham, with letters from
Torcy, presumably to win support at Court for his own conduct.[29]
Swift tried once more to breach the rift in the ministry, but the dispute
grew more bitter, until there was an explosion in the Cabinet on 28
September.

In this meeting the ministers angrily discussed the whole conduct of the
peace negotiations and the respective merits of each other's policies.
Buckingham was highly critical of the whole tenor of the negotiation
and he accused the leading ministers of selling their country's interests
for a paltry armistice. Bolingbroke accused Oxford of irresolution and
Dartmouth of incompetence. He suggested that the matter should be put
to the test, by an appeal to public opinion through a general election.
On this, though for different reasons, Buckingham, Harcourt and
Shrewsbury were prepared to support him, but the idea was opposed
by Oxford, Dartmouth and Poulett. The Lord Treasurer's reply was
crushing. He openly upbraided Bolingbroke for going beyond his
instructions and for misconduct in Paris. The Secretary was charged with
seeking to make a separate peace and with making open-handed promises
to the French, which had made them reluctant to come to terms with the
allies. All this had delayed the chance of a general peace. With the Dutch
now willing to come into the negotiations, the ministry must insist on the
fortress of Tournai for the Dutch Barrier. This withering attack convinced
Harcourt, Bolingbroke's friend, though he was by instinct a trimmer, to
come out against a separate peace. Buckingham and Shrewsbury probably
joined him in deciding against an immediate dissolution.[30] Left un-
supported, Bolingbroke was forced to back down. He was compelled to
tell Strafford that the French had interpreted incorrectly the remarks
which he had made to them in Paris.[31] To Torcy, he had to write an
apologetic letter, admitting that Britain would support the Dutch
pretensions.[32] Bolingbroke had clearly failed to by-pass Oxford, whose
peace policy had always envisaged an eventual agreement with the
Dutch.

Oxford's attack on Bolingbroke at this Cabinet meeting did not stop
with his criticisms of the Secretary's handling of the peace negotiations. He
believed that Bolingbroke had met the Pretender and had allowed the

French to think that the ministry sympathised with the Jacobite cause. The Lord Treasurer regarded this as the height of folly. He even hinted to the Court at Hanover that Bolingbroke would be dismissed. In the event, some kind of reconciliation was patched up, yet again. Bolingbroke retired to Bucklebury for a few days, to lick his wounds, the Queen cried all night, and Lady Masham left Windsor in a rage.[33] An open rupture had only narrowly been averted and further disputes between Dartmouth and Bolingbroke, at least, were inevitable. Bolingbroke did, in fact, conduct a deliberate campaign to oust Dartmouth from the peace negotiations or at least so to intimidate him that Dartmouth would follow his lead. This was noticed by Erasmus Lewis, who reported to the Lord Treasurer: 'I have been this morning with my Lord Dartmouth, who tells me Lord Boling- broke treated him last night on two or three occasions in so rough a manner that he believes it will be impossible for you to find any expedient to keep them together.' Dartmouth believed that Bolingbroke had grown too powerful to be dismissed and so he offered his own resignation.[34] This was the last thing that Oxford wanted, and so, with the support of the Queen, he persuaded Dartmouth to soldier on. He thus confirmed his authority over the Cabinet and his overall control of the peace negotiations. Although the Queen was not so well-satisfied with his conduct as pre- viously, he was still the dominant influence at Court. When six new knights of the garter were created, Oxford and five minor Tory peers received the honour. Bolingbroke did not receive this coveted reward, but had to be content with the post of Lord Lieutenant of Essex. His efforts to dominate the ministry and its policies had failed.

This defeat did not mean that Bolingbroke's power and influence were insignificant. The Cabinet spent weeks discussing both the general peace offers, which would be acceptable to the allies, and the new projected Barrier Treaty for the Dutch. The Lord Treasurer was unable to resolve these disagreements. This allowed the more decisive Bolingbroke to devise a Barrier Treaty which was studded with reflections on the over- generous terms which the Whigs had negotiated with the Dutch in the treaty of 1709, and which was intended to cut down the advantages to Dutch trade in the Netherlands to a bare minimum.[35] It was also Boling- broke, this time supported by the Queen herself, who pressed for the dispatch of an ambassador to Versailles, to speed up discussions on the vexed problems of North America and the trading concessions to Britain.[36] The first choice for this embassy was the Duke of Hamilton, a strange candidate, in view of his known Jacobite sympathies. Possibly as a result of a Whig plot, Hamilton was killed in a duel, before he could leave for France.[37] He was replaced by Shrewsbury, a Hanoverian sympathiser, though Matthew Prior continued to do all the spade work. Bolingbroke himself was able to resume his role, of instructing Prior and of corresponding with the French, on the government's behalf. Whatever his lack of concern for the interests of the allies, he was determined to protect Britain's interests in Newfoundland, Nova Scotia and Cape Breton Island. When the French employed delaying tactics, hoping that Britain would accept poorer terms, rather than allow the negotiations to drag on, Bolingbroke waxed indignant. He ordered Matthew Prior to pass on this warning to the French:

> We stand indeed on the brink of a precipice, but the French stand there too. Pray tell Monsieur de Torcy from me, that he may get Robin [Oxford] and Harry hanged; but affairs will soon run back into so much confusion, that he will wish us alive again. To speak seriously, unless the Queen can talk of her interest as determined with France, and unless your Court will keep our allies in the wrong, as they are sufficiently at this time, I foresee inextricable difficulties.

Three days later he added: 'Make the French ashamed of their sneaking chicane; by heaven, they treat like pedlars, or, which is worse, like attornies.' When words did not have the desired effect on the French ministers Bolingbroke warned them that, in the next session of parliament, supplies would be voted for a new campaign. The French then gave way, though they put a good face on it.[38]

The Treaty of Utrecht was not an unsuccessful peace, as the next two decades were to show, but it had many unsatisfactory features. These were largely due to the pressure in Britain to conclude a peace quickly, the ministry's need to accomplish it to survive, and the rivalry between Oxford and Bolingbroke. The Lord Treasurer had resisted Bolingbroke's attempts to sign a separate peace, but he had been compelled to bring strong pressure to bear on the allies in order to bring them to the conference table. He had at least connived at the notorious 'restraining orders' to Ormonde and he had joined Bolingbroke in blatantly betraying Prince Eugene's plans to the French.[39] Though he eventually succeeded in getting the Dutch to join in the peace negotiations, he had not safeguarded their commercial interests and they had been compelled to accept a reduced barrier in the Netherlands. He had shown himself almost as willing as Bolingbroke to ditch the Austrians, who were left to make a separate peace after Britain had taken the richest pickings and had given up Spain to the Bourbon claimant. Both the ministers had done little, and that late and with obvious reluctance, to remove the Pretender from France.[40] What Oxford did hesitantly and under pressure, Bolingbroke did cheerfully and willingly. The Secretary was prepared, without much compunction, to secure the best terms for Britain at the expense of the other allies and even to wash his hands of the Catalans, who had supported the allied cause in Spain.[41] Several of his decisions were wide open to substantial objections. The agreement over Newfoundland was not watertight and the commercial treaties with both France and Spain, which he had done most to arrange, were conspicuous failures.

Thus, there was a strange paradox about the Treaty of Utrecht. Oxford had controlled the negotiations to a greater extent than Bolingbroke. The main outlines of Britain's gains had been decided before the Secretary was even aware that any discussions were in progress. Bolingbroke's efforts to arrange a quick and, if necessary, a separate peace were successfully resisted by the Lord Treasurer. The final treaty was, therefore, more the work of Oxford, though his methods had been devious, tortuous and less than frank. He had tended to get caught up in the threads of his own cunning diplomacy. In contrast, Bolingbroke saw clearly what the grumbling, discontented Tories were demanding and how far they would support his policy of safeguarding the particular interests of Britain, at the expense of those of her European allies. His later defence of the statesman-like qualities of the treaty, and his open admission of some of its weaknesses, were deliberately made as an appeal to a new generation and an admiring posterity.[42] At the time, he had been prepared to close his eyes to inconvenient problems and he had sought to erase unpalatable facts, in order to achieve the kind of peace which would satisfy Tory opinion at home and bolster his own political reputation. In the last stages of the negotiations he made the running and finally clinched a peace which was popular and relatively successful, if weak in some of its provisions and 'perfidious' in some of its implications. Bolingbroke had counted upon the evident willingness of a majority in Britain to desert the allies and to make friends with France. He had accomplished much, though there would have been even more unsatisfactory features, but for the persistent rear-guard action of the Lord Treasurer.

The French procrastination during the final stages of the peace negotiations caused the ministry considerable trouble on the home front. The Whig opposition continually sniped at the discussions taking place at

Utrecht, while the Tory backbenchers protested at the ministry's failure
to clinch the peace. The ministers began to lose their nerve and the
differences between Bolingbroke and Oxford again came into the open.
Once more, Bolingbroke's solution to the problems facing the ministry
was to urge bolder action. Abroad he threatened the French with a
renewal of the war and at home he demanded the dismissal of all the
Whigs still in office. General Cadogan, his old friend, lost all his posts, in
January 1713, but neither Bolingbroke nor the Tories in general were
satisfied with this isolated gesture. Bolingbroke was particularly anxious to
dismiss two other Whigs, Lord Chief Justice Parker and Lord Cholmondeley, the Treasurer of the Household, both of whom had openly
opposed the peace.[43] What gave an added edge to Bolingbroke's discontent with Oxford's conduct and leadership were the clandestine meetings
which the Lord Treasurer continued to arrange with the Whig leaders.
Oxford was not necessarily plotting to betray his Tory colleagues. He
may have been trying to smooth the way for the new parliamentary
session by offering to hold back attacks on those Whigs still in office or on
the late Whig ministry's record, if the opposition would only accept the
peace. Nevertheless, there were rumours that he intended to ditch the
Tories, once the peace was safely signed. Bolingbroke was distinctly uneasy, for he could not expect to come to terms with the Whigs. On 3
March 1713 he protested to Shrewsbury: 'I cannot help saying, in the
fullness of my soul to your Grace, that if we do not establish ourselves,
and the true interest of our country it is the Queen's and Treasurer's
fault.'[44] The pressure from Bolingbroke and the other Tories was such
that Oxford was again forced to make concessions. Several Whigs were
dismissed and Bolingbroke's friends, Harcourt and Francis Atterbury,
were promoted to the Lord Chancellorship and the Bishopric of Rochester,
respectively. A reconciliation between Oxford and Bolingbroke was
again 'arranged', though this was largely agreed to in order to carry the
peace through the new session of parliament.

When parliament at last met, in April 1713, the peace proved more
popular than the ministers had anticipated, and there was little serious
opposition to it. The Tory backbenchers were delighted, for the peace led
to a reduction in the armed forces and a cut in the burdensome land tax.
This excellent start to the session may have lulled the ministers into a false
sense of security, for they were not prepared for the disaster which struck
when the treaty of commerce with France came under discussion.
Bolingbroke was deeply engaged in this treaty, which he felt would lead

to closer relations with France. This political and diplomatic aim led him to pay less attention to the implications of, and reaction to, the commercial terms, which he allowed his crony, Arthur Moore, to negotiate. Articles eight and nine, and, to a lesser extent, article ten, were soon seized upon by critics of the treaty. The eighth article established that Britain and France should give the most favourable trading concessions to each other, but the other two articles seemed to benefit France more than Britain. By article nine, the general tariff between the two countries was reduced to the level of 1664, though the French were allowed to make exception to the import of wool, sugar, salted fish and whale produce from Britain, while Britain had not yet decided which exceptions she would make. Article ten did not give British tobacco, sent to France, more favourable treatment than that from other countries. Despite the unsatisfactory nature of these articles, Bolingbroke laid great store on this treaty. Though he envisaged some opposition to these clauses, he hoped parliament would ratify the whole treaty.[45] In its early stages the bill to ratify the treaty had the united support of the ministry, yet the second reading was passed by only twenty-five votes. This should have served as a warning to Bolingbroke, especially as the opposition included some Tories; and a positive flood of petitions, from merchants and traders throughout the country, was raining down on the Commons. The gist of all these petitions was that some improvement in trade with France would not compensate for the much greater damage which would be done to Britain's trade in wool and other textiles. In contrast, the defence of the treaty was neither widely canvassed nor forcibly made. Bolingbroke and his supporters seemed unable to combat the economic arguments of the opposition and they were not prepared to reveal their primary motive for pushing on with the treaty. The Secretary was well versed in the value of propaganda and he could have employed his own and Swift's highly effective pen, but to proclaim his desire for closer relations with France would cast suspicion on his loyalty to the Hanoverian succession.

More petitions and more Tory defections could not persuade Bolingbroke to abandon the treaty. He had staked his reputation on it and he was temperamentally opposed to retreat, manoeuvre and conciliation. The crisis came on 18 June, when the Commons met in committee to discuss amendments made to the limited bill, which aimed to ratify the much criticised eighth and ninth articles of the treaty. Though the ministry again appeared united, defeat came after Sir Thomas Hanmer, the most

widely respected Tory backbencher, rose to attack the eighth and ninth
articles. The March Club followed his lead and the bill was narrowly
defeated by 194 to 185 votes. There were many abstentions, but some
72 Tories voted with the opposition. The scale of this rebellion was so
large that Oxford was suspected of deliberately undermining his rival's
cherished treaty of commerce. Bolingbroke certainly laid the blame at the
Lord Treasurer's door: 'The reason of this majority was, that there had
been, during two or three days' uncertainty, an opinion spread, that
Lord Treasurer gave up the point.'[46] There is, however, very little
evidence to substantiate such a charge against Oxford. The worst construction which can be put on his behaviour was that he failed to speak out
clearly enough to dispel the rumours that he was against the bill.[47]
In the Commons all his relatives and adherents spoke and voted for the
bill, and William Stratford believed that the defeat had surprised and
troubled the Lord Treasurer.[48] Nevertheless, it is important to remember
that Bolingbroke held Oxford personally responsible for the defeat.
Bolingbroke never questioned his own failure to manage the Tory rebels.
He thought that the Lord Treasurer's machinations, not the effects of the
eighth and ninth articles on the Tory backbenchers nor his own dubious
reasons for wanting the treaty, fully accounted for its defeat. The Tory
rebels, in fact, were convinced that the treaty did not serve Britain's best
commercial interests, and they disliked the idea of closer links with France.
To many of them, friendship with France suggested Jacobite sympathies.
Hanmer and his Tory followers were soon known as 'Hanoverian'
Tories. Their revolt against the treaty of commerce heralded a major split
in the Tory party on the basic issue of the succession.

The ministry, reeling from this blow, was further embarrassed by a
rebellion of Scottish peers over the new malt tax, which they interpreted
as an infringement of the Union, and by a Whig address to have the
Pretender removed from Lorraine. It was with considerable relief that the
ministry was able to prorogue parliament in July. This short, but crucial,
session of 1713 marked an important stage in the fortunes of the Tory
party and in the struggle between Oxford and Bolingbroke. The Tories
had been rewarded with the peace, a reduction in their tax burden, and
more places in the administration, yet they were more divided than at any
time since the tack of 1704. The fundamental split over the succession
was now the greatest political issue of the day. For years the Tories had
refused to face up to the problem of who would succeed Anne, even after
it was obvious that she would never produce an heir to the throne.

While the war was in progress it saved the Tories from embarrassment, for it diverted political attention away from this issue; but the peace, and the manner of negotiating it, brought the problem to the forefront of all political discussions. Some Tories had always been sympathetic to the Jacobite cause and more of them began to contemplate a Stuart restoration, when they realised that the peace, which they had so fervently desired, had in fact alienated the Hanoverians, the legal heirs to the throne. An increasing number of other Tories, starting with Nottingham's defection in December 1711, and culminating in the major rebellion against the treaty of commerce, led by Sir Thomas Hanmer, had begun to fear that the manner of the peace negotiations was but the first step in a calculated campaign to bring over the Pretender. Nearly all the Tories had wanted an end to the war, however, and so they did not put too much pressure on the ministry to bring it into line with their own views on the succession, until the peace was safely concluded. The Whigs, for their part, rallied even more effectively on this issue. Their efforts to oppose the peace had not won much support in Britain, either within parliament or without, but they were absolutely united in favour of the Hanoverian succession and determined to fight for it, if necessary. Despite their numerical weakness, the Whigs could profit from the deep fissures appearing in the Tory party and from the failure of the ministry to offer a clear lead to the Tory rank and file or to the nation at large, on this fundamental issue. These developments affected the relationship between Bolingbroke and Oxford. To carry on his administration, the Lord Treasurer had to rely increasingly on the support of his Tory backbenchers, but he would not take Bolingbroke's advice to place his trust in them. Bolingbroke's personal setback, in June 1713, had only served to convince him that it could have been avoided if only greater concessions had been made to the Tories earlier. Further concessions now might avoid a split over the succession problem. In many ways he was deluding himself. He always had a tendency to believe that boldness made awkward problems vanish. Since he was not personally committed in principle, either to the Pretender or to the Hanoverians, he believed other Tories would follow him in opting for the successor who would benefit the party. In his estimation, the only real obstacle to a solution of the succession problem was the Lord Treasurer. Once he had been removed, Bolingbroke was confident he would face little resistance to his own plans from the Tory backbenchers. Thus, the succession problem grew more serious the longer Oxford held onto power, and the bitter rivalry between

Bolingbroke and the Lord Treasurer kept pace with the developments within the Tory party. Oxford had resisted Bolingbroke's challenge for more than two years, but, increasingly, his touch became unsure and his aims even less clear. The initiative passed to Bolingbroke, though he was to find the Lord Treasurer the master of defensive tactics and still far too influential at Court.

CHAPTER 7

Bolingbroke's Bid for the Leadership

NONE of the Tory ministers could have been pleased with the short parliamentary session of 1713. After the weeks of tension waiting for the peace to be signed, the ministry had seen its programme split the Tory party wide open. Divided among themselves, the ministers now found themselves facing a serious rebellion on their own backbenches. This revolt, led by a man of Sir Thomas Hanmer's stature, posed a greater threat than the peevish discontent of the October Club. The new split had appeared over differences of principle rather than of tactics. At first the disagreement seemed to be only about the treaty of commerce with France, but, increasingly, the main issue was the thorny problem of the Protestant succession. With a general election imminent the Tory leaders ought to have been striving to re-establish some measure of harmony and discipline. Instead, in the summer of 1713 Bolingbroke mounted his most serious challenge for the leadership. Though claiming that he had no wish to separate his interest from that of the Lord Treasurer, he was clearly leading a faction, which included Harcourt, Atterbury, Lord Chief Justice Trevor and Lord Bingley, the Chancellor of the Exchequer.[1] Bolingbroke was also angling for Shrewsbury's support. Having told him of the dissension within the ministry, he added: 'I will only say thus much, that I wish heartily you was here, because it will very soon be time for those, who must in honour and good sense unite in the same measure, to come to some peremptory resolution; and that resolution cannot, ought not to be taken, until your Grace is amongst us.'[2]

The Secretary, despite his failure to carry through the commercial treaty, still believed that he could treat with Oxford on an equal footing. The Lord Treasurer feared that Bolingbroke's plan would restrict his initiative and his ability to take independent action. Bolingbroke wanted to organise a group of ministers to counterbalance Oxford's authority more effectively. This veritable junto would, at the very least, reduce the Lord Treasurer's authority to that of one voice among equals.[3] In fact,

Bolingbroke seemed ready to dictate to his rival. On 27 July 1713 he wrote him a long letter, complaining that the attacks from the disaffected Tories were the product of ministerial negligence. He listed three faults, which needed remedying at once. The Tory party required greater encourage- ment and firmer leadership. Too many places were still held by opponents of the ministry and Oxford monopolised power, when his proper role was to supervise the other ministers. In an imperious tone, Bolingbroke virtually commanded the Lord Treasurer:

> Separate, in the name of God, the chaff from the wheat, and consider who you have left to employ; assign them their parts; trust them as far as it is necessary for the execution each of his part; let the forms of business be regularly carried on in Cabinet, and the secret of it in your own closet. Your Lordship would soon find those excellent principles, laid down in the Queen's Speech, pursued with vigour and success.[4]

Bolingbroke even made suggestions about the disposal of Cabinet posts. He was anxious to keep Bromley as Speaker, instead of seeing him promo- ted to ministerial rank, where he would be able to offer Oxford greater support. To his colleagues Bolingbroke voiced similar complaints of the Lord Treasurer's conduct. While sympathising with Lord Strafford, who had not received his proper allowances from the Treasury, he explained that Oxford had not yet reimbursed him either for the expenses of his trip to France in 1712.[5] In a letter to Matthew Prior he wrote of his intense dis- satisfaction with Oxford's perpetual state of indecision, which was playing into the hands of the Whig opposition:

> Our enemies are in themselves contemptible, and our friends are well inclined. The former have no strength but what we might have taken from them, and the latter no dissatisfaction, but that we might have prevented. Let the game which we have, be wrested out of our hands; this I can bear; but to play, like children, with it, till it slips between our fingers to the ground, and sharpers have but to stoop and take it up; this consideration distracts a man of spirit and not to be vexed in this case, is not to be sensible.[6]

This attitude naturally caused offence in the Lord Treasurer's circle, especially as Oxford was very ill in July 1713. William Stratford was amazed at Bolingbroke's demands, but at the beginning of August he really feared that the Lord Treasurer might be overborne.[7]

Stratford soon reversed his opinion, when he saw how successful Oxford was in thwarting Bolingbroke's schemes to dominate the ministry.

Satirical Whig print attacking Bolingbroke

The picture on the wall shows Bolingbroke writing
dispatches to France while in bed with his mistress. She
was reputed to be Anna Maria Gumley, who later married
William Pulteney.

Queen Anne's procession through the Strand
to celebrate the signing of the Treaty of Utrecht

Bolingbroke in his parliamentary robes

Bolingbroke in Viscount's robes for George I's coronation

When the ministry was recast in mid-August the new appointments strengthened the Lord Treasurer's hand. The Bishop of Bristol retired and was replaced by Dartmouth as Lord Privy Seal. William Bromley, an ally of the Lord Treasurer's, filled the vacant Secretaryship of State. Francis Gwyn, who had joined the Harley camp in 1710, was appointed Secretary at War. With the changes in the Scottish administration, the Lord Treasurer was even more successful. The Earl of Mar became a third Secretary of State, with special responsibility for Scotland. This was a deliberate rebuff for Bolingbroke, who had been trying to extend his authority over Scottish affairs.[8] At the same time Lord Findlater was appointed Lord Chancellor of Scotland, a move which diminished the patronage of Lord Harcourt, Bolingbroke's closest friend in the ministry. Even with minor appointments, the Lord Treasurer was able to reward his friends, Lord Lansdowne, Lord Denbigh and Thomas Foley. In contrast, Bolingbroke made few gains. He himself was moved to the senior Secretaryship of State, while two of his followers, Sir William Wyndham and Sir John Stonehouse, were appointed Chancellor of the Exchequer and Comptroller of the Household, respectively. Wyndham replaced another supporter of Bolingbroke, Lord Bingley, and Stonehouse's position did not carry with it any real political influence. Bolingbroke had, in fact, lost ground in the battle for the leadership. Once more the Lord Treasurer had effectively demonstrated his greater influence with the Queen, an advantage which could always checkmate any move Bolingbroke could make.

The Lord Treasurer scored two further successes in the late summer of 1713. After repeated attempts he managed to persuade Sir Thomas Hanmer to stand as the ministry's candidate for the Speakership in the new parliament. Since Hanmer had previously refused all tempting offers of a place and had led the rebellion against the commercial treaty with France, this was a notable achievement and a tribute to Oxford's political management. A more personal triumph for Oxford was the marriage of his son to the daughter of his late friend, the Duke of Newcastle. She was the greatest heiress in England, a fact which, of course, did not escape Bolingbroke's notice. He commented sourly to Matthew Prior: 'He [Oxford] has established his family now beyond what he could expect, and I am heartily rejoiced at it: let him establish the Queen's administration on a sure and lasting principle, and I think I have virtue enough to acquaint him of any reward I may be thought to deserve; I could take the trouble of contributing to such a work, as full and recompense [in itself].'[9] Over this

E

marriage, however, Oxford did take a fatal step. Too anxious to secure the interests of his family, he irritated the Queen by pressing her to allow his son to inherit the late Duke of Newcastle's titles.[10] Bolingbroke was not slow to see that here, at last, was an opportunity of weakening Oxford's influence with the Queen, particularly as his rival began attending the Court less frequently. He had long recognised that the Queen's regard for the Lord Treasurer was the principal obstacle to his own advancement to the leadership of the ministry and the Tory party. Once Bolingbroke began to curry favour with the Queen, which was only made possible by Oxford's neglect, the Lord Treasurer began to fear that his position was not impregnable.

All these signs of malaise in the ministry and of divisions within the Tory party did not appear to augur well for the general election, which was held in the autumn of 1713. Yet the most reliable evidence points to a rather unexpected result: an increased Tory majority. This remarkable Tory victory was eloquent testimony that a majority of the voters was naturally inclined to favour the Tories. Divisions within the party had not been able to eradicate this natural preponderance. The chief reason for the Tory victory was the immense relief of the country gentlemen that the war had at last been concluded with substantial British gains. The reduction in the land tax, a consequence of the peace, also made the Tories very popular with the squirearchy. The Tory party, however, despite its great victory, did not emerge from the elections as a united force. There appeared staunchly pro-Hanoverian and stolidly Jacobite elements, which broke away and began to operate almost as separate forces. After the 1713 election the committed supporters of the Pretender in the Commons numbered between eighty and one hundred. About half of these were prepared to act as an independent unit under the leadership of Sir John Pakington, George Lockhart and William Shippen. Many of the remainder hoped that the ministry would give a lead by renouncing or arranging to by-pass the Act of Settlement. The Hanoverian Tories had already emerged in the last parliament under the leadership of Sir Thomas Hanmer and the Earl of Anglesey. In all, there were probably seventy Hanoverian Tories in the new parliament. They rarely acted as a united body and were not unequivocally opposed to the ministry. A clear pro-Hanoverian lead might have reconciled many of them to the administration.[11]

The 1713 election results and these fundamental divisions within the Tory party affected the relative strength and the future prospects of

Oxford and Bolingbroke. In the last parliament the Lord Treasurer had won over many of the younger high Tories, who had once followed Rochester, Nottingham and William Bromley. Now he found two important groups breaking away from his control. The Jacobites had never accepted his policies nor his leadership, but they had not previously acted as a separate unit. The Hanoverian Tories had previously rallied to him rather than to Bolingbroke, but in this new parliament they had their own leaders and they took a more independent line. The threatened disintegration of the Tory party inspired Bolingbroke to renew his efforts to oust Oxford, in order to pave the way for the reunification of the party under his own leadership. This was to prove a vain ambition, but in the process Bolingbroke did manage to increase his own personal following in the Commons. He had already drawn off some of the members of the old Harleyite group, including Harcourt, Lord Masham and Sir John Stone-house. Not surprisingly, he attracted the more partisan Tories, particularly those with Jacobite sympathies. To established supporters such as Sir William Wyndham, he was able to add men like Henry Campion, Sir Edward Knatchbull, William Collier, Richard Cresswell and Sir William Barker. A group of Scottish members, notably John Carnegie, James Murray and Sir Alexander Cummings, rallied to him as did the clients and friends of peers such as Beaufort and Masham.[12] Bolingbroke also increased his group of personal adherents by his activities in the general election of 1713. As Lord Lieutenant of Essex, he appointed no less than 47 deputies, of whom 14 were elected to parliament in 1713.[13] For his former borough of Wootton Bassett, he procured the return of two Tory clients. Thus, Bolingbroke's base was widening and, together with the overwhelming success of the Tories in general, he was encouraged to step up his bid for the leadership. The divisions in the Tory party only served to make the task seem more urgent and necessary.

The huge Tory majority increased Bolingbroke's confidence that the ministry would have no alternative but to abandon Oxford's moderate course in order to rally the support of the backbenchers. He urged the Lord Treasurer to pursue a more vigorous policy: 'I am sorry there is little show of government when the difficulties we have to struggle with require that all the powers of it should be exerted.'[14] Though he professed himself full of personal regard for Oxford and ready to obey his commands, he was caustic in his references to the Lord Treasurer's close friend, Lord Dartmouth. A fortnight later Bolingbroke was assuring Oxford: 'I see an opportunity of giving new strength, new spirit to your administration, and of cementing a firmer union between us, and between us and those who must support us. . . Believe me for once, what I always am, and have been to you, sincere, however I may have been too warm and your Lordship, allow the expression, too jealous.'[15] Bolingbroke was not in a position to ditch the Lord Treasurer, but, despite his professions of loyalty, he now regarded himself as an equal, with whom Oxford should be prepared to concert measures. When the Whigs gained a majority in the Irish parliament Bolingbroke advised Oxford not to allow it to sit.[16] To one of his lieutenants, George Clarke, he confessed his plans for a pronounced Tory policy in Britain: 'I own to you, Sir, tho' I have not used to be very sanguine, that I begin to reckon upon a clear Tory scheme, more concert and better method. Should we prove so happy, our friends must do their part in making the administration easy in Parliament.'[17]

There was some justification for Bolingbroke's imperious language and growing confidence. Despite his defeat over the ministerial changes in the summer of 1713, he was at last seeing signs of a reduction in Oxford's power. This was primarily due not to changes in the Tory party, but to the Queen's growing dissatisfaction with Oxford's conduct. The Lord Treasurer had gone off to Wimpole for his son's wedding and then proceeded to stay away from the Court for some time, because of the sudden death of his daughter, the Marchioness of Carmarthen. Bolingbroke seized this opportunity for assiduous attendance on the Queen at Windsor Castle. His first objective was to win over Lady Masham, the royal favourite. She was virtually bribed by a share of the Asiento contract and a part of the large sum to be derived from the three explanatory articles of the treaty of commerce with Spain,[18] that had the effect of doubling the duty paid on goods imported into Spanish territory. This treaty was ratified on 28 November 1713, and it was during November and December 1713 that it became clear that Bolingbroke was now more influential at Court. William Stratford warned Oxford's son:

> On the 22nd of this month I made a visit for one day at Bucklebury. I there learnt that the gentleman [Bolingbroke] was much out of humour whilst he was there, and amongst other signs of it, broke out into these expressions against your father, 'I and *Lady Masham* have bore him upon our shoulders, and have made him what he is, and he now leaves *us* where *we* were.' I know my old friend will rant sometimes, but the person he joined with himself made me take notice of the expression. I must leave it to others to make reflections on it.[19]

John Aislabie even believed that it would soon be time to salute the new favourite. He told James Grahme that during Oxford's absence Bolingbroke had attended Windsor with 'unusual assiduity' and was putting on 'premier airs'. Schütz, the Hanoverian envoy, made similar observations.[20]

The Queen was certainly becoming disgruntled with the Lord Treasurer's lethargy and his apparent neglect of his official duties. Oxford was too grief-stricken to heed the warning and he continued to stay away from the Court. This played straight into Bolingbroke's hands, especially as Oxford was still absent when the Queen fell ill shortly before Christmas 1713. Bolingbroke asked Oxford to come to her bedside and the Lord Treasurer's friends were amazed at his continued absence.[21] As soon as the Queen recovered sufficiently she made it plain that she was most dissatisfied with his conduct and it was confidently predicted that he would resign. When the Queen's illness recurred, in mid-January 1714, the Tory leaders could no longer doubt that they must prepare for the Queen's death or else the Whigs would outmanœuvre them over the succession. Bolingbroke warned Lord Anglesey, a leading Hanoverian Tory, that the Queen 'had but one life, and whenever that drops, if the Church interest is broke, without concert, without confidence, without order, we are of all men the most miserable. The Whigs will be united, and ready to take any hint which their leaders shall give.'[22] The Secretary had no definite solution to the succession problem, but he did have an immediate objective, to unite the Tories under his leadership. With this, and with constant vigilance in debate in both Houses, he believed the Tories could meet any Whig challenge.[23] Oxford replied by labouring to re-establish his influence with the Queen. Clearly, Bolingbroke had recovered some ground since his humiliation in August 1713, but there was still no immediate prospect of his leading the ministry.

The Queen's illness naturally brought the succession problem to the forefront of politics. This suited the Whigs, who were united in favour of the Hanoverian succession and who could afford to play upon the obvious divisions within the Tory party on this issue. The ministry tried to counter the Whig propaganda, by sending emissaries to Hanover with protestations of loyalty. Yet the ministers could hardly complain when the Hanoverian royal family remained suspicious of their intentions. Both Oxford and Bolingbroke had been communicating with the Pretender for some time.[24] During these tentative negotiations neither minister went so far as to pledge positive action and both contented themselves with vague promises. Probably neither minister was sure how far the other had committed himself. After September 1713 Bolingbroke opened a separate channel to the Pretender through d'Iberville, the new Envoy-Extra-ordinary from France. This dabbling in Jacobite intrigue exacerbated the bitter rivalry between the two ministers. Oxford was probably most alarmed at what the rash and ambitious Bolingbroke might be plotting with the Pretender. Yet, ironically, both the Pretender and Torcy were pinning their hopes on Oxford. It has even been argued that Bolingbroke was no more deeply engaged than the Lord Treasurer in the Jacobite cause.[25] Nonetheless, while Bolingbroke, just as much as Oxford, insisted that nothing could be done until the Pretender changed his religion, he was more sympathetic to Jacobitism than Oxford ever was. He would have been satisfied had the Pretender's conversion to Protestant-ism been purely nominal. In the new parliament he sought the support of the Jacobite wing of the Tory party and never dashed their hopes of eventually setting aside the Act of Settlement. To the last, he hoped that he and the Tory party could choose the successor who would confirm them in place and power.[26]

The succession problem was the one issue which had to be resolved, if the Tory party were to survive as a coherent group and if Bolingbroke were to become its leader. The magnitude of the problem did not escape contemporary witnesses. In March 1714 Sir John Perceval noted in his journal: 'The Torys were now in two parties, those who submitted them-selves entirely to the ministry's measures, and those who showed a doubtfulness and distrust, and declared openly their adherence to the Hanover Settlement. The Jacobites in the habit of Tories made a third party.'[27] Bolingbroke was prepared to see the Hanoverian Tories attack Oxford's leadership, while at the same time he was telling the Jacobites that it was Oxford who prevented anything being done for the Pretender.[28] Setting these Tory splinter groups against the Lord Treasurer might have helped to turn him out of office, but it did not assist Boling-broke himself to devise a policy which would really unite the Tory party. When the new parliament met, Bolingbroke had still not defeated Oxford nor rallied the Tories behind his own banner. His political future and that of the Tory party were far from secure.

In the first few weeks of the new parliament the intense rivalry of the two leading ministers was obscured by their need to combine against the Whig onslaughts on the late peace and on the dangers threatening the Hanoverian succession. In the Commons their supporters cooperated in expelling Sir Richard Steele from the chamber for his criticisms of the peace in his contributions to *The Englishman* and in his pamphlet, *The Crisis*. In the Lords, Oxford and Bolingbroke personally defended the ministry's record on the Protestant succession. Behind the scenes, however, the contest for the leadership was still being fought out with grim determination on both sides. While Oxford was full of complaints of neglect and betrayal by his ministerial colleagues, Bolingbroke was pressing for a more vigorous policy, which might unite the Tory party. He told Lord Strafford: 'All that can be done is doing, to prevail on our friend, my Lord Treasurer, to alter his measures, to renew a confidence with the Tories, and a spirit in them, and to give a regular motion to all the wheels of government. I am sanguine enough to hope that we shall prevail. Indeed, it would be a pity to lose by management what none can wrest by force out of our hands.'[29]

Since Bolingbroke was still unable to topple the Lord Treasurer, he had to cooperate with him, even to effect some kind of superficial reconciliation. His hand was forced by two circumstances. First, though the Secretary had now won over Lady Masham, he had not yet fully converted the Queen. He had angrily expostulated to Her Majesty that it was impossible to tell whether the Lord Treasurer were a Whig or a Tory.[30] The Queen was beginning to see sense in Bolingbroke's policies, but she still did not trust him. Moreover, she had considerable proof of Oxford's unequalled ability at parliamentary management and she believed that only he could save her from the unpleasant prospect of capitulating once more to the Whigs. She therefore insisted on a reconciliation between her two contending ministers. In the second place, despite all his efforts, Bolingbroke could not command an impressive array of Tories. Prominent Jacobites, such as George Lockhart, were not convinced that he was sincere in his professions of loyalty to the Pretender, though they hoped he might yet prove true to the cause.[31] The leaders of the Hanoverian Tories, the Earl of Anglesey and Sir Thomas Hanmer, appeared more willing to trust and support Oxford. The bulk of the 'Church Party', whose primary concern was to uphold the interests of the Church of England, and which included stalwarts such as William Bromley, Charles Caesar, Justinian Isham and Sir George Beaumont, had failed to rally behind Bolingbroke's demand for a more positive Tory policy. They were no doubt offended by Bolingbroke's flagrant immorality, his shameful treatment of his wife and his ill-concealed contempt for the doctrines of the Church of England itself. His ambition, his rashness and his lack of integrity prevented him commanding their devoted support. It was significant that, apart from Francis Atterbury, no leading Churchman seriously supported Bolingbroke. In fact, the Secretary, apart from a few friends of integrity and ability, such as Lord Harcourt and Sir William Wyndham, was left with a rag-bag of supporters; the inexperienced, the self-seeking and the second-rate. His cause must have inspired little confidence, when he had to depend upon men of the calibre of Arthur Moore, Sir John Stonehouse and Edward Knatchbull. The comparison with the supporters of the Lord Treasurer was stark and invidious. Until Bolingbroke could widen the basis of his support, he had to tolerate Oxford's continued leadership of the ministry. He was compelled to admit his inability to oust the Lord Treasurer at this stage. 'I most sincerely desire to see your Lordship, as long as I live, at the head of the Queen's affairs, and of the Church of England party,' was one of his flattering and hypocritical remarks to Oxford, in March 1714.[32]

Largely as a result of the Queen's insistence, some kind of tenuous agreement was restored and Tory morale at once revived. Even Anglesey seemed prepared to rally to the ministry. An important outcome of this ministerial rapprochement was the decision to push ahead with a policy of rooting out prominent Whig officers from the armed forces. This had been Bolingbroke's objective for some time and he had already had some success in this direction. In January he had personally informed the Whig Admiral Byng that he was to be placed on half-pay and left out of the commission of the Admiralty.[33] The army, however, was the main target for ministerial revenge. In March 1714 the Cabinet resolved to dismiss the Duke of Argyll from all his places and to order the Earl of Stair and several colonels in the Guards to sell their regiments. Plans were laid for sweeping changes among the regiments on the Irish establishment, while the ministers worked hard to convert other officers with promises of suitable rewards. In Scotland, for example, the army was shown how officers loyal to the present ministry prospered. The Earl of Orkney was made governor of Edinburgh Castle and George Hamilton became the new Commander-in-Chief in Scotland. This whole policy of remodelling the army[34] was a triumph for Bolingbroke. It suited his general strategy and he took a great interest in it. In addition, he personally selected the army officers who were to be sent to supervise the destruction of the fortifications of Dunkirk,[35] for he knew that the Whigs would not hesitate to make political capital out of any reports about the slow progress of the demolition. Bolingbroke was not satisfied with the extent of this initial onslaught on his Whig opponents, who he believed had been immune from attack for too long. He wished to show the Tory backbenchers that they could rely on him to protect the party's interests. On 4 April Sir Edward Knatchbull recorded in his diary an account of an important meeting between ministers and backbenchers:

> We had a meeting by summons from Mr Bromley at his office where Lord T[reasurer], Lord Bolingbroke, Lord Chancellor, the Speaker and about 30 gentlemen of the House of Commons [were present], when the Lords proposed that we should exert ourselves and not let a majority slip through our hands, and that we should meet twice a week for a mutual confidence and that the Queen was determined to proceed in the interest of the Church, etc., and my Lord Bolingbroke farther added afterwards that she would not leave a Whig in employ.[36]

The enthusiastic welcome which many Tories gave to the removal of Whig army officers encouraged Bolingbroke to press for similar policies, designed to win their approval and support. Literally within days of his enforced reconciliation with Oxford, he was again rocking the boat and challenging for the right to steer. The Lord Treasurer's private discussions with moderate Whigs, such as Lord Halifax and Lord Cowper, only served to increase Bolingbroke's alarm about the essential weakness of his position. The sudden storm over the succession, which arose in April 1714, made him determined once more to safeguard his own political future at Oxford's expense and before the Queen's death could threaten his whole career. The succession problem was raised in vital debates in both Houses and by the demand from the Hanoverian envoy for a writ to summon the Electoral Prince to England, in order to secure the Hanoverian inheritance. On 5 April Anglesey castigated the peace in the House of Lords and claimed that the ministry was endangering the Protestant succession. This alarming attack posed a major challenge to the ministers, but unfortunately it provoked different responses from them. Oxford opted for caution and hoped to avoid any vote being taken. Bolingbroke wanted to pick up the gage thrown down by Anglesey. While Oxford spoke scarcely a word during the debate, the Secretary defended the ministry 'with much warmth and quickness'. At least nine Tory peers rebelled, but a motion that the Hanoverian succession was not in danger was narrowly passed after Harcourt wisely cloaked it in the royal prerogative, by adding the words 'under her Majesty's Administration'.[37] Bolingbroke hoped for a more vigorous defence of the ministry's conduct

when the succession problem was debated in the Commons. He planned
his strategy with a handful of close friends, including Sir William Wyndham, Arthur Moore and Sir Edward Knatchbull. When Knatchbull
pointed out the difficulty of rallying the dispirited Tories, while so many
Whigs still enjoyed office, Bolingbroke replied that 'if there was one
Whig in employment at the rising of this session he would give anyone
leave to spit in his face if he would keep his seals 2 months after
the session'.[38] This might have satisfied Knatchbull, but it did not prevent
Sir Thomas Hanmer leading another revolt of Hanoverian Tories against
the ministry when the succession problem was debated on 16 April.
On this occasion over eighty backbenchers voted with him.[39] This
alarming split in the Tory party was paralleled by the divisions which
appeared within the ministry when Baron Schütz demanded a writ to
summon the Electoral Prince to the House of Lords as Duke of Cambridge.
The demand placed the ministers in a cruel dilemma, since they risked
alienating either the Queen or the Hanoverian family. Bolingbroke,
hoping to ingratiate himself with the Queen, opposed granting the writ,
but Oxford, Harcourt and Dartmouth believed that it could not be
refused.[40] The result was a compromise. Schütz was told that the writ
could be collected, but the Hanoverian Court was left in no doubt that
the Queen would resent it, if he in fact called for it. The Hanoverians
took the hint and Schütz was recalled.

Browbeating the Electoral family was no substitute for a clear ministerial
policy. This was all the more necessary as events in parliament were
rapidly getting out of control. The Commons criticised the peace with
Spain, passed a Place bill without a division, and even defeated a Supply
bill. The events of April convinced Bolingbroke of the need for a determined policy, in order to retrieve the worsening situation before it was
too late. The reconciliation with Oxford, arranged so recently, had been
quickly destroyed. On 21 April he appealed to the Lord Treasurer to make
an example of Heneage Finch, Nottingham's nephew, who was voting
regularly with the opposition, while still retaining a Court appointment.[41]
To Lord Strafford he wrote: 'My Lord, let us act like men of courage and
public spirit; let those who guide the helm answer for the course of the
ship, but let us hand the sails, and do our part of the work, without
reproach.'[42] Oxford's reply was to press for a more clearly defined Hanoverian policy, which would rally Anglesey, Hanmer and their supporters
to his side and might also placate the moderate Whigs. He was no longer
supreme at Court, however, and could not dislodge Bolingbroke. Unless

he could achieve this, his other efforts would not command enough confidence for him to dominate parliament and his ministerial colleagues.

Bolingbroke's problem was to find some kind of policy which would unite the Tory party. It was virtually impossible to do this on the succession issue. Bolingbroke was not averse to leading a Tory party which had been converted to Jacobitism, but he knew this could never be achieved if the Pretender refused to renounce Catholicism. In a pungent phrase, he warned the Pretender that the country would rather accept the Grand Turk than a Roman Catholic as King of England.[43] While the Pretender remained firm in his attachment to his faith, Bolingbroke had to make preparations to meet an eventual Hanoverian succession. The Electoral family had been annoyed at the separate peace negotiated at Utrecht, but it would be compelled to accept Tory ministers, if a strong, united Tory party was in firm control of the levers of power when the Queen died. Therefore, instead of grasping the nettle of the succession problem, Bolingbroke sought to unite the Tories on enough other issues so as to strengthen their hold on political power. His plans were to oust the Lord Treasurer, to make a clean sweep of all the Whigs still in office, and to face any successor with a Tory party firmly entrenched at Westminster and throughout the Church, the administration and the country at large. Then, as leader of the Tories, he himself would be in a strong position to negotiate terms with either of the rival claimants to the throne.

All these ambitious schemes hinged on Bolingbroke being able to gain a victory at Court. For the thrusting Secretary this was an agonisingly slow process. He had clearly replaced Oxford in Lady Masham's favours and he was slowly winning over the Duchess of Somerset, another royal favourite, whose daughter was married to Sir William Wyndham.[44] By the early summer the two rivals were almost on an equal footing at Court. Bolingbroke planned to tip the scales in his favour by convincing the Queen that he had the greater support among the rank-and-file Tories. His first move in this direction was something of a blunder and Oxford almost thwarted him. The Secretary decided to press for a motion in parliament that the Hanoverian troops should not be paid their arrears, because of their refusal to obey Ormonde's orders after the cessation of arms in 1712. He probably came to this decision after a great number of Tories had gathered at his office, in order to insist that these arrears should not be paid.[45] When the motion came before the Commons all Bolingbroke's supporters voted for it, but Oxford's followers were divided, probably because the Lord Treasurer had not given them a clear lead. Even so, the motion was only narrowly carried by eight votes. In the Lords, Oxford took the plunge and opposed the motion, claiming that he had the Queen's approval to do so. Bolingbroke tried to counter this by offering to take Anglesey to the Queen, in order to hear her personally oppose the payment of the arrears.[46] Though he carried the day, it was only at the cost of a public dispute with the Lord Treasurer and the loss of favour at the Court of Hanover.

Bolingbroke was more confident of success with the Schism bill, which he promoted with the support of Atterbury and Harcourt.[47] Atterbury, at least, had genuine, if partisan, religious convictions, but Bolingbroke was much more concerned with uniting the Tory party and furthering his own career. He knew that the Queen and the Tory backwoodsmen would delight in this attack on one of the main strongholds of nonconformity, the Dissenting Academies. It would also place Oxford, with his well-known sympathy for the Dissenters, in an invidious position. Finally, it offered the prospect of driving a wedge between the Whigs and the Hanoverian Tories, thus enabling him to draw the latter to his side. These hopes were not entirely unfounded. In the Commons the bill was piloted through its various stages by Sir William Wyndham, Bolingbroke's lieutenant. Though the severity of the measure was slightly reduced, allowing the Dissenters to teach their children to write, the bill passed through the House with large majorities. The equivocal behaviour of Oxford's relatives annoyed many Tories; there were Harleyites on both sides and also among the abstainers.[48] In the Lords, on 4 June, Bolingbroke championed the measure, saying 'it was a Bill of the last importance, since it concerns the security of the Church of England, which is the best and firmest support of the monarchy'.[49] Anglesey and Abingdon, the two leading Hanoverian Tories in the Lords, spoke up for the bill, while Oxford refused to commit himself and left the House without voting. His close friends, Dartmouth, Foley, Mansell and Poulett, all showed sympathy with the Dissenters.[50] All this was useful ammunition for Bolingbroke, in his campaign to damage the Lord Treasurer's standing with the Queen and the Tory party. Yet it was not all gain, for the opposition passed several amendments, which weakened the impact of the bill. On the third reading the majority was a mere five votes. Boling-broke may have pleased the Queen and the Tories, but he had not achieved a complete triumph.

Other events soon proved that he was not yet in control of the parliamentary situation, particularly with regard to the succession problem.

In the Commons, Ralph Freeman, a leading Hanoverian Tory, suggested that the Queen's proclamation, offering a reward of £5,000 for the arrest of the Pretender, if he landed in Britain, should be amended to raise the reward to £100,000. He evidently believed that the ministry was luke-warm in its hostility to the Jacobite cause and so the government had to let it pass without a division. In the Lords, Bolingbroke himself was surprised when the opposition moved an amendment requesting the Queen to have the Pretender removed from Lorraine. The Secretary was not even in the House at the time and, when he hastily returned, he was too late to turn the tide. To demonstrate his loyalty to the Hanoverian succession, he moved for a bill to make it high treason for anyone to enlist soldiers in the Pretender's service. The Whigs were delighted to commit Bolingbroke on the succession issue and a bill was immediately ordered. The Secretary's supporters boasted that he had turned the tables on his opponents, but other commentators asserted that he was roughly handled in the debate. He was certainly not in control of the situation for, though he actually chaired a committee on the bill, he could not prevent amendments making it more difficult for British troops to serve either the Pretender or the King of France.[51]

Bolingbroke's greatest failing, however, and the one which rendered him unfit to lead the ministry, was his inability to pilot bills of supply through parliament with the skill displayed on such occasions by the Lord Treasurer. At one stage the Committee of Ways and Means was uncertain about precisely what financial expedients it should adopt to raise a mere £150,000. Apparently, this was the result of various Tory malcontents attempting to embarrass the government.[52] Nevertheless, one commentator actually thought the whole fiasco had been skilfully engineered by Bolingbroke, so that he could accuse the Lord Treasurer of negligence and of losing control of the Commons, and then step in himself to retrieve the situation.[53] In fact, Bolingbroke was alarmed at this delay in passing the money bills. He sent for George Lockhart, who was one of those Tories opposing the Supply bills, and angrily warned him that nothing could be done for the Pretender until Oxford was defeated, and that this was not possible during the session.[54] The Lord Treasurer was also per-fectly aware of this and he was deliberately spinning out the session as long as possible, particularly once Bolingbroke came under attack over the treaty of commerce with Spain. When the Malt bill finally came before the Lords it was Harcourt, not the Lord Treasurer, who hastily rounded up every available peer to help steer the bill through the House.[55]

The Lord Treasurer was clearly fighting a vigorous campaign, even if he was on the defensive. His greatest weapon was still his influence with the Queen. For years he had been her greatest political confidant and the Queen had always appreciated his moderation, his honesty and his financial and political ability. His private papers are full of draft memoranda of the various arguments which he used to combat Bolingbroke in his discussions with the Queen. He warned her of the dangers to which she would be exposed should he fall. There would be no money, no credit, and the whole Church interest would believe that she planned to support the Pretender's cause. She risked everything by listening to the advice of Bolingbroke, Harcourt and Lady Masham.[56] In these confrontations the Lord Treasurer could stress Bolingbroke's overweening ambition. He could also make much of the Secretary's failure to manage affairs in parliament and of his general untrustworthiness. The last argument was very effective. It was strongly rumoured that Oxford was in a position to arraign Bolingbroke for plotting a Jacobite restoration.[57] The Secretary was also losing credit with the Queen, because of his ill-treatment of his wife. In order to placate Her Majesty, he had promised to return to his wife.[58] Bolingbroke's personal morality had always contrasted ill with that of Oxford and of the Queen. His dubious financial dealings also compared unfavourably with the strict honesty of the Lord Treasurer. Unfortunately for Bolingbroke, it was the sudden highlighting of precisely this aspect of his character that made the Queen cling to Oxford. A major scandal arose over the financial terms of the Spanish commercial treaty and Bolingbroke himself was implicated. This played straight into Oxford's hands. He planned to use it in order to ruin Bolingbroke's shaky reputation with the Queen.[59]

The treaty of commerce with Spain, which had been ratified in November 1713, was most unsatisfactory and its weaknesses were largely due to the inexperience and hasty negotiations of Bolingbroke and his advisers. It clearly did not defend the interests of British merchants and was, indeed, actively hurtful to some of them. The main parliamentary attack, however, came not on the principal terms of the treaty, but on some of the more shady aspects of the treaty. Its critics looked askance at the way $22\frac{1}{2}$ per cent of the profits from the trading clauses of the treaty were assigned to the Queen. It was generally believed that Bolingbroke and Lady Masham were to profit from this arrangement. The whole question was highlighted when the Court of the South Sea Company began to investigate a shady deal, by which an additional cargo was to be put aboard the first licensed ship destined for the Spanish West Indies, in accordance with the terms of the Asiento. Arthur Moore, the friend and financial adviser of Bolingbroke, was implicated in this piece of sharp practice. The Secretary tried to forestall further inquiries by informing the company that the Queen was willing to surrender her share of the Asiento. When the company continued its investigations Oxford made it quite clear that he had had no part in the negotiations and so his hands, at least, were clean. Arthur Moore was found guilty of a breach of trust and voted incapable of serving the company again.[60]

Bolingbroke was well aware that these developments could destroy his bid for power. Even before the Lords took up the affair he was contemplating the possibility of having to resign at the end of the session.[61] Oxford did his best to force the Secretary's hand. On 2 July Robert Monckton, one of the Commissioners of Trade and Plantations, and a close friend of the Lord Treasurer, denied that his Board had any responsibility for the three explanatory articles of the commercial treaty, which the Lords were now examining.[62] Oxford himself voted to hear the objections of the merchant community. This brought his dispute with Bolingbroke onto the floor of the House. During the debate 'it was observable that there was not a word said either by the Lord Treasurer or any of his friends in defence of the peace [with Spain] so that all readily conclude that the Lord Treasurer endeavours to sacrifice Lord Bolingbroke'.[63] Further damage was done to Bolingbroke's sagging reputation, on 8 July, when William Lowndes, the Secretary to the Treasury, confessed to the Lords that he was only the nominal assignee for the Queen's share of the Asiento. It was strongly suspected that the real beneficiaries were Bolingbroke, Lady Masham and Arthur Moore.[64] Even after the Queen resigned her share the Lords continued the attack. Bolingbroke desperately needed to end the session, in order to prevent any more damaging disclosures. Fortunately for him, the debates in the Lords had been spun out by the detailed investigations into the commercial treaty. This allowed the Secretary to push through the last money bill, the Lottery, despite the obstructive tactics of the Lord Treasurer. On 8 July this bill was passed and next day, on Bolingbroke's advice, the Queen prorogued the session.[65] It had been a close shave.

These last damaging disclosures in the Lords and the precipitous prorogation of parliament revealed Bolingbroke in a poor light and, as far as he was concerned, fatally postponed the fall of Oxford. A week or so before, there had been a welter of speculation about ministerial changes

and Bolingbroke's impending triumph. William Stratford feared that
Bolingbroke was winning converts. The Duke of Ormonde had gone over
to him, Anglesey might yet be bribed by the post of Lord Lieutenant of
Ireland, and even Bromley might not stand firm under pressure. Swift was
also informed about the capture of Anglesey and about the rumour that
Abingdon and Trevor would also serve in the new ministry. By this
account, however, Bromley would fall and so would Poulett. Another
report indicated that Sir William Wyndham, Henry Campion and Sir
Constantine Phipps would be appointed Secretary of State, Chancellor of
the Exchequer and Attorney-General of Ireland, respectively, while
Bolingbroke would take over the Treasury.[66] If these reports were true,
then the Secretary had indeed made headway, though he still had not won
over many supporters of integrity or administrative talent. The final
debates in the Lords probably lost him some of these new adherents.
There was certainly no sign of him rallying significant numbers of both
Jacobites and Hanoverian Tories to his banner. Instead, there was renewed
speculation about yet another ministerial reconciliation. Observers were
convinced that Oxford would continue his fierce rearguard action.
Harcourt despaired of ever ousting the Lord Treasurer, virtually
abandoned the struggle, and went off into the country.

Bolingbroke did not give up the contest so readily. He continued to
advise the Queen to dismiss Oxford and he used every opportunity to
blast the Lord Treasurer's reputation. To Lord Strafford he sent a damning
indictment of the state of affairs under Oxford's leadership:

> My dear Lord, the Queen's affairs are in a deplorable state, by that glorious
> management, with which, it seems, no man must presume to find fault; we
> are fallen into contempt abroad, into confusion at home; with a vast majority of
> the nation on our side, we are insulted by the minority; and with the merit of
> having made a good and popular peace, we are reproached by those who lie
> under the guilt of attempting to prolong a ruinous war. It is a great while
> since I have thought that this could never be, was not our leader in a secret
> with our enemy; and, I believe, that there is hardly a Whig or Tory in
> Britain, that is not of the same opinion.[67]

As he disseminated such swingeing criticisms it was generally expected that
Bolingbroke would soon replace his rival and there were widespread
rumours of the composition of his proposed ministry. It was agreed that
Bolingbroke himself would not be made Lord Treasurer; a damning
indictment of his financial ability and honesty. The Treasury would be

put into commission and among the names canvassed for the new Board were the leading figures who could be expected to support a Bolingbroke administration. These included Wyndham, Henry Campion, James Brydges, Jack Hill, Sir John Pakington, Lord Bathurst, Lord Lexington, Lord Masham and, surprisingly, the Bishop of London. Lord Trevor was expected to become Lord President, Atterbury to be Lord Privy Seal, and Ormonde, Lord Lieutenant of Ireland.[68] 'A motley crew' is the most favourable description which could be applied to this ministry. Apart from Harcourt and, perhaps, Wyndham and the Bishop of London, Bolingbroke had few supporters able to combine ability with integrity. Trevor, Masham, Lexington, Bathurst and even Ormonde were second-rate, Campion and Pakington were 'wild men' from the backbenches, and the idea of Brydges and Hill at the Treasury must have alarmed everybody, including their best friends and colleagues. Even Wyndham lacked experience and the Bishop of London was not an able politician, though he was a skilled diplomatist. A ministry based on such talent lacked credibility and could not inspire any confidence. After months of endeavour Boling-broke had not succeeded in winning over Hanmer or Abingdon, while Bromley, Dartmouth, Poulett and Buckingham sided with Oxford. Anglesey's position remained equivocal, but Shrewsbury wisely stood aside from the conflict. He was much too cautious to join a ministry which was virtually scraping the barrel for talent.

Nevertheless, despite the poor quality of Bolingbroke's proposed ministry, the Secretary was at last able to persuade the Queen to dismiss his rival. On 24 July it was strongly rumoured that the Treasury was to be put in commission and that this would be made up of Bolingbroke's supporters. Yet still the 'uncertain timorous nature of the Queen'[69] led her to hesitate before dismissing a man who had served her so long and so faithfully. It was not until 27 July that she parted at last with her Lord Treasurer, complaining 'that he neglected all business; that he was seldom to be understood; that when he did explain himself, she could not depend upon the truth of what he said; that he never came to her at the time she appointed; that he often came drunk; that lastly, to crown all, he behaved himself towards her with ill manner, indecency, and disrespect'.[70] These charges were the results of months of malicious insinuation by Bolingbroke and Lady Masham, but they were not entirely without foundation. Oxford had begun to drink heavily, had not fully recovered from the death of his daughter, and his grip on financial and political affairs had not been so sure in recent months. Matthew Prior in Paris, who was by no

means hostile to the Lord Treasurer, despite his friendship with Bolingbroke, had complained that he did not receive adequate directions from
Oxford on the conduct of his affairs.[71] Yet it is hard to believe all these
charges. Oxford had fought a very skilful rearguard action, in order to
deny Bolingbroke victory, and he had almost prevented his rival from
passing the necessary Supply bills in time to prorogue parliament, before
there were any damaging disclosures in the debate on the Spanish commercial treaty. It is even more difficult to believe that the Lord Treasurer,
the most subtle and experienced politician of the age, could have treated
the Queen with so little respect. More likely, Bolingbroke had poisoned
the Queen's mind and exaggerated all Oxford's faults. The Queen had
certainly taken a great deal of convincing. When she did pluck up enough
courage the strenuous effort was at least partially responsible for her last
and fatal illness. Her decision was something of a surprise to Bolingbroke
himself. He had to summon Harcourt hastily to London to put the
finishing stroke to Oxford and to concert plans for the new ministry.

To Bolingbroke's everlasting bitterness, his triumph was short-lived;
almost non-existent. The Queen could not be persuaded to promote
him to the Lord Treasurership and, to crown his disappointment, she fell
mortally ill almost within hours of dismissing Oxford. The Secretary lost
his nerve in this crisis and virtually threw in the towel. His plans to unite
the Tories and to place his personal adherents in all the major posts of
responsibility remained unfulfilled and time was fast running out. He
therefore took the extraordinary step of trying to arrange a deal with the
Whigs. James Stanhope, William Pulteney and James Craggs were
surprised to receive an invitation to dinner with the Secretary, but they
accepted; Robert Walpole was in Norfolk and missed the bizarre encounter. To his astonished guests Bolingbroke protested his attachment to
the Hanoverian succession. James Stanhope, who had been his friend in the
days of his Grand Tour of Europe, replied that the Whigs expected
deeds not words. As a first step, he suggested that Marlborough and
Orford should be given command of the army and navy, respectively.
As a parting shot, he added the threat: 'Harry! You have only two ways of
escaping the gallows. The first is to join the honest party of the Whigs, the
other to give yourself up entirely to the French King and seek his help for
the Pretender. If you do not choose the first course, we can only imagine
that you have decided for the second.'[72] Bolingbroke was crushed by this
reply and incapable of the decisive action required to retrieve the situation.
Ironically, after months of complaints about Oxford's failure to give a

clear, vigorous lead, Bolingbroke could only drift helplessly with the tide. In contrast, the Whigs acted efficiently and with great determination, in order to safeguard the Protestant succession. Argyll and Somerset promptly appeared at the Privy Council meeting, on 30 July, when they learned of the serious nature of the Queen's illness. There they combined with Oxford in calling for a full meeting of the Privy Council, which brought in Lord Somers and other leading Whigs.[73] The Council agreed unanimously to recommend to the dying Queen that Shrewsbury should be made Lord Treasurer. Bolingbroke quietly acquiesced in this decison and even took the message to the Queen himself.[74] With her acceptance of this advice, all Bolingbroke's schemes crashed in ruins, much to the delight of Oxford's supporters.

When the Queen died, on 1 August 1714, the Hanoverian succession was assured. The Whigs were united and prepared to fight, if necessary. The Tories were hopelessly divided and incapable of decisive action. Oxford threw his weight behind the Hanoverian Tories. Bolingbroke meekly followed his example, though he tried to pass off his despair with a philosophic shrug: 'The Earl of Oxford was removed on Tuesday; the Queen died on Sunday. What a world is this and how does Fortune banter us.'[75] He at once took the oath of allegiance to George I and helped to prepare for his arrival; even lighting a bonfire to celebrate his accession.[76] There is no reliable evidence that Atterbury put forward the suggestion, which Bolingbroke rejected, of proclaiming the Pretender. In fact, when parliament was hastily reassembled it was Bolingbroke's lieutenant, Sir William Wyndham, who moved to vote the Civil List for George I. His supporters spoke against Walpole's motion to pay the Hanoverian troops their arrears since 1712, but they did not press their opposition to a vote.[77]

It was too late to curry favour with the new Court. The King's list of Regents, or Lords Justices, excluded both Bolingbroke and Oxford, though it included the leading Hanoverian Tories, Nottingham, Anglesey and Abingdon. Bothmer, who had no reason to like Bolingbroke, discovered that the Secretary had been planning a defensive alliance with France, Spain and Sicily. This smacked of Jacobite intrigue and it was rumoured that even more damaging papers had been discovered. At the end of August, Bolingbroke was dismissed and his office sealed up. At first he tried to put on a bold front, claiming that he had intended to resign at his first audience with the King and that he was suffering from the gross misrepresentations of his enemies.[78] In a letter to Atterbury he tried to pass off the blow lightly: 'To be removed was neither matter of surprise nor of concern to me; but the manner of my removal shocked me for at least two minutes.' He wrote in a less facetious, but no more truthful, vein to Swift: 'After a greater blow than most men ever felt, I keep up my spirit, am neither dejected at what has passed, nor apprehensive at what is to come.' By 11 September he was telling Lord Cowper that he planned to retire from politics.[79]

Bolingbroke decided it would be prudent to spend a few days in the country and he did not put in an appearance when George I landed. He did return for the coronation, on 20 October, when he saw the new King for the first time. Lady Cowper was one of the fascinated spectators at this encounter: 'The King, seeing a face he did not know, asked his name, when he did him homage; and he (Lord B.) hearing it as he went down the steps from the throne, turned round and bowed three times down to the very ground.'[80] Shortly afterwards Marlborough introduced Bolingbroke to the King.[81] The former Secretary began to hope that all might not yet be lost. Even at this late stage a united Tory party could force its attentions on the King. Swift encouraged him and even suggested another attempt at coming to terms with Oxford.[82] Bolingbroke was well aware of the dangers if the Tories remained disunited, but there was no immediate prospect of holding them together, even when the Hanoverian succession was an accomplished fact. In some despair, he wrote to Atterbury: 'The grief of my soul is this: I see plainly that the Tory party is gone. Those who broke from us formerly, continue still to act and speak on the same principles and with the same passions. Numbers are still left, and those numbers will be increased by such as have not their expectations answered. But where are the men of business that will live and draw together?'[83]

Though this was an attempt to throw the blame for the divisions within the Tory party onto Oxford's shoulders, it was a sound diagnosis of the party's present situation and its future prospects. Shrewsbury, Nottingham and Anglesey had deserted to the Court, the first of many secessions from the Tory ranks. At least Bromley, Hanmer and Ralph Freeman refused to serve a ministry dominated by the Whigs,[84] but the greatest stumbling blocks remained. The Tories lacked the united leadership, the strict discipline and the coherent political philosophy necessary to weather a period in the wilderness of opposition. Nothing could bring Oxford and Bolingbroke together. If anything, their mutual hostility increased. Bolingbroke even feared that Oxford would provide the Whigs with evidence of his negotiations with the Pretender. When his insincere offer of friendship was rebuffed by Oxford he abandoned the attempt forever.[85] The Tories faced the general election and the developments of 1715 more disunited than ever, and with their leaders engaged in mutual recriminations.[86] Bolingbroke was once more to prove incapable of dealing with such a serious political crisis.

CHAPTER 8

Jacobite and Hanoverian

BOLINGBROKE, despite all the evidence to the contrary, still vainly hoped that a strong Tory party could force George I to reduce his reliance on the Whigs. He put his faith in a Tory victory in the general election of 1715. Unfortunately the Tories were in a poor state to combat the Whigs in the elections. Their leaders were hopelessly divided, the backbenchers were still not united on their attitude to the new dynasty, and the party was rapidly alienating George I. Atterbury tried to rouse all the old Tory prejudices by calling upon the electors to defend the Church of England and the landed interest. The Whigs had more powerful arguments against the late peace and the present Jacobite sympathies of some of the Tories. With the powerful support of the Court the Whigs naturally won a sound majority. Yet the Tories won over 200 seats, more than the Whigs had done in 1713. If they had been united, disciplined and well led, as the Whigs had been then, the Tories might have made a recovery after a few years in opposition. Instead, they soon showed that the party was disintegrating and threatened with extinction.

Although there was now no chance of his making a quick political comeback, Bolingbroke did not immediately panic. The seizure of Lord Strafford's papers, in January 1715, first gave him serious cause for alarm. Then, in February, his old crony, James Brydges, warned him that the Whigs might be planning violent measures against the late Tory ministers.[1] Bolingbroke feared that Oxford might provide his Whig opponents with evidence to convict him of Jacobitism. His friends already saw that his fears were exceeding his good sense and Ormonde urged him to keep up his courage.[2] Bolingbroke attended the new parliament in March to defend his past conduct. When the Whig peers proposed to address the King to recover the reputation of the kingdom abroad Bolingbroke moved to substitute *maintain* for *recover*. He 'expressed the deepest concern for the memory of the late Queen, which, he said "he would do all in his power to vindicate; that he had the honour to be one of her servants, and if he had done anything amiss he would be contented to be punished for it; but that he thought it very hard to be censured and condemned without being heard" '.[3] The Whigs secured a comfortable majority as they did in the Commons where Sir William Wyndham led the Tory opposition in the first days of the session. Bolingbroke was concerned at the strength and vindictiveness of his opponents, but his nerve did not fail him until the ministry ordered the seizure of Matthew Prior's papers in Paris. He at once inquired of the French whether they had ever reported his conversations with them to others, particularly to Oxford. If they had, then he believed his head might be in danger. Torcy tried to reassure him, but d'Iberville acknowledged that the Dutch and Austrians were seeking revenge on Bolingbroke and that Marlborough was urging his former protégé to withdraw, at least temporarily.[4] When the Whig ministry finally asked Bolingbroke to surrender his own papers[5] he decided to flee to France. He made his arrangements in great secrecy. His first concern was to protect his wealth. He borrowed £20,000 from James Brydges, using his estates as security. These lands were then conveyed to six trustees, all political friends, who were to hold them for his wife, who accepted his debts to Brydges and others. The personal effects which he could not take with him, such as household goods, coaches and horses, were also conveyed to his wife.[6] Having completed these arrangements Bolingbroke appeared at a London playhouse, on Saturday, 26 March, but then, disguised as a servant of one of the French ministers, he fled to France next day, just in time to avoid arrest.[7]

Bolingbroke's flight was an enormous blunder. Once again he had revealed a tendency to lose his nerve, to panic in a crisis. To do him justice he was by nature very highly strung and there had been considerable political gossip, in February and March 1715, that the Whig ministers had found enough information among the papers they had seized to hang one or two of the late ministry.[8] Nevertheless, it was a fatal mistake. Oxford was in as much potential danger but stayed to face the storm. Several prominent supporters of the new ministry, including Cowper, Marlborough, Nottingham and Stanhope, had expressed a preference for saving Bolingbroke at Oxford's expense.[9] Moreover, the Whigs naturally took Bolingbroke's flight as confirmation of his guilt, while the Tories were embarrassed and dismayed. The Earl of Stair, the new Minister-Plenipotentiary, later ambassador, in Paris, learned from a London correspondent:

All our discourse here at present runs upon Lord Bolingbroke's sudden retreat. It was yesterday we had the news of his arrival at Calais. All your Whigs, excepting those of bloody vengeful tempers, seemed pleased he's gone. The court without risk gain their ends thereby as much as if he had lost his head, but the Tories are exceeding angry with him for deserting them at a time when they want a head so much.[10]

Bolingbroke had expected these reactions and sought to combat them. Shortly before his flight he had protested to his father that there was no truth in the Whig accusations that he had engaged in Jacobite intrigues.[11] When he fled the country he left a letter, addressed to Lord Lansdowne, which attempted to justify his conduct:

> You will excuse me, when you know that I had certain and repeated informations from some who are in the secret of affairs, that a resolution was taken by those who have power to execute it, to pursue me to the scaffold.
>
> My blood was to be the cement of a new alliance; nor could my innocence be any security, after it had been once demanded from abroad, and resolved on at home, that it was necessary to cut me off. Had there been the least reason to hope for a fair and open trial, after having been already prejudged, unheard by the two houses of parliament, I should not have declined the strictest examination.[12]

Despite his exaggerated claims Bolingbroke's letter did alleviate the worst Tory fears. Swift learned that it had 'done a great deal of good, and we have not lost a man by his going. It was a great surprise to his friends at first, but everybody is now convinced he would have been sacrificed had he stayed.'[13] Pamphleteers rushed to Bolingbroke's defence. His whole conduct was lavishly praised in *A Letter to the Right Honourable the Lord Viscount Bolingbroke* and his part in the peace negotiations was defended in *The Representation of the Right Honourable the Lord Viscount Bolingbroke*.

After committing the grave mistake of fleeing to France, Bolingbroke's wisest policy was to lie low, protesting his innocence and his loyalty to the Hanoverian succession, until he had learned the outcome of the Whig investigations. This appeared to be his intention. When he arrived in Paris he sought in vain to wait upon Lord Stair to clear himself of any suspicion of having come to join the Pretender. When Stair refused to see him he sent him a long letter, explaining his decision to leave England, which he asked the ambassador to forward to the King. His first concern was to deny that his flight was confirmation of his desire to betray the Hanoverian succession:

In the midst of many misfortunes there's not one which can afflict me more sensibly than to have my withdrawing from England misconstrued by the King, and a resolution, which in the present conjuncture appeared necessary for my security, be looked on to proceed either from a consciousness of past crimes or from an intention to commit new ones. I therefore take the liberty to apply myself to you and to beg that you will represent to His Majesty that wherever I am I carry along with me a heart full of duty to his person and zeal for his service. The contrary may perhaps have been suggested and against those arrows shot in the dark the most innocent are not secure, but I dare boldly affirm that no proof can be produced that I was ever embarked in any design to subvert that establishment for the settling of which I gave my vote in parliament and to the maintenance of which I have so frequently sworn. Had I apprehended a charge on this head alone I should have now the happiness of being in my native country.

The dangers he feared were the product of party rancour raised because of the many momentous decisions which had to be taken by the Queen's last ministry. He himself was directly concerned in the making of the peace which made him many enemies, but he maintained that he never had the direction of the government's policies and that he only obeyed the Queen's express commands. The only errors which could be directly attributable to him were the result of an excess of zeal and a lack of experience. His flight should not be presumed to be evidence of guilt, since there were many other cases of innocent men fleeing persecution. If the King would but command him he would retire from the public scene and his conduct would be beyond reproach.[14]

The ambassador, who had been warned from London to observe Bolingbroke's activities, was unimpressed by the declaration. He was convinced that Bolingbroke would soon join the Pretender. To allay such suspicions Bolingbroke obeyed the entreaties of his friends who urged him to leave the vicinity of the courts of Louis XIV and the Pretender.[14] When he had settled at Bellevue, near Lyons, he wrote to his friend George Clarke, that he had moved from Paris to save his friends embarrassment on his account. His conscience was clear, he averred, but he was grateful for the good opinions and the loyalty of his Tory friends. With their support and perhaps with the assistance of the rising tide of public dissatisfaction he hoped he might yet defeat the malice of his enemies. For the moment he confessed that he had no plan of action.[15] While he waited for the Whigs to act and looked for signs of growing discontent with the new regime, he refused to commit himself to the

Pretender's cause. Though he listened sympathetically to the pleas of the Jacobites, he would not be drawn too quickly into their conspiracy. He even claimed that he had lost all political ambition and that he would be happy to live in peaceful obscurity.[16] The last man to remain inactive when events were rapidly moving to a climax, Bolingbroke at last took the plunge in July 1715, accepting an earldom from the Pretender and becoming his Secretary of State.

Events were soon to prove that this was an even greater blunder than his original decision to flee from England. He now unequivocally declared his betrayal of the Hanoverian succession, an act which he was to repent for the rest of his life. Bolingbroke's gross miscalculation was largely due to his lack of patience and excess of political ambition. His lack of judgement, however, was highlighted by later developments, which he could not see at the time but which have seemed obvious to his critics ever since. His rash decision was taken because of two changes in British politics. As Bolingbroke himself later claimed in his *Letter to Sir William Windham*, he was driven to this course by the decision of the Whigs to impeach him on a charge of high treason. His critics maintain that the impeachment process did not begin until after his decision to join the Pretender. However, the committee investigating his conduct had been meeting since April and it was regularly predicted that this would result in charges of high treason. In fact, Robert Walpole first announced the impeachment on 10 June, nearly a month before Bolingbroke's decision to join the Pretender.[17] With a Whig majority in both chambers a verdict of guilty was a mere formality. The other reason for Bolingbroke's decision was his genuine desire to serve the Tory party. He had always believed that the Tories represented the majority of the country gentlemen, the backbone of the nation, and he claimed that Jacobitism was their only refuge now that they had been virtually proscribed by the Hanoverians. The new royal family was certainly unpopular and in the early summer of 1715 there were riots and disturbances in several counties. Far from the scene, Bolingbroke evidently exaggerated their significance, but he was dependent upon the reports of his Tory friends in England. They too miscalculated, with less justification, for Wyndham, Lansdowne, Mar and Ormonde were all involved in Jacobite intrigues. Like Bolingbroke they were over-anxious for a rapid political comeback and allowed ambition to cloud their judgement.

Once Bolingbroke had joined the Pretender as his Secretary of State he set about his new duties with characteristic energy and enthusiasm.[18]

Though he realised some of the mischiefs under which the Pretender's cause laboured, he quickly suggested remedies and was confident that he would make the Whigs repent their attacks on him. He soon learned that his optimism was misplaced. The whole Jacobite adventure of 1715–16 was dogged by misfortune and mistakes. Any military expedition to Britain would require considerable French support if it were to succeed, but Bolingbroke found it more difficult to gain French assistance than he had ever imagined. For a time the French government cautioned patience, then, at the end of August 1715, Louis XIV died and a vital prop of the Jacobite cause crumpled. Bolingbroke later claimed: 'My hopes sunk as he declined, and died when he expired.'[19] The Regent, the Duke of Orleans, had his eyes on the throne itself and refused to alienate Britain by committing himself to the Jacobite cause. Though he turned a blind eye to some of the Jacobite preparations, he obstructed the more obvious plans for the expedition and would not give the large-scale support which was essential to the Pretender's success. Bolingbroke turned to Spain and Sweden, but their minor efforts could not make up for the loss of France's financial and military backing. The Jacobite cause was finally doomed by a complete failure to coordinate and harness the efforts and energies of the Pretender's supporters and sympathisers. Bolingbroke found himself only one servant among many. His advice and counsel were frequently ignored or countered at the Pretender's Court, often by men and women of little ability and of less experience of political conditions in Britain, though with more years of service in the Jacobite cause. Bolingbroke had specifically advised that the rebellion must be a concerted rising and that this was not possible until the English Jacobites were ready, but the Earl of Mar made a unilateral decision to raise th estandard of revolt in Scotland. The Pretender had no alternative but to assist this undertaking.

In planning the Pretender's embarkation Bolingbroke clashed with the other political advisers at Court. When shown the text of the declaration which the Pretender proposed to issue to his British subjects, Bolingbroke clearly warned him of the utter necessity of obtaining support in England. He was adamant that the Pretender must put himself at the head of the Tories and he assured him that this could only be achieved by a firm undertaking to protect the Church of England:

Certain it is that to keep up a party in England at this time and to disarm your enemies of their strongest weapon, your Majesty must link unto your own cause, that of the Church of England, of the Tory party, and of your sister's memory. Others may perhaps represent things to you as they wish them, but I shall, as long as I have the honour to serve you, represent them as they are.[20]

Bolingbroke followed this up with another lesson on political conditions in England. He instructed the Pretender that the theory of divine right was no longer enough to uphold his cause. Britain had changed much since 1688 and the clock could not now be turned back. Since the Pretender's declaration had not been amended to his satisfaction he refused to counter-sign it. Potential supporters in England would observe:

> that there is no promise made in favour of the Church of Ireland, and that even the promise which relates to the Church of England is very ambiguous, and liable to more than one interpretation . . . In this case, Sir, I should not be able to answer it to the world, or to my own conscience, if my name had in any degree contributed to weaken that security which all your friends expect, and will certainly insist upon, both for the Church of England and for that of Ireland. I serve your Majesty with an entire zeal and upon that bottom which can alone restore you and the monarchy. Was I to go off from that bottom, which I am incapable of, I should become useless to you.[21]

There could be no clearer evidence that Bolingbroke was not prepared to betray the major constitutional and religious developments achieved since the Revolution. The Pretender must come to terms with the new type of Tory, who had abandoned divine right, but who was more than ever attached to the Church of England. Bolingbroke was ready to betray the Hanoverians, but not the Tory party. He wanted power, but his ambition was limited by some political principles.

With the Pretender intent on joining Mar in Scotland and with the failure to mount a successful expedition to the west of England, Boling-broke had to agree to support the rebellion in the Highlands. He recognised that a victory in Scotland would not ensure ultimate success and that a war in England was now inevitable, but there seemed no alternative. After three months of delay and irresolution the Pretender at last sailed for Scotland, only to find a bare 4000 troops and a lost cause. Bolingbroke was blamed for the failure to send him adequate supplies and reinforce-ments and, on his return to France, the Pretender dismissed his Secretary of State in March 1716. This decision resulted in mutual and unsavoury recriminations. Bolingbroke's Jacobite critics drew up detailed written charges, accusing him of failing to perform his duties as Secretary of State.[22] The general burden of these criticisms was that Bolingbroke was difficult of access and deaf to desperate pleas from his Jacobite colleagues. He ignored urgent requests for arms and ammunition from both the Earl of Mar and the Pretender. In all his affairs as Secretary of State he had shown a lack of discretion, giving away secrets when drunk and not refraining from attacks on the other servants of the Pretender even when sober. When he could not get the full support of the French ministers or the English Tories he had made little effort to save the Jacobite rebellion from ignominious defeat. Bolingbroke was the last man to allow such personal criticisms to go unanswered. He wrote four letters defending his conduct.[23] In the first letter he claimed that the Pretender was using him as a scapegoat for the failure in Scotland. The shortage of powder was not responsible for the disaster and he had managed to procure some, but too late to send to Scotland. In his second and fourth letters he bitterly criticised the fools and meddlers at the Pretender's Court, who could not match his honesty and prudence. Only in the third letter did he attempt a reply to all the specific charges levelled against him. His strenuous efforts to provide the necessary supplies for the expedition had been hampered by the lack of cooperation from the French Court, the chronic shortage of money and the inefficiency of other servants of the Pretender. He was not concerned by his dismissal, 'being from the first resolved to serve upon a Protestant and English bottom, or not to serve at all'.

Bolingbroke's decision to join the Pretender has invariably been condemned by historians. Conversely, his conduct as the Pretender's Secretary of State and his decision to abandon Jacobitism have usually been defended by these same writers. They have accepted Bolingbroke's own defence, especially in his *Letter to Sir William Windham*, and the Duke of Berwick's opinion that the dismissal of Bolingbroke was an enormous blunder:

> To cast a public stigma upon him, and seek to blacken his character with the world, is an inconceivable proceeding, . . . I was in part a witness how Bolingbroke acted for King James whilst he managed his affairs, and I owe him the justice to say that he left nothing undone of what he could do; he moved heaven and earth to obtain supplies, but was always put off by the Court of France; and though he saw through their pretexts and complained of them, yet there was no other power to which he could apply.[24]

Only the most recent historian of the Jacobite movement has accepted the accusations against Bolingbroke, particularly the counter-charges made after Bolingbroke wrote his four letters defending his conduct.[25] Bolingbroke knew about the shortage of supplies and failed to remedy the defect, though other Jacobites managed to ship small quantities to Scotland. He would not cooperate with his colleagues, he gave away vital secrets when the worse for drink, and even corresponded with the Duke of Marlborough in England. To these charges could be added, it has been claimed, Bolingbroke's deliberate misrepresentation of the Pretender's declaration, which quite clearly guaranteed the Church of England, and of his religious principles, which were not bigoted. Berwick's defence of Bolingbroke should be ignored since he himself had betrayed the Jacobite cause. Some of these accusations can be accepted. Bolingbroke had a loose tongue after too much wine and he was quite capable of exercising his wit on the foibles of his Jacobite colleagues. Lord Stair, the British ambassador, had kept a spy on Bolingbroke's tail and no doubt his indiscretions reached London, though there is no evidence that he deliberately betrayed secrets.[26] The defence of the Pretender's religious views and of his original declaration for his British subjects carries little conviction, for Bolingbroke's charges have been substantiated from other sources. The major problem concerns Bolingbroke's efforts to provide arms and ammunition for the army in Scotland. His letters were full of protestations that he was doing all he possibly could, and he was normally an industrious and efficient minister. It was also significant that the Duke of Ormonde took the lead in getting rid of Bolingbroke, though he had not been directly involved in the Scottish expedition.[27] Yet, by the winter of 1715–16, Bolingbroke may well have lost confidence in the whole Jacobite cause. He was shocked by the loss of French support and seemed as anxious not to antagonise the Regent as to send supplies to Scotland. Nevertheless, while there might have been some grounds for criticism, nothing Bolingbroke could have done would have saved the Pretender's cause. There is some justification for believing that Bolingbroke was the public scapegoat for the fiasco.

Bolingbroke, with his highly developed instinct for political survival, opened himself to much greater criticism by the alacrity with which he abandoned Jacobitism and curried favour with George I and his Whig ministers. It is fair to point out, however, that the British government deliberately sought to make use of him and to encourage him to betray the Jacobites in the hope of some future reward from a grateful George I. Within days of Bolingbroke's dismissal James Stanhope informed Lord Stair in Paris that the government had heard that Bolingbroke might be prepared to abandon the Jacobites and betray their secrets. This would obviously weaken the Pretender's cause and seat the Hanoverians more firmly on the throne. Stanhope allowed Stair considerable freedom of action, for he gave him to understand that the King authorised him to offer Bolingbroke 'all suitable hope and encouragement' in return for his services.[28] Lord Stair, who rapidly came under Bolingbroke's spell, gave him too much encouragement, for he led him to expect a rapid pardon. The Whig ministers, particularly Stanhope and James Craggs junior, had to warn Stair that their insecure position in parliament made the corres- pondence with Bolingbroke 'very ticklish'. There were too many discon- tented, even neutral, Whigs, who would not stomach Bolingbroke's return so soon after the 1715 rebellion.[29]

To expedite his return to England Bolingbroke endeavoured to make himself useful and, if possible, indispensable to the Whig government. He recognised that the only card in his hand was his influence with some of the Tory opposition. He could strengthen the ministry's position by counter- acting Jacobite propaganda and by persuading some of the Tories to lessen their hostility to the present government. If he were seen to be openly betraying his former Jacobite colleagues, however, he would lose all credit with the Tories. He therefore told the ministry that he could not speak out publicly against the Pretender or give the government such confidential information as would implicate individual Jacobites.[30] These scruples were for public consumption. He was quite prepared to betray all either to the King or to the Duke of Marlborough and to trust to their discretion. Lord Stair approached Marlborough in a private capacity:

> Your Grace will see that I have writ to Mr Secretary Stanhope upon the subject of Lord Bolingbroke. You'll see the conditions he puts there, which he thinks necessary to preserve his reputation with his friends, but these reasons don't regard your Grace. He orders me to tell you, that he will have no reserves of any kind with you, that he will tell you all he knows, that he will depend upon your protection and be entirely governed by your advice. He will likewise freely tell the King everything he knows, and do everything to deserve His Majesty's pardon; but he would avoid being put into the hands of some persons who may have personal ill will to him, and would give such persons no hold on him to bring him to a public examination before the council. In my humble opinion his intentions are very sincere to do the King and his country all the services he can to make amends for the false steps he has made. He speaks to me already with great freedom, and tells me he will give me an account of everything he knows as soon as he hears from England that he may hope for the King's mercy.[31]

This letter rips to shreds the notion that Bolingbroke was too honourable to betray all the actions of individual Jacobites. He was quite prepared to do anything to salvage his political career, but feared that public betrayal of his former Jacobite colleagues would win some Whig support at the expense of losing all influence with the Tories. He was concerned that his betrayal should be secret not ineffective.

With the approval of the ministry Bolingbroke began to contact the Tories in parliament. On 13 September 1716 he advised his old friend, Sir William Wyndham, not to enter into any new political engagements until he had met him. He warned him that the Jacobite cause was desperate, its supporters were miserable wretches, and their measures weak.[32] While admitting the reasonableness of Bolingbroke's opinions, Wyndham argued that he could not abandon the Tories. Their prejudices and obstinacy were deeply ingrained and, since he was already suspected by them, he felt unable to act a more conspicuous role at this juncture.[33] Wyndham's caution was perfectly understandable, for Bolingbroke's *volte-face* had certainly been remarkable while his policies over the last year or two had hardly been consistent. Bolingbroke, moreover, was also labouring under the calumny heaped upon him by the Jacobites. The articles which they had drawn up against him were disseminated in England. Mar was anxious to avoid a paper war, which might discredit the Jacobite cause, but he was confident that these charges, backed by private letters, would condemn Bolingbroke. The Pretender himself recognised Wyndham's importance by writing him a personal letter justifying his dismissal of Bolingbroke. Wyndham appeared convinced and Bolingbroke began railing against the Jacobites for ruining his credit with his Tory friends in England.[34] Jonathan Swift, like Wyndham, feared Bolingbroke had been too ready to betray his former Jacobite colleagues: 'I should be sorry to see my Lord Bolingbroke following the trade of an informer, because he is a person for whom I always had, and still continue, a very great love and esteem. For I think, as the rest of mankind do, that informers are a detestable race of people, although they may be sometimes necessary.'[35]

To combat this successful campaign of vilification Bolingbroke redoubled his efforts to justify his whole conduct during the last five years. He wrote several letters to his Tory friends urging them to abandon Jacobitism as the only means of ending their sojourn in the political wilderness. In a letter to Swift he wrote of his desire to lead the Tories out of the cul-de-sac of Jacobitism: 'They are got into a dark hole, where they grope about after blind guides, stumble from mistake to mistake, jostle against one another and dash their heads against the wall, and all this to no purpose. For assure yourself, that there is no returning to light;

James Edward Stuart, the Old Pretender

John Dalrymple, 2nd Earl of Stair

The Château de la Source

Madame de Villette, 2nd Viscountess Bolingbroke

no going out, but by going back.'[36] To quieten Whig fears he promised to abandon party politics and to eschew any action which would distress the King's government. By the end of 1717 he had prepared for circulation among his Tory friends private copies of his celebrated *Letter to Sir William Windham*. In this, one of his most powerful works, he sought to justify his conduct since 1710, to wean the Tories from any commitment to Jacobitism, and to reduce the political temperature which threatened the future of the Tory party and himself. About one third of the work defended his conduct from 1710 to his flight to France in 1715. He admitted that the Treaty of Utrecht was far from perfect, but argued that it had been the best peace which could be obtained against tremendous opposition at home and abroad. With regard to the succession he claimed that the Tories, like himself, did not turn to Jacobitism until they had lost their offices and places, and were menaced by the vengeance of the Whigs. Since the Queen's last ministry had failed to secure the political fortunes of the Tory party, Bolingbroke had to blame these shortcomings on someone other than himself. The obvious scapegoat was Robert Harley, Earl of Oxford, but the blame for Bolingbroke's espousal and then rejection of Jacobitism could not be laid at Oxford's door. With some justice he claimed that he left England because he feared that the Whigs would impeach him. With less justification he asserted that his sole motive in joining the Pretender was to serve the Tory party. The failure of the Jacobite rebellion was not his responsibility. The death of Louis XIV and the refusal of the Regent to support the venture was a mortal blow. The Pretender himself was incapable of decisive action: 'He talked to me like a man who expected every moment to set out for England or Scotland, but who did not very well know which.'[37] His entourage and agents were disorganised and ill-prepared. The information which they received from England and Scotland was inaccurate and over-optimistic. Yet when the expedition failed all the blame had been heaped on his head because of his failure to resolve insoluble problems. Bolingbroke left none of his readers in any doubt that, in his opinion, any future Jacobite venture had even less hope of success. The Pretender must be abandoned or he would ruin the Tory party.

Bolingbroke was to spend the rest of his life repeating his defence of his conduct as Secretary of State to Queen Anne and the Pretender. His *Letter to Sir William Windham* was his fullest and most powerful reply to his many critics, but it is also valuable for an understanding of Bolingbroke's attitude to the Whig and Tory parties in the light of the failure of

F

Jacobitism. In his self-imposed task of restoring the fortunes of the Tory party he pursued two objectives, which, though they were connected, were not entirely compatible. On the one hand he had to win the confidence of his former Tory allies and persuade them to renounce openly all sympathy with the Jacobite cause. On the other, he had to allay any Whig suspicion that he might so revive and refurbish the Tory party that it would become a serious rival for political power. The first was the more obvious task and the one which would ingratiate him with the Whig ministers and the Hanoverian Court. His declared loyalty to the Tory party might counteract the impression sedulously created by Jacobite slanders. He skilfully accused his critics of abandoning their former principles, especially their loyalty to the Church of England, in order to serve the Pretender, whereas he had only turned Jacobite to serve the Tory party: 'I own the crime of having been for the pretender in a very different manner from those, with whom I acted. I served him as faithfully, I served him as well as they; but I served him on a different principle.' The Pretender was a religious bigot, who could not be trusted to defend the Church of England, whose security was so dear to the Tories. He warned them that they were

> grossly deluded in their opinion of this prince's character, or else that they sacrifice all, which ought to be esteemed precious and sacred among men, to their passions. In both these cases I remain still a tory, and am true to the party. In the first I endeavor to undeceive you by an experience purchased at my expense and for your sakes: in the second, I endeavor to prevail on you to revert to that principle from which we have deviated.[38]

Bolingbroke was thus embarked on his long career of trying to reshape the Tory party so that it could cope with altered circumstances. He was also showing some awareness of just how this new situation was affecting the old Whig-Tory alignment. Of course, to ingratiate himself with the present Whig government, he had to announce that his principal desire was to promote the national interest. This involved apologising for the previous excesses of the Tory party, including his own, and implying that these were the product of exaggerated divisions between Whig and Tory. The partisan Tories had threatened the Bank of England, the East India Company and the moneyed interest in general, but they would never have subverted their property: 'The intention of those, who were the warmest, seemed to me to go no farther than restraining their influence on the legislature, and on matters of state.'[39] His own actions, combined with the warmth of his temper and his unguarded expressions, had rightly antagonised the Whigs and increased party strife. The Whig opposition had been just as guilty of perpetuating political disputes by their actions in 1714–15. There was a lesson to be learned by both parties. The Whigs, however, were not convinced that Bolingbroke had really repented of his former actions, though, as Lord Stair reported, he frequently repeated his decision to serve the whole nation and not merely a party interest:

> In talking of his going back into England, I told him, whenever you come into England you'll clap yourself at the head of the Tory party and endeavour to distress the government. He answered me, My Lord, I am sick of parties. I'll give you my word, if ever the King pardons me, and allows me to return into my country, I will think myself in duty bound and gratitude obliged to support his Majesty's measures, whatever my own sentiments may happen to be, and after what I shall owe to the King if I am allowed to return, no man can think it strange that I am his servant without reserve. Without his mercy I could not be there, and I never will use what the King gives me against himself, and I will at no time pretend to judge what measures are most for the King's interest. The King shall judge and I will follow his sentiments with the implicit obedience that is due to the obligations I shall owe.[40]

Bolingbroke was never to display, and was probably incapable of, such excessive, almost servile, loyalty. He was primarily seeking a pardon, but he was also weighing up the current political situation in the light of the old Whig–Tory rivalry. It was doubtful whether he was yet prepared to acknowledge that the party alignment was unrealistic and unnecessary, though he was beginning to take stock of its effect on his personal ambitions. The continued rivalry and hostility between Whig and Tory was clearly preventing his own return to politics. Eventually, in seeking to overcome the major problems facing not only himself but also the Tory party after 1715, particularly the problem of ending the Whig monopoly of power, he was compelled to deny the validity of the old party dichotomy. He had not learned this lesson as early as 1717, but he was coming to grips with the problem and was beginning to grope towards the answer.

Living in exile, unsure of his political future and without many political friends, Bolingbroke naturally protested at the calumny of the Jacobites, the lingering suspicions of the Tories and the unrepentant hostility of the Whigs. Yet his adversity was a valuable political lesson. It sharpened his political wits and intensified his study of the political situation in Britain. He gained insights into the new political world of the Hanoverians, which might have been denied to him had he been involved in regular parliamentary battles. In the past he had often been an excellent judge of the drift of public opinion, but he had failed to grasp the wider significance of the political contest in Anne's reign. His enforced exile gradually rammed home the precise nature of the Whig supremacy and the bleak political future of the Tory party and himself if they failed to move with the times. Though he was never to come up with the successful answer, Bolingbroke did learn the nature and the scope of the problem, of how to prevent the Tories becoming a permanent opposition faction, and he became adept at suggesting expedients and possible solutions. His delayed return to politics enabled him to fashion a stronger opposition to the Whig oligarchy than was possible immediately after 1715.

The Tories in fact proved remarkably deaf to Bolingbroke's exhortations and warnings in his *Letter to Sir William Windham*. Sir William, Lord Lansdowne and other former Tory colleagues were not impressed with Bolingbroke's conduct or his explanations. The Jacobites began to take heart, believing he could not hurt their cause: 'Bolingbroke, we hear, is like to play the part of a complete scoundrel, and it seems he has lost all sense of honour, honesty and shame, but sure he is too well known by friends to be able to do hurt, and those he now courts by those vile ways cannot but despise him.'[41] Bolingbroke was very distressed by Wyndham's rejection of his defence and he railed at the madness of the Tories for remaining tainted with Jacobitism. Yet he was not entirely without hope. His old friend Lord Harcourt, who had managed to make his peace with the Whigs, sent him encouraging news. The Tories were turning away from Jacobitism in ever growing numbers, led by those old stalwarts William Bromley and Sir Thomas Hanmer. It only needed a really able leader to convert the majority of them. Bolingbroke, who always underrated the difficulty of managing the Tory squires, was confident that he could provide the necessary leadership if he could only pick up the threads of his political career: 'Parties are like flocks of sheep, they will stand sullen, and be run over, till they hear the bell-wether, and then they follow without knowing very well where.'[42] It was this qualified optimism which persuaded him to complete his *Letter to Sir William Windham* and have his secretary, Brinsden, distribute copies to leading English Tories early in 1718. It did not have the quick success he had anticipated.[43] His task of converting and re-educating the Tory party, even a part of it, had to be measured in terms of years not months.

As long as he was unable to control any Tory votes in the Commons

Bolingbroke could put little pressure on the Stanhope ministry, which had a precarious majority and serious problems of its own with which to contend. Indeed, Bolingbroke's hopes of a quick return to politics were continually thwarted by the failure of the Whigs to establish a stable ministry, which could afford temporarily to alienate its backbench support by recalling a Jacobite who had been so deeply involved in the 1715 rebellion. Several factors had prevented the electoral success of the Whigs being translated into a secure ministry. Most of the old Whig leaders died early in the new reign, leaving a new power struggle involving, principally, Stanhope and Sunderland on the one hand and Townshend and Walpole on the other. Their personal differences were exacerbated by the undue influence of the Hanoverian ministers on George I and by the repeated quarrels between the King and the Prince of Wales. Several political problems provided ample fuel for these conflicts. The leading Whig politicians were sharply divided on how far to support the interests of Hanover, particularly when this involved British action in the Baltic, and several domestic issues, notably the Peerage bill and the South Sea Bubble, also threatened to fragment the Whigs. Not until 1723, after the deaths of Stanhope and Sunderland and after domestic problems had been largely solved, was there a Whig ministry with a secure majority. In his efforts to stabilise Stanhope's ministry and to put it on a firmer foundation Bolingbroke advised it against measures which would antagonise the Tory opposition and play into the hands of Stanhope's Whig opponents. He warned of the danger of rousing the Tories by attempting to repeal the Occasional Conformity and Schism acts: 'If the ministers are driven into it, they will raise a cursed storm. A multitude of Tories who are not for the Pretender, and who may be rendered as affectionate as any men in Britain to the King's service will be shocked at it.'[44] The breach between the King and the Prince of Wales threatened to hinder his pardon by complicating the whole political situation. When the ministry was defeated on the Peerage bill he feared this would weaken its power to serve him. 'I confess to you, my dear Lord,' he lamented to Stair, 'the ill success of the Peerage Bill astonishes me. To open the session with such an attempt and not to have told noses better, is most unaccountable management. There is no room to expect that the ministers after this defeat should be able to exert much influence over their party. I fear a good deal of disorder and expect no good either to the public or to particular persons.'[45]

While the opposition of Tories and discontented Whigs embarrassed the ministry and jeopardised its control of the Commons, little could be done to effect Bolingbroke's pardon. Other concessions, which did not need parliamentary approval, were granted. The French Regent was asked to consider Bolingbroke as under King George's protection. Bolingbroke's secretary and general agent, Brinsden, was allowed to visit England to protect his master's financial interests, complicated by the death of his wife in November 1718. The King had refused to sequester Bolingbroke's estates as punishment for his role in the 1715 rebellion and he had created Bolingbroke's father Viscount St John, partly to compensate for Bolingbroke's loss of his title.[46] To do more than this required the consent of parliament. In its present precarious position, having just seen Townshend and Walpole go into opposition, partly because of personal disagreements but also because of differences over the government's foreign policy, the Stanhope ministry was reluctant to do anything which would lose it the backing of even more Whig votes. To bring in a bill to repeal Bolingbroke's attainder would certainly have caused a rebellion on the government's backbenches. Though not all the ministers were as willing to assist Bolingbroke as Lord Stair and James Craggs evidently were, the difficulties in the way of a pardon and a reversal of Bolingbroke's attainder were not counterfeited.[47] With discontented Whigs in opposition, independent, even loyal Whigs, ready to rebel on this particular issue, and Bolingbroke's failure to get the Tories to back the ministry, the government had every reason not to risk defeat for a recent traitor to the Hanoverian succession. Bolingbroke was distressed by the failure to do anything for him in the 1717–18 session, but his hopes rose and pressure increased from him and Lord Stair as each of the next few sessions approached. Before the 1718–19 session James Craggs thought something might be done for Bolingbroke, though he admitted that such a move might disoblige forty or fifty of the ministry's supporters in the Commons. Near the end of the session he was claiming that Cadogan had so inflamed the opposition and that the Tories were so obstinate in their hostility that the ministers risked being sent to the Tower even if they merely offered to solve those problems over Bolingbroke's estates, which had been created by the death of his wife. When Stair suggested that the government might consider pardoning the Earl of Mar, who appeared ready to desert the Pretender, Craggs reminded him of the difficulties already encountered in trying to serve Bolingbroke and warned him to proceed with extreme caution. Though the ministry might be able to help Bolingbroke in the next session, he warned Stair that 'our madmen, blown up by our knaves, would, I am afraid bounce like bottled ale at a negotiation with Mar'.[48] In the event the ministry was even weaker in the next session. Robert Walpole, who played a prominent part in defeating the government's Peerage bill, specifically attacked the ministry for planning to help Bolingbroke. Writing on the bill he criticised the Earl of Oxford and 'his rival in guilt and power [who] even now presumes to expect an act of the legislature to indemnify him, and qualify his villany!'[49]

Frustrated at repeated failure, Bolingbroke unwisely offered to bribe Craggs, believing that it was in his power to persuade a sufficient number of M.P.s to grant Bolingbroke's request for the repeal of his attainder. Craggs, who was not averse to making money by virtue of his office, reacted strongly. He knew he could not perform what Bolingbroke desired, with or without the benefit of extra funds, and he resented the implication that he had not previously been doing his best for Bolingbroke. The ministry's difficulties were real enough and he instructed Lord Stair to make this truth quite clear to Bolingbroke:

> I am not a little nettled at the pretty proposition contained in the latter part of your letter. I am to receive from Sir M[atthew] Decker [a banker] £10,000 without giving any receipt or account of it. I cannot be so weak to imagine that anybody has thought it proper for me to take members aside and offer them £500 more or less if they would be for repealing York's [Bolingbroke's] attainder, as far as the £10,000 would go, and therefore I take it in the plain sense that somebody supposes I have credit enough to get this matter through the house of commons, but am such a rogue, that, notwithstanding all my promises and professions, I will take no pains in it without a sum of money, as likewise that I am judged by this same friend or friends of York's [Bolingbroke's] to be susceptible of such an offer. I vow other people's heads or mine is turned, but I am sure my heart is not changed. Pray tell York [Bolingbroke] that I will take very hearty pains to serve him, but I desire for once to be a little sufficient, and say that I can judge much better how and when to serve him than all his other friends put together.[50]

Craggs made no serious effort to help Bolingbroke after delivering this rebuff, but he was not acting out of mere pique. The ministry's defeat on the Peerage bill had at last convinced it that it must broaden its base of support. The Tories could not be bought, but Walpole and Townshend, the leading Whigs in opposition, were prepared to come to terms. Their entry into the ministry blighted Bolingbroke's hopes. Walpole had been one of the strongest opponents of his return to a political career. Bolingbroke recognised the changed circumstances and tried to resign himself to more years in exile. He would have to remain in retirement until the political storms blew over. The greatest burden, particularly for a man of his temperament, was the constant uncertainty. He believed that he had already been left in doubt long enough, but he tried to resign himself to the fact that the situation was outside his control and that he could only await a favourable turn of events.[51] In March 1721 Lord Harcourt finally drafted a bill for Bolingbroke's restoration, which he believed the Earl of Sunderland would support and which Walpole might not oppose. Walpole in fact proved hostile to his political restoration, though he claimed that he would have been prepared to allow Bolingbroke the right to inherit his father's estates if the Whigs had not been unalterably opposed to even this concession.[52] In the event the disaster of the South Sea Bubble put an end to any suggestion of assisting Bolingbroke in the immediate future. The ministers were so harassed by the opposition in parliament that a bill to repeal Bolingbroke's attainder would have been political suicide. To make matters worse Craggs and Stanhope died during this crisis and Walpole emerged as the leader of a new ministry. Lord Stair had already left his embassy in Paris, and Bolingbroke was left with little influence with the new government.

Bolingbroke's proud, ambitious and impatient spirit was mortified by the repeated frustrations of his dearest wish, to resume his parliamentary career. He had had ample opportunity to recognise that his disappointments were the direct result of the continued prejudices and disputes of Whig and Tory parties. The obstinacy and hostility which they engendered threatened to ruin his career. It was this discovery, and not merely his first-hand observations of Walpole's system ten years later, which impressed on him the necessity of ending party divisions. By the 1730s he was describing what was virtually an accomplished fact, the ending of a real Whig-Tory contest, but before 1720 he opposed the rivalry of the parties principally because of their effect on his personal career. His letters were increasingly dominated by his awareness of the problems posed by the malignancy of the party spirit. As early as June 1717, when he was admitting to Lord Stair that the hostility of enraged Tories and malcontent Whigs was hindering his return to England, he observed:

I have more than fulfilled all the imaginary obligations of party and if ever we came to state the debtor and creditor the balance will be found very much on my side. Besides in the plan which I have formed for the rest of my life I shall have no regard to either party. I will rather fly my country once more than continue in it at the expense of being a bondslave to Whig or Tory.[53]

A few months later he was claiming that there was no difference between those Tories, who had renounced the Pretender, and the Whigs and that he was prepared to contribute to break all opponents of the King.[54] In August 1718 he accepted that there might be differences between the wild men of the parties, but argued that the King could break free from the shackles of Whig or Tory by choosing moderates from both parties who would put the interests of the nation first.[55] Such a policy was reminiscent of Robert Harley's ideas in Anne's reign: a recognition of Whig-Tory divisions, but a need for the government to rest on the more moderate elements of the two parties. Bolingbroke, however, in the changed circumstances of George I's reign, developed his ideas beyond this point. He was becoming convinced that, in contrast to Anne's reign, the party alignment could actually be ignored. In 1719 he believed that the European situation was so favourable that 'the honest endeavours of a few men would be sufficient to set our government at home on a foot not to be shook by every blast of the humour and passions of parties'.[56] His hostility to party and his conviction that British politics need no longer be dominated by the Whig-Tory contest for power was quite marked before ever he returned to challenge the supremacy of Walpole. In his rural retreat he confessed that he forgot that he had ever been a Tory and was 'ready to imagine that there never was any such monster as party'.[57] When he came to oppose Walpole, Bolingbroke had spent ten years observing the realities of the contemporary political contest in Britain. He had not only learned from the damage which party prejudices could inflict on his own career, he had also applied himself to philosophical studies which helped him to understand the origin and nature of civil government, the dangers inherent in partisan conflict, and how often men's principles were mere rationalisations of their prejudices and passions. Chastened by political adversity and with his ability enlarged by philosophical studies, Bolingbroke was a much more formidable and significant opponent by the time he eventually returned to contest Robert Walpole's supremacy.

CHAPTER 9

From Politics to Philosophy

I

FOR ten frustrating years, from 1715 to 1725, Bolingbroke schemed to make a political comeback. Yet, despite all his endeavours, he liked to pretend that he was content with his enforced retirement and that exile held no terrors for him. All the time that he was writing a stream of letters to Lord Stair, pestering and pleading with him to further his cause with the ministry in London, Bolingbroke was assuring his friends that he was resigned to his fate. He told them that he was retreating from the world and was no longer interested in the affairs of busy politicians. In one letter to Swift he claimed: 'As to my present [circumstances] my fortune is extremely reduced; but my desires are still more so. Nothing is more certain than this truth, that all our wants beyond those which a very moderate income will supply, are purely imaginary; and that his happiness is greater, and better assured, who brings his mind up to a temper of not feeling them, than his, who feels them, and has wherewithal to supply them.'[1] Bolingbroke's calm, philosophical letters, to Swift and Charles Ford, contrast sharply with his clamorous, abject appeals to Stair and the British ministers. The stark comparison is not merely further evidence of Bolingbroke's hypocrisy and affectation. He was also endeavouring to convince himself. He realised, almost unconsciously, that his anxiety to return to politics was at odds with his ambition to appear an heroic, a truly aristocratic, figure. His reason sought to control, to disguise, even to deny his passions. While the attempt can appear ludicrous, it also reveals his persistence and even his courage.

In 1716, when his political career was in ruins and when his spirit must have been sorely oppressed, Bolingbroke wrote his first treatise, a work designed to show the world and to convince himself that he could triumph over a cruel fate. This was his *Reflections upon Exile*,[2] a work which has usually been dismissed as a false and puerile description of his state of mind. It was, indeed, a loose paraphrase of Seneca's *De Consolatio ad Helviam*, with additions and examples culled from other Roman writers, such as Cicero and Plutarch. Many of the sentiments were bound to appear ridiculous, coming from a man so eager to return home. The loss of riches, honour and reputation, he claimed, did not concern him. He could be happy in any country. All that was required to bear the burden of exile was a courage born of philosophy. A man was only unhappy when his desires exceeded his expectations and opportunities. If he reduced his demands to what he could attain, then he would achieve happiness and contentment. Such sentiments, shallow as they were, give a useful indication of Bolingbroke's desire to accept his fate and of his new interest in philosophy. The mere fact that he felt compelled to write such a work showed that he was prepared to wrestle with misfortune and put a brave face on his inner despair. His examples of exiled heroes of the past were meant to inspire him to emulate them and to convince others that he too was bravely suffering under an unjust fate. Besides the search for consolation in study, now that his public career was in ruins, there was also the desire to arrive at a workable philosophy of life. Already, in his first work, there were traits appearing which were to run through all his later philosophical essays. He laid great stress on the importance of being guided by 'unprejudiced reason':

It is a good rule, to examine well before we addict ourselves to any sect: but I think it is a better rule, to addict ourselves to none. Let us hear them all, with a perfect indifferency on which side the truth lies: and, when we come to determine, let nothing appear so venerable to us as our own understandings. Let us gratefully accept the help of every one who has endeavored to correct the vices, and strengthen the minds of men; but let us choose for ourselves, and yield universal assent to none . . . It is much harder to examine and judge, than to take up opinions on trust; and therefore the far greatest part of the world borrows, from others, those which they entertain concerning all the affairs of life and death.[3]

Bolingbroke did not claim that reason alone was sufficient to solve all life's problems, for he stressed the value of experience and example, but he did believe that the mind was the best guide in the pursuit of wisdom and virtue.

Another theme in this work, which Bolingbroke was to develop later, was the immutability of the laws of nature; the stable element in the fluctuating tide of human affairs. The beauty of nature and the mind of man were constant factors, the results of general principles, despite the variety of laws, customs and fortune to be seen in the world. A third strand, which appeared in all Bolingbroke's later works, was his stress on the virtue of a certain stoicism in the face of misfortune, and an intellectual humility, which did not presume to be able to control all the affairs of man. These were not the sentiments of the dedicated rationalist, bent on reshaping the world:

> The darts of adverse fortune are always levelled at our heads. Some reach us, some graze us, and fly to wound our neighbours . . . This established course of things it is not in our power to change; but it is in our power to assume a greatness of mind as becomes wise and virtuous men; as may enable us to encounter the accidents of life with fortitude, and to conform ourselves to the order of nature, . . . Let us submit to this order, let us be persuaded that whatever does happen ought to happen, and never be so foolish as to expostulate with nature. The best resolution we can take is to suffer what we cannot alter, and to pursue, without repining, the road which Providence, who directs everything, has marked out to us.[4]

Bolingbroke's philosophical studies were continued when he failed in his strenuous efforts to resume his public career. Towards the end of 1716 the Duke of Berwick introduced him to the social and intellectual life of Paris, where he mixed with aristocrats interested in a wide range of studies, such as the Matignons, the Torcys, the Maréchal d'Huxelles and Madame de Ferriol, and with genuine scholars, such as Pierre Joseph Alary, Lévesque de Pouilly, Voltaire, the Abbé Asselin, the Abbé Conti and the British mathematician and philosopher, Brook Taylor. In such a wide circle, he came into contact with ideas of people who were playing a crucial role in the development of the French Enlightenment. Bolingbroke also met Marie-Claire de Marcilly, Marquise de Villette. Though she had been a widow for nine years, and had reared three daughters, she was able to attract and hold Bolingbroke, who had been a notorious rake, for the rest of her life. In January 1717 he moved with her to Marcilly, near Nogent-sur-Seine, and early in 1719, within a few months of the death of his wife in England, he married her in the private chapel of Lord Stair at Montfermeil. In order to protect her financial interests in Britain, now that she was married to an attainted traitor, the public marriage ceremony was delayed until 1722.[5] Meanwhile, in December 1720, he and his second wife leased the Château de la Source, near Orleans, where he spent much of his time, until his return to England in 1725.[6] This rural retreat did not prevent him from making frequent visits to Paris, where he joined in the literary and philosophical discussions at Alary's new Club de l'Entresol, or inviting his aristocratic and scholarly friends to stay with him. It certainly encouraged him to pursue seriously his new interests in history, philosophy and religion.

From about 1717 to 1720 Bolingbroke's principal interest was the study of history, a subject in which he received considerable instruction from Pierre Joseph Alary. From him Bolingbroke received a constant supply of books and regular answers to many queries which he raised.[7] He read such classical historians as Polybius, Pliny, Lucan and Sallust, but he also studied more modern historians, such as Guicciardini and Machiavelli. At first, however, he concentrated on a study of ancient history and the problems of discovering a reliable chronology for this period. It was some time before he complained of the futility of a study where the concrete evidence available was so slight, and where there seemed to be only flimsy traditions and contradictory testimonies. By November 1721 he told Brook Taylor that he was coming to the end of his studies into remote antiquity, because of his dissatisfaction with its historical and chronological foundations. Two years later he confessed to him that he had examined the bases of the existing system of chronology and the evidence for the events of ancient history, only to find that they were based on loose sand. He was resolved not to continue these labours, when his efforts would undoubtedly go unrewarded.[8] In all his later writings on history Bolingbroke concentrated on the period since the late fifteenth century. From that date, he considered that there was enough tried and tested information to enable him to write serious history. By 1724 he was planning a history of Europe from the sixteenth century to 1713.[9] Nevertheless, his earlier studies had not been in vain. All his later works were full of classical illustrations and allusions, and he was always ready to use his knowledge of antiquity to give weight to his arguments about more recent events. Moreover, he had learned a great deal about the historian's greatest problem, the question of reliable testimony. Early tradition was oral and hence unreliable, unless it could be substantiated by other evidence: 'Nothing can be less credible than all that we read in ancient story, about the Assyrians for instance. It is a wild heap of inconsistent traditions which cannot be reconciled, nor verified for want of a historical criterion.'[10] History, if it were to be authentic, must, he decided, be based on the evidence of several witnesses who could be trusted. Even then it could only be regarded as highly probable and not as the absolute, unchallengeable truth. Bolingbroke was clearly developing an historian's critical judgement and no modern historian would quarrel with this following statement:

> Now to constitute the authenticity of any history, these are some of the conditions necessary. It must be written by a co[n]temporary author, or by one who had co[n]temporary materials in his hands. It must have been published among men who were able to judge of the capacity of the author, and of the authenticity of the memorials on which he wrote. Nothing repugnant to the universal experience of mankind must be contained in it. The principal facts, at least, which it contains, must be confirmed by collateral testimony, that is, by the testimony of those who had no common interest of country, of religion, or of profession, to disguise or falsify the truth.[11]

In addition to his historical studies, Bolingbroke was attracted by philosophy, a subject which increasingly absorbed his attention, especially from about 1720. In this field he regarded Lévesque de Pouilly as his chief guide, though he frequently discussed his ideas with Alary too. Pouilly helped to direct a monthly journal, *L'Europe Savante,* dealing with the arts and sciences. He visited Bolingbroke at La Source and stayed with him in England for over a year, after Bolingbroke's return in 1725. It was Pouilly who inspired Bolingbroke to subject man's knowledge to critical study, in order to discover what was true or most probably true. Bolingbroke, who never displayed any intellectual humility, was soon claiming to have rejected an immense number of errors. After he had made what he considered was a rigorous scrutiny of the whole problem of human knowledge, he was confident that he now knew what was attainable.[12] Man could not always aspire to complete certainty, but he could often arrive at a very strong probability: 'Though we cannot have, strictly speaking, a certain knowledge of any fact whereof we have not been ourselves witnesses, yet are there several such facts whereof we cannot doubt. High probability must stand often in lieu of certainty, or we must be, every moment, at a loss how to form our opinions and to regulate our conduct.'[13] In this pursuit of truth he gave priority to experimental philosophy rather than to metaphysical speculation.[14] Unlike Pouilly, he rejected the Cartesian approach of deductive reasoning from hypotheses and innate ideas as a means of discovering the truth. Reason alone could never resolve difficulties. The senses had to be used and this involved observation and experiment. Bolingbroke thus became a disciple of the empiricism of John Locke and Isaac Newton. This involved a rejection of the *a priori* reasoning of Descartes, in favour of the inductive, *a posteriori*, method.[15] Though he stressed this in all his works, he could on occasion lapse into the *a priori* method himself. While he never fully accepted the Cartesian philosophy to which Pouilly introduced him, Bolingbroke was, nevertheless, so far inspired by it as to attempt to impose a systematic pattern upon his stray reflections. This love of clarity, order and design was also due to his fascination with Newtonian physics.[16] He wanted his philosophy to achieve the beauty and order of Newton's explanation of the universe, though he feared that no system of philosophy could reach such a standard of perfection.[17]

In his philosophical studies Bolingbroke concentrated on the problems of religion and morality. The interest in Stoicism and natural law that he had revealed in his *Reflections upon Exile* was expanded into a wider discussion of human frailty and God's omnipotence. Onto his philosophical foundations he built up his structure of natural religion. This Deism was as apparent in his early essays, *The Substance of Some Letters to M. de Pouilly* and *A Letter occasioned by one of Archbishop Tillotson's sermons*, as in his later, more famous, philosophical essays, which he addressed to Alexander Pope. In these first works he affirmed that there were sufficient proofs of the existence of one Supreme Being, the first intelligent cause of all things. Natural phenomena were clear evidence of the 'existence of an all-perfect, self-existent being, the source of all existence, invisible and incomprehensible'.[18] This God of natural law had infinite wisdom and power, but there was no evidence that He actually interfered in human affairs. Since Bolingbroke believed that God was distinct, even remote, from the world, he had to reject the notion of particular providence. His emphasis on the necessity of evidence and proof led Bolingbroke not to deny the power of God, but to suggest that man was incapable of ever fully understanding the nature and attributes of God. It was presumptuous for man to define God, for this put human limits on the Almighty. He constantly urged intellectual humility, which he himself rarely practised, and deplored the outlook which made man the measure of all things. The powers of the human mind, and the extent of human knowledge, should not be exaggerated.[19]

His study of the basis of morality and religion led Bolingbroke into an attack on the evidence, cited by divines and theologians, for their particular ideas of God. He was especially critical of the opinions of Moses and the Jews of the Old Testament. There was no evidence that Moses was the author of the Pentateuch or that the Jews merited God's special concern. He denied that the books of the Old Testament were divinely inspired and, therefore, they could not legitimately be called the word of God.[20] Nor was Bolingbroke entirely satisfied with the New Testament. He believed that St Paul had distorted the primitive purity of the Gospels, with additions from pagan religions. The concept of the soul, and the belief in a system of rewards and punishments in an after-life, had come from Greek and Egyptian sources. There was no evidence that Moses had accepted such ideas. Even the doctrine of the Trinity was not based on the clear authority of the Gospels, but was a later embellishment. Bolingbroke concluded that: 'There are gross defects, and palpable falsehoods, in almost every page of the Scriptures, and the whole tenor of them is such as no man, who acknowledges a Supreme, All-perfect Being, can believe it to be his word.'[21]

Bolingbroke rejected what he regarded as the false accretions to the purity of Christianity, but he never regarded himself as an atheist. He professed a harmless rationalism, a belief in a Supreme Being, based on the evidence of natural law; a system which can best be described as Deism. Atheists and free-thinkers he regarded as dangerous, because they would loosen the bonds of society; but he was also dissatisfied with orthodox or revealed Christianity, which was 'a lofty and pompous structure, erected close to the humble and plain building of natural religion'. His intention was not to demolish religion altogether, but to base it solidly on that truth, which could be established by the free use of reason: 'The faculty of distinguishing between right and wrong, true and false, which we call reason or common sense, which is given to every man by our own bountiful Creator, and which most men lose by neglect, is the light of the mind, and ought to guide all the operations of it.' His avowed aim was to prevent religion being perverted to purposes so contrary to its true intention and first design. When he went so far as to claim that divine revelation was evident by the test of reason, he was obviously trying to allay the fears of his friend, Jonathan Swift, that he would discount divine revelation entirely. He did in fact come close to this; and he never stated in his later essays that revelation was consonant with the test of reason.[22]

By rejecting the divine revelation of the Bible, Bolingbroke had to face the problem of the origins of moral principles. He considered this in another of his early works, *Reflections concerning Innate Moral Principles*.[23] In this he claimed that morality or compassion, that love of others which is the basis of all moral principles, was not innate and given by God, because it was not common to all men. Rather, it was the result of education, customs and laws. Such moral principles were the result of experience and instruction, which were gained after birth and were not instinctive. Having accepted the opinion of Locke that ideas were the result of external impressions and were not innate, Bolingbroke proceeded to confuse the issue. He also accepted Descartes' view that man has an intuitive knowledge of his own existence and from this there springs one innate moral principle: self-love, which leads man to seek pleasure and avoid pain. It was this 'blind' principle which could lead men to acquire compassion and other moral virtues, but first it had to be guided by reason. The human mind was capable of gathering experience from external impressions and so it was able to realise that other men had a similar love of pleasure and fear of pain. A man could thus acquire a sympathy for others and could make their misfortunes his own. In this manner he could graft a moral character on to his natural self-love. Bolingbroke believed that the proof of his argument was that it explained why moral principles were not universal. Reason, which was necessary to guide man's self-love towards moral principles, was not the same in all men and was never perfect in any of them:

> If reason were completely formed in all men, which is far from being the case, or if it met with no opposition from the passions, then in all such, whose reason is as completely formed as our rank in the universe permits, self-love would become the source of virtues, the source of human happiness . . . but in the human state, the only one we know anything of, those means are in great measure imperfect, and consequently produce their ends but in a very imperfect manner.[24]

This treatise was typical of Bolingbroke's ventures into philosophy. He applied his intelligence to the philosophic systems erected by greater thinkers, in this case John Locke and Descartes. He took from them what he was looking for, in order to support a particular argument which he was trying to make. He never created a coherent system of philosophy and so he was frequently inconsistent. In this treatise he accepted Locke's view that ideas were the result of impressions received from the external world, but he did not go so far as to assert that man's mind at birth was a veritable *tabula rasa*. In his later philosophical essays he proved even more contradictory, for he claimed that benevolence, which is little different from what he had earlier described as compassion, was innate. His whole concept of natural law also ran counter to his argument, in this treatise, that there were no principles of universal application.

II

Bolingbroke began his philosophical studies, partly from a genuine love of learning, but mainly because his active mind and restless ambition made him wish to shine in some other field, now that his political career seemed over. Yet he became so attracted to philosophy that, even after his return to active politics in 1725, he continued his studies. Since his philosophic development underpinned the rest of his career, it needs to be studied here. The fruits of this further research comprised nearly half his published works. Though they did not appear until 1754, nearly three years after Bolingbroke's death, most of these philosophical essays were the result of his studies in the decade after his return from France. The four principal essays were dedicated to Alexander Pope and were described as the product of their conversations, largely from the years 1725–35. There were certainly several mentions in his letters of preliminary essays, written in the early 1730s, though these were revised during Bolingbroke's second prolonged residence in France after 1735.[25]

Bolingbroke's first steps in philosophy were guided by Alary and Pouilly. Much of his later work was a natural development from these tentative beginnings. Though he gained in knowledge and experience, he did not radically depart from the views expressed in his earliest works. He was not exaggerating unduly when he replied to Swift's criticisms: 'You say that you could easily show, by comparing my letters for twenty years past, how the whole system of philosophy changes by the several gradations of life. I doubt it. As far as I am able to recollect, my way of thinking has been uniform enough for more than twenty years. True, it is, to my shame that my way of acting has not been always conformable to my way of thinking.'[26] In his later essays, despite his claims to have conducted original research and to have arrived at independent conclusions, Bolingbroke never lost his dependence on other scholars. Very often he concealed his debt to particular philosophers, by refraining from citing their works or by attacking some of their opinions, while relying on them in other respects. Among the influences on his philosophy were Pufendorf, Spinoza, Bayle, Malebranche, Bacon, Locke, Shaftesbury, Archbishop William King, Sir William Temple, Charles Leslie and the leading Deists, Toland, Collins and Lord Herbert of Cherbury. It is not clear how far he knew all their works at first-hand. He certainly read the works of Locke,

Hobbes and Bacon with great thoroughness, but his knowledge of many of the ancient philosophers, and even of recent writers, such as Leibnitz and Spinoza, was probably second-hand. Even Newton and Descartes probably came to him through the works of commentators.[27] His knowledge was large, but less extensive than he claimed. Though he shared with the Cartesians a love of clear and fundamental principles, his own philosophy was neither coherent nor consistent. While preferring the inductive, *a posteriori* method, and frequently criticising the *a priori*, inductive or speculative reasoning of Descartes, he can often be found using the latter approach. He stressed the value of Locke's empiricism and he was a great admirer of his *Essay on Human Understanding*, but he disagreed with him on both natural law and the origins of civil government.[28] Of all the philosophers he had read, he had the greatest contempt for Plato and the metaphysical speculations of the neo-Platonists, yet he himself was a strong advocate of one of their central concepts, the Great Chain of Being. With other philosophers he was just as selective, without ever creating a philosophical system of his own.

Bolingbroke's philosophical essays were largely concerned with religion, morality and the nature of civil government.[29] His major criticisms were levelled at the metaphysical speculations of the Platonists and the artificial theology of orthodox Christianity. His principal aim was to erect an alternative ethical and religious system, based on reason and natural law. He attacked metaphysics, because it rested too much on hypothesis and was not susceptible to rational proof. The imagination must not go beyond knowledge founded on experience or on such near certainties as were immediately deducible from experience. It was because the clergy had indulged in too much wild speculation that they were able to distort and corrupt the natural theology of primitive Christianity. Theologians had made the simple both obscure and artificial; and there was a real need to return to the clarity and purity of the Gospels. This corruption of Christ's teaching had begun with St Paul, who had introduced pagan practices and his own personal theories of predestination and unlimited passive obedience. In succeeding generations, theologians and clergy had engaged in violent scholastic disputes over various religious doctrines, such as those of redemption and the Trinity, none of which was actually derived from the Scriptures. They had also been consistently anxious to increase their temporal power and to involve themselves in politics and government, whereas it was evident that Christ's kingdom was not of this world. As a result of their secular ambitions and their interminable disputes:

'The scene of Christianity has been always a scene of dissension, of hatred, of persecution, and of blood.'[30]

It was not merely the interpreters and practitioners of religion who were attacked by Bolingbroke. He took issue with the Bible itself. His fundamental argument was that there was insufficient proof that it was the word of God, for its claim to be divine revelation could not answer the test of reason. The Old Testament, in particular, came under sustained criticism from Bolingbroke. Most of it could not be verified and it rested on such absurdities as the notion that the Jews were the chosen people and were often the beneficiaries of God's direct intervention and particular providence. With regard to the New Testament, Bolingbroke was much less severe in his criticisms. He never categorically denied all miracles, especially those performed by Christ, but he never appeared to give them much credence. The divinity of Christ was never explicitly asserted and Bolingbroke seemed to regard him as a great religious teacher and, in some vague, indefinable sense, a special messenger of God.[31] Bolingbroke's inhibitions, which prevented him making an open and sustained assault on Christianity, were only partly due to a failure of nerve, for he was prepared to admit that 'no religion ever appeared in the world, whose natural tendency was so much directed to promote the peace and happiness of the world'.[32] Moreover, he always maintained that the criticisms which could be justifiably levelled against Christianity should not lead to its downfall. Though he was a critic of organised religion, from a theological and philosophical standpoint, Bolingbroke was convinced of its social and political utility. Christianity improved men's standard of behaviour, by promoting public and private morality. It was of inestimable value to any government, for it encouraged obedience to the law; always providing, of course, that there was only one national religion: 'To make government effectual to all the good purposes of it, there must be a religion; this religion must be national and this national religion must be maintained in reputation and reverence; all other sects must be kept too low to become the rivals of it.' Men with an enlightened philosophy, such as himself, might reject orthodox Christianity, as inconsistent with reason, but the majority of mankind needed some form of external discipline to enforce a civilised moral code: 'Many things absurd in belief, and ridiculous in practice, were necessary to attach the greatest number of men and women, and especially of the vulgar to Christianity; ... men of sense and knowledge ought to consider and distinguish what is for them and what for the vulgar.'[33] Religion was so valuable, as a social and political instrument, that it could not be left to the clergy. It must be controlled by the civil authority.[34]

Since he had rejected divine revelation, Bolingbroke was faced with the problem of how to arrive at an ethical code and a philosophy of life. Nor was he satisfied that other philosophers had produced a satisfactory alternative. For example, he was always suspicious of the kind of reasoning which was based upon imagination and speculation;[35] and he not only took Descartes and all theologians to task, but regarded Plato as the inspiration of a great deal of later metaphysical fantasy.[36] In old age he warned the youthful Earl of Huntingdon that he was wasting his time, reading the *Dialogues* of Plato: 'It will not be hard to show you that this poetical philosopher poisoned the very roots of knowledge, and to convince you both by reason and example that no writings have contributed so much to misguide men in the conduct of their understanding, the men of greatest genius and on the most important subjects of philosophy.'[37] Moreover, despite his admiration of the empiricism of Locke and Newton, Bolingbroke was never a complete rationalist nor the epitome of the Age of Reason. Many of his philosophical doctrines, for example, were quite old-fashioned; he accepted such concepts as the law of nature and the Great Chain of Being, which had lengthy pedigrees. His principal disagreement with the rationalists of the Enlightenment, however, was that he recognised that the capacity of the human mind was not the same in all men and that even the greatest men were subject to spells of passionate, irrational behaviour. Reason was never infallible nor ever capable of attaining perfection. In his early works he had already admitted that man had intellectual limitations and should not presume to know or understand God fully, while, in his later essays, he frequently emphasised the limited capacity of the human mind: 'Reason not being given to all alike, and being very imperfectly given to those who possess the greatest share, our wisdom and our happiness are very imperfect likewise, and the state of mankind is, upon the whole, a very imperfect state.' Nature had almost certainly created better specimens of rationality than man, according to Bolingbroke, and it was very doubtful whether any man had reached the limit of even human reason. When men view the wonders of the universe 'can we be stupid or impertinent and vain enough to imagine that we stand alone or foremost among rational created beings? We must be conscious, unless we are mad and have lost the use of our reason, of the imperfection of our reason?'[38] In view of his own nature, it was not surprising that Bolingbroke held such a relatively pessimistic view.

Though he regarded his own mind as superior to that of the majority of mankind, he knew that it could often be overborne by his passionate temperament. He believed that there would always be a conflict between these two aspects of man's nature, his reason and his passions; and he was never confident that the former would always triumph.

Bolingbroke, therefore, cannot be included among those optimistic rationalists who believed that the human mind could fathom all philosophical problems or create a perfect world; but his philosophy did rest on a firm conviction that man should be guided, as far as possible, by his reason. Because man was unable to achieve perfection, was not a sufficient reason for him to abandon himself to irrational behaviour. An attempt must be made to control the passions, at least so far as a man's public life was concerned. This, Bolingbroke confessed to Wyndham, must be the aim of all those who wished to lead mankind:

> In the ordinary course of private life, you know how much indulgence I have for my passions, my fancies, my weaknesses. How much of it is, according to my system, a part of wisdom to give great way to them, and pay little regard to common notions, received customs ... so terrible to many persons. But in the great turns of private life, and in every part of public life, I condemn this indulgence, and I respect the opinion of mankind. I mean that opinion which is founded in judgement, and will last; not the momentary applause or censure of the vulgar.[39]

Above all, a man's religion and philosophy of life must be guided by, and consonant with, reason. He was convinced that this was the case with natural law and natural religion.

The concept of natural law could be traced from both the Stoics and the early Christians. It asserted that the moral law, which men ought to obey, was derived from the law of nature and not from the decisions of human society, that could compel men to act in certain ways, but could not provide the inward moral sanction. Bolingbroke was convinced that this law of nature could be discovered *a posteriori*, from experience and observation. The scientific discoveries of Newton and others had revealed both the order and beauty of nature, and the wisdom and power of the Creator. By studying the world about him man could learn the moral obligations, in both secular and religious life, which God had imposed upon him. Religion and morality were, therefore, derived from nature by the exercise of human reason and not from the divine revelation of the Bible. Because God had created the world, then natural law was of divine origin. It was the same for all men, at all times, and was the source and criterion of all human laws. Since it was founded on reason, it rested on stronger proofs than Christianity and artificial religions:

> In short natural theology rests on better foundation than authority of any kind, and the duties of natural religion and the sins against it, are held out to us by the constitution of our nature, and by daily experience, in characters so visible, that he who runs may read them . . . The religion of nature, and therefore of the God of nature, is simple and plain: it tells us nothing which our reason is unable to comprehend, and much less anything which is repugnant to it. Natural religion and reason are always agreed, they are always the same, and the whole economy of God's dispensations to man is of a piece. But religions, founded in the pretended revelations . . . grow voluminous and mysterious, oppose belief to knowledge, and when they cannot stand a reasonable examination, escape from reason by assuming that they are above it.[40]

In his efforts to guide the young Earl of Huntingdon's education, Bolingbroke was adamant that he must start with the study of natural law, 'the law of laws'. It was the law which all believers must follow, since it was the product of God's wisdom and the result of His will. It was also the law for all unbelievers, since the system of private and public morality, which it enjoined, was based on the scientific evidence of nature itself.[41]

Like other philosophers who confidently affirmed the existence of natural law, Bolingbroke never explained precisely what it was nor how human reason derived such laws from the world of nature around them. However, he did explain what he believed the law of nature revealed about God and about the code of ethics by which man should live. In his estimation, an examination of the physical universe, and every work of nature, proved the existence of God. It was from His work in creating the world, not from the activities of His Son on earth, that man could know anything of God. Man must be careful, however, not to impose his own image on God. It was presumptuous to give God such moral attributes as goodness, justice and truth, not only because these were only known from man's association with other men, but because it meant that man had decided what God could or could not do. All that man could be certain of, was that God was 'a self-existent Being, the first cause of all things, infinitely powerful, and infinitely wise'.[42] Having willed the world to exist and to continue, God did not continually interfere in the lives of men. The world now operated by a general providence or general laws – the laws of nature. These, therefore, not only proved the existence of God but were the only manifestation of God known to man. Early, primitive Christianity had been simply a republication of the law of nature, though its simplicity and purity had been distorted thereafter.

Bolingbroke believed that, since God was infinitely wise and powerful, He would only have created a perfect world. This optimistic view was at odds not only with his pessimism about man's capacity for acting reasonably, but with the evident evil in the world. Bolingbroke got round this problem by developing his argument that God did not interfere in the affairs of man. It was only man's conceit which led him to believe that the world was created solely for man or that God had sent His Son to earth, to show man the road to salvation. The world was rather one vast linked design, the Great Chain of Being, and man was only one part of this structure. There was an infinite gradation of forms of being, both above and below man; and it was impossible for man to realise the significance of them all. Nor was it essential that each should impinge directly on the others. Thus, the sins of man were but part of the immense variety of creation. Man could not appreciate the total pattern of the universe nor the significance of the role which evil played in it. If he had been capable of following all the ethical principles of the law of nature he would not have been human. Bolingbroke buttressed this opinion with other arguments. If God were denied moral attributes, then the problem of evil no longer existed. God was not just, in the human sense of the word. He had given man free will and so He was not responsible for man's misuse of it. Besides, Bolingbroke claimed, with his optimistic streak clearly evident, the amount of evil in the world had been exaggerated. Man was not only essentially good, but was more often happy than sad. If it were otherwise, he would not be so reluctant to leave the world.[43]

Despite his rather cavalier attitude towards the problem of good and evil in the world, Bolingbroke did believe that man should live by an ethical code. He had already made it abundantly clear that it was not enough simply to cite the moral code derived from the divine revelation of the Bible. Nor did he believe that the sins and inequalities of this life would be judged and redressed in a life to come. With his distaste for the doctrines of purgatory and eternal punishment, and dissatisfied with the evidence for the immortality of the soul, Bolingbroke could not rely on a system of future rewards and punishments, to enforce a moral code in this life. He admitted that the concepts of a future state, and of a time of judgement, were useful in restraining vice and encouraging virtue among the vulgar masses, but it could have no effect on men of superior reason, such as himself. Men of this kind must live by the principles of natural law. By the use of their reason they could perceive the fundamental principles of benevolence and sociability. In his *Reflections upon Innate Moral Principles* Bolingbroke had denied that there were any universal moral principles, except self-love. Now he claimed that self-love when guided by reason, or, in other words, enlightened self-interest, led man to benevolence and sociability, because by these actions man was benefiting himself as well as others. Thus, the intelligent observance of the law of nature produced happiness, while the transgression of this law resulted in misery. The law of nature, by enjoining benevolence and sociability, did not lead to the principle of self-denial. Its impositions were few. It forbade such evident sins as idolatry, blasphemy, murder, theft, sodomy and bestiality, but it recognised man's natural passions, instincts and affections. Reason must be used to discriminate intelligently, between sin and legitimate pleasures. True happiness, as distinct from mere pleasure, resulted from a nice balance between passion and reason. While an excess of passion was dangerous, reason itself was not the sole guide, but only a moderating influence.[44] Once more Bolingbroke returned to the conflict which most beset him personally: the problem of bringing his own reason and passion into fruitful harmony.

With his intense and abiding interest in politics, Bolingbroke's studies in philosophy naturally extended to discussions on the nature and origins of political society and civil government.[45] His political theories stemmed from his strong attachment to the concept of natural law. All moral distinctions, he claimed, were rooted in the law of nature and were not merely the creations of civil authority. This natural law was God's basic law and so it ought to determine both the actions of all men in authority and the laws of any political society. It was the duty of princes and magistrates to promote public and private morality, by enforcing a strict observance of the law of nature. Human law ought always to follow the precepts of natural law, for these were always clear, reasonable and of universal application. Similarly, human governments ought to seek to conform to rational first principles, in order to promote the greater happiness of society. England's ancient constitution, which had its origins in Anglo-Saxon society, was an example of the ideal government based on first principles, and every administration should aim to adhere to its precepts. Bolingbroke, however, never expected men would conform exactly to the laws of nature and he expected them to be equally fallible in their efforts to create an ideal government. Though he always praised men who used their reason and attacked those consumed by prejudice, particularly the clergy, he never imagined that men would be entirely rational. Therefore, since men were imperfect and they often allowed their passions to cloud their reason, then no government could ever be perfect. However, just as man was obliged to assert control over his passions and to keep the law of nature always before him, so governments must conform, as far as possible, to the ideal constitution. Bolingbroke did not expect, or even believe in the possibility of, a Utopian society or government. He believed that all governments, even when they approached the ideal, as with the English system in 1688, were subject to change and decay. Vigilance and virtue could slow down this process and might lead to another form of government, approaching the standards of the ideal constitution, but they could not permanently establish a perfect system of government.[46] Too often the actual situation was even worse than this, for the men who achieved political power were too often factious spirits dominated by passion. This imposed an even greater burden on men of reason, who must resist the threat of a rapid decline from an acceptable form of government.

The concept of natural law, particularly as it was interpreted by Aristotle and Lord Shaftesbury, influenced Bolingbroke's theories on the origins of civil government. He believed men were naturally benevolent and sociable, disliking solitude and seeking human conversation and company. This sociability was produced by self-love and the need to satisfy mutual wants, and so naturally led men into family units. Since sociability was a natural characteristic of man, then some form of civil society had always existed. Reason enabled men to recognise the obligations of natural law, to administer justice, and to keep compacts. It also persuaded some men to seek long-term happiness, rather than fleeting pleasures. As reason replaced instinct, then the social circle widened and large artificial civil societies were created.[47] In maintaining that natural society embodied a form of political society, Bolingbroke rejected Hobbes's description of the individualistic anarchy and ruthless competition, the nasty, short and brutish life, that had preceded the creation of civil society. Instead, he asserted that some kind of subordination and order had been characteristic of the paternalistic family groupings of natural society.[48] Nor could Bolingbroke fully accept Locke's view that consent was the only legitimate basis for political obligations. In his opinion the original contract of a civil society was not arranged by a decision of all the individuals in the community. It was more usually a covenant by the heads of important families, though it could be the result of fraud or conquest. Civil government was an artificial creation, but its purposes and aims were little different from those of natural society. It was an extension of the family, and the ruler had similar paternalistic duties to the head of a family. The members of a family were not all free and equal, nor were artificial governments based on a democratic contract.[49]

Artificial governments, once established, tried to promote the happiness of all subjects, by studying the precepts of the law of nature. The first rulers had often been great philosophers and legislators. Those who were in positions of authority had to consult the needs of the governed, rather than their own desires. The rulers generally had superior reason and could seek long-term results; they did not simply submit to the demands of the people. The primary duties of a government were to maintain peace and order, and administer justice. Locke had claimed that its chief functions were to protect rights and property, but Bolingbroke did not accept this new concept. It was not congenial to his aristocratic and paternalistic theory of government, that followed naturally from his theory of the Great Chain of Being, with its hierarchical order of society. He did not accept Locke's premise that all men, as individuals, consented to the formation of a civil government and so retained their original freedom and equality. In his view natural society had always required the exercise of authority by a few leaders and the submission of the majority of its members. Men must accept their station in life and the particular functions and duties incumbent upon them. Popular liberty and social equality had never existed in natural society and so could never be part of the original contract, which established an artificial political society. Thus, Bolingbroke's contract theory looked back to the traditional concept prevalent in the middle ages. The contract required the government to consult the good of the people. This was in conflict with the newer concept of government, that demanded that it should defend individual rights and property, and acknowledge the existence of legitimate self-interest.[50] In Bolingbroke's system the ruler's authority did not come from below, though he received public consent by doing what was best for the people. This required that he should not alter the common law or threaten the liberty of the people. When he failed to serve the public interest, then

those who had made the artificial contract, that is the natural leaders, the
men of independent property, could break it and reassert their paternal
authority. This was what had been done in the Revolution of 1688. Thus,
while Bolingbroke rejected the notion of divine right, he did not accept
Locke's particular justification of the Revolution.[51]

CHAPTER 10

The Return to Politics

ALL his life Bolingbroke showed a genuine love of study and a strong desire to shine in literary and intellectual circles. His philosophical interests after 1716 were taken seriously. While he never became a good philosopher, this was not because of any lack of application or ambition. He tackled major problems which were exercising the minds of the greatest philosophers of the age. Though he was reticent about making his works public during his lifetime, Bolingbroke believed that he might have an impact on posterity. The publication of his unorthodox views might have frustrated his political ambitions, but when he and his political enemies were off the stage he hoped that his merits might then receive their due acclaim. Only his intimate circle were fully aware of his moral and religious views during his lifetime. He undoubtedly profited from the superior knowledge of Alary, Pouilly and Brook Taylor, while he in turn influenced the work of Voltaire, Swift and Pope. Neither his parliamentary allies nor his political enemies, however, could be trusted with a full knowledge of his unorthodox opinions. Clearly, philosophy was an important but still only a secondary interest for Bolingbroke. His real objective was political power. Though his ambitions in this direction were often frustrated, they remained insatiable until the end of his days.

Bolingbroke had thrown himself into his historical and philosophical studies with considerable enthusiasm, but he never relented in his campaign to persuade the British government to reverse his attainder and to allow him to return to politics. His efforts had been frustrated by the intransigence of both Whig and Tory backbenchers. By the early 1720s he had won over a section of the Tories, notably the followers of Sir William Wyndham, Lord Bathurst and Lord Gower, but the majority remained suspicious of a politician who had betrayed two kings within a year. Nor could these Tories reconcile themselves to the Whig-supremacy and accept Bolingbroke's advice to cooperate with some of the leading Whigs. Party prejudices as well as party labels survived the death of Anne.

173

To confound Bolingbroke's ambitions even further the Stanhope-Sunderland ministry had a precarious majority. If they assisted Bolingbroke they would play into the hands of the dissatisfied Whigs, ably led by Walpole and Townshend. It was not until the leading Whigs could accommodate their differences that a ministry could emerge which would risk the wrath of the malcontent Whigs for Bolingbroke's sake.

Bolingbroke had laid great store on the ability of Lord Stair in Paris, and Stanhope and Craggs in London, to effect his return to politics. By 1722 their endeavours had come to nought. Stair had left his embassy, and Stanhope and Craggs did not long survive the financial crash of the South Sea Company. Bolingbroke was then faced with negotiating with a new Whig ministry dominated by Walpole, Townshend and Carteret. At first he openly contacted all three, but he soon realised that Carteret was not on good terms with the other two leading ministers. Though he continued his negotiations with all three, he engaged in the dangerous game of secretly appearing to favour one side against the other. The Whig ministers in their turn used him to gain a political advantage. Carteret showed a more genuine interest in helping Bolingbroke and he was supported by Lord Harcourt, Bolingbroke's old Tory colleague, who had just been appointed to the Privy Council.[1] Walpole and Townshend had no real desire to assist Bolingbroke, but by 1723 the opposition in parliament was so weak that they could not resist some concession to him without irritating the King, who had long promised to do something for Bolingbroke. To reveal their implacable hostility to Bolingbroke would only have benefited Carteret. Thus, after years of uncertainty and bitter disappointments, Bolingbroke was finally pardoned on 25 May 1723, but he was not released from all the penalties and forfeitures incurred under the Act of Attainder of 1715.[2] He was free to return to England because he would no longer face charges of treason, but he had not regained all his political and civil rights. His estates, his title and his seat in the Lords were still forfeited.

Though his restoration was not yet complete, Bolingbroke was much encouraged by his success and renewed his efforts to pick up the threads of his political career. He promised Townshend that if he were allowed to return to the political arena he would earn the ministry's trust. Townshend refused to be drawn into any new commitment. A full restoration would rest with parliament and not merely with the King or his ministers.[3] Undeterred, Bolingbroke lost no time in returning to England, where, in July 1723, he acknowledged his profound obligations to his old colleague,

Lord Harcourt.[4] He could count on Harcourt's further assistance, but he soon found that he still had plenty of political enemies. Many Whigs threatened to oppose any bill which would allow him to enter parliament again. The Prince of Wales refused to see him on the pretext that he should first present himself to the King, who was in Hanover for the summer.[5] Even Carteret was careful not to commit himself too much on Bolingbroke's behalf for fear of weakening his own position. Walpole was frankly hostile. He told Bolingbroke quite plainly that he would not antagonise parliament for his sake. Bolingbroke tried to ingratiate himself with Walpole by offering to break with Carteret and to lead Wyndham, Bathurst and Gower into Walpole's camp. In his tough, forthright manner Walpole had warned Bolingbroke that he was acting most unwisely. If he expected his political salvation from a Whig parliament he must not give the impression of negotiating to bring a pack of Tories into office. If this became widely known his cause would indeed be desperate and so Walpole suggested that Bolingbroke should inform his Tory friends that he had decided that it would be inopportune to press the ministry at this stage.[6] Walpole described this blunt advice as his ultimatum to Bolingbroke. The Whigs must first be consulted before anything was done for Bolingbroke and he would only weaken his case if he tried to appeal over their heads to the King in Hanover.[7] Townshend, like Walpole, was concerned about retaining Whig support and he persuaded the King to oppose Bolingbroke's intention of visiting Hanover to press his case personally.[8]

Bolingbroke left England and promised to conduct himself in a manner which would cause no offence.[9] His visit had taught him one valuable lesson. Carteret's influence was restricted to the Court. Walpole and Townshend held the keys to the parliamentary situation because of their influence with a majority of the Whigs. No bill to repeal Bolingbroke's attainder could be passed against their determined opposition in parliament. Bolingbroke had to weaken their resolve. The death of the Duke of Orleans gave him the opportunity to assist the Walpole-Townshend interest with the new French Regent and to destroy the credit which Carteret was trying to build up. Carteret sent his agent, Sir Luke Schaub, to Paris to persuade the Regent to grant a dukedom to the Marquis de la Vrillière, whose son was planning to marry the daughter of the Countess of Darlington, one of George I's German mistresses. Walpole and Townshend, who favoured the rival mistress, the Duchess of Kendal, decided to counter this move and sent the former's brother, Horatio

Walpole, to Paris. Bolingbroke offered to help Walpole's brother, but the latter, while making use of Bolingbroke's information, would not let him control the negotiations. He agreed that Bolingbroke could introduce him to the Duke of Bourbon and his entourage, but he also opened a direct channel of communication for himself. Bolingbroke had to be satisfied with the roles of messenger and informer. To weaken Carteret's credit with King George he exaggerated Schaub's indiscretions at the Regent's Court. To increase his own influence he offered his advice directly to Walpole and Townshend. They ought to win the Regent's goodwill by helping him to combat his rivals at the French Court. Bolingbroke could perform this task if he were not so obviously a proscribed man without real influence with the British ministers. While regularly trying to damage the reputations of Schaub and Carteret, he asked Walpole and Townshend not to betray his role. To convince them that he was indispensable he tried to show that Horatio Walpole was out of his depth and that he relied on the wrong French courtiers. If he were not better advised he might allow Schaub to succeed or he might disoblige the Regent. In fact, Walpole was able to prevent Schaub securing the dukedom, though the marriage went ahead. Schaub was recalled and Horatio Walpole was appointed ambassador to France. Bolingbroke had not proved indispensable and he had to be content with offering advice and information to Horatio Walpole.[10]

Bolingbroke loved diplomatic intrigue and he had wanted to play the role of a European statesman, but his primary aim in these negotiations was to assist Walpole and Townshend to combat Carteret's influence with George I. Though his role was much smaller than he fondly imagined, this objective was attained. Carteret was sent out of the way by his new posting as Lord Lieutenant of Ireland. Townshend, who had been more concerned than Walpole to get rid of his fellow Secretary of State, was grateful for the assistance Bolingbroke had given. He informed him that he believed that the majority of the Tories would not now oppose his restitution and that the opposition Whigs, though implacable, were now too weak to defeat the measure by themselves. The real obstacle was the number of Whig supporters of the ministry, who might rebel against a measure designed to allow Bolingbroke to resume his political career. They were not yet satisfied that he would ever accept a Whig ministry. Bolingbroke's prudent conduct and the persuasive powers of Harcourt, Townshend himself and other friends of Bolingbroke might lead them to revise their opinion.[11] Meanwhile, Townshend and Harcourt did try to

Robert Walpole

William Pulteney, 1st Earl of Bath

Frontispieces of *The Craftsman*

Bolingbroke
in about 1730

Sir William Wyndham

help Bolingbroke overcome his financial problems. His second wife, Madame de Villette, had some £50,000 invested in England, but her banker, Sir Matthew Decker, refused to let her draw on it. He claimed that, since parliament had not yet restored Bolingbroke's forfeited estates and privileges, this money might be regarded as part of Bolingbroke's personal estate and therefore subject to confiscation. Townshend regarded this as a piece of sharp practice. Harcourt advised Lady Bolingbroke to seek the Duke of Bourbon's aid.[12] In the summer of 1724 she was allowed to visit England, where she regained her money. She was also received at Court, but failed to make much impression on the King.[13] Her devotion to Bolingbroke was such, however, that she bribed the Duchess of Kendal with some £11–12,000 to use her influence on the King to procure her husband's restoration.[14]

George I, pressed by the Duchess of Kendal, by Harcourt and possibly by Townshend, was now willing to fulfil his earlier promises to Bolingbroke to reward his loyalty to the Hanoverian dynasty. Walpole, however, remained unalterably opposed to Bolingbroke's return to politics. He did not trust Bolingbroke's promises not to lead the Tories against the Whig ministry and not to stir up the old party rancour. Walpole's fears and suspicions were shared by many Whigs and he made use of this fact to dissuade the King from a full restoration of Bolingbroke's political rights. Walpole's motives were a mixture of sound political judgement, a genuine desire to avoid political unrest, and bitter personal antagonism towards Bolingbroke. His influence and his arguments inhibited the more generous instincts of the King.[15] It was agreed that a bill should be prepared to reverse Bolingbroke's attainder only so far as it affected his right to own and inherit property. His political rights, his title and his seat in the Lords were not to be restored. Bolingbroke agreed to accept this partial restoration, though it was much less than he had anticipated. He even pretended to accept the ministry's explanation: 'If these promises are short of those offers which were made me several years ago, it will be however an entire satisfaction to me, that this difference must arise from the temper of party, and from the circumstances of affairs, since no man will, I am sure, affirm that it arises in any degree from my conduct.'[16] In fact, his resigned acquiescence could not disguise his bitter disappointment. He never forgave Walpole for frustrating the fulfilment of what he had been promised over so many years. For the rest of his life he claimed that a full restoration had been desired by the King and could have been forced through a relatively docile parliament.[17] Only Walpole had

G

prevented it. This betrayal gave him an excuse in his turn to dishonour his agreement not to oppose the King's ministers. Thus, Walpole's suspicions were confirmed. Though he was partly responsible for this result, it is hard to imagine that he and a fully restored Bolingbroke could long have remained in support of the same ministry.

The bill to allow Bolingbroke to inherit the estates of the St John family in Wiltshire, Surrey and Middlesex, and to purchase landed property in his own right, was planned for the 1724–25 session, though the beneficiary was in suspense for several weeks fearing that the ministry would again disappoint him.[18] The ministry decided to delay the introduction of the measure until 20 April, hoping that many backbenchers would by then have left for their estates. It adopted the procedure of letting Lord Finch, a Hanoverian Tory in Anne's reign though now in alliance with the Whigs, present the Commons with a petition to allow Bolingbroke to inherit or purchase real or personal estate in the kingdom. The members were informed that Bolingbroke had given testimony of his fidelity and allegiance to the King for some time. Robert Walpole then intervened to second his proposal and to tell the House that the King was in favour of this gesture to a subject who had proved his loyalty for the past seven years. This assertion did not prevent a warm debate in which several Whigs voiced their hatred of Bolingbroke. Sir John Cope called him an enemy of God and man, and a standing threat to the Protestant succession. He was ready to denounce the ministers too, but a friend pulled him down before he could blurt out enough to send him to the Tower. His intemperate behaviour did not inhibit other Whigs from indulging in character assassination at Bolingbroke's expense. Captain Vernon described him as a complicated villain. Paul Methuen, though a placeman, opposed the petition and repeated all the charges levelled against Bolingbroke in 1715. Walpole endeavoured to take the heat out of the debate by reminding the House that the bill would not reverse the attainder, but merely suspend some of its penalties. Bolingbroke, he stressed, would not regain his title nor his seat in the Lords and so he would remain stripped of political influence. As he, Walpole, had taken a principal part in prosecuting Bolingbroke in 1715 so now he was ready to temper justice with mercy. Bolingbroke had repented of his past sins and had helped to confound recent Jacobite conspiracies. Walpole's arguments did not still all the Whig criticisms, but they probably accounted for the absence of the Jacobites from the debate. William Shippen and his group could not support the petition of a man who had betrayed the Pretender, though they were also loath to approve of the original attainder of 1715. The Hanoverian Tories played little part in the debate, leaving the Whigs to quarrel among themselves. Only Sir Thomas Hanmer and Dr John Friend seemed prepared to speak a few words on Bolingbroke's behalf. When the petition was approved by a majority of two to one some 52 Tories voted for it, though five opposed it and the Jacobites abstained.[19] Evidently not all the Tories were reconciled to Bolingbroke's conduct. Wyndham and Bathurst had tried to rally them in favour of the petition before the debate, but without success. The Jacobites were adamant that they could not support Bolingbroke. A few, like Charles Caesar and Sir Christopher Musgrave, were ready to oppose the petition, though most of them agreed to abstain with William Shippen and Thomas Strangeways.[20]

Bolingbroke's bill was read for the first time on 26 April 1725. Four days later it was amended in committee so as to preserve the family's estates for Bolingbroke's half-brother should he die without issue. On 3 May, Lord William Pawlet, an intransigent Whig and an old opponent of Bolingbroke, suggested an additional clause to disable Bolingbroke from ever sitting in either House and from any office or place of profit or trust under the Crown. This vindictive clause was opposed by Walpole and defeated by 154 to 84 votes. There was no pressing necessity for it since the existing bill did not in fact restore Bolingbroke's political rights. The bill met no further obstruction in the Commons and the Court party was much too powerful for the opposition in the Lords. Three Whig peers did denounce this 'extraordinary and undeserved bounty and reward' for a traitor to the Protestant succession and another three Whigs joined in the protest after the successful third reading. They maintained that Bolingbroke's actions from 1710–16 had clearly amounted to treason whereas his subsequent conduct had not convinced them that he could be trusted. The Tory peers voted with the majority, except for the eccentric Duke of Wharton, the notorious Jacobite son of the staunchest of Whig peers, and his fellow Jacobite, the Earl of Scarsdale.[21] The bill received the royal assent on 31 May 1725 and within weeks Bolingbroke had left La Source forever and returned to England. He did not receive an ecstatic welcome. Pope and Swift were delighted and so was the group of Tories led by Wyndham, Bathurst and Gower. Other Hanoverian Tories, particularly the friends of the late Earl of Oxford, were not ready to welcome him with open arms. He soon gave them further cause for complaint when he became embroiled in an unsavoury legal wrangle over his former estate at Bucklebury. His first wife had conveyed this to her nephew and godson in return for the payment of Bolingbroke's debts. Bolingbroke had no strong claim to the estate, but on his return he began to chop down the trees and hedges, apparently in a vindictive effort to reap what small profit he could before the estate reverted to the son of his brother-in-law, Robert Packer.[22] Though he did not relinquish his claim to the estate until 1733, he had to find a new home. His father still lived and so he could not yet inherit any of the family estates. Instead, he fixed upon the manor house at Dawley, near Uxbridge, Middlesex. There he gave the impression of retiring unconcerned from the public scene, but he was more like Achilles sulking in his tent. Anxious to avoid any suggestion of conspiring with the opposition, he was hoping that the ministry might yet relent and secure the restoration of his political rights. William Stratford, that old critic of Bolingbroke and a staunch friend of the Harley family, observed his conduct: 'I have sure and certain intelligence that he is resolved to have done with the Tories and to observe no measures with them, but to throw himself entirely into the opposite party.'[23]

The parliamentary session of 1725–26 persuaded Bolingbroke to take a more active role in British politics. Walpole refused to countenance any further action on his behalf and there was no prospect of re-entering parliament while Walpole was the leading minister. His position had seemed impregnable in the last session, but now there were signs of a reviving opposition. In February 1725 Bolingbroke had agreed with Wyndham's description of the opposition in the Commons as 'people who expect they know not what, who are ready to be angry, they know not why, and eager to act, tho' they have neither plan nor concert'.[24] Before the next session, however, William Pulteney, a former Whig minister, went into opposition when Walpole preferred the Duke of Newcastle for the vacant Secretaryship of State. Pulteney was a politician of some ability, well versed in financial affairs and an excellent speaker and debater. A man of wealth, with social position and social graces, he appreciated the value of public opinion and soon became a popular opposition spokesman. In parliament he at once became the leading Whig opponent of Walpole. At the same time the Treaty of Hanover, by which Britain reversed her foreign policy and became an ally of France, provided a major issue on which to contest Walpole's policies. It offered the disgruntled Whigs, the Hanoverian Tories and the Jacobites an opportunity to combine in opposition to the ministry. In fact, they failed to take it and the government survived the session with a large majority.

Nevertheless, it had encouraged Pulteney to seek an accommodation with the Tories to further his own ambitions. Bolingbroke too was ready to open tentative negotiations with a view to organising a more effective operation.

Bolingbroke hated suspense, could never remain inactive, and had lost none of his political ambition. Yet, as he made clear to Harcourt, he would not concert action with Pulteney while there was any chance that the ministry would serve his interests:

> I have very much esteem for Mr Pulteney. I have met with great civility from him, and shall, on all occasions, behave myself towards him like a man who is obliged to him. But, my Lord, I have had no private correspondence, or even conversation with him, and whenever I appeal to the King, and beg leave to plead my cause before him, I will take care that his ministers shall not have the least pretence of objection to make to me in any part of my conduct. I will only say upon this occasion, that if I had caballed against them, there would have been other things said than were said, and another turn of opposition given.[25]

This was an unmistakable warning to the ministry that they must buy off Bolingbroke or see him lead his Tory friends into Pulteney's camp. Walpole disregarded the threat and Bolingbroke was driven into joining the opposition. On 5 December there appeared the first issue of *The Craftsman*, a journalistic venture which heralded the birth of a formidable opposition to Walpole. Bolingbroke opened his own campaign in January 1727, with three essays in *The Occasional Writer* and *The First Vision of Camilick*, his first contribution to *The Craftsman*.

Having taken the plunge into opposition politics, Bolingbroke knew he had to defeat Walpole in order to return to power. It was a daunting prospect. Walpole had the confidence of the King, an impregnable majority in the Lords and a commanding influence in the Commons. Bolingbroke had to forge a united opposition from the most unpromising materials. Had the politics of the period been merely a contest of 'ins' and 'outs' he would have had little difficulty in getting cooperation among the opposition factions. In fact, the parliamentary position was still bedevilled by Whig and Tory disputes. In 1715 the disorganised and demoralised Tory party seemed to have committed suicide, but though it had lost any chance of holding power, it had not disappeared from the scene. It died a lingering death as its years in the political wilderness slowly drained it of men of ability. Leading politicians like Nottingham and Harcourt, and place-hunters such as James Brydges and Arthur Moore, had tried to come to terms with the Whig supremacy and the Hanoverian succession. A steady stream of ambitious backbenchers – men like Sir Edward Knatchbull, Sir Robert Raymond and Lord Finch – defected, became first 'independents', and then gradually indistinguishable from Whigs. Nevertheless, throughout Walpole's ministry there were between 140 and 180 recognisable Tories in the Commons. Apart from the ministerial Whigs they were potentially the strongest group in the House. Unfortunately, they laboured under severe handicaps. They had lost most of their men of ability and ambition. The majority were country gentlemen with no real desire for office. Moreover, they had no distinctively Tory issue on which to oppose the ministry. Walpole had judiciously defused two emotive issues by reducing the land tax and refusing to countenance any attack on the privileges of the Church of England. Thus, the Tories had neither would-be courtiers in their ranks nor the policies of an alternative government. As backbench squires they contented themselves with negative criticisms. They attacked the number of placemen in the Commons, the growth of corruption, the size of the standing army and the danger of continental alliances. In Anne's reign both parties had had a Court and a Country wing. By 1726 the Tories were without a potential Court leadership and were rapidly becoming a natural and permanent section of the Country opposition. The position, however, was still not completely hopeless. There were some men of ability and integrity, who had not yet defected to the Whigs. Unfortunately the Tories had not healed the divisions so evident in Anne's reign. There was a Jacobite faction, which included able parliamentarians such as William Shippen, Sir John Hynde Cotton and Sir Watkin Williams Wynn. The Hanoverian Tories were fragmented into three groups. Bolingbroke's friends, Wyndham, Bathurst and Gower, led the largest faction, but able survivors of Oxford's group, men of the calibre of William Bromley and Lord Strafford, had not forgotten old quarrels. Men like Sir Thomas Hanmer and Lord Abingdon operated independently and were not reconciled to Bolingbroke either.

To fuse the Tories into an organised, coherent group was a major task, but Bolingbroke also had to cooperate with the opposition Whigs. Men like William and Daniel Pulteney did not differ with Walpole on any question of principle. Their hostility was the product of frustrated ambition. They had little in common with the Tories, whom they suspected of harbouring Jacobite sympathies. While they would use their votes to bring down Walpole they had no desire to see any Tories in

office. If Bolingbroke were to defeat Walpole he had to replace hostility
with cooperation and forge the disparate elements of the opposition into
a potential governing party. To achieve this he inspired the most important
and fascinating opposition campaign of the eighteenth century. He fought
Walpole on two levels. On the one hand he looked about him for any and
every expedient and issue, real or imagined, which could be used to
embarrass Walpole and weaken his hold on power. In this battle he himself fought through the press, but had to rely on his friends and allies in
parliament to follow his advice. A much more significant contest was
waged on a theoretical and philosophical level. In his search for a viable
programme he eventually elaborated important ideas and concepts of
opposition, which raised the whole level of the debate above the more
obvious and very real contest for power.

The Opposition to Walpole: 1. Bolingbroke's Platform

THOUGH often regarded as an ambitious, self-seeking adventurer, Bolingbroke showed in his opposition to Walpole a clear vein of political principle. Once more he revealed his genuine concern for the interests of the landed gentry, particularly for the fate of the middling and lesser squires, who were not advancing so fast under the Whig supremacy as the great landowners and the City financiers. He also seized upon and highlighted many genuine grievances against Walpole's mode of government, such as the increasing number of placemen in parliament and the infrequency of elections, with which he personally had considerable sympathy. Thus, while Bolingbroke's main ambition in life was to achieve political power, he also wished to safeguard the interests of a particular segment of the political nation and the fortunes of men with whom he had always identified himself. His political writings should be seen primarily as a means to both these ends. However, partly because of the experience and intellectual polish he had acquired during his years of exile and partly because of the need to broaden the basis of his support, these writings did reflect more generally on the problems of government, political parties and opposition. Nevertheless, this was not enough to make them great political or philosophical works in their own right. When Bolingbroke's works are divorced from their political context they lose much of their value. When seen in relation to his political ambitions and to the political obstacles which he had to overcome, they assume a much greater significance. Viewed in this manner, they become important guides to the problems which vexed politicians, particularly those in opposition, from the Revolution to the Reform Bill, and even beyond. Party and opposition, patronage and corruption, limited monarchy and the balanced constitution, were all subjected to critical analysis and close scrutiny by Bolingbroke during his long campaign against Walpole. He has often been accused of expressing commonplace ideas, and he did indeed get many of his ideas from earlier writers such as Charles Davenant and James

Harrington, but he made them more widely known and he brought them more into the public arena by constant and forcible reiteration. Moreover, while political disputes frequently revolve around slogans, shibboleths and platitudes, such controversies can still involve major questions of general principle. This was the case with Bolingbroke's writings. Though he produced neither a comprehensive political treatise nor a coherent body of works, but was involved instead in a journalistic campaign to oust Walpole and destroy the mode of government which he sustained, Bolingbroke could justly claim that his efforts were not ephemeral polemics: '. . . the writings of the *Craftsman* have not been confined to these subjects, that are personal or temporary. The cause of the British constitution hath been pleaded through the whole course of these papers; every danger to it hath been pointed out; every security, or improvement of it, hath been explained and pressed.'[1]

Before he departed once more for France in 1735 Bolingbroke wrote most of his political essays for *The Craftsman*, though he also wrote separate pamphlets on particular topics. *The Craftsman* began in December 1726 and was published throughout Bolingbroke's campaign against Walpole. Several other politicians, notably William Pulteney, besides various journalists and literary figures, also contributed to its pages. There is considerable doubt as to which articles were written by Boling-broke and his contribution has often been over-estimated. By 1736 over 500 articles had appeared in it and Bolingbroke had contributed about one fifth of them.[2] The most important of these formed two series, which Bolingbroke acknowledged as his compositions. In 1730–31 he wrote 24 essays, which formed his *Remarks on the History of England*, and in 1733–34 he contributed a series entitled *A Dissertation upon Parties*.[3] These, aug-mented to some extent by his miscellaneous essays and pamphlets, must form the basis of any assessment of his contribution to the opposition press campaign against Walpole before 1735. After that date he wrote more systematic treatises such as *The Idea of a Patriot King*, which, while they were often an elaboration of ideas first expressed in *The Craftsman*, were written in altered circumstances. By then he had virtually acknowledged his inability to oust Walpole and he was thinking more in terms of influencing a new generation. His philosophical essays, however, were also the product of his years of active opposition to Walpole. His campaign against Walpole, as seen in his contributions to *The Craftsman*, developed along three main lines. He looked for suitable issues which would help him to construct a broadly based political platform and to unite the disparate elements hostile to Walpole. He tried to destroy the old distinctions of Whig and Tory, that kept the opposition divided. Thirdly, he laboured to create a new party, which would be able to proclaim itself the defender of the constitution and the nation's liberties. In his philosophical essays, in which he discussed the origins and nature of government in more general terms, Bolingbroke added a fourth dimension to his opposition to Walpole. We must now look more closely at these four strands in Bolingbroke's campaign against his great rival.

I

In his efforts to unite the disgruntled Whigs and the fragments of the Tory party into an effective opposition against Walpole it was not surprising that Bolingbroke should search for some common principles or at least some shared prejudices and vested interests. It was significant that he refrained from raising the cry of 'the Church in danger', which had been such a potent political weapon in Anne's reign. This was not simply due to the lack of opportunity. Religious issues, in particular the privileged position of the Church of England, did not excite such passionate debates as twenty years earlier and Walpole did skilfully avoid antagonising the clergy or the High Church squires. Nevertheless, there was always heated discussion when the Dissenters petitioned for the repeal of the Test and Corporation Acts. They did so in the 1732–33 parliamentary session, yet *The Craftsman* did not join in the debate. Bolingbroke may have learned his lesson about the incalculable political repercussions arising from religious ferment and he may have been inhibited by his personal religious opinions, but his real motive in ignoring the issue was fear of a Whig-Tory split. In his *Dissertation upon Parties* he maintained that religious differences had been the basis of party distinctions in the seventeenth century. Since his declared aim was to unite Whig and Tory, he was naturally anxious not to foment religious disputes. To placate his Whig allies he even went so far as to accept the qualified toleration of Dissenters then obtaining, and to admit his previous mistake in persecuting them. Apparently, 'experience hath removed prejudice'.[4]

There was one old plank in the Tory platform that Bolingbroke could successfully renovate and even extend. This was the dismay and fear registered by many of the landed gentry at the rising influence of financiers, stockjobbers and the moneyed interest in general.[5] The Tories had long mistrusted the new financial system which the Revolution had created around the National Debt, public credit, the stock-market, the Bank of England and the great chartered corporations like the East India Company. With good reason they and Bolingbroke had believed that these new vested interests were attached to their Whig opponents and were actively undermining the financial, social and political status of the squirearchy, the backbone of the Tory party. In his *Letter to Sir William Windham* Bolingbroke had justified the hostility of the over-taxed and heavily mortgaged Tory squires to the moneyed men, who had profited in the late wars against France:

> The bank, the East-India company, and in general the moneyed interest . . . enjoyed advantages so much greater than the rest of their fellow subjects. The mischievous consequence which had been foreseen and foretold too, at the establishment of those corporations, appeared visibly. The country gentlemen were vexed, put to great expenses and even baffled by them in their elections: and among the members of every parliament numbers were immediately or indirectly under their influence . . . But that which touched sensibly, even those who were but little affected by other considerations, was the prodigious inequality between the condition of the moneyed men and the rest of the nation. The proprietor of the land, and the merchant who brought riches home by the returns of foreign trade, had during two wars bore the whole immense load of the national expenses; whilst the lender of money, who added nothing to the common stock, throve by the public calamity, and contributed not a mite to the public charge.[6]

By the time Bolingbroke took up the cudgels against Walpole the plight of the lesser gentry and even of the middling gentry had worsened in relation to the great landed families and the leading financiers. Despite the years of peace and the reduced land tax, some small squires went to the wall and saw their estates bought up by the moneyed men and the great Whig aristocrats, who were the beneficiaries of government offices, places and pensions. In contrast to the Whig oligarchy the middling Tory gentry, who depended solely on their rents, found times much harder during the agricultural depression of the 1730s and 1740s. The fears and prejudices of the Tories were no doubt exaggerated, and there were some Tory gentlemen who were still quite wealthy and economically secure, but there was enough solid economic justification to perpetuate their political fears. The great financial crash of the South Sea Bubble in 1720 and the later collapse of the Charitable Corporation in 1732 confirmed their suspicions about the dangers and mysteries of speculation. The

Septennial Act made parliamentary seats more valuable and therefore more expensive. The Tory complaints of wealthy financiers and stock-jobbers buying up the seats once held by respectable country gentlemen, which had been voiced by Bolingbroke and Swift in Anne's reign, gained a much wider currency during the 1720s when many small landowners were compelled to sell out. There was thus some justification for the complaints of William Stratford, who was not the wildest of Tories, when he protested, during the 1727 election campaign, that unknown stock-jobbers were swarming throughout his part of the world, and that they were offering incredible sums for the votes of the freeholders. The Whigs were shamelessly encouraging them and they would undoubtedly succeed in displacing men with a real stake in the area. He feared that the new parliament would include more of these pernicious upstarts than placemen and that they would be even more ready to sacrifice the interest of the nation as a whole.[7]

On this particular question Bolingbroke had always sympathised with the attitudes, aspirations and frustrations of the Tory gentry. In his opposition to Walpole he capitalised on their smouldering resentments and their nostalgia for the days when politics and society had appeared to be the preserves of the landed interest. His writings embodied the political philosophy of the declining gentry. In *The Craftsman* he wrote many articles critical of the privileges of the great monopoly trading companies: 'A charter is no sooner granted to a select number of people, but immediately arises a set of men called governors, sub-governors, directors, stock-jobbers, &c.'[8] The whole system of paper credit, he argued, created a new class of men without any real stake in the country. They were gradually buying up more parliamentary seats and were threatening to engross the whole wealth of the nation. The process, begun at the Revolution, must be stopped before it ruined the nation and beggared its inhabitants. These alarming prognostications were a constant theme of Bolingbroke's essays:

It is impossible to look forward, without horror, on the consequences that may still follow . . . What will happen, when we have mortgaged and funded all we have to mortgage and to fund; . . . when we have mortgaged all the product of our land, and even our land itself? . . . Who can answer, that a scheme, which oppresses the farmer, ruins the manufacturer, breaks the merchant, discourages industry, and reduces fraud into [a] system; which beggars so often the fair adventurer and innocent proprietor; which draws continually a portion of our national wealth away to foreigners, and draws most perniciously the rest of that immense property that was diffused among thousands, into the pockets of a few; who can answer that such a scheme will be always endured?[9]

Bolingbroke's defence of the landed interest against the advances of the moneyed men was a constant factor in his career. His fears were shared by most of the landed gentry of the age, though they in fact held on to much of their economic, social and political power. A few Whig landed families and some Whig financiers certainly prospered in a spectacular fashion and some of the lesser farmers and squires went under, but the majority of the gentry survived the economic pressures of heavy taxation and agricultural depression relatively unscathed and were able to prosper in turn from the more favourable economic climate of the later eighteenth century. Nor was their social and political power in their own localities ever seriously threatened despite the expansion of the central bureaucracy. The economic and political trends since the Revolution appeared unfavourable for the gentry, but they stopped far short of the disastrous. At the time this was not so obvious and the new world of public credit was certainly growing, while remaining mysterious to many squires. Bolingbroke's hostility to the financial revolution may have been exaggerated, but it was sincere and it tapped the genuine fears of many country gentlemen. This allowed him to appeal to all the Tories, Jacobite or Hanoverian. It also enabled him to make common cause with some of the opposition Whigs. The Country Whigs had always included men of landed estates, such as Sir Wilfrid Lawson, Samuel Sandys and Sir Thomas Pengelly, who in their economic and social life were indistinguishable from many Tory country gentlemen. Moreover, this programme enabled Bolingbroke to attract the support of the smaller traders, especially of London, who resented what they regarded as the extravagant privileges and exorbitant powers of the great monopoly trading companies. During Bolingbroke's years of opposition to Walpole the ministry's control over the common council of London was steadily weakened. Sir John Barnard, a City M.P., became a principal opposition spokesman and Bolingbroke's personal friend, John Barber, became Lord Mayor of London in 1732. These London supporters of the opposition played a vital role in the success of the campaign against the Excise scheme.[10]

Always on the look-out for allies against Walpole, Bolingbroke broadened his economic platform to include the interests of the trading community. It was only partly an expedient to fit the occasion. Bolingbroke had constantly stressed the importance of trade to the country's wealth and power. In his contributions to *The Craftsman* the defence of the country's trading interest was almost as conspicuous as his concern for the landed gentry. 'Trade is of that general use and importance to every country,' he wrote in December 1728, 'that whatever relates to it can never be unseasonable, nor too often discussed; especially in this nation, which has so great a dependence on it.'[11] To draw a sharp contrast with the ministry's close relations with the financial interest and the great trading companies, Bolingbroke stressed the opposition's concern for the freedom of trade and the destruction of restrictive and exclusive trading privileges: 'All exclusive companies are generally allowed to be prejudicial to the nation, as they lessen our exports and navigation, and enable men to set their own price upon such commodities as they import, which must give our rivals in trade a very great advantage over us in those particular branches.' Stocks and shares, Bolingbroke claimed, attracted too much of the nation's wealth and diverted vital capital away from the trade of the country, which was the only true way to enrich the nation. 'Hath not trade decay'd ever since stock-jobbing flourished and met with encouragement? Have not our manufactures diminished, our imports and exports in general declined, and our poor become more numerous for want of employ?'[12] Whenever the political situation at home or diplomatic developments abroad threatened the interests of the traders, Bolingbroke was quick to seize his opportunity. He wrote regularly of the need to defend and indeed to extend Britain's colonies, which he regarded as essential markets and suppliers of raw materials. The government was not doing enough, he charged, to thwart the commercial ambitions of the French, Spanish and Dutch. Britain must retain all her naval outposts, particularly Gibraltar, and she must protect her merchants from the depredations of rival powers.[13] As early as 1728 Bolingbroke was criticising the operations of the customs office, especially in the application of the Navigation Acts.[14] When Walpole's Excise scheme played into his hands he did everything possible to unite the whole trading community behind the opposition's censure motions. He emphasised the need for the landed gentlemen to join forces with the merchants to defeat this measure. The gentry should not imagine that trade was none of their concern, for the wealth of the whole nation depended upon it flourishing. Nor must they be seduced into supporting the excise by Walpole's promises to reduce the land tax. The landed gentlemen must not regard the traders as a threat to their interests. Their real opponents, the men who had been buying up estates, were those who 'have raised large fortunes by the publick funds; to which this method [the excise] of laying taxes, and borrowing sums upon the produce, will give a larger scope'.[15] His sense of urgency and frequent repetition of this argument showed that the opposition, as late as 1733, was still not as united as Bolingbroke would have liked. After six years of opposition the Tory squires had not been persuaded to identify their interests with the traders, most of whom were Whigs.

Bolingbroke was not content merely to defend the economic interests of the men of estates and the merchants against the encroachments of the financiers and stockjobbers. Influenced by his reading of Polybius and Machiavelli, and of James Harrington and the 'neo-Harringtonians', he believed that the results of what he regarded as dangerous economic developments extended into the political sphere.[16] Those who possessed a real stake in the country, the owners of land and property, were the true citizens and the natural leaders of society, and government existed to protect their interests. Their property gave them both independence and responsibilities and so they alone could act in the best interests of the nation. Unfortunately, since 1688 their position, and with it the natural political and social hierarchy, had been undermined by the rise of the moneyed men and the increase in the numbers of those who held government places and pensions. These parasites enriched themselves at the expense of the gentry and the merchants and acquired power without either independence or responsibilities. These inferior men, who depended on others to protect their wealth and who were yet in a position to leave the country with their paper money, were able to undermine the traditional harmony and balance of the political order. The rise of such men, accompanied by the enervating effects of luxury and extravagance, destroyed virtue and led to the collapse of even the greatest states.[17]

According to Bolingbroke, the natural results of a situation where money, rather than merit or rank, carried the greatest political influence were the corruption of the government and the corresponding loss of liberty. By using government patronage and the secret service money, the royal ministers could bribe a larger number of M.P.s. They, in turn, would vote for more places, pensions and secret service money, and so enable corruption to be carried a stage further. Men bribed by office would be corrupt in office. The government would be weak, inefficient and expensive, but would still be able to destroy freedom and liberty. A packed parliament was worse than no parliament at all, because men would be seduced by the illusion of liberty instead of struggling to secure it.

In the past the English had lost their freedom whenever the sovereign or the royal ministers had been able to subvert the independence of parliament. They had usually justified their actions by claiming that corruption was a necessary expedient of government: the only means to smooth the relations between the executive and the legislature. Bolingbroke's readers were meant, of course, to identify Walpole with such practices.[18] He drove the point home by warning of the danger of a chief minister forming a corrupt alliance with the great financiers and moneyed companies in order to buy votes in every constituency. This would destroy the freedom of elections and undermine the constitution. The minister could buy up seats and so control these members, who could then unseat every honest member in a disputed election case. 'In fine, to what dangerous uses may these companies be made subservient, by corrupt and enterprizing ministers? . . . Have not all Ministries an influence over those companies; and may they not by their means be able to influence the elections of every city, and trading town in England? And what may we not justly apprehend from such a formidable, complicated power; which may, one time or other, destroy our happy constitution?'[19] Corruption on this kind of scale had undermined the liberty of Ancient Greece. A wise administration could only stand on its own merits and not on the power of bribery. The electors could ensure that they got such a government by voting for opposition candidates. They should vote for men of principle, for men who attacked the practice of bribery in elections and who wanted annual or at least triennial parliaments.[20]

Bolingbroke's attacks on the corruption of the Walpolean system were echoed by many other critics, including the small radical wing of the Whigs, the Commonwealthmen. These charges were not, in fact, simply the political expedients of a wily opposition, even though Bolingbroke was so strongly motivated by personal ambition. Such fears were perfectly understandable. In Anne's reign the number of dependable placemen in the Commons had been about 60 to 70, but the figure had doubled by 1727. Moreover, since the Septennial Act the cost of elections had gone up considerably, while the number of contests had been reduced. This seemed to confirm that money, rather than merit or rank, won parliamentary seats. These developments were the natural result of the administration's need to secure a reasonable majority in parliament and its inability to rest on the support of the Whig or Tory party. The dissolution of these parties made the growth of 'corruption' inevitable. If he had been prime minister Bolingbroke would probably have taken the same course as Walpole.[21] Yet this does not mean that there was no principle at stake. Many men, besides Bolingbroke, really feared that the increasing number of placemen and the extensive use of money to win elections were destroying the constitution. It seemed to strengthen the power of the Crown, for the King chose his own ministers, who then appeared to corrupt parliament.[22] In fact, ministers could never bribe a majority of the Commons and were dependent upon the support of the independent backbenchers, but this was not so obvious to men who saw their cherished bills, to reduce the number of placemen and to end bribery in elections, defeated by a seemingly all-powerful minister.

There was obviously a real fear, which Bolingbroke was able both to express and to harness to his political cause. He was able to rally the strongest opposition to Walpole behind measures aimed at reducing the number of placemen, ending electoral corruption and ensuring more frequent elections. Walpole had to use all his undoubted political expertise to ward off these threats. At times he had to allow place bills through the Commons, knowing he could kill them more easily in the Lords. In 1729 and 1733 he had to accept acts against corrupt practices in elections, though he made sure that they were never implemented. But even the enlarged opposition vote on such issues was not a victory for Bolingbroke's policies. What he was doing on these occasions was rallying the backbenchers to the old Country policies of reducing the power of the executive. He was not creating the kind of opposition which could become an alternative government. Many of the backbenchers, who supported Place bills and triennial parliaments, had no desire to be in office and no inclination to support any ministry, even if it included Bolingbroke or Pulteney. Whig-Tory alliances on these Country issues had been known in Anne's reign. They were not a sign then that Whig and Tory divisions had ended and they were no proof now that Bolingbroke had united the disparate elements opposed to Walpole.

The same drawback applied to Bolingbroke's other successful endeavours to increase the opposition vote. He was able to tap the average backbencher's dislike of an expensive foreign policy and a large standing army. In several of his essays he warned of the danger that a wicked minister might use a standing army as an instrument of tyranny.[23] There was little need to remind his readers of the examples of Cromwell and James II. As recently as Anne's reign the Duke of Marlborough had become very unpopular because of his excessive pretensions to control the army. During his years of opposition to Walpole, Bolingbroke was

presented with several opportunities to attack the ministry for signing
treaties which involved Britain in defending the King's German territories and hiring German mercenaries. Even when the Treaty of Seville
meant a reduction in the size of the army Bolingbroke was able to arouse
popular prejudices by protesting that the foreign mercenaries should be
the first troops disbanded: 'Why should foreigners take the bread out of
the mouths of Englishmen? . . . to disband our countrymen and maintain
foreigners in pay, at the same time, is what sticks in English stomachs,
and may be call'd a saving that tends to poverty.'[24] Arguments such as
these could certainly appeal to backbenchers, whether they called themselves Whigs or Tories, but for an ambitious politician they were mere
expedients and not genuinely alternative policies. They did not endear
Bolingbroke to the King nor did they ensure that Whigs and Tories could
unite on a constructive programme. By increasing the opposition vote,
they did not necessarily solve Bolingbroke's problem of how to unite his
potential allies into a force capable of replacing Walpole.

II

The disparate elements in opposition to Walpole had not been cemented
into a coherent, organised party by Bolingbroke's efforts to find broad
interests on which to unite them. Only the hostility to the influence of
the moneyed men and to the corruption of parliament had provided the
kind of policy which could bring Whigs and Tories together. It was
hardly a programme which could be implemented by any administration
and so it was unlikely to carry Bolingbroke and Pulteney into office with
a parliamentary majority behind them. The opposition could never find
an effective programme while it remained divided by old Whig-Tory
prejudices. Bolingbroke realised that he had to counter the accusations of
the Walpole camp that the opposition was tainted with Jacobitism and
riddled with faction. His own past career lent weight to these charges
and served to aggravate the divisions within the opposition. He advised
the public to discount Walpole's practice of attaching the epithet 'Jacobite'
to the whole opposition. The spirit of Jacobitism was now dead and the
principles of 1688 were now accepted by the opposition. Indeed, it could
be argued that it was the ministry which was betraying the Revolution.[25]
The Tories had combined with the Whigs to accomplish the Revolution
Settlement and, in doing so, had purged themselves of the old doctrines of

divine right and passive obedience. They too now recognised the King as a public servant, whose trappings of office and majesty did not amount to a divine sanction and whose duties to his subjects were as clear as their obligations to him. The King was nothing more than a supreme magistrate chosen for the convenience of the community, which wanted the executive power to be vested in a single person. His crown, sceptre and throne distinguished him from his subjects and appealed to the vulgar, but they were only the symbols of office and a reminder of the services which the King was expected to perform.[26]

Bolingbroke was not merely trying to dissociate the opposition from William Shippen's irrelevant Jacobitism, but trying to persuade the followers of Pulteney and Wyndham that even the labels Whig and Tory had lost the real meaning they had once had. There had once been valid distinctions between the two parties. Their real difference had been over religion, a dispute which went back to the reign of Queen Elizabeth, but there was now an excellent opportunity of reconciling all Protestant groups if men would cease fighting old, irrelevant battles.[27] Even at the height of the Whig-Tory disputes, in the last years of Charles II's reign, the divisions between the two parties had been exaggerated by excessive zeal. The Whigs had not all been republicans and Dissenters and the Tories had not all supported the introduction of absolutism and religious intolerance.[28] These differences had all been settled by the Revolution and it was absurd to use the same party labels to describe the present contest for power:

> . . . the proper and real distinction of the two parties expired at this era, and . . . although their ghosts have continued to haunt and divide us so many years afterwards, yet there neither is, nor can be any division of parties at this time, reconcilable with common sense, and common honesty, among those who are come on the stage of the world under the present constitution, except those of churchmen and dissenters, those of court and country.[29]

The majority of the former Whig and Tory parties, Bolingbroke claimed, was now united in defence of liberty and in opposition to the handful of Jacobites on the one hand and Walpole's mercenary detachment on the other.[30] The only people anxious to retain the old, obsolescent party labels were the factious spirits around Walpole, who were only interested in promoting their own selfish ambitions at the expense of the whole nation. The opposition, Bolingbroke urged, must not allow themselves to be seduced by Walpole's rhetoric and his cunning attempts to divide his opponents along the old Whig-Tory lines. To do so would be to play into his hands and risk the destruction of the Revolution principles upheld by all the followers of Wyndham as well as by the supporters of Pulteney. The dangers were too great to be ignored:

> If the [old party] distinction should remain, when the difference subsists no longer, the misfortune would be still greater; because they, who maintained the distinction in this case, would cease to be a party and would become a faction. National interests would be no longer concerned; at least on one side. They would be sometimes sacrificed, and always made subordinate to personal interests; and that, I think, is the true characteristic of faction.[31]

In Bolingbroke's estimation, the political arena no longer witnessed a battle between Whigs and Tories, but a contest for power. The question was not which party should be in office, but whether a corrupt faction or the honest representatives of the interests of the whole nation should govern the country. Walpole and his hirelings were not upholding Whig principles but feathering their own nests by ignoble and dishonest means. All men of good will, whether they were known as Whigs or Tories, must combine to save the nation from this exercise of arbitrary power under the guise of Revolution principles. To triumph over such a well-entrenched faction required its opponents to rise above the narrow spirit of party. The defence of liberty required a new party, a 'Country Party', which would embrace the interests of the whole nation and which would end the need for the old parties or the corrupt faction now in power. Bolingbroke even claimed that the present opposition embodied the aspirations of the nation:

> A ferment, or spirit, call it which you please, is raised; but, I bless God, it is not the blind and furious spirit of party. It is a spirit, which springs from information and conviction, that has diffused itself not only to all orders of men, as you observed, but to men of all denominations. Even they who act against it, encourage it. You cannot call it toryism, when such numbers of independent Whigs avow it. To call it whigism would be improper likewise, when so many tories concur in it. He, who should call it jacobitism, would be too absurd to deserve an answer. What is it then? It is, I think, a revival of the true old English spirit, which prevailed in the days of our fathers, and which must always be national, since it has no direction but to the national interest.[32]

Bolingbroke's analysis of contemporary politics was both sophisticated and essentially accurate. The notion that parliament resounded to the conflict of the Whig and Tory parties was unreal and the serious contest was between Court and Country. A shrewd awareness of political realities, however, was not enough to create an effective opposition to Walpole. Indeed, by itself, it would have hindered Bolingbroke's plans. He had illustrated and effectively assisted the decline of the positive attributes of Toryism. It was no longer attached to Jacobitism, divine right, passive obedience and non-resistance, and had ceased to exalt the royal prerogative. The Tories therefore no longer had a Court programme. The survivors of the old Tory party were left supporting a Country policy which, if continued, would keep them permanently in opposition. Moreover, Bolingbroke was in danger of getting the worst of both worlds. He had rejected the idea of opposing Walpole on a Whig or Tory basis, but he had not convinced his allies of the wisdom of following his example. Many opposition Whigs were still unhappy working in harness with former Jacobites like Bolingbroke and Wyndham. Despite all Bolingbroke's endeavours, Walpole's smear campaign, particularly his indiscriminate use of the term 'Jacobite' when referring to his opponents, continued to strike home. The Tory backbenchers too were not as ready as Bolingbroke to abandon their old prejudices and attachments, however unrealistic. To get over these two obstacles – the restrictive nature of the old Country programme and the survival of Whig-Tory prejudices – Bolingbroke had to rally the opposition behind a new constitutional banner. His national party, the new Country Party, had to have a positive appeal, which would cut across the old Whig-Tory divisions and give it an irresistible claim to power. It had to be able to oppose Walpole, and to show the real value of defeating his designs, while remaining loyal to the Hanoverian succession and the principles of 1688.

III

The old Country programme was distinctly limited, with its emphasis on resistance to the exorbitant demands of the executive. Bolingbroke's new Country Party wanted to preserve the whole constitution and end the unnatural division between Court and Country, sovereign and subjects. Queen Elizabeth had shown that the Crown could work in harmony with the people for the benefit of the whole nation.[33] Such a prosperous alliance occurred whenever both the monarch and the citizens, whom Bolingbroke identified with men of property, defended the natural liberties of Englishmen. Bolingbroke claimed that there was an ancient constitution, which had existed since Saxon times, and which was based on free institutions, notably parliament. This freedom could not be guaranteed unless the people resisted the efforts of weak kings and their evil advisers. Corrupt, scheming and factious ministers had destroyed liberty in the reigns of Richard II, James I and Charles I, when these monarchs had failed to cooperate with the majority of their subjects. In certain other periods, notably the reigns of Edward III, Henry V and Queen Elizabeth, the ancient constitution had been restored by the efforts of both the Crown and the nation. The Revolution of 1688 had followed such precedents. It did not mark a new era or define new liberties. The people had merely regained their rightful inheritance and had defeated James II's attempts to subvert the ancient constitution. Bolingbroke believed that it was time for a new cry to arms. By dint of an extensive system of corruption Walpole's faction was endangering the victory so recently won.

Bolingbroke's thesis was stated at length in his *Remarks on the History of England*.[34] It was not an original concept, for the opponents of Stuart absolutism in the seventeenth century had often claimed to be defending traditional English liberties. In the reign of Charles II it was the Whigs like Algernon Sidney who appealed to the freedom of the ancient constitution, and royalists, notably Dr Robert Brady, who argued that the Norman Conquest had established a new form of monarchical government, which did not guarantee the people's liberties. Bolingbroke not only rejected the old Tory interpretation of English history and accepted the Whig view, but clearly rejected Brady's approval of such an unlimited monarchy. By an ironic reversal of roles, Walpole replied by accepting Brady's argument that in the medieval world commoners had had no property and no freedom. Walpole was intent on proving that the Whigs had secured the nation's liberty for the first time at the Revolution and that only the Whigs could safeguard it now. Men of Bolingbroke's stamp had been ready to destroy the Revolution Settlement in 1715 and must never be trusted again. Though Brady's scholarship ultimately proved more accurate, Bolingbroke and Walpole were not really concerned with the truth of these differing historical interpretations. Bolingbroke used the notion of the ancient constitution as a base from which to launch attacks on Walpole's system. The latter posed as the only embodiment of Revolution principles and the staunch defender of hard-won liberties.[35] Another paradox was inherent in Bolingbroke's particular notion of the ancient constitution. There were two interpretations of how this constitution had been formed. The conservative view, accepted by Sir Matthew Hale in the seventeenth century and by Edmund Burke in the eighteenth, held that the ancient constitution was the result of immemorial custom and the product of innumerable adjustments to particular circumstances. It was therefore the product of history and not the work of one legislator. There was no one, original model of this constitution and it was therefore absurd for a discontented parliamentary opposition to demand that this constitution should be restored. Those politicians and opposition groups who wanted to widen the political representation and to resist the power of the Court, and who demanded a return to the ancient constitution, usually implied that there was such an original model which was based on rational first principles. It was therefore possible to say that this constitution had degenerated under a particular government and that this government should be reformed until it conformed to the basic principles of this original model.[36] Bolingbroke accepted this second interpretation, but he gave it an illiberal twist. His ancient constitution was not the result of an original contract based on natural rights and the product of general consent, which had enshrined the liberties of all men, but rather a concept rooted in natural law and in the traditions and experiences of Anglo-Saxon society, that had produced a government which was paternalistic, aristocratic and dominated by the men of landed property. The nation's liberties were best protected by resisting the rise of new interests and by returning to the traditional ruling classes. It was the liberties of the men with a stake in the country that ensured a free parliament and protected the rights of the ordinary people. This was clearly an attempt to adapt a 'Tory' philosophy to a world dominated by the Whig interpretation of the constitution.

Bolingbroke's particular theories of the ancient constitution stemmed from his efforts to convince the Tory squirearchy and the malcontent Whigs of the need to oppose Walpole's system of government. His personal ambition and his genuine concern for the social, economic and political rights and privileges of the gentry led him to pose as the champion of liberty and to out-Whig the Whigs. In depicting Walpole as a traitor to the Whig cause, which had always asserted the rights of parliament against the Crown and the royal ministers, and in supporting the standard Country programme aimed at reducing ministerial authority, electoral corruption, the management of parliament and the size of the standing army, Bolingbroke hoped to link hands with the radical Whigs (the Commonwealthmen or Country Whigs) as well as with the Tory backwoodsmen and the ambitious Whigs out of office. Together, as the representatives of the whole nation, they could challenge the corrupt oligarchy now in power. With Walpole's faction threatening the nation's liberties, the country had the right to form an opposition which was designed to protect the constitution from such dangerous encroachments. The opposition, which Bolingbroke wished to lead, was not to be a mere party or faction contending for office, but the nation carrying out its sacred duty to preserve its liberties. This new Country Party was not only opposing a particular government for narrow ends, but defending the ancient constitution. It posed as a loyal opposition; protecting the King from the dangerous advice of his corrupt ministers, but not threatening the constitution nor the Hanoverian dynasty.[37] Bolingbroke claimed that he would support any government which followed the precepts of the constitution, but would resist any minister who endeavoured to pervert it by introducing new laws and practices which violated both its principles and its spirit.[38] His task was to justify opposition in an age when the Court party always accused its opponents of being crypto-Jacobites ready to overthrow the present establishment and when most men abhorred the idea of a regular, formed opposition consistently criticising the government of the day. Both Whigs and Tories had refused to see any virtue in the existence of contending parties in the state and had always accused their opponents of being a mere faction. They had hoped that the ideal of national unity and unanimity would be achieved by the complete defeat of their opponents. Thus, Bolingbroke's Country Party was not only claiming to be trying to save the King from the bad advice of his corrupt and factious ministers, a cloak adopted by all critics of the administration of the country over the centuries, but asserting its right to be regarded as the defender of the constitution and, as such, the party to whom the King ought to turn to save the nation. It was not motivated by selfish ambition or the desire to dictate to the King, but by the highest ideals.

According to Bolingbroke, the extent to which a particular government threatened the constitution decided what kind of opposition was both legitimate and permissible. Ordinary errors of judgement by the royal ministers did not justify sustained opposition, only specific criticisms, but a spirited people, he urged, must be vigilant in the defence of its liberties. If the constitution itself were threatened by a corrupt administration then the nation must assert its full power in parliament or even outside it, though it had no right to overthrow the present royal family or to reduce the royal prerogative because of the sins of ill-designing ministers. By putting his case in this light, Bolingbroke hoped to link his theory of the ancient constitution with the prejudices of the country gentlemen. Many of these were reluctant to challenge the King's legitimate authority and few of them were prepared to accept the need for a regular opposition. Their commendable loyalty and independence, Bolingbroke advised, must not permit them to allow a corrupt faction to impose on them and the nation at large. As the men of property with a real stake in the country, it was their clear moral duty to uphold the constitution. Their traditional and rightful authority in parliament could only be exerted if they constantly strove for more frequent elections, the reduction of the number of pensioners and placemen and the ending of the government's corruption of M.P.s and voters. They should remember that a ministerial faction could pose a greater threat to the constitution when it allied with the moneyed interest. Financiers and stockjobbers depended upon the favour of the ministers and could never be trusted to defend the nation's liberties.

Bolingbroke was skilfully elevating the prejudices of those country gentlemen who disliked Walpole's ministry into the highest constitutional principles. He was also grappling with the problem of creating a legitimate opposition. The ancient constitution required that the Court should identify its interests with those of the country and this implied a conditional contract. If the King, however unwittingly, allowed his ministers to corrupt parliament and create divisions and factions within the nation then he must accept the consequences. In an extreme case, where the independence of parliament had been completely destroyed, the people could restore the constitution by force. To make certain of averting such a calamity, Bolingbroke maintained, it was necessary to have freely elected and independent parliaments, through which the Country Party could defend the constitution. Only by an effective opposition campaign could factious ministers be replaced by honest men from the Country Party. Bolingbroke, however, never envisaged and did not advocate a permanent opposition, an alternative government able to criticise the existing administration as a matter of course and ready to replace it at any time. His concept of opposition implied that once the honest men of the Country Party had replaced the previous ministers then all abuses would be remedied and there would be no need for the continuation of a formed opposition. It would not be needed again unless and until the government were once more dominated by an ambitious faction ready to undermine the constitution for its own selfish ends. Bolingbroke's suggestion, that the constitution might, in an emergency, have to be restored by force, did not lead him to the conclusion that the Country Party could force the sovereign to appoint his ministers from their ranks. The principle of resistance in extreme circumstances had triumphed at the Revolution, but not even the staunchest Whigs accepted the notion of a regular opposition. Bolingbroke and, even more, his Tory allies never openly advocated a policy of infringing the monarch's prerogative to choose his own ministers.[39]

In order to illustrate how Walpole was undermining the constitution, Bolingbroke had to explain how difficult it was to maintain the country's liberties and how easily a faction could threaten them without arousing immediate opposition. The British constitution was that of a limited monarchy, which depended upon the delicate relationship, indeed the precarious balance, between Crown, Lords and Commons. Such a limited monarchy or mixed constitution avoided the dangers of tyranny and anarchy, but a slight change in the balance which maintained it could swing the pendulum in either direction. The love of power was natural and insatiable, so it must be assumed that ambitious men would frequently disturb this balance. Thus, even in this, the best form of government, there was a perpetual danger to liberty. Each of the three vital components of the constitution must resist the encroachments of either or both of the other two.[40]

Bolingbroke's discussion of the balanced constitution was sometimes ambiguous and this had led to some confusion over whether he adhered to the traditional notions of mixed government or was advocating the more original theory of the strict separation of powers.[41] Mixed governments avoided the dangers inherent in absolute monarchies, aristocracies and democracies, by combining the benefits of all three in a legislature of Crown, Lords and Commons. The theory of the separation of powers gave these three institutions (Crowns, Lords and Commons) three separate functions (executive, judicial and legislative). In some places Bolingbroke did seem to be implying some kind of separation of powers when he maintained that Crown, Lords and Commons must retain a certain independence: 'In a Constitution like ours the safety of the whole depends on the Balance of the parts and the Balance of the parts on their mutual independency on one another.'[42] If one part increased its power it would ruin the balance, and so each must retain its special powers and privileges in order to hold the others in check and in balance:

As they constitute a limited monarchy, so the wisdom of our government has provided, as far as human wisdom can provide for the preservation of it, by this division of power, and by these distinct privileges. If any one part of the three which compose our government, should at any time usurp more power than the law gives, or make an ill use of a legal power, the other two parts may, by uniting their strength, reduce this power into its proper bounds, or correct the abuse of it; nay, if at any time two of these parts should concur in usurping, or abusing power, the weight of the third may, at least, retard the mischief, and give time and chance for preventing it.[43]

Though there was a suggestion here of the separation of powers, Bolingbroke was also describing how they might cooperate. Bolingbroke made it clear that he believed in a mixed constitution when Walpole's *London Journal* ridiculed his Utopian scheme of advocating 'government by powers absolutely distinct, and absolutely independent'.[44] He emphasised that the legislative function was shared by the Crown, Lords and Commons, and that it could not be exercised by one without the cooperation of the others. This made each one dependent upon the other two, but, unless each had sufficient power to protect its own special rights and privileges against any attempted usurpation by one or both of the others, then there would be no balance and harmony in the constitution. The limited monarchy and mixed constitution would be replaced by the supremacy of one of the original three components. There had to be both a constitutional dependency, in which the three parts worked together, and a mutual independency, by which they preserved their rights inviolate. There was not a strict separation of functions, but disinct powers vested in each institution in order to hold the others in check and in place. In reply to the *London Journal* he wrote:

> The constitutional dependency, as I have called it for distinction's sake, consists in this; that the proceedings of each part of the government, when they come forth into action and affect the whole, are liable to be examined and controlled by the other parts. The independency pleaded for consists in this; that the resolutions of each part, which direct these proceedings, be taken independently and without any influence, direct or indirect, on the others. Without the first, each part would be at liberty to attempt destroying the balance, by usurping or abusing power; but without the last, there can be no balance at all.[45]

To avoid future misunderstandings Bolingbroke was careful to explain in his other essays that the three parts of the constitution cooperated to enact a law, but were each free to withhold consent.[46] In describing the functions of the King, for example, he wrote in Newtonian imagery: 'He can move no longer in another orbit from his people, and, like some superior planet, attract, repel, influence, and direct their motions by his own. He and they are parts of the same system, intimately joined and cooperating together, acting and acted upon, limiting and limited, controlling and controlled by one another.'[47]

In praising the merits of limited monarchy and in expounding the absolute necessity of preserving inviolate the special privileges of the three parts of the constitution, Bolingbroke could invest his opposition to Walpole with noble principles. The new Country Party, which he was endeavouring to forge out of malcontent Whigs and Hanoverian Tories, would have a duty to oppose a corrupt faction and would profit from a coherent ideology. Though Bolingbroke had considerable success in terms of political philosophy and was able to provide the Court-Country dichotomy with an ideological basis, he had not solved the practical problem of how to defeat Walpole. Most of his difficulties stemmed from his whole concept of the constitution, which was essentially static. He believed that there was one correct mixture or balance, which had to be maintained at all costs. A constitution was always subject to inadvertent decay or deliberate corruption and could only be preserved by the utmost vigilance. The correct balance of the English constitution, he argued, had been restored in 1688 and the effort to prevent it decaying again presented Bolingbroke with two major problems. In the first place he maintained that the rise of the moneyed interest and the extension of the executive's powers of patronage had enabled a corrupt faction at Court to undermine the independence of the Commons and to subvert the Revolution Settlement. Walpole was threatening to upset the balance of the constitution:

> We all know that there are mercenary and abandoned wretches amongst us, who have dared to plead for a dependence of the parliament on the crown; not for that dependence of the several parts of the government on one another, which our constitution hath formed, and on the preservation of which the freedom of our governemnt entirely rests; but for the most indirect, the most iniquitous, as well as dangerous dependence imaginable; for a dependence, to be created by corruption, which must always produce effects as infamous as its cause.[48]

Merely to recognise that Walpole was not acting according to the letter and spirit of the Revolution did not preserve that constitutional settlement.

Nor did Bolingbroke's ideology suggest new methods by which Walpole could be defeated. He had not made any practical advances on the old Country programme. He was still reduced to advocating the exclusion of placemen, the abolition of corruption and resistance to the demands of the executive. Although in his political theory the constitution could only be safeguarded by the cooperation of Court and Country, in practice he was urging the latter to resist the encroachments of the former. The complete identification of the interests of King and parliament remained a pious hope. Bolingbroke's Country ideology was not the programme for an alternative government, but the watchword of a permanent opposition.

Bolingbroke's second intractable problem was the product of his almost schizophrenic view of the Revolution. While he struggled to preserve the constitution restored in 1688, his hatred of the financial revolution, which had sprung almost inevitably from that settlement, knew no bounds. He deplored the financial and political practices which developed from that balance he was always praising. His defence was that the intentions of the Revolution were being perverted by constitutional practices never envisaged by the architects of that settlement. The whole system of public credit, for example, was arranged by a faction, he maintained, whereas the political revolution had been accomplished by a united people. There was some justification for this view. The Revolution had not been accomplished to create a new system of public credit, to strengthen the central bureaucracy, nor to bring about various financial innovations like the Bank of England. It was very largely the need to seat William III more firmly on the throne and to finance the long struggle against Louis XIV, that William III's accession inaugurated, that led to the changes associated with the financial revolution and the growth of the administration. The Whigs had accepted the need and supported the changes. The Tories, who had only reluctantly accepted William himself, had never accepted the need for these developments and had strongly opposed them. Nevertheless, Bolingbroke's continued hostility to these developments led him to exaggerate the political impact of the financial developments since 1688. He also failed to recognise that the constitutional settlement itself would have proved unworkable without closer financial and political links between Crown and parliament. The new system of public credit had helped the Crown to finance its policies, but it had also ensured parliamentary control of the purse strings. This was paralleled in the political sphere by the gradual development of the practice of having ministers appointed by the Crown but also responsible to parliament and envisaged

by the men who had accomplished the Revolution, but they did help to
promote the better understanding between Crown and parliament that
these men had wanted. Both processes meant that the ministers had to
achieve the confidence of Crown and parliament. This considerable feat
could be made easier by the use of placemen, patronage and mild forms of
'corruption'. Bolingbroke feared, not unreasonably, that the executive's
progressive destruction of the independence of parliament would tilt the
balance in favour of the Crown. In fact, he grossly over-estimated the
Court's ability to influence parliament. The House of Commons was
never at the mercy of the ministers and, in essence, retained its independence. Later in the century it was to follow Bolingbroke's advice and
curb the royal influence, but this did not restore the 1688 settlement. It
tilted the constitutional balance in favour of the Commons. Bolingbroke
can be forgiven, however, for not being able to predict future developments. In the age of Walpole he was not alone in his fears for the constitution, but he was unable to translate this alarm into effective action.
He could not freeze the constitution at 1688.

IV

In his articles in *The Craftsman* Bolingbroke not only indulged in polemics
and propaganda, but became involved in a serious analysis of the contemporary political scene. He examined and discussed not only the issues
which would immediately appeal to his parliamentary allies, but the
wider problems of party and opposition, of mixed government and
the balanced constitution. This led him to make the occasional remark on
the nature and aims of government itself and the origins of political society.
He mentioned, for instance, that the aim of government was to promote
the national interest by achieving the happiness of all members of the
community and that all government began and ended with the consent of
the people.[49] In discussing the limits on the King's power he wrote:
'The settlements, by virtue of which he governs, are plainly original
contracts. His institution is plainly conditional, and he may forfeit his
right to allegiance, as undeniably and effectually, as the subject may forfeit
his right to protection.'[50] Such serious and philosophic topics could not
be expounded at any length in a partisan journal like *The Craftsman*,
but Bolingbroke did pursue his investigations further during his years of
opposition to Walpole. The fruits of his research appeared in his philo-

sophical essays, published posthumously in 1754. These ideas were an extension of, and a new dimension to, his opposition platform. The political theories, which had appeared in *The Craftsman*, were now underpinned with a general philosophical basis.[51]

Some of the links between Bolingbroke's philosophical studies and his programme of opposition to Walpole were rather tenuous and should not be overstrained. Nevertheless, it can be argued that his philosophical ideas, for example his contempt for metaphysical controversies and his desire to keep religion firmly under state control, were tapped by him in order to further his plans to develop a truly secular political ideology. The Country Party, which he created to oppose Walpole, was never allied to one religious doctrine or sect. Its avowed objectives and principles were secular. This rather reactionary and élitist party of aristocrats, squires and writers would probably have accepted Bolingbroke's conviction that reason rarely managed to control the passions and so those who possessed superior reason should govern the masses. Claiming to have a superior, cultivated mind Bolingbroke never wished to appear as an obscurantist backwoodsman, but his sympathy with the Age of Reason was more apparent than real. His deepest philosophic commitments were to the concepts of an older order, to the law of nature and the Great Chain of Being, which had their roots in Renaissance humanism and much older philosophies. Similarly, in politics, he stressed such traditional notions as mixed government and the ancient constitution. The law of nature and the Great Chain of Being were both concepts which enjoined man to accept his role in the universe and individuals to be content with their allotted role in society. The efforts of moneyed men to ascend the social scale were an act of rebellion against the natural order of things. The landed men were the natural leaders of civic life and to alter this arrangement was to threaten the whole fabric of society. Bolingbroke's Deism had a shorter ancestry than the concept of natural law, but he never advocated its general adoption. His view of Deism like his attitude towards republicanism was that both were good in theory and might be intellectually preferred by men of superior reason, but that they were both impracticable for the masses. Just as in religion and ethics Bolingbroke wished to revive the virtues of primitive Christianity and enlightened self-interest, so in politics he wanted to revert to the traditional framework of society dominated by the men of landed estates, whose moral leadership and self-interest benefited and safeguarded the nation at large. By the exercise of his reason man could discover the law of nature and bring some order out of moral chaos. In the same way reason could lead men from barbarism to the laws of civil government. Self-love would persuade men to obey the laws of nature and the political expression of self-love was patriotism and the defence of liberty. Bolingbroke's attack on the temporal ambitions of the Church was matched by his contempt for the doctrines of divine right and non-resistance. He supported an hereditary monarchy for the same reasons that he accepted a national church: given an imperfect world they were valuable aids to political stability. Finally, it might be argued that Bolingbroke's emphasis on the tried and trusted role of the landed classes in government and society, and his evident distaste for such dangerous political and financial innovations as the National Debt and the Bank of England, were akin to his marked preference for the *a posteriori* method of experiment and observation over the speculative, *a priori* approach.

While some of these suggestions can only be tentative, there are much stronger reasons for believing that Bolingbroke's theories on the origins and nature of civil government were very closely connected with his political theories. His rejection of Locke's contract theories and Locke's concept of natural rights parallelled his assault on the Walpolean system of government. He did not regard individual freedom, self-interest and competition as being of positive benefit to civil society. They produced the moneyed upstarts who threatened the natural order of society, the Great Chain of Being and, with it, the stability of the government. Society was divided inevitably between the leaders and the led. The former should be those in whom reason predominated over passion. The men of calm, deliberate reason, the aristocracy of talent, coincided with the independent men of landed property. These were the few designed to govern. The vulgar masses were passionate, ill-informed, superstitious, and incapable of judgement. It was their duty to obey. The only natural democratic element was the relative equality of the leisured, well-born men of independent means. The landed gentry had made the original contract and they should defend the constitution and help the sovereign to rule through their power in parliament. Bolingbroke had rejected the Tory doctrine of divine right and he was prepared to accept the prevailing Whig theory of a social compact, even to the extent of acknowledging the people's right to resist an arbitrary or tyrannical sovereign, but his patri- archal society dominated by the landed classes can be seen as an attempt to adapt Tory philosophy to a new world dominated by the Whig philosophy of Locke. His Country Party was meant to embody the virtues

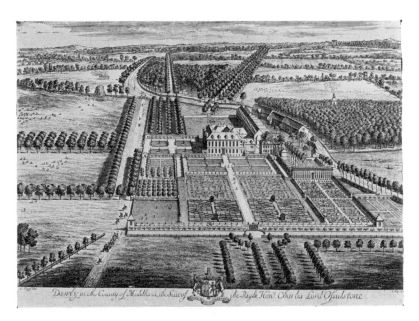

Engraving of Dawley Estate

Bolingbroke hunting

Alexander Pope

Voltaire

and power of the Tory squirearchy. The leaders of it, and therefore the men who should act as the King's ministers, were men of the most superior reason, educated in the fundamental principles and philosophy of government. Bolingbroke, of course, believed that he matched these requirements, while Walpole quite clearly did not. He told Swift:

> The greatest part of the men I have seen in business, perhaps all of them, have been so far from acting on philosophical principles, that is, on principles of reason and virtue, that they have not acted even on the highest principles of vice. I have known many, whose vanity and whose avarice mimicked ambition. The greatest part of the men I have seen out of business, have been so far from practising philosophy, that they have lived in the world arrant triflers; . . . But for all this, I think that a man in business may practise philosophy as austerely to himself, and more beneficially to mankind, than a man out of it.[52]

V

Bolingbroke's opposition to Walpole was in many ways a personal battle for power. Certainly his first objective was to displace Walpole and return to an active parliamentary career. Yet a study of all his political writings inspired by this hostility to Walpole gives his actions a wider dimension and a more profound significance His agile mind, seeking any stratagem to rally the opponents of Walpole, ranged over the major political problems of the day. He contemplated which issues could be used against men in office, he examined the real basis of political conflict, and he laboured to forge a loyal opposition against a new and foreign dynasty, which looked upon all its critics as potential Jacobites. Above all, he expressed in eloquent and forceful language the widespread fears of the backbench squires and the London coffee-house intelligentsia concerning the new world which had appeared since the Revolution. The rapid extension of the central bureaucracy, the development of the system of public credit, joint-stock companies and the stock-market, and the growth of corruption and patronage in politics, alarmed many men besides Bolingbroke. For them, Walpole was the principal villain as well as the greatest beneficiary of the new system. With some justice, Bolingbroke could complain that Walpole was betraying the very Whig principles he so frequently mouthed. Walpole, the defender of the Revolution, the upholder of the rights of parliament and the enemy of absolute monarchy, was now using royal power to corrupt the freedom of parliament and to

H

destroy the nation's liberties. 'Here are pretended Whigs arguing for arbitrary power, passive obedience and hereditary right.'[53] It was not a gross exaggeration to distinguish Walpole as a 'new Whig', who had betrayed the 'old Whig' principles of 1688. Even on specific issues Walpole had retreated from the Whig position. He refused to antagonise the Church of England by repealing the political restrictions on the Dissenters, he pandered to the landed gentry by reducing the land tax, and he resisted the demands to curb France's continental ambitions.

Nevertheless, Bolingbroke's political platform failed to carry complete conviction or to ensure ultimate success. Fatal flaws and intractable problems remained. All his complaints against Walpole's system were exaggerated. The bureaucrats of the central administration had not penetrated far into local government. The financial revolution greatly strengthened the nation and it was, in essentials, guided and contained by the politicians. The corruption of parliament had not made it a mere cypher, a rubber stamp for ministerial decisions. Throughout Bolingbroke's life, the aristocracy and landed gentry controlled local affairs, were the leaders of society and dominated parliament. They, not the ministers, were ultimately in control. Without the support of the independent back-benchers, Walpole could never have survived so long in office. They certainly disliked some of those developments which Bolingbroke attacked and they had still not entirely tamed the new system of credit, but they did not really believe that their world was collapsing about their ears. The social and economic tension between the landed and the moneyed interests, which had threatened to become acute in Anne's reign, never became fundamental or deep enough to divide the politically conscious into two inimical factions. By the 1730s many of the richer landed men, Tory as well as Whig, were beginning to invest in the money market and some financiers had bought estates. Only the hardest-hit of the small Tory squires and the impoverished Anglican priests really accepted Boling-broke's platform, and these two groups were a declining element in the Commons and a declining influence in elections. It was Bolingbroke's frustrated ambition which made his tone so shrill and his arguments so alarmist. Years later Horace Walpole wrote, with pardonable exaggera-tion: 'Last night at Strawberry Hill, I took up, to divert my thoughts, a volume of letters to Swift from Bolingbroke, Bathurst, and Gay; and what was there but lamentations on the ruin of England, in that era of prosperity and peace, from wretches who thought their own want of power a proof that their country was undone! Oh, my father! twenty years of peace, and credit, and happiness, and liberty, were punishments to rascals who weighed everything in the scales of self.'[54] Despite Bolingbroke's ability to stimulate their nostalgic longing for a mythical past, an ancient constitution and a Country Party ideal, the majority of the independent backbenchers preferred Walpole's phlegmatic pragmatism, which gave the country peace, stability and prosperity. Bolingbroke's naked ambition, his notorious past and his inability to inspire trust and confidence all worked against him. The opposition Whigs never really wanted him back in office. The Tories were more ready to listen to his criticisms of the new world, for many of the lesser squires were the victims of recent economic and political developments, though some of them detected the exaggeration and still distrusted Bolingbroke. The independent backbenchers would support attacks on placemen and corruption, but would not further Bolingbroke's personal ambitions. His much-vaunted Country Party was destined for permanent opposition as a sullen and rather toothless watchdog of the constitution. Bolingbroke had helped to give the opposition to Walpole an ideology and a greater political and historical significance, but he had not found a way of really uniting it nor a means of combating the power at Walpole's disposal.

CHAPTER 12

The Opposition to Walpole: 2. Bolingbroke's Tactics

I

UNABLE to sit in either the Lords or the Commons, Bolingbroke could not personally lead the opposition to Walpole, though he was able to reach a wider audience through his pen and to indulge in some intrigues at Court. In his retreat at Dawley, where he ostentatiously painted the hall with farm implements to suggest rural seclusion,[1] he continued his study of philosophy and regularly entertained his literary and academic friends. His patronage of literature, his brilliant conversation and his undoubted charm and grace attracted an impressive circle of admirers. When Swift came over from Ireland in 1726 and 1727 he was able to meet Bolingbroke, while Alexander Pope, John Gay and John Arbuthnot were all regular visitors at Dawley. With these and other companions from his political circle Bolingbroke discussed philosophy, theology and literature. Alexander Pope was astonished at the learning and scholarship which his friend had acquired in France. The Earl of Orrery later described him as a changed man after his years of exile: 'a philosopher equal to any of the sages of antiquity. The wisdom of Socrates, the dignity and ease of Pliny, and the wit of Horace appeared in all his writings and conversation.' This was excessive praise indeed, but there is no reason to reject Bolingbroke's own claim that he had abandoned his life of pleasure and now took a more serious view of life.[2] That he aspired to practise philosophy and to influence posterity can also be allowed, but his reputed disdain for politics was sheer pretence.[3] It is a distortion of the evidence to view Bolingbroke's literary circle as simply a gang of hack political journalists, but it is true that he and his friends had all been ready to serve Walpole and, when they were not treated as they thought they deserved, they sought vengeance with the pen.[4]

Bolingbroke's political theories and prejudices, even many of those philosophical ideas which underpinned his opposition to Walpole, were shared by or transmitted to his literary circle. The work of his Dawley friends echoed his own attacks on the moneyed men, the extension of corruption and the decline of liberty, and reiterated some of his views about society and government in general. Jonathan Swift had always supported the landed interest in Anne's reign, notably in *The Conduct of the Allies* and in his contributions to *The Examiner*. Bolingbroke had encouraged him to produce these biting attacks on the moneyed interest and he now suggested that Swift should write for *The Craftsman*, though he advised him not to revive other old Whig-Tory disputes.[5] Indirectly, he also influenced Swift's greatest work, *Gulliver's Travels*, which appeared in 1726 at the very beginning of the campaign against Walpole. Through the medium of Gulliver's voyage to Lilliput, Swift defended the conduct of the Tories in the last years of Anne's reign. It has been argued by Arthur Case and others that Swift, by portraying Gulliver in the role of Bolingbroke, implicitly justified his friend's actions, including Bolingbroke's flight to France in 1715. If Bolingbroke had not fled, like Gulliver, then he would have been sacrificed by a malicious faction at Court. Moreover, it is clear from all the voyages in *Gulliver's Travels* that Swift shared and sometimes anticipated Bolingbroke's attacks on Walpole. He constantly remarked on how luxury, the expansion of the system of public credit, the increase in the number of placemen and the undue influence of money in parliamentary elections would undermine the constitution. Corruption was upsetting the balance achieved by the Revolution and was destroying the nation's liberties. A dishonest faction controlled parliament and the Court, while men of estates, who were men of rank and integrity, were neglected and abused. Swift feared that under Walpole the corruption and avarice which had grown since 1688 would continue its rapid advance.[6]

Swift's political views, like those of Bolingbroke, had their origin in Anne's reign, but they had been sharpened by his virtual exile in Ireland and by his correspondence with Bolingbroke in the years after 1715. He had even come to share many of Bolingbroke's philosophical views, though, as a devout Anglican, he rejected his friend's criticism of divines and orthodox Christianity.[7] In book four of *Gulliver's Travels*, the voyage to the Houyhnhnms, Swift expressed the same view of man's limited capacity for acting rationally as Bolingbroke put forward in his philosophical essays. Men could not live solely according to their reason, but they must seek to act rationally or they would sink back into the sub-human condition of the Yahoos.[8] At times Swift was rightly sceptical of Bolingbroke's exaggerated claims that he could remain utterly unmoved by the slings and arrows of misfortune, but at other times he wished he could emulate him.[9] Bolingbroke believed that Swift was too pessimistic about the ability of any man to control his passions. A few superior spirits, among whom Bolingbroke numbered himself, could achieve peace of mind by the unaided powers of reason. Thus, while he welcomed the manner in which *Gulliver's Travels* attacked the Walpolean system of government, he criticised parts of it. Pope, his great admirer, explained to their common friend, Swift, that Bolingbroke regarded this work 'as a design of evil consequence to depreciate human nature, at which it cannot be wondered that he [Bolingbroke] takes most offence, being himself the most accomplished of his species, and so losing more than any other of that praise which is due both to the dignity and virtue of men'.[10]

Bolingbroke's influence on Alexander Pope also extended to his political views and to the wider sphere of philosophy. Indeed, he probably had closer relations with Pope than any other in his circle. They had become friends in the last years of Anne's reign and had corresponded regularly during Bolingbroke's exile in France. After Bolingbroke's return Pope was able to visit him constantly, for his own home at Twickenham was in easy reach of Dawley. He was intensely, even pathetically, grateful for Bolingbroke's friendship, and Bolingbroke grew to love him as his greatest disciple. Several of Pope's works, even his imitations of Horace, were inspired or influenced by Bolingbroke's suggestions and ideas. In *The Dunciad* Pope ridiculed a society full of knaves and fools, which was presided over by the 'Great Dunce', undoubtedly Walpole himself. The *Epistle to Bathurst* attacked the moneyed men who endangered the established order of society and *The Epilogue to the Satires* praised the love of liberty. Pope was evidently susceptible to the charms of Bolingbroke's many-sided genius and to his brilliant conversation and personality, though he was probably influenced more by Bolingbroke's philosophy than by his politics. There can be no doubt that the two friends regularly discussed such topics as metaphysics and religion,[11] and Bolingbroke later dedicated his philosophical essays to Pope, but the extent of his direct influence on Pope's most philosophical poem, *An Essay on Man*, has always been a subject of controversy.[12] While Pope did not simply versify Bolingbroke's prose, he did accept some of his friend's basic philosophical assumptions. He acknowledged the perfection of the universe and the infinite gradations of the Great Chain of Being. Man should not exalt his place in the hierarchy and cut himself off from the lowly animals. Individuals too should accept their allotted place in society and not presume to upset the divine order. Thus, the notions which underpinned Bolingbroke's political theories and his objections to Walpole were shared by Pope. The *Essay on Man* was in fact dedicated to Bolingbroke and in it Pope described him as his 'guide, philosopher, and friend'.

The third of the really important members of Bolingbroke's literary circle was John Gay. As early as 1714 he had dedicated a poem, *The Shepherd's Week*, to Bolingbroke. After losing money in the South Sea Company disaster and after being humiliated by the offer of a very minor Court post in 1727, it was hardly surprising that he launched into an attack on the corruption and manipulation which had become, in his eyes, a common feature of a commercial society. With charm and wit he contrasted the honest, simple, natural life of the countryside with the venal, unstable and artificial life of the town. *The Beggar's Opera* depicted the fate of the poor and the landed gentry in a corrupt, money-dominated world and some of its characters could be identified with contemporary politicians, including Walpole. Its whole theme was that the love of money, and its misuse through bribery and corruption, upset the natural social order, the Great Chain of Being. Gay's satire so infuriated the government that his next play, *Polly*, was banned before it could be performed. More gentle and inoffensive than Bolingbroke, Swift or Pope, Gay did not generally attack Walpole quite so directly or forcefully as they did, but he accepted their general alarm at the pernicious effect of money on government and society. His *Fables*, however, were more specific than his plays in their unkind references to Walpole and his corrupt, factious style of government, and in their espousal of liberty and patriotism.[13]

George Lyttelton was also influenced in his politics and his writings by Bolingbroke, though he was a late addition to his circle and did not grow to prominence until the 'Patriot' opposition was formed in the later 1730s. Lyttelton's *Persian Letters* (1735) revealed a preoccupation with the political and constitutional problems which were at the heart of Bolingbroke's opposition to Walpole. They attacked the new economic order, which allowed moneyed men to prosper while country gentlemen were racked by high taxes. There was also praise for the balance of the ancient constitution. Queen Elizabeth's reign had seen this balance achieved and the

1688 Revolution had seen it restored, but now it was threatened once
more. This time it was not the royal prerogative but the undue influence
of money which menaced the constitution. The opposition must therefore
endeavour to defend the nation's liberties. Lyttelton's friend, Henry
Fielding, wrote the most pungent personal attacks on Walpole in his
series of plays from *The Welsh Opera* to *The Historical Register* (1731–37),
but there is no evidence to show that he was closely connected with
Bolingbroke's circle.

Voltaire, on the other hand, did visit Bolingbroke and Pope during their
campaign against Walpole, but the precise nature of his association with
them is shrouded in mystery. As a rising young writer Voltaire had visited
Bolingbroke at La Source in 1722 and, for a time, he had been captivated
by the brilliance of Bolingbroke's mind, personality and conversation.
He described Bolingbroke as a man who combined all the erudition of
England with all the politeness of France, who knew the history of
Ancient Egypt as well as that of England, and the poetry of Virgil as
much as that of Milton.[14] He even wrote a poem which included fourteen
lines of lavish praise of Bolingbroke.[15] The latter was almost as enthusiastic
about Voltaire, praising both his charm and his work.[16] By the time the
poverty-stricken Voltaire visited England in 1726, however, the friendship had evidently cooled, despite Voltaire's claim that Bolingbroke had
offered him every possible assistance.[17] In 1731 Voltaire dedicated his
tragedy, *Brutus*, to Bolingbroke[18] and this defence of liberty against the
ambitions of a would-be tyrant might have been inspired by Bolingbroke's
campaign against Walpole, but there is no evidence to suggest that Voltaire placed his considerable satirical gifts at the disposal of the opposition
while he was in England. On the contrary, it has been suggested that
Voltaire deliberately joined Bolingbroke's circle in order to act as Walpole's spy. Impoverished, anxious for patrons, and unwilling to alienate
the British government as well as the authorities in France, he was no
doubt reluctant to lend his pen to the opposition's campaign, but the
accusation that he betrayed his friends has never been substantiated.[19]
Walpole in fact seemed unwilling or unable to employ writers of genuine
talent to defend his policies.

II

Bolingbroke was both a more prolific and a more effective critic of
Walpole than any of his immediate circle, talented though they were.

While they wrote works of art with political overtones, Bolingbroke wrote overt political tracts. He contributed nearly one hundred articles to *The Craftsman*, the chief opposition journal and one of the most famous of political journals. Edited by Nicholas Amhurst, it appeared weekly after the first few months of production and had a regular sale of several thousand copies during the parliamentary session. The able pens of the best opposition writers, including William and Daniel Pulteney, employed both wit and satire in hard-hitting attacks on Walpole and his policies. Though Bolingbroke wrote less than one fifth of the articles during his years of opposition to Walpole, he did contribute the two most important series, his *Remarks on the History of England* and his *Dissertation upon Parties*. He also supplied over fifty occasional pieces to *The Craftsman* as well as writing several separate pamphlets. *The Craftsman* as a whole was so effective that the government issued eight writs against it in four years. In November 1729 the publisher, Richard Francklin, was at length brought to trial, but the jury was packed by John Barber, the Tory Lord Mayor of London and a friend of Bolingbroke, and Francklin was acquitted amidst public rejoicing. In 1731 the government again prosecuted him and made sure it had a jury of its own political persuasion. This time he was sentenced to a year's imprisonment, fined £100, and compelled to find large sureties for his good behaviour over the next seven years. In addition to these attempts to silence *The Craftsman*, the government supported several journals to put over its own case to the public.[20] The *London Journal*, *Daily Courant* and *Free Briton* all kept up a running fight with the opposition's journal. Despite the greater resources and influence of the government, it was an unequal fight. The writers in the government's service were inferior to the talented journalists working for the opposition and they were more ready to descend to scurrilous personal attacks. Swift, with some justice, complained: 'It is certain that Walpole is peevish and disconcerted, stoops to the vilest offices of hireling scoundrels to write Billingsgate of the lowest and most prostitute kind, and has none but beasts and blockheads for his penmen, whom he pays in ready guineas very liberally.'[21] Lord Hervey himself admitted almost as much: 'All the best writers against the Court were concerned in the *Craftsman*, which made it a much better written paper than any of that sort that were published on the side of the Court. The two best of these writers were Lord Bolingbroke and Mr Pulteney.'[22]

Unable to match the opposition writers, the government press resorted to character assassination. They levelled their big guns at the most able and prolific journalists in opposition, William Pulteney and Bolingbroke. Pulteney was not only the principal Whig speaker in the Commons in opposition to Walpole, but a regular contributor to *The Craftsman* and the author of many individual pamphlets on the major issues of the day. The government replied to him by claiming that he had betrayed his Whig principles merely out of thwarted ambition. His only genuine disagreement with Walpole was caused by his omission from the Cabinet and yet in revenge he now associated with Jacobites. The attacks on him became so personal that he replied in kind and eventually fought a duel with Lord Hervey.[23] Bolingbroke, however, was never quite reduced to scurrilous personal attacks and, Pulteney's weighty contribution notwith-standing, he produced the most profound and forceful critiques of Walpole's system. These were reproduced in local newspapers like the *York Courant* and the *Newcastle Courant*. His opponents recognised his importance and concentrated their attacks on him. The government's prosecution of *The Craftsman* began with the journal's sixteenth issue, Bolingbroke's *Vision of Camilick*, and thereafter Bolingbroke's major contributions were always singled out for attack by the government press. When Bolingbroke finally gave up writing for *The Craftsman*, not only did that journal lose its special character and prestige, but even the ministry's *Daily Gazetteer* paid him a reluctant tribute: 'It was an honour to wrestle a fall with him; . . . besides he afforded matter to discourse about, for he wrote upon all the great arguments of politicks.'[24] While Bolingbroke was active in the field, his opponents were much less generous. Frequently unable to reply to his serious criticisms, they resorted to vicious personal attacks. In view of Bolingbroke's past conduct there was no shortage of targets. The *Daily Courant* of 26 December 1733 asked the public to compare him with Walpole:

> . . . behold a man who bravely fled from the justice of his country, which he had seen raised to the highest pitch of glory and terror; and afterward as it were in a moment of time by his unparalleled skill and address reduced to the lowest degree of infamy and contempt, to behold this man poorly and basely cringing for pardon, which was no sooner extended to him, but he thinks himself qualify'd to write *Dissertations on Parties,* to read weekly lectures on politics, and to spread his rage against a certain person.[25]

Lord Hervey and Sir William Yonge wrote special pamphlets with the express purpose of destroying Bolingbroke's reputation.[26] They examined his conduct in Anne's reign and in 1715–16, and accused him of betraying all those who had tried to serve him. Bolingbroke replied in a tone of studied moderation.[27] He defended his flight in 1715 by urging that persecution had driven him into the arms of the Pretender. There was no truth in the assertion that he was trying to subvert the constitution. Redress, not revenge, was his primary aim. His pardon, he maintained, had been granted without application to George I. This claim was a calculated and deliberate lie. His remark that he was without political ambitions and only interested in a quiet retirement was just as false and produced an ironic rejoinder, instancing all his efforts to achieve power.[28] Even when he had quite evidently lost his campaign against Walpole his opponents made every effort to destroy his credit and drive him once more out of the country. On 22 January 1735 the *Daily Courant* began a series of essays, entitled 'The Reasonableness and Necessity of driving Bolingbroke out of the Kingdom', and his whole past career was blasted in *The Grand Accuser the Greatest of all Criminals.*

Bolingbroke not only assailed Walpole's ministry in the press; he also tried to ruin his standing at Court. His early challenge to the Earl of Oxford's leadership in Anne's reign had convinced him of the necessity of royal favour or at least access to the Closet. Just as he had won over Abigail Masham years earlier, he now tried to exert influence over first the Duchess of Kendal and then Henrietta Howard, Countess of Suffolk, the mistresses of George I and George II respectively. Bolingbroke maintained that he was cheated of success in 1727, for George I would have dismissed Walpole had he ever returned from his final trip to Hanover in the summer of that year. A short time before the King's death in 1727, Bolingbroke did secure an audience with George I, during which he endeavoured to show the King how unfit Walpole was to serve him. When he left he apparently handed the King a written statement of his criticisms of Walpole. Though he claimed that he had convinced George I, Walpole maintained that the King had been unimpressed and had even handed over Bolingbroke's memorial to him.[29] Walpole exaggerated his own lack of concern at Bolingbroke's ability to discuss politics with the King, but there is no evidence to support Bolingbroke's opinion that George I was ready to part with his minister.[30] In the next reign Bolingbroke had even less success at Court. Lady Suffolk, George II's mistress, was on good terms with several of Bolingbroke's circle, including Swift, Pope and William Chetwynd, and she eventually married his friend, George Berkeley,[31] but she lacked the necessary influence to promote his cause. When she lost royal favour in 1734 it was strongly rumoured that her dismissal followed her intrigues with Bolingbroke,[32] but her own denial carries conviction.[33] There is not the slightest evidence that George II ever contemplated restoring Bolingbroke to political favour.

The real contest against Walpole had to be fought out in parliament. The opposition's press campaign did succeed in making Walpole unpopular, but Bolingbroke's own contribution, significant though it was, failed to unite the disparate elements hostile to Walpole. If Walpole's hold on power were to be shaken, then Bolingbroke and his allies had to devise parliamentary tactics capable of translating the minister's unpopularity into an opposition majority in the Commons or in the constituencies. In this task Bolingbroke could not play a public role, because he could not speak in either House. Instead, he was confined to operating by remote control, suggesting issues and supplying information on which the opposition leaders in parliament could act. The merits and significance of the opposition's platform owed much to Bolingbroke, but his contribution to the parliamentary campaign has usually been exaggerated. The opposition leaders in parliament, undergoing the heat of political battle in long-drawn-out debates for session after session, were not negligible figures, mere puppets being manipulated by the scheming Bolingbroke. Many of his Whig allies cooperated with him, but for their own political motives and on their own terms. William Pulteney, though ambitious, self-interested, and over-intent upon points in debates, was a considerable political figure in his own right. An experienced ex-minister and an excellent orator, knowledgeable about finance and well versed in foreign affairs, his spirited opposition caused Walpole some anxious moments. His Austrian ally, Count Palm, with whom he discussed European affairs, believed that his Whig followers numbered nearly a third of the Commons and that his popularity was even greater outside parliament.[34] Pulteney was ably seconded in numerous debates by Samuel Sandys, a frequent speaker on bills of supply and the leading Country Whig. He had nothing to learn from Bolingbroke about the need to reduce the number of placemen and to fight corruption. Nor did Bolingbroke have any influence with such rugged characters as Sir John Barnard, Francis Child and George Heathcote, who were among Walpole's most outspoken critics in the merchant community. John Barber, the friend of Swift, seemed to be Bolingbroke's sole ally among the influential London merchants. In the Lords, Bolingbroke had little contact with opposition Whigs such as Coventry and Lechmere, or even Carteret. He was the personal friend of a few Whig peers, notably Chesterfield, Stair, Marchmont, Essex and Cobham, but his impact on their political conduct was not always great. Essex could not be persuaded to desert Walpole, while Chesterfield did so for his own reasons. Stair and Marchmont were more influenced by Bolingbroke's politics, but, as Scottish peers, they could be kept out of the House by Walpole, because he was always able to control the choice of the sixteen Scottish representative peers.

Bolingbroke did not fare much better with the Tories in opposition. The older Hanoverian Tories, led by William Bromley, Sir Thomas Hanmer and Ralph Freeman, distrusted him and endeavoured to ignore him. William Shippen, the leading Jacobite, and a tenacious, outspoken and honest opponent of Walpole, would never have followed Bolingbroke's lead. Only Sir William Wyndham's followers in the Commons were amenable to Bolingbroke's ideas and directions, but they were never under his direct leadership. Wyndham himself was not simply Bolingbroke's mouthpiece, despite his great admiration for him. He was inspired by Bolingbroke's political philosophy and sometimes primed with his lordship's arguments, but he was also a competent speaker and a parliamentarian of considerable experience. A complete nonentity would not have stood up to Walpole as he did. Above all he inspired confidence and trust, even among his Whig opponents; a feat Bolingbroke could never have accomplished. Arthur Onslow, the Speaker, had a high regard for Wyndham. Though Onslow believed that Bolingbroke instructed Wyndham on foreign affairs and improved his debating skill, he also described Wyndham as a man of grace and dignity, who could rally the country gentlemen more effectively than anyone else in the Commons.[35] Chavigny, the French ambassador, who was in close touch with the opposition, described Wyndham as a man of integrity, with great credit among the Tories. He also added that Walpole would have bought Wyndham if he could, but that Wyndham would only act with Bolingbroke.[36] Lord Hervey held a similar opinion of Wyndham:

> He was far from having first-rate parts, but by a gentleman-like behaviour and constant attendance in the House of Commons, a close application to the business of it, and frequent speaking, he had got a sort of parliamentary routine, and without being a bright speaker was a popular one, well heard, and useful to his party. Lord Bolingbroke's closet was the school to which he owed all his knowledge of foreign affairs, and where he made himself master of many facts that got him attention and gave him reputation in Parliament, though they were not introduced with that art, expressed with that energy, nor set

off with that eloquence that would have attended them could his school-master have delivered them without a proxy.[37]

Bolingbroke had much less effect on the surviving Tory peers. The majority of them, including Strafford, Compton, Abingdon, Berkeley of Stratton and the second Earl of Oxford, harboured grudges from Anne's reign. The Jacobites, Orrery, Scarsdale and Lichfield, could not forgive his more recent conduct. Only Bathurst, Bingley and Gower were as attached to him as Wyndham's group in the Commons. Of these Bingley was ambitious but ageing, while Gower was able but indolent. Only Bathurst, an effective speaker and a skilled tactician, could make Bolingbroke's influence felt in the Lords.

III

It took some time for Bolingbroke and his allies to make much impression in parliament. The opposition was still divided on the old Whig-Tory lines and there was no major issue on which to criticise Walpole. In these early stages Bolingbroke's role was largely confined to political journalism. His anonymous contributions to *The Occasional Writer*[38] did sting Walpole into protesting against malicious libels when, in March 1727, he was defending his handling of Treasury affairs. Walpole acquitted himself so well that a few Tories, including Sir Edward Knatchbull, a staunch supporter of Bolingbroke in 1714, voted for the ministry.[39] A few days later the opposition combined to assail the ministry's rumoured intention of restoring Gibraltar to Spain, an issue which Bolingbroke was quick to exploit in *The Craftsman*.[40] When the King died in the summer of 1727, Walpole found himself out of favour with George II for a short time and the Tories paid court to the new King.[41] Bolingbroke himself publicly advised the King to remove Walpole permanently from office,[42] but his suggestions went unheeded. In the general election campaign which followed the accession of George II, Bolingbroke unsuccessfully attacked the use of undue government influence. When petitions were heard against some of the results Bolingbroke indicted the ministry for the use of bribery in elections and the corruption of members to persuade them to defeat valid complaints. He followed this up with attacks on the way the great financial institutions, the Bank and the great chartered trading companies, used their power to subvert the country's liberties.[43]

Walpole's reinstatement, buttressed by a secure majority in the election, helped to reduce the divisions in the ranks of the opposition. The first two or three parliamentary sessions of the new reign saw the achievement of much closer cooperation between the Whig malcontents, the Jacobites and the Tories. For the first time Jacobites such as William Shippen were prepared to concert measures with staunch Hanoverian Tories such as William Bromley and Sir Thomas Hanmer.[44] Much of this improved cooperation was due to the existence of important issues in the realms of trade and diplomacy, which enabled the opposition to force the ministry on to the defensive. In the 1728–29 parliamentary session the major debates revolved around the condition of British trade and the problem of negotiating a satisfactory settlement of various disputes with Spain. These were inter-connected, for Britain's trade with the Spanish West Indies and Americas and her possession of Gibraltar were the principal causes of her disputes with Spain. Bolingbroke exploited both issues. On the question of trade he seized the opportunity to unite the opposition by accusing the ministry of neglecting this vital source of wealth. While the government, he claimed, was prepared rigorously to enforce the Navigation Acts and to prosecute merchants who unwittingly broke the law, it was quite content to allow corrupt practices to flourish in the customs office and especially at Gibraltar.[45] Most of his criticisms, however, were reserved for the government's preference for the great trading companies at the expense of the smaller traders. By urging the need to investigate the conduct of the South Sea Company and the operation of the Asiento, he could appeal to the prejudices of Whig traders and Tory squires. By censuring the government for allowing the fleet to remain inactive, while the Spaniards ill-treated British traders with impunity, he could tap self-interest and patriotism at the same time. The independent members might come to fear that the government's weakness would embolden the French and the Dutch to threaten British colonies throughout the world.[46]

The opposition's campaign, however, was hampered by the complexity of the European diplomatic situation which caused divisions within its own ranks as well as between the leading ministers. Walpole and Townshend differed in their response to the recurring disputes with Spain and the Emperor. Britain was at odds with the Emperor over the Ostend Company in the Austrian Netherlands, that threatened to compete with the East India Company, and at odds with the Spanish, who demanded the return of Gibraltar and Minorca and who were dissatisfied with the trading concessions granted to Britain in 1713. These problems threatened to become much more serious when the Emperor and the Spanish temporarily forgot their own interminable disputes and agreed to support each other in their disputes with Britain. Townshend responded to this danger with ambitious plans for defensive alliances with the other European powers. His first step in this direction was the Treaty of Hanover in 1725, which linked Britain with France and Prussia. Walpole disliked this diplomacy, which was expensive and continually threatened to bring about dangerous confrontations. It forced him to raise the land tax to four shillings in the pound, to hire Hessian troops and to defend Gibraltar from Spanish attacks. He preferred to open negotiations with the Austrians at Soissons and with the Spanish at Seville in order to resolve their old disputes and their differences with Britain peacefully and to ease his own problems in the Commons. The opposition failed to widen the breach between Walpole and Townshend, because it too could not agree on a united policy but was also in contact with both the Austrians and the Spanish. Pulteney was on very close terms with the Austrian ambassador, Count Palm, while Bolingbroke alarmed both Pulteney and Wyndham by his efforts to get information from his friends in France.[47] The complexity and uncertainty of European affairs did not prevent the opposition from accusing the government of indecision, though its attacks failed to carry conviction when it could not agree on an alternative policy. Bolingbroke contented himself with negative criticisms of the ministry's conduct of diplomacy. He maintained that the real problems were of recent origin. The ministry had mishandled affairs since the Treaty of Hanover in 1725 and could not claim that it had inherited its diplomatic headache. It appeared to have no conception of the various negotiations between the great European powers and had been caught unprepared by the new friendship between Spain and Austria, and the breach between France and Spain. The country's trade was suffering from both the depredations of the Spanish and the concessions granted to the Ostend Company in the Austrian Netherlands. Britain's trading privileges and her colonies, especially Gibraltar, were in grave danger. Both the first Treaty of Vienna, which had allied Spain and the Emperor, and Britain's negotiations with the Emperor at Soissons threatened her interests.[48]

Despite this onslaught, the opposition was not particularly effective until the government had committed itself to a definite policy. In November 1729 Britain signed the Treaty of Seville, which appeared to solve both the Austro-Spanish disputes in Italy and the British-Spanish trading quarrels in the Caribbean. Walpole hailed this as a diplomatic triumph, but it caused an irreparable breach with Townshend and it aroused the suspicions of several City merchants and many country gentlemen. As a result the opposition in the 1730 session was more substantial than at any time since the first two years of Walpole's administration. In the debate on the Treaty of Seville the opposition mustered 129 votes, a marked increase. The employment of Hessian troops was unnecessary, the opposition claimed, if the treaty were adequate, and it was a breach of the Act of Settlement if they were needed solely for the defence of Hanover. On this issue Walpole's majority dropped to 79, the lowest since he came to power.[49] Bolingbroke broadcast these criticisms beyond the confines of parliament. He attacked the treaty for its failure to safeguard Britain's trading interests and even over the arrangements for the disposal of the Italian duchies. Though he offered qualified approval of the plans to reduce the size of the army, he wrote scathingly of Hessian troops being paid while English forces were disbanded.[50] These objections were soon relegated to secondary importance when Bolingbroke and the opposition found that the case of Dunkirk was a much better stick with which to beat the ministry.

In the autumn of 1729 Bolingbroke toured the Netherlands and northwest France, visiting Ostend and Calais. This visit and his connections in France probably led him to suspect that the French were rebuilding the harbour and fortifications of Dunkirk contrary to the terms of the Treaty of Utrecht. At his own expense he organised further investigations of Dunkirk itself and sent over his own secretary Brinsden to make a full report.[51] Bolingbroke and Sir William Wyndham believed that this could be political dynamite, but, to have the maximum effect on the independent members, they thought it should be sprung on the ministry before Walpole could take remedial action. To ensure that Walpole was kept in the dark, Wyndham invited about thirty of his supporters to dinner to discuss what issues they could take up with the ministry, but he said absolutely nothing about Dunkirk. If Walpole had any spies at the table, then he would have been lulled into a false sense of security.[52] This subterfuge was continued, on 10 February 1730, when Wyndham asked for a debate on the state of the nation, but refused to ask for any particular papers in case this gave the ministry an excuse to put off the debate for several days. When he was granted the debate Wyndham opened quietly about the state of foreign affairs and the condition of Britain's trade before dropping his bombshell: 'I have in my hand an account that Dunkirk harbour is restoring to its former condition and there are several credible persons, masters of ships, now waiting at your door to be examined to it.'[53] This revelation aroused considerable indignation among the backbenchers and Walpole was compelled to hear evidence, though he did add the proviso that no vote should be taken until Colonel Armstrong returned from an inspection of Dunkirk. Several ships' captains were then called in to give evidence of French operations to clear Dunkirk harbour. This seemed so convincing that many independents wavered in their allegiance to the ministry. When Lord Perceval was sounded out by a government whip two days later he warned him: 'If the Ministry endeavour to hinder our enquiry to throw cold water on it, or to justify the Court of France, they will become exceedingly unpopular, and lose the few independent persons who yet stick by them.'[54] Walpole received a further setback when about sixty of his supporters refused to oppose a Place bill introduced by Samuel Sandys. At last Bolingbroke and Wyndham had discovered a major issue which might dent Walpole's majority. The case of Dunkirk had rattled the independent backbenchers, though Wyndham unwisely failed to press for an immediate debate on the evidence from the captains despite Pulteney's advice to keep Walpole on the defensive.[55] The minister skilfully avoided a division and gained a breathing-space which he used to get himself off the hook.

Colonel Armstrong's report and all the diplomatic papers on Dunkirk could not be presented to the Commons for at least two weeks, though, in the meantime, Wyndham's other accusations about the ministry's handling of foreign and commercial affairs were debated on alternate days. By the time the debate on Dunkirk was resumed, on 27 February, Walpole had been able to lobby many independent members and to secure a letter from the French consenting to destroy the clandestine fortifications at Dunkirk. He also got the loyal chairman of the Committee of the Whole House to accept that the Commons should debate the ministry's motion, that the French Court should be asked to demolish any unauthorised works at Dunkirk, rather than Wyndham's more embarrassing motion, that the French had violated the Treaty of Utrecht.[56] Even this watered-down motion was debated until 3 a.m. and the ministry, to please the independent members, accepted an amendment to drop the reference to 'unauthorised' and simply ask for the reduction of Dunkirk. To weaken the resolve of the independents Walpole made great play of Bolingbroke's clandestine and suspicious role in bringing on the whole debate. Sir Edward Knatchbull reported that Walpole accused Bolingbroke of deliberately engineering the whole turbulent discussion.

Montesquieu, who was present at the debate, commented on the venom of Walpole's attack, which arraigned Bolingbroke as an ungrateful wretch ready to betray even those who served him. One of the independents whom Walpole was seeking to influence, Lord Perceval, noted in his diary: 'Sir Robert Walpole hinted that Lord Bolingbroke was at the bottom of this enquiry concerning Dunkirk, and had sent for the evidences produced by Sir William Wyndham, five of whom were actually under prosecution for smuggling; but rogues he thought should have no credit given them.'[57] Walpole thus cleverly introduced Bolingbroke's name to divide the opposition and stung Wyndham into rushing to his friend's defence. Wyndham reminded Walpole that he had once been sent to the Tower for corruption, but he also gave the ministry the opportunity to turn the debate away from the central issue, Dunkirk, and into a discussion on Bolingbroke's past conduct. Henry Pelham declared to the House that there was no comparison between Walpole's actions and the evident treachery of Bolingbroke. In Anne's reign Walpole had been wrongfully accused by a party which had later betrayed the Protestant succession, whereas Bolingbroke 'falsified his oaths, and laid schemes to overturn the Government, to ruin all that was dear to us, and set up the Pretender, and when discovered, dared not stand a Parliamentary enquiry, but fled his country, and entered the Pretender's service'.[58] Horace Walpole believed that the 'zeal, fire, and good sense' of Henry Pelham 'created an universal spirit, flame, and resentment against Bolingbroke in the whole House'.[59] Certainly many uncommitted members rallied to the ministry, which triumphed by 270 to 149 votes. The minority, however, was sufficiently large to worry Walpole, especially when the opposition carried the Place bill through its third reading. The minister counter-attacked by playing on the divisions between the opposition groups. This was best done by tarnishing the reputations of the opposition leaders and accusing them of following the advice of a traitor to the Hanoverian succession, Bolingbroke. Every M.P. was given a copy of affidavits sworn by two of the opposition witnesses in the Dunkirk debate, to the effect that the opposition leaders in parliament – Wyndham, Sandys and William and Daniel Pulteney – had all concerted measures with Bolingbroke. Wyndham and William Pulteney both issued public and private denials, but they failed to convince many of the backbenchers.[60] Thus, Bolingbroke had found an issue on which to weaken the government's majority, but also learned that his name alone might be used to divert the attack, however justified it might be. His past conduct could be used to discredit the opposition's legitimate criticisms of Walpole's foreign policy.

To avert this situation and to recover lost ground Bolingbroke endeavoured to bring the discussion back to the fortifications of Dunkirk. If members would ignore Walpole's polemics and concentrate on the indisputable facts they must find the minister guilty of neglecting the country's interests. In *The Case of Dunkirk Faithfully Stated and Impartially Considered*, published shortly after the parliamentary debates, Bolingbroke reviewed the efforts made in Anne's reign by the Tory ministers to force the French to destroy the harbour and fortifications of Dunkirk and warned his readers of the dangers which would threaten Britain's trade if the present ministry allowed the terms of the Treaty of Utrecht to be set aside and Dunkirk to be rebuilt. He argued that the ministers had always been aware of the French efforts to restore Dunkirk since 1727, but they had not made any serious representation to the French Court though frequently pressed by the Dutch to do so. Only when the opposition had instigated their inquiry into the state of Dunkirk in February 1730 and had provided overwhelming evidence to support their case did the ministers take any action. The French had then promptly agreed to demolish the new works at Dunkirk. If the French offer were genuine, then the government could have obtained this result three years before. If the French were not to be trusted, then it was fortunate for the country that the opposition had warned of the grave danger in time. The opposition could be trusted to maintain its vigilance to ensure that both the British and the French ministers fulfilled their obligations. But for the opposition the country would have been in great danger through the negligence of the ministry and the dishonesty of the French. Thus Bolingbroke sought to deny Walpole any credit for securing the French promise to desist from restoring Dunkirk.

During the next parliamentary session Bolingbroke and the opposition failed to find another such issue to attract support away from Walpole. Bolingbroke tried to justify his own past conduct both in *The Craftsman*[61] and in a separate pamphlet, *A Final Answer to the Remarks on The Craftsman's Vindication*, since Walpole had been able to exploit this in the previous session. It was not an easy task to explain away his past to the satisfaction of the independent backbenchers. Bolingbroke wisely preferred to keep the discussion about general policies. He wished to contrast the noble aims of the opposition with the threat to the nation's liberty posed by the present corrupt and tyrannical ministers. To this end, and to unite the disparate elements of the opposition, he wrote his celebrated *Remarks on the History of England* in a series of essays in *The Craftsman* running intermittently from September 1730 to May 1731. The *Remarks* examined English history in order to bring out the dangers of royal favourites, corrupt ministers, financial jobbery, continental alliances, military ventures in Europe, French ambitions, etc.; all meant to make the reader aware of all these dangers in the contemporary situation with Walpole in power. There was also a more serious, underlying theme aimed at uniting the opposition. Bolingbroke recognised that the opposition must accept the 1688 Revolution and with it a limited monarchy and the balanced constitution. The Tories must reject divine right, abandon the Stuart cause and join their Whig allies in defending English liberties. Accepting the principles of 1688 did not, in Bolingbroke's view, mean that the opposition had no fundamental differences with Walpole. The Revolution, achieved by both Whigs and Tories, had restored the ancient constitution; the kind of ideal balance between freedom and stability which had existed in Elizabeth's reign. The opposition was prepared to defend this balanced constitution, which was now seriously threatened by the widespread corruption practised by Walpole. In this sacred duty the independent country gentlemen ought quite clearly to act with the opposition. Walpole's system was a betrayal of the Revolution and of Whig principles.

In parliament itself foreign affairs remained the principal subject of debate, but Walpole proved too successful to be seriously embarrassed by the opposition's criticisms. By deciding to negotiate with the Emperor, even at the cost of alienating France, he was able to improve on the Treaty of Seville with a new agreement at Vienna in March 1731. This appeared to settle the interminable Austro-Spanish disputes, while giving Britain the additional bonus of the suppression of the Ostend Company, which had seemed a potential threat to her trading interests. The opposition had tried to undermine Walpole's efforts by exposing the early negotiations at Vienna by means of 'The Hague Letter', published in *The Craftsman* on 13 January. The information was fed to the opposition by the French representative in London and so Bolingbroke was accused of writing this particular essay.[62] In fact, he did not contribute this particular piece. It was probably the work of Pulteney or one of his Whig allies. The disclosure succeeded in embarrassing the government, who protested to the French and arrested Francklin, the printer of *The Craftsman*. In doing so, the ministers over-reacted. Once the negotiations at Vienna were successfully completed the opposition's case collapsed and the independents rallied to Walpole. The opposition did achieve some success with typically Country issues, on which it could rally the independent backbenchers, but this was not the same as generating permanent hostility to Walpole's ministry. In the debate on the Hessian troops in British pay, on 3 February 1731, the opposition mustered 164 votes, a significant minority, but the issue was largely fought out by the second-rank troops on both sides. Walpole, Wyndham and William Pulteney were all conspicuously silent.[63] Two weeks later a Pension bill was actually carried through the Commons without a division,[64] but Walpole was often content to let the backbenchers vent their spleen on such measures, knowing that their gesture could be neutralised by the ministry's majority in the Lords.

The opposition recovered strongly in the 1732 session when Walpole gave them a first-class issue on which to make a stand. The minister planned an important financial overhaul. The salt duty, which had been abolished in 1730, was to be restored. The excise scheme, which had applied to tea, chocolate and cocoa ever since 1724, was to be extended to wine and tobacco. The revenue thus gained would enable him to placate the country gentlemen by reducing the land tax to one shilling in the pound. Despite this deliberate sop to the backbenchers and the merits of the more efficient system of excise duties, Walpole found he had given the opposition a useful stick with which to belabour him. There were strong complaints, particularly from William Pulteney, that the salt duty would require an army of Revenue Commissioners to collect and would hurt the poor most. The ministry was surprised to see its majority cut to less than forty votes. When the bill was reported from the committee the government's majority slumped to twenty-nine. This greatly encouraged the opposition which went on to pass another Pension bill. In an effort to divert the landed interest from Walpole's offer to reduce the land tax, the opposition introduced a Qualification bill which would force members to prove that they had the right property qualifications to allow them to sit in the Commons. Walpole narrowly defeated this bill, but he raised a storm of protest when he suggested that wealth invested in the public funds should be regarded as the equivalent of landed property. He wisely withdrew the amendment.[65]

Bolingbroke took little interest in the debates of this session, but he was far from inactive. He had made friends with Chavigny, the new French ambassador in London. It was to be a relationship which would supply him with ammunition against Walpole, but which was ultimately to blast his political career once more. Soon after his arrival in England, Chavigny had succumbed to Bolingbroke's personality and many-sided talents. Despite the evident displeasure of the British Court, he became a regular visitor to Bolingbroke's home at Dawley.[66] Together they discussed both foreign affairs and domestic politics. While Pulteney and Wyndham were aware of these meetings and sometimes took part in the discussions, Bolingbroke often met Chavigny alone and held the reins of all their important negotiations. In their discussions about the European diplomatic situation Bolingbroke often spoke of Austrian affairs. With considerable foresight he criticised the government's undertaking at the second Treaty of Vienna to support the succession of Maria Theresa. He believed it was an engagement which might drag Britain into yet another war on behalf of the Empire.[67] Over domestic issues Bolingbroke spent much time explaining to Chavigny how he hoped to unite the opposition and prevent some of its leaders being seduced by tempting offers from the Court. The opposition, he claimed, could never be united on Tory principles or merely on shared resentments. He hoped to use honest Whig principles to destroy Walpole's corrupt system.[68] All his views were promptly reported to the French Court, along with lavish praise for Bolingbroke's ability. Chavigny regarded him as the great spirit behind the opposition, but the ambassador was so hostile to Walpole that he did not mind consorting with the minister's greatest enemy. Certainly he felt no inhibitions about meeting Bolingbroke for wide-ranging political discussions. Despite this, he told the French Court that he was acting with all possible discretion and he even claimed that he was maintaining better relations with the ministry than with the opposition.[69] This opinion was not shared by the British government, which began to protest at his behaviour. Horatio Walpole accused Chavigny of fomenting trouble with the opposition and in one outburst he wrote:

> ... he has constantly frequented those persons that are most inveterate against his majesty's government and administration, acted in a strict confidence with them, and especially with lord Bolingbroke and his particular intimates; has received his intelligence from them, given the most malicious turns, in prejudice to those that serve his majesty, to everything that has passed in parliament; and constantly alarmed the rest of the foreign ministers, as if the government was in the greatest danger, or at least the administration could never stand. He lives, eats, and drinks with the enemies of the king's

government, and after a bottle, carries his liberty so far as to joyn with them, as we are informed, in talking treason . . . In short, he is, as I hinted before, the creature of lord Bolingbroke, his devoted admirer and disciple, describes him as the ablest, the honestest, and the best of men, and every body that is no friend to that lord is a knave, a fool, or the weakest of men in monsieur Chavigny's eyes. In concert with this lord, this French minister has, as we have good reason to believe, undertaken to foment a convulsion in this government, and a war in Europe . . . He has undertaken in concert with lord Bolingbroke, as we are informed, to engage to foment a war, as far as is possible, as what may embarrass this nation, and in consequence the ministry extremely.[70]

The ministry obviously kept a close watch on Chavigny's conduct, and Bolingbroke warned him that his letters might be intercepted and decyphered.[71] In view of the danger Bolingbroke was incredibly stupid to compromise himself in the way he did. In the first place he freely discussed the Pretender's cause with Chavigny. He and Wyndham mentioned several times that the Tories had not become reconciled to the Hanoverian succession and he suggested ways in which the Stuart cause could be revived. There could be no going back on the principles of the Revolution and a restoration could only be accomplished by act of parliament. The Protestant religion would also have to be guaranteed. Meanwhile, the Pretender might win new friends in Britain, if he left Rome for Switzerland and tried to conceal his religious bigotry. The Pretender's son, if wisely educated, would have an even better chance of succeeding to the throne. The main obstacles to a restoration were the financiers and the system of public credit propping up the Hanoverians.[72] Bolingbroke never at this stage made any clear plan to further the Jacobite cause and these remarks were probably idle conversation much exaggerated by Chavigny. Nevertheless, Bolingbroke was taking enormous risks. To make matters worse he became a pensioner of the French government. In December 1732 he complained to Chavigny that he was discouraged at the financial cost of opposition and that the money he needed to carry on his campaign against Walpole was greater than his expected inheritance from his father. Chavigny suggested to the French Foreign Minister, Chauvelin, that France should help finance the opposition provided Wyndham was also brought into the arrangement. Chauvelin agreed that it would be a wise investment to have a stake in the opposition, but he too stipulated that Wyndham should come into the bargain.[73] Wyndham probably demurred, for no agreement was struck at this time. It was agreed that Lady Bolingbroke's daughter by her first marriage should be helped with her expenses at a convent, where the nuns were expected to have a private income,[74] but it was not until after the critical session of 1733 that Bolingbroke became fatally embroiled with the French.

In the 1732 session Walpole had been served a warning that there would be considerable opposition to his financial schemes, especially his plan to extend the excise to wine and tobacco. Undeterred, he went ahead with his arrangements and *The Craftsman* began to whip up opposition to them long before the new parliamentary session of 1733. From 4 November 1732 it opened a major campaign on the threat to British liberties posed by a general excise. The administration of this, it was claimed, would require an army of government officials, who would poke their inquisitive noses into private homes and businesses. They would extend the central bureaucracy into local affairs and also corrupt elections and increase the number of placemen in the Commons. By December, London and several provincial towns had instructed their members to resist in the Commons any plan to extend the excise. In London the opposition was particularly fierce. The Whig, Sir John Barnard, was to lead the London opponents of the scheme in parliament, but in the City it was Bolingbroke's friend, John Barber, the Lord Mayor, who coordinated the petition to the Commons.[75] All this activity had several independent members bending to the popular outcry, even before the session opened, yet Walpole remained confident of his ability to present his scheme in a favourable light and of his capacity to dominate the Commons.

With the political world in a state of tremendous excitement and with the opposition facing its greatest opportunity for years of giving Walpole a bloody nose, Bolingbroke was surprisingly slow to exploit the situation. Although in January 1733 he was credited with writing one of the best pamphlets against the excise,[76] there is in fact no evidence that he composed a separate essay at this critical juncture. Pulteney was much more active, contributing half a dozen separate pamphlets and numerous essays in *The Craftsman*. Never an expert on financial and commercial matters, Bolingbroke had burned his fingers before on such issues and he hesitated to join the fray on this particular occasion. His sympathies were primarily with the plight of the lesser gentry rather than with the problems of the merchant community, and he may not have relished opposing a scheme which would help to reduce the land tax. It was not until 17 February 1733, by which time he had become convinced that Walpole had given his opponents a first-rate issue on which to unite the opposition, that he came out strongly against the excise. He realised that he could use the economic grievances of the merchants, the local jealousies of the Tory squires and the backbenchers' hostility to placemen, to unite the opposition in the noble cause of defending British liberties. His main task was to convince the landed gentlemen that their interests were threatened by Walpole's scheme. The gentlemen of England, he maintained, must make common cause with the merchants in order to save the country's liberty. They must resist Walpole's cunning efforts to divide the opposition by offering to reduce the land tax. This was the burden of his first essay on the excise scheme:

> I can't help observing that it hath always been the method of ill-designing men to endeavour to divide the people, whom they would enslave; and therefore [I] am not surprized to hear revived, upon this occasion, the invidious distinction of the landed and trading interest, which in reality are always united.

The gentry must not be seduced into believing that the scheme would reduce their own tax burden overall and they must bear in mind the danger of losing 'the quiet and undisturb'd possession of our own houses'.[77] In another article he warned them that their real enemies were the moneyed men and government placemen, who would both benefit by the extension of the excise: 'I must once more beg the landed gentlemen to consider the danger to their own liberties and estates from this farther extension of the laws of excise.' Besides, they must bear in mind how many of them sat for borough seats where the voters would be hard hit by Walpole's scheme.[78] As he began to perceive the effect of this campaign against Walpole, Bolingbroke shrugged off his earlier inhibitions and became a leading critic of the excise. The landed interest could not abandon its political responsibilities when the government was tampering with the rights of large sections of the community even if the gentry were not directly involved.[79]

Walpole laid his plan for an excise on tobacco before the Commons on 14 March 1733, when, despite his forceful defence of the scheme, the motion for bringing in a bill to put his proposals into effect was carried by only 265 to 204 votes in a very full House. This was the greatest vote the opposition had ever mustered, but even this and the evidence that several Court peers, including Chesterfield, Cobham, Bolton, Scarborough and Wilmington, were ready to defect on this particular issue, did not dissuade Walpole from pressing on with his plans. Only when the government's majority was reduced to 56 on the first reading, on 4 April, and slumped to an alarming sixteen the next day did Walpole give way. His utmost concern was to prevent this defeat becoming a rout. He did manage to defeat the move to hear the City of London's counsel speak against the measure, but he was forced to postpone the next reading of the bill until 12 June, which was a skilful way of dropping it without suffering a defeat in the Commons. This tactical retreat was met with intense jubilation and Walpole himself was jostled by an angry mob which had surrounded the Commons. The opposition's triumph ended with the government's decision to give up the excise scheme. Having bowed to the inevitable, Walpole at once set about canvassing the independent members about the danger of letting his opponents into office. He was particularly alarmed at the motion to appoint twenty-one Commissioners to investigate any frauds in the customs, for the opposition put up a list which included the staunchest critics of the government.[80] With a superb display of political management Walpole secured the election of his list of twenty-one placemen. It was an astonishing triumph which surprised even his supporters. His revived majority mortified and divided the opposition, for there had been strong disagreements among their leaders about this plan to inquire into the alleged abuses in the customs service. Lord Perceval, an independent member himself, believed that the move had cost the opposition many uncommitted backbenchers. Pulteney had foreseen trouble with the neutral Whigs and so he had drawn up a list composed entirely of Whigs, including some friendly towards the government. Wyndham had rebelled against this suggestion and had insisted that he and several other Tories should be included in the opposition list. When Pulteney reluctantly complied he placated his Tory allies, but lost the support of the independent Whigs. Independents, such as Lord Perceval, still suspected that the Tories were not loyal to the Hanoverian dynasty.[81]

This was an indictment of the opposition's attempts to create a united party. Walpole skilfully exploited these divisions and exposed the opposition as an uneasy alliance of old Tories and Whig malcontents. He made much of the Jacobite element among the opposition and emphasised Bolingbroke's political record in order to frighten the independent backbenchers. On the day before the vote for the lists of Commissioners to investigate the customs he had called together some 263 M.P.s, to whom he gave a long, detailed explanation of his decision to abandon the excise scheme. He warned them against allowing the opposition to overthrow the government just because of this success. They must look about them and see the kind of men who were leading the campaign against him. Such men were not merely interested in rectifying abuses in the customs. Rather, a push was being made at the administration itself with the design of throwing the whole government of the country into confusion. Lord Bolingbroke, who had once been convicted of treason, was at the bottom of the present scheme and so it was necessary for all the friends of the present administration, of the 1688 constitution and of the House of Hanover to vote for the same list. If they divided their vote by supporting some men from both lists, they would open the door to enemies of the government as it was now established.[82] According to Lord Hervey's account of this meeting, Walpole admitted that he deserved to be reproached for having contributed to Bolingbroke's freedom to disturb the country: 'I did not then believe it was possible for any individual in human nature to be entirely devoid of all shame, truth, or gratitude; . . . do not you blindly and inconsistently contribute now to let the Legislature by proxy receive laws from him, whose crimes have made you divest him of that share which the Crown once thought to give him in all the deliberations of Parliament.'[83]

The opposition in the Commons was dejected by the ease with which Walpole had extricated himself from the greatest crisis he had faced in ten years. For the rest of the session they were despondent and divided. Even when Sir John Barnard, aided by Sir William Wyndham, managed to get his bill 'to prevent the infamous practice of stockjobbing' through the Commons, he did so in a House which was almost empty. Suitably encouraged, Walpole was able to kill this measure in the Lords by numerous amendments.[84] When in May 1733 the Commons discussed the allowance to be granted to the Princess Royal, upon her marriage, the opposition was again split on how best to proceed. Lord Perceval commented: 'I was pleased to see on this occasion the discontented Whigs separate from the Tories and Jacobites, because 'tis an evidence that they are not absolutely linked together, though they join on all occasions to distress the Ministry, having personal spleen against Sir Robert Walpole, because he does not admit them to employments.'[85] In the Lords, however, the situation was more favourable than ever. As soon as Walpole had survived the excise crisis he turned on those Court peers who had voiced their opposition to the scheme. The King was persuaded to dismiss Chesterfield and Clinton, and to warn several other peers about their future conduct. Given this accession of strength the opposition, led by Bolingbroke's friend, Lord Bathurst, decided to bring up an old griev-

ance, the uses to which the confiscated estates of the directors of the
South Sea Company had been put. On 24 May the ministry tried to
thwart the inquiry, but failed on a tied vote, seventy-five peers on either
side. The opposition included not only the old stalwarts and new recruits
such as Chesterfield, Marchmont and Stair, but staunch Court peers
such as Argyll and Scarborough.[86] After considerable lobbying Walpole
narrowly defeated further attacks. He then struck out ruthlessly. Bolton,
Cobham, Marchmont, Montrose and Stair all lost their places and the
first two lost their regiments. These peers were all Hanoverian Whigs and
were a great acquisition for the small Whig opposition group in the Lords
led by Carteret. For the first time Walpole had to face an effective
opposition among the peers. Bolingbroke, however, could only regard
this development as a mixed blessing. Chesterfield, Marchmont and
Stair were personal friends, but they were anxious to emphasise their
Whig principles and to clear themselves of any taint of Jacobitism. They
enabled the group of malcontent Whigs led by Carteret and Pulteney to be
less dependent than formerly on their Tory allies and thus widened the
divisions among the opposition. As was the case with their friends in the
Commons, these opposition Whig peers remained distinct from the Tories,
even to the extent of setting up a special club to which they refused to
admit Tory peers such as Bathurst and Gower.[87]

With a vital general election due in 1734, Bolingbroke resolved to
destroy once and for all what he regarded as the false and dangerous
distinctions of Whig and Tory. In all his earlier works he had tended to
attack Walpole as a corrupt minister threatening the country's liberties.
As a counter to this he had urged the opposition to compose its differences
and to end the old Whig-Tory disputes. Now his planning took a more
positive turn and he undertook the task of creating a truly united opposition, a national Country Party to defend the interests of the country at
large. It was a much more positive programme and an advance on his
earlier thinking or any of the ideas emanating from the other opposition
leaders. In a long letter to the Marquis de Matignon on 30 June 1733 he
explained his aims in the present circumstances of the opposition. The
ministry had a majority in parliament only because of the support of a
mercenary band of backbenchers seduced by offices and places. If the
opposition could only unite properly it would be formidable in the
Commons and even stronger in the country as a whole. The weakness
and corruption of Walpole ought to persuade the opposition groups to
form a national party devoid of all old, invalid distinctions. Bolingbroke

admitted that there were still three separate factions in opposition to Walpole. There was a small group of members who were Jacobites more by habit than by principle. They lacked numbers, a general plan, or even detailed tactical projects. A larger section of the opposition claimed to be interested in the welfare of the nation, but their real aim was simply to change the composition of the ministry by forcing their way into office. Bolingbroke clearly included many of the malcontent Whigs in this category. The Tories on the other hand were the largest party in opposition in his estimation and had the support of the bulk of the nation. This group wanted another administration which would follow different policies. Once invidious party labels disappeared this group would engulf the other two opposition groups and form a truly national party. Unfortunately, these party labels still existed though, in Bolingbroke's opinion, genuine party distinctions had not survived the Revolution. There were no politicians now on the public stage who had been active before that date and no party sincerely or irrevocably attached to the Stuart cause. The corruption and threat to liberty inherent in Walpole's system could lead to another revolution, if measures were not quickly changed. Much would depend upon his own ability to unite the opposition.[88]

Having clearly perceived his task Bolingbroke set about accomplishing it. From October 1733 he began a series of articles in *The Craftsman*, which ultimately formed his *Dissertation upon Parties*. This ranks as perhaps his greatest work and as one of the finest political tracts of the eighteenth century. In it he showed that an effective and legitimate opposition could only be based on the national interest. This required that party labels should be generally regarded as obsolete and divisive. In a long history of the rise of the Whig and Tory parties Bolingbroke traced their origins to the religious and constitutional issues which had divided England since the sixteenth century. These differences had once been genuine enough, though often exaggerated maliciously by factious spirits and unwittingly by honest men in the heat of controversy. Real distinctions, however, had ended at the Revolution when both parties had forgotten their differences and combined to defend the nation's interests. It was no longer possible to describe the political contest in parliament as a struggle between Whigs and Tories. Only Walpole subscribed to this myth, in order to discredit his opponents as Jacobites. In fact, the real division was between a corrupt ministry and the nation at large, not between Whig and Tory:

These associations are broken; these distinct sets of ideas are shuffled out of their order; new combinations force themselves upon us, and it would actually be as absurd to impute to the Tories the principles, which were laid to their charge formerly, as it would be to ascribe to the projector [Walpole] and his faction the name of whigs, while they daily forfeit that character by their actions. The bulk of both parties are really united; united on principles of liberty, in opposition to an obscure remnant of one party [the Jacobites], who disown those principles, and a mercenary detachment from the other [Walpole's Whigs], who betray them.[89]

There was now no division into parties reconcilable with common sense or common honesty. The Tories had abandoned all those constitutional principles, including the doctrines of divine right, hereditary succession and non-resistance, which had once distinguished them from the Whigs. The Revolution Settlement was accepted by honest Tories as well as honest Whigs. If only members opposed to Walpole would recognise this truth, then a truly national party could be created which would safeguard the liberties of 1688 now threatened by Walpole's faction. 'It is time therefore that all who desire to be esteemed good men, and to procure the peace, the strength, and the glory of their country, by the only means, by which they can be procured effectually, should join their efforts to heal our national divisions, and to change the narrow spirit of party into a diffusive spirit of public benevolence.'[90]

Bolingbroke continued in the same vein in his other articles in *The Craftsman*, which were meant to prepare the ground for the 1734 general election. In these contributions he addressed the voters, whereas his *Dissertation upon Parties* was aimed at the members of the parliamentary opposition who stubbornly refused to forget old Whig-Tory quarrels. Bolingbroke warned the voters that the threat to their liberties from a corrupt ministry ought to arouse their hostility far more than minor party differences. At least all the opponents of Walpole were united in their view of the constitution. They rejected doctrines of divine right and passive obedience, and opposed the growth of the royal prerogative and arbitrary power. Though members of the opposition might be distinguished by the labels Whig and Tory, they were all united in support of a limited monarchy, a balanced constitution and a return to the sound principles of the Revolution. To achieve their goal they needed the support of the voters, who were urged to remember the excise scheme and to elect only those candidates who could be counted upon to resist government encroachments on their fundamental liberties.[91] In a separate pamphlet,

The Freeholder's Political Catechism, he took the voter through an indoctrination course on the principles of the new opposition. If liberty and freedom were to be safeguarded, then the constitution restored at the Revolution must be defended against the corruption of the present ministry. This constitution was based on a limited royal prerogative, the rule of law and the independence of the three branches of the government, which together promulgated the nation's laws. To protect it the voters must resist government interference in elections, refuse all bribes and elect the honest opponents of the present minister.

In his urge to exploit any issue and seize every opportunity, however dubious, Bolingbroke made a fatal, even a criminal error. Hard-pressed to sustain the momentum of his attacks on Walpole, he decided that his opposition campaign, and perhaps his own rather precarious finances, needed an infusion of French gold. Without more money he might have to abandon the struggle or curtail his press campaign. On 1 July 1733 Chavigny, the French ambassador, suggested to his government that Bolingbroke was ready to accept a French pension of £3000 a year. He regarded this as a cheap price to pay for a man with such influence with the opposition and such valuable knowledge of foreign affairs. The French government, he urged, should take up the offer, but he warned of the great need to keep the transaction secret.[92] Chauvelin, the French Foreign Minister, wrote a personal letter to Bolingbroke, approving of his opposition to Walpole and agreeing that the minister was betraying Britain's real interests. He accepted Bolingbroke's interpretation of the state of the opposition and offered to assist it, and to foster cooperation between the Whigs and Tories and between Britain and France.[93] Bolingbroke was not satisfied with mere promises of support and he began to press for concrete evidence of French goodwill, in the form of a subsidy which he could control and use. Chavigny supported his efforts and suggested to the Foreign Minister that Bolingbroke should receive an initial payment of £10,000 or £11,000. Chauvelin finally agreed to this and expressed his conviction that Bolingbroke would perform valuable services.[94]

Bolingbroke had now committed himself to financing the opposition with French money. In doing so, he gave himself a hostage to fortune. If once discovered by Walpole the minister could finally destroy Bolingbroke's credit and depict the opposition as the creatures of the French. With Bolingbroke's past record this would have led once more to charges of treason. On the mere evidence of the French pension such an

Frederick, Prince of Wales

George, Lord Lyttelton

accusation would not have been entirely accurate, for Bolingbroke was using the money to finance a campaign he had long been fighting and which was not in itself treasonable. Nevertheless, the decision to accept French money was damning evidence of unbridled ambition and political recklessness. To compound the offence Bolingbroke spoke too freely on very delicate subjects in his discussions with Chavigny. He was prepared to listen to Chavigny's efforts to advance the Jacobite cause and he constantly offered suggestions and advice on this dangerous subject and on foreign affairs.[95] Discussing the prospects of Jacobitism could have been construed as bordering on treason and giving his opinions on foreign affairs was almost as culpable, since France was then at war over the question of the Polish succession. Bolingbroke expressed his dislike of the Austrians, a prejudice he had held since Anne's reign, and he hoped that his fellow-countrymen and the Dutch would not be so unwise as to ally once more with the Emperor.[96] He thus encouraged the French to believe that the opposition would strive to keep Britain out of the war and so give France a freer hand in Europe. For his part, the French Foreign Minister began to regard himself as the paymaster of the opposition and therefore as a proper person to advise it on how to conduct itself in parliament when foreign affairs were the subject of discussion. Naturally his main aim was to keep Britain out of the European conflict and so he urged Chavigny to instruct the opposition, through Bolingbroke, to force the ministry to remain neutral and to refuse the Austrians any subsidies. The opposition should be encouraged to support a policy of mediation and to examine scrupulously the ministry's conduct to ensure that it pursued this policy itself. If necessary, the opposition should intimidate and hamstring the ministers by opposing and even frustrating any warlike measure such as a decision to raise a larger army. Although this advice was clearly in France's interests, Chauvelin maintained that the opposition would be serving Britain.[97] Far from showing any hesitation, Bolingbroke accepted this advice so readily that he asked the French for evidence which he could use to demonstrate the irregularity, the weakness and the iniquity of the ministry's diplomacy in the affair of the Polish succession.[98] Such reckless conduct almost defies belief. Bolingbroke was risking his political career once more. The ministry learned something of his correspondence with Chavigny and Chauvelin, enough to discredit him, but not enough to expose his foolish and near-treasonable conduct.[99] A show-case trial, like Bishop Atterbury's in 1723, would not only have ruined Bolingbroke, but would have destroyed the opposition. Walpole was not the man to have

I

let such an opportunity slip and so he could not have had full details
of Bolingbroke's financial arrangements with the French government.
He knew of Bolingbroke's meetings with Chavigny, he probably
suspected that Bolingbroke had some correspondence with the
French Court, and this, with Bolingbroke's past record, was enough
to demolish Bolingbroke's dubious standing with the independent backbenchers.

IV

Though Bolingbroke was prepared to take great risks to strengthen the
opposition, he could not paper over the divisions between the Whig and
Tory opponents of Walpole. As a result, the opposition failed to push
home the advantage it had temporarily gained during the crisis over the
Excise bill. In the 1734 session the early debates on foreign policy and the
size of the army showed that the opposition had no clear alternative to the
policies pursued by Walpole and its spokesmen were frequently at odds
with each other.[100] Most backbenchers preferred the minister's strategy of
keeping up the strength of the armed forces, while avoiding any intervention in the War of the Polish Succession. The opposition fared no
better on what should have been more favourable issues. When the
opposition petitioned against the excise on tea, which had existed for
several years, it could only muster 155 votes. In the debate on the King's
right to dismiss army officers without a court martial, William Shippen
refused to question the royal prerogative and defected. The almost annual
Place bill and Qualification bill were both defeated in the Commons in
this session. Such failures resulted in mutual recriminations by the opposition leaders. Pulteney lashed out at the Tories for still being too much
attached to the doctrine of passive obedience and hostile to the principles of
the Revolution.[101] Bolingbroke's friend, the Earl of Stair, prayed that these
fatal divisions might be healed before the opposition threw away its
chance to overthrow Walpole. He believed that the Tories now seemed
disposed to cooperate fully with their Whig allies in preparation for the
general election. This had not always been the case, Stair argued, though he
did admit that some of the opposition Whigs were equally guilty of
reviving old party prejudices. A united opposition could get the better of
Walpole in the elections and there could be no shortage of issues on which
to attack the ministry. The fears and prejudices of the opposition, he

concluded, were a greater obstacle to success than the power of Walpole and the Court.[102]

Stair hoped that at least the opposition would be able to unite on a motion to repeal the Septennial Act. This had always been a source of grievance to the Tories, who believed that more frequent elections would reduce the Court's ability to corrupt the voters. Bolingbroke appealed to these sentiments when, in the spring of 1734, he wrote *The Craftsman Extraordinary; in which the Right of the People to Frequent Elections of their Representatives is fully consider'd*.[103] Wyndham insisted that the opposition should bring in a bill of repeal and the honour of introducing it was given to young William Bromley. Pulteney had been opposed to its introduction, but had bowed to the pressure from Bolingbroke and Wyndham. His speech in favour of the bill made little impact on the Commons and failed to satisfy the Tories.[104] The highlight of the debate was the clash between Wyndham and Walpole. The Tory leader protested about ministerial interference with the freedom of elections in general and savaged Walpole's personal reputation in particular. Walpole replied in kind. He ignored the real issue at stake and instead launched a blistering attack on Bolingbroke. He described him as:

. . . an anti-minister who thinks himself a person of so great and extensive parts, and of so many eminent qualifications, that he looks upon himself as the only person in the kingdom capable to conduct the public affairs of the nation . . . all these [opposition] gentlemen, with respect to their political behaviour, moved by him, and by him solely; all they say either in private or public, being only a repetition of the words he has put into their mouths, and a spitting out of that venom which he has infused into them; and yet we may suppose this leader not really liked by any, even of those who so blindly follow him, and hated by all the rest of mankind . . . suppose him continually contracting friendships and familiarities with the ambassadors of those princes, who at the time happen to be most at enmity with his own. And if at times it should happen to be for the interest of any of those foreign ministers to have a secret divulged to them, which might be highly prejudicial to his native country, as well as to all its friends; suppose this foreign minister applying to him, and he answering I will get it you, tell me what you want, I will endeavour to procure it for you. Upon this, he puts a speech or two in the mouths of some of his creatures, or of his new converts . . . Let us farther suppose this Anti-minister to have travelled, and at every court where he was, thinking himself the greatest minister, and making it his trade to betray the secrets of every court where he had before been; void of all faith or honour, and betraying every master he ever served.[105]

Walpole had clearly discovered some evidence of Bolingbroke's offers to advise the French on British affairs, but he was probably not aware of the extent of Bolingbroke's commitment to the French Court. Bolingbroke himself began to fear that Walpole might be ready to impeach him once more. This probably encouraged him to leave England in 1735, though from the safety of France he denied that he had ever had any treasonable correspondence with the French and he declared his readiness to return at any time to defend himself.[106] By that time it was also clear that Walpole did not have enough evidence to convict him on such a charge. Nevertheless, in view of Bolingbroke's past conduct and the unsettled state of Europe due to the War of the Polish Succession, Walpole's hints in 1734 were enough to shatter the remains of Bolingbroke's reputation with the independent backbenchers. This in turn drove a deep wedge between the Whig and Tory groups in the opposition. The former were beginning to regard Bolingbroke as a serious liability.

Bolingbroke's fall was delayed by the opposition's desire not to aggravate its problems just prior to the general election. The opposition's electoral prospects looked distinctly rosy, if it could avoid further disputes among its leaders. This opinion was confirmed by the opposition's success in the debate on the ministry's undue influence on the election of the sixteen Scottish peers. On this issue the opponents of the ministry mustered sixty votes, a very large minority. Bolingbroke himself did everything possible to regain credit with his political allies by proving his ability to unite the opposition. For the debate over the election of Scottish peers, Bolingbroke provided one of his friends, probably Stair, with suggestions for criticising the ministry. He argued that the Court's interference in these elections and its ability to corrupt many members in the Commons too would destroy the constitution and vest absolute power in the Crown. The Lords must defend the constitution:

> If the alarm is taken, and the indignation of your Lordships expressed in time against ministers who shall presume to influence in any manner the election of peers for Scotland, and much more against such audacious men as shall dare by themselves or their undertakers, to nominate the Sixteen Peers, before hand, and to impose by their arbitrary will a list of these on the other peers who are to elect them; we may reasonably hope that a stop will be put to such infamous and dangerous practices, and the fatal consequences of them will be prevented. But we apprehend on the other hand that the silence of this House when a point of so great importance is proposed, may have the dismal effect of encouraging some wicked and desperate ministers to attempt by menaces,

promises, places, pensions, bribes, and all the means of seduction and corruption such an undue influence as has been mentioned.[107]

During the election campaign Bolingbroke continued with his efforts to hold the opposition together. He put the finishing touches to his *Dissertation upon Parties* and he urged the voters to elect men of integrity who refused to accept their orders from a corrupt minister.[108] In the event, Bolingbroke failed to cement the opposition or to salvage his career. Walpole won the general election, though with a reduced majority in the Commons, and he swept the board in the election of the sixteen Scottish peers. The opposition's high hopes were disappointed, but at least it could count upon between 180 and 210 members in the Commons and in the Lords it had a talented if reduced minority. Bolingbroke's services were no longer needed. The opposition had largely accepted his platform at least in theory, and could now hope to survive without him. He had served his turn and was regarded by many as a liability.

Walpole was quick to see that Bolingbroke had lost his influence with the Whig opposition and he showed no mercy to his rival. He instigated a savage press campaign to destroy the last vestiges of Bolingbroke's credit with Pulteney and to divide the opposition once more on Whig and Tory lines. Bolingbroke's Jacobite past and his relations with Chavigny were fully exploited in pamphlets like *The Grand Accuser – The Greatest of All Criminals* and in a whole series of newspaper articles. Starting on 22 January 1735 the *Daily Courant* began to publish essays on 'The Reasonableness and Necessity of driving Bolingbroke out of the Kingdom.'[109] When his *Dissertation upon Parties* was published in book form, with an ironic dedication to Walpole, it was attacked by all the ministerial journals.[110] Bolingbroke may have taken Walpole's strong hints because he feared a parliamentary investigation into his conduct. His financial position was also precarious while his father lived and for this reason too he may have decided on a return to France.[111] A third reason was undoubtedly his loss of credit with Pulteney and the opposition Whigs, which made it impossible for him to act effectively against Walpole. Pulteney had never been on good personal terms with Bolingbroke. He resented his ally's intimacy with Chavigny and he also seriously disagreed with him over foreign affairs. Whereas Bolingbroke was anxious to keep Britain out of the war in Europe, the opposition Whigs began to press for British assistance to the Emperor.[112]

Bolingbroke was most reluctant to admit that he was being forced to leave the country either by Walpole or Pulteney. His decision to retire to France, he told Wyndham, was his own free choice. He was neither depressed by the reduction of his fortune nor was his spirit broken by constant disappointments.[113] In his attacks on Walpole, he had always acted for the true interests of his country and without any thought of personal ambition or private prejudice. Now he believed he could serve the opposition best by retiring:

> You are grown to be a formidable minority within doors, and you have a majority without. I am still the same proscribed man, surrounded with difficultys, exposed to mortifications, and unable to take any share in the service, but that which I have taken hitherto, and which, I think, you would not persuade me to continue to take in the present state of things. My part is over, and he who remains on the stage after his part is over, deserves to be hissed off.[114]

Whatever gloss Bolingbroke tried to put on his retreat, his disappointment showed through. He could not camouflage his failure. His departure from the scene left the opposition more prone than ever to a split along Whig and Tory lines. Bolingbroke had fought a major campaign against Walpole, he had given the ministry some hefty blows, but he had not been able to create a new Tory ideology.

Even after his retreat to France, however, Bolingbroke did not abandon his attempts to defeat Walpole and to destroy his system of government. As we shall see in the next chapter, he helped to develop the new Patriot programme, which aimed to rally the opposition behind the Prince of Wales. It was hoped that the heir to the throne would, upon his accession, dismiss Walpole and reverse this minister's policies. Such expectations were never realised, for Bolingbroke continued to face the same intractable problems as during his active campaign against Walpole and the Prince of Wales was even less capable of solving them. Thus, Bolingbroke did not bring the Tories back to power and never saw his Country Party in office nor the Patriot programme implemented. Indeed, by an ironic twist, he served the malcontent Whigs better than the Tories. The latter increasingly retreated into the position of a permanent Country opposition, whereas the discontented Whigs were given a respectable opposition platform, which they did not intend to carry through, but which occasionally helped them to rally enough independent support to push a few of them into office.

CHAPTER 13

The Spirit of Patriotism

NEAR the end of May 1735 Bolingbroke left England with Lord Berkeley, who needed to travel because of his health, and in June he settled at Chanteloup, near Amboise, in Touraine, northern France. During his stay there he made several visits to Paris, where he sought out Lord Waldegrave, the British ambassador, hoping to keep in contact with the Court in London.[1] Within a year he had reconciled himself to a long stay in France and moved to Argeville, near Fontainebleau, where he lived until his final return to England in 1744. He did pay several visits to England before that date, mainly to settle his financial affairs and to keep in contact with his friends. His father lived until 1742 and so Bolingbroke's financial position remained precarious. He was forced to sell Dawley, but he was mortified to discover that prospective buyers resisted his attempts to clinch a quick deal, hoping that he would be compelled to reduce his price. Unable to live very long off his capital and reluctant to take on any more debts, he feared he would have to accept less than Dawley was worth.[2] From July 1738 to mid-April 1739 he stayed at Twickenham with Alexander Pope while he tried to negotiate the sale of his small estate. After protracted discussions he eventually got a reasonable price.[3] During this visit Bolingbroke probably left with Pope the manuscripts of his new works on politics, which he agreed could be circulated among his closest friends. Pope feared that he might never see his great friend again, but Bolingbroke visited him again in 1742 and 1743–44 when he came over to secure his inheritance after the death of his father. In 1744 he was able to resettle at his ancestral home at Battersea.

In his rural retreats in France, Bolingbroke once more lived like a country gentleman and retired scholar. While his enemies accused him of importing cargoes of prostitutes, he protested that his greatest pleasure was hunting wild boars in the forest of Fontainebleau. His letters to his friends were certainly full of requests for the best horses and hounds they could find him.[4] Yet he was not isolated from the world. He had many

French friends, particularly the Marquis de Matignon and Chavigny, and he welcomed a succession of visitors from England. Lord Berkeley stayed several months with him, and the Duke and Duchess of Queensberry settled in the same area for some time. Lord Chesterfield, Lord March-mont, Lord Essex and the Countess of Denbigh all visited him while Wyndham, Lord Gower and John Hynde Cotton all asked him to guide and advise their sons during their visits to France.[5] When not welcoming friends, Bolingbroke kept busy with his books and studies. He revised his philosophical essays and at last attempted his long-planned history of his own times.[6] As with his first exile in France, he claimed that he was entirely satisfied with his retirement from politics: 'Without giving myself any airs of false humility, or false philosophy, I do myself and the world justice. A long chain of events has made us very unfit for one another. The world, I dare swear, does not regret me; and after looking into it again for ten years together, I saw nothing which can make me regret the world.'[7] He tried hard to convince Wyndham that he had grown tired of politics some years before his decision to leave England and that he had not retreated to France because of his failure to defeat Walpole:

> Whatever appearances may have made you and others believe, I have been more tired of the world these four years at least than the world can have been of me. But tho' I am tired of the world I am not tired of myself. Unfit for the one, I can live comfortably with the other . . . But I have always intended to retire totally, not only from the business, but from the commerce of the world, and the conversation of mankind . . . Do not imagine these to be melancholy thoughts, produced by disappointment, and effects of the spleen.[8]

Such protestations cannot be accepted at face value, yet Bolingbroke's chagrin did not prevent him from engaging in serious study. His first effort, however, had little to commend it. Entitled *Of the True Use of Retirement and Study*,[9] this short essay was dedicated to Lord Bathurst, probably in 1736. In it he reiterated some of his fundamental philosophical principles. The universal factor in the world was the law of nature. Human reason too was the same everywhere, but it was constantly being distorted by prejudice and passion. Men must seek to free their reason from such restrictions and improve it by continual vigilance. It was possible for the greatest of men to achieve this in the busy world, but success came more often to the man who retired from the world, where prejudices and passions were everyday temptations. Bolingbroke believed that he had always improved his reason while active in politics, for he had never abandoned his love of study nor was he a stranger to profound philosophical reflections:

> But my genius, unlike the demon of Socrates, whispered so softly, that very often I heard him not, in the hurry of those passions by which I was transported. Some calmer hours there were: in them I hearkened to him. Reflection had often its turn, and the love of study and the desire of knowledge have never quite abandoned me. I am not therefore entirely unprepared for the life I will lead, and it is not without reason that I promise myself more satisfaction in the latter part of it, than I ever knew in the former.[10]

Though he was now nearly sixty Bolingbroke did not believe that it was too late to return to his studies, particularly as he confessed that he would not bother to read the huge number of worthless books written by mere pedants. His aim, as it had been nearly twenty years before, was the ambitious project of discovering the first principles of philosophy and the fundamental facts of life. His boast was that he would reason for himself and not be deluded by the specious ideas and superficial notions of other philosophers. The real objects of study should be God, oneself and other men, and the relationship between all three. This, he told Bathurst, would be his happy task for the rest of his life. He was not concerned at his retreat from active politics: 'Happy is he whose situation and circumstances give him the opportunity and means of doing it!'[11] This shallow work lacks intrinsic merit and fails to carry conviction. Bolingbroke was once again seeking to convince himself, and others, that he had no regrets at having to abandon politics. His excessive rationalism and over-optimism always emerged when he was trying to cover up his real emotions. Yet, despite himself, he betrayed his yearning for a political comeback even at this late date. He assured Bathurst: 'In the midst of retreat, wherever it may be fixed, I may contribute to defend and preserve the British constitution of government, and you, my lord, may depend upon me, that whenever I can, I will.'[12]

Bolingbroke's study of history was much more serious and valuable, although the underlying political motivation can be clearly recognised and indeed was explicitly acknowledged. His great ambition was to justify his own conduct by a detailed history of his own times, but he was continually frustrated in his efforts to procure the necessary documentary evidence.[13] Unable to complete such a work, he wrote instead a history of Europe, mainly from 1659 to 1713, to which he prefixed his reflections on the study of history itself. The narrative section was probably intended as the introduction to, or a substitute for, his history of his own times. It was probably joined to his reflections on the nature of history, when he failed to complete his major task.[14] His *Letters on the Study and Use of History*[15] certainly reads like two separate works. It was dedicated to Lord Hyde, in November 1735, but it was not until 1738 that Alexander Pope was allowed to have several copies printed from the original manuscript to hand around among Bolingbroke's intimate friends in England.[16]

The first five of Bolingbroke's *Letters on the Study and Use of History* present his reflections on the nature of history. As such they bear traces of his earlier studies in philosophy. He repeated his distrust of the history and chronology of ancient times. The only evidence available for the early history of nations could be described as myths and fables. In particular he cast doubts upon Old Testament history, which relied too much on oral tradition. Moreover, churchmen had always engaged in deliberate and systematic lying and so the early history of the Jews, and even of the Christians, must be suspect:

> ... history has been purposely and systematically falsified in all ages, and that partiallity and prejudice have occasioned both voluntary and involuntary errors even in the best ... ecclesiastical authority has led the way to this corruption in all ages, and all religions ... If the foundations of Judaism and Christianity have been laid in truth, yet what numberless fables have been invented to raise, to embellish, and to support these structures according to the interest and taste of the several architects?[17]

Bolingbroke was always prejudiced against Biblical history, but he wisely understood the necessity to check historical evidence and to assess its authenticity and value. He had no patience with mere compilers and annalists, who simply amassed facts and placed them in chronological order. History should not be studied for amusement nor to increase one's store of knowledge. The true and proper object of the study of history was the constant improvement of private and public virtue. The function of history was not simply to describe how men acted in the past, but to inculcate moral and practical lessons, to promote social virtues and to provide a basis for future action. The study of history sharpened the wits, concentrated the mind and strengthened judgement. It could influence the development of a man's character, by ridding him of ill-conceived prejudices and narrow-minded intolerance, and it could help him to understand how the past had shaped the present. The future statesman would learn to distinguish the causes and results of particular events, but he should also seek to understand the underlying principles. By doing so he could set up for himself a general system of ethics and politics. History was therefore philosophy teaching by example.[18]

Bolingbroke clearly believed that history should have a practical value. This utilitarian view, combined with his suspicions about the veracity of much historical evidence, led him to stress the importance of studying recent history. He believed that his own world had been largely shaped since the Renaissance and Reformation and so this was the period which required serious study. All history had some value, Bolingbroke admitted, but a man could only devote a limited amount of time to the study of history and so he should concentrate on the material, which was based on accurate evidence and which was directly relevant to his station in life. This would force him to spend most of his time studying recent history:

> Man is the subject of every history; and to know him well, we must see him and consider him, as history alone can present him to us, in every age, in every country, in every state, in life and in death. History, therefore, of all kinds, of civilised and uncivilised, of ancient and modern nations, in short, all history that descends to a sufficient detail of human actions and characters, is useful to bring us acquainted with our species, nay, with ourselves ... [but] as soon as we have taken this general view of mankind, and of the course of human affairs in different ages and different parts of the world, we ought to apply, and, the shortness of human life considered, to confine ourselves almost entirely in our study of history, to such histories as have an immediate relation to our professions, or to our rank and situation in the society to which we belong.[19]

Bolingbroke's preoccupation with contemporary politics is even more evident in the last three of his *Letters on the Study and Use of History,* which give a narrative account of European diplomacy from the sixteenth century. Letters seven and eight treat the period 1659 to 1713 in considerable detail. His intention was not to write impartial history but to defend his own conduct and that of the Tory ministry in making the Treaty of Utrecht. With some justice, he claimed that the Whigs might have made a satisfactory peace in 1706. By 1710 Spain was clearly lost and Britain could no longer bear the enormous costs of the war in the pursuit of ever-expanding objectives. To have continued the war would have been expensive in blood and treasure, while complete victory would always have eluded the allies, because France's power could never have been permanently reduced. Yet when the Tory ministry tried to make peace it had to contend with the obstructive tactics of the Whig faction at home and the hostility of selfish allies abroad. In these difficult circumstances the final peace was the best obtainable and was in strict accordance with the original aims of the Grand Alliance. Bolingbroke was not satisfied with re-fighting old Whig-Tory battles. He was also anxious to renew his attacks on the Walpolean system of government. The new financial interest had expanded and prospered ever since the war of William III's reign: 'They who got by the war, and made immense fortunes by the necessities of the public, were not so numerous nor so powerful as they have been since. The moneyed interest was not yet a rival able to cope with the landed interest either in the nation or in parliament.'[20] These developments since the Revolution threatened to corrupt the people and to undermine the constitution: 'The trade of parliament, and the trade of funds, have grown universal . . . Few know, and scarce any respect, the British constitution: that of the Church has been long since derided; that of the State as long neglected; and both have been left at the mercy of the men in power, whoever those men were . . . Public and private virtue, public and private spirit, science and wit, decline all together.'[21] Despite these references, Bolingbroke's special pleading and political message was skilfully masked by the appearance of impartiality. With an eye on more recent political developments, he was prepared to criticise some of the excesses of the Tory party before 1714. He was lavish in his praise of William III, who was given the credit of having defended and saved the liberties of England and of much of Europe. The parliamentary attacks on the size of the standing army in the last years of William's reign and the criticisms of the Partition Treaties, in which Bolingbroke himself had participated, he now realised were factious and unwarranted: 'I repeat it again; I cannot see what king William could do in such circumstances as he found himself in after thirty years struggle, except what he did.'[22] William III was the great Whig hero, the Revolution Settlement had restored the ancient constitution, and patriotism was to be the keynote of the opposition to Walpole. In such circumstances, Bolingbroke was wise to confess past mistakes. This would placate the opposition Whigs and might persuade the Tories to accept some of the developments since 1688 as inevitable.[23]

Bolingbroke and the Tories could never accept that the system of public credit and the rise of the moneyed interest had been natural consequences of the Revolution. Their prejudices were too deeply rooted for them to come to terms with these unwelcome developments. It was the principal issue which distinguished them from the Whigs and divided them from both Walpole and their own parliamentary allies. Even when giving his views on the nature of history, in the first half of his *Letters on the Study and Use of History,* Bolingbroke could not avoid digressing to lament the disastrous results of the rise of the moneyed men since 1688:

> Few men at that time looked forward enough to foresee the necessary conse-
> quences of the new constitution of the revenue, that was soon afterwards
> formed; nor of the method of funding that immediately took place; which,
> absurd as they are, have continued ever since, till it is become scarce possible
> to alter them. Few people, I say, foresaw how the creation of funds, and the
> multiplication of taxes, would increase yearly the power of the crown, and
> bring our liberties, by a natural and necessary progression, into more real,
> though less apparent danger, than they were in before the revolution . . . The
> notion of attaching men to the new government, by tempting them to
> embark their fortunes on the same bottom, was a reason of state to some: the
> notion of creating a new, that is, a moneyed interest, in opposition to the
> landed interest or as a balance to it, and of acquiring a superior influence in the
> city of London at least by the establishment of great corporations, was a
> reason of party to others: and I make no doubt that the opportunity of
> amassing immense estates by the management of funds, by trafficking in
> papers, and by all the arts of jobbing, was a reason of private interest to those
> who supported and approved this scheme of iniquity, if not to those who
> devised it.[24]

Despite all his protestations to the contrary, and all his efforts to renew his studies in history and philosophy, Bolingbroke was clearly still captivated by contemporary politics. He was unable to disguise his interest in the opposition to Walpole or in the War of the Polish Succession. Walpole kept Britain out of this war, but Bolingbroke gave him little credit for this neutrality or for his attempts to bring about peace. In December 1735 he told his brother-in-law, Robert Knight, that the ministers claimed the merit of trying to end the war in Europe, but their policies would ruin the nation, because of their enormous expense, and would never disentangle her from the many engagements she had with Hanover and other continental powers. Their conduct had been foolish and iniquitous, and they could not escape the consequences.[25] In the following spring he contributed a short series of articles to *The Craftsman,* in which he poured scorn on the ministry's peace formula whereby France would secure Lorraine. This would upset the balance of power, by extending French territory to the Rhine, thus increasing the threat to the Germans and the Dutch. Walpole, who had criticised the Treaty of Utrecht so severely, was evidently prepared to accept a worse peace.[26] Bolingbroke was again allowing his hostility to Walpole to impair his public assessment of the diplomatic situation. In private he was much less critical of the peace negotiations. The Emperor had emerged from the war relatively unscathed and many people in Britain would be relieved that the European situation was not more threatening. Even in these personal letters, however, he was unwilling to concede that any of this was due to Walpole's diplomacy.[27]

The continued success of Walpole, his own failure, and what he regarded as the steady erosion of Britain's liberties, preyed on Bolingbroke's mind.[28] He could never admit that Walpole had the confidence of either parliament or the nation. Nor could he accept that his own diagnosis of the country's ailments was in any way at fault. The opposition to Walpole had failed because it had stubbornly refused to adopt the remedies, which he had prescribed. The leaders of the discontented Whigs had failed to cooperate with the Tories. They had remembered old grievances and were only motivated by the desire for office. The Tories and the honest patriots had the right policies, but had neglected to organise a systematic, vigilant opposition. Bolingbroke complained to Lord Bathurst that the opposition wasted its energies on internal disputes and old issues. Honest men must forswear factions of any kind and resolve to defend the constitution on the principles laid down at the Revolution, but inadequately safeguarded. 'I would rather be a dog, my Lord, and bay the moon than be obliged to roar and rant eternally in that note which the humour, the passion, the ignorance, and the incapacity of a party sets. The only popularity worth having is that which will sooner or later arise from the steady pursuit of national interests.'[29]

Bolingbroke was still confronted by the major political problems thrown up by the Hanoverian succession and the Whig supremacy. The contest between Whigs and Tories had to be abandoned, because the Court would ensure the permanent defeat of the latter. The factious struggles of 'ins' and 'outs' meant abandoning political power to the Whigs. Even the more ideological, permanent clash of Court and Country allowed the former to hold the initiative and monopolise political office. If he were to achieve power Bolingbroke had to create an opposition which was a genuinely alternative government. It must not be a mere faction, ambitious for the fruits of office, nor simply a watchdog capable of frustrating the more unpopular measures of the King's ministers. This was the problem which Edmund Burke was still trying to answer nearly forty years later.

Bolingbroke believed that he had come near to the solution with his Country Party, based on the patriotic desire to defend the nation's liberties. He failed to recognise, or at least he refused to admit, that an opposition of this kind was only a watchdog of the constitution and not an alternative government. It could criticise passively and it could defeat a ministry, but there was nothing to ensure that it would replace the former ministers. In his estimation, its failure was due to the vast amount of patronage at Walpole's disposal, to the weakness and selfishness of the opposition leaders, and to the general decay of the spirit of patriotism. This was the burden of *A Letter on the Spirit of Patriotism*,[30] which he addressed to Lord Cornbury in 1736. While he expressed some despair at the continued success of Walpole, his indestructible optimism still showed through. 'Patriotism' might still save the day. This was not just self-interest or chauvinism. It was grounded on sound first principles, on the universal law of nature no less. Civil government must conform as near as possible to these basic principles. Bolingbroke admitted that this was no easy task and, at a time when many men had been corrupted, it might prove well-nigh impossible. Fortunately for the good of the nation, a few superior spirits had refused to succumb to the minister's blandishments. Among this group Bolingbroke listed himself and the friends to whom he sent his treatise:

> These are they who engross almost the whole reason of the species; who are born to instruct, to guide, and to preserve; who are designed to be the tutors and the guardians of human kind . . . Such men cannot pass unperceived through a country. If they retire from the world, their splendor accompanies them, and enlightens even the obscurity of their retreat. If they take a part in public life, the effect is never indifferent.[31]

The majority of men had allowed themselves to be bribed and corrupted by a faction which had enriched its own members while impoverishing the nation. This process had continued for so long that only the example of a dedicated few could now reverse it. Unfortunately, these superior spirits had failed to recognise the seriousness of the situation. Their opposition had been faint and unsteady, more of an adventure than a sacred duty. Excellent opportunities, like that of the Excise crisis of 1733, had not been seized, because of the opposition's indolence or inactivity. It was not enough, Bolingbroke argued, to perceive the abuse and suggest a remedy. The right prescription must be applied with the utmost determination. Too many of the present leaders of the opposition had only pretended to desire a reformation of the government. Their real interest was power. Other leaders had been honest, but easily misled. It was the duty of a new generation of superior spirits to wrest power out of wicked hands, by their industry, application and perseverance. The opposition must be just as organised as the ministry. Only then could it reap the fruits of its more honest policies:

> Sure I am, they do not act like wise men, unless they act systematically, . . . a party who opposed, systematically, a wise to a silly, an honest to an iniquitous, scheme of government, would acquire greater reputation and strength, and arrive more surely at their end, than a party who opposed, occasionally as it were, without any common system, without any general concert, with little uniformity, little preparation, little perseverance, and as little knowledge or political capacity.[32]

Bolingbroke had pinpointed some of the failings of the opposition to Walpole, but his suggested remedy can only be regarded as the counsel of despair or sheer wishful thinking. He had defined the threat to the constitution in realistic terms. The root problem was the shift in the balance of wealth and property, which was creating a new financial class closely tied to the Court. This enabled the ministers to corrupt parliament, which had previously represented the landed men. The latter had been independent, because of their property and their control of local justice and the local militia. While they had been able to safeguard the constitution, the new moneyed men and dependent placemen were prepared to see the nation's liberties subverted. Bolingbroke's remedy for this practical difficulty was moral exhortation. The opposition had no chance of reversing the Court's policies, or of changing the balance of wealth, until it could rouse the nation to defend its liberties. A few men of virtue and right reason might combat the passions and prejudices of weaker men. Corruption must be destroyed by a revival of patriotism and public morality. This could only be inspired by the determined and systematic opposition of a new generation of politicians. Young men such as Lord Cornbury, George Lyttelton, Lord Cobham, Lord Polwarth and the 'Boy Patriots' might have escaped the corrupting influence of Walpole's regime. Bolingbroke, however, had made some advance in the concept of opposition. At least he had recognised the need for a regular, systematic opposition and he implied that its moral authority would oblige the ruler to bring it into office, once he had been persuaded of the wisdom of removing the previous ministers. Bolingbroke had not insisted that this must be done, for this would be an infringement of the royal prerogative of a kind which neither he nor most of his potential allies were prepared to contemplate. The King's hand was to be forced by moral persuasion, and the need for opposition would end when the King clearly perceived his moral duty.

The *Letter on the Spirit of Patriotism* was Bolingbroke's way of shifting blame for the failure of the opposition to Walpole onto the shoulders of his late allies. In his heart he must have known that this situation would not be changed by a few young patriots, and he continued to express dissatisfaction with the opponents of Walpole.[33] His fertile mind was soon considering the possibility of the next king dismissing Walpole. As early as January 1736 he expressed the hope that Prince Frederick would eventually renounce his father's ministers.[34] When, a year later, Prince Frederick quarrelled with George II over the size of his personal allowance, Bolingbroke was quick to see the opportunity which this breach created. He may have encouraged the opposition to support the Prince's request for an allowance of £100,000 a year, but, if he did so, he failed to persuade all the Tories to follow his advice. The opposition minority totalled over two hundred votes, but some 45 Tories refused to infringe the royal prerogative.[35] Bolingbroke feared that the opposition was once again throwing away its chances, and he had little confidence in the character of the Prince. When the breach in the royal family was widened, in the autumn of 1737, by the Prince's decision to have his first child born in his own home instead of at Court, Bolingbroke believed Frederick had acted rashly and had then hastily apologised. Nothing could be expected of him unless he built up a reputation sufficient to offer a lead to the rest of the nation: 'Whilst you have weak princes on the throne, some cabal or other will draw the whole wealth of the nation, and the whole power of the state, to itself. Whenever you have an able prince there, he will soon find means of being directly or indirectly, the proprietor of both.'[36]

By the beginning of 1738 the political tide could be seen to be turning against Walpole. Queen Caroline, Walpole's strongest supporter at Court, had died, the merchant community was indignant at the government's failure to protect its ships from the Spanish coastguards in the Caribbean, and Walpole and the Duke of Newcastle were at odds over the

conduct of foreign policy. There were promising issues on which to rouse
public opinion against the ministry and there was also the possibility of
dividing Lord Hardwicke and the Pelham brothers from Walpole.
Bolingbroke maintained his pretence that he was not interested in taking
an active role in politics again, but in reality he was furious at the opposition's inability to capitalise on its opportunities of embarrassing Walpole.
He complained about the lack of concert between the Whigs and the
Tories, and protested that the leaders were so inactive that they allowed
their rank-and-file supporters to grow despondent at the slightest adversity.
When he visited England himself, in 1738, he could hardly credit the
foolishness of the opposition nor contain his indignation. He confessed to
Lord Denbigh:

> I never was more disgusted at politics in my life than since my being in this
> country. Every man talks of them, and tells of nothing else, but I scarce meet
> with any man who talks sense about them . . . I renounce them as I do the
> Devil and all his works. The spirit you saw decline here is now extinct, and
> that of Jacobitism rises anew among the Tories, and that of the narrow,
> interested party, knaves and fools, among the Whigs.[37]

Despite his evident disgust at the conduct of the opposition leaders,
Bolingbroke's eye for the main chance had already convinced him
that a few able men gathered around the Prince of Wales might succeed in
making his cause both powerful and popular, while the reversionary
interest offered the tempting prospect of political office in the next reign.[38]
Bolingbroke was already in contact with Lord Stair, who had been
advocating a united opposition, led by Prince Frederick, for some months,[39]
and George Lyttelton, who had become the Prince's secretary and personal
favourite. Lyttelton had been friendly with Bolingbroke ever since he
joined the opposition, when he entered parliament in 1734. His *Persian
Letters* (1735) had echoed many of Bolingbroke's ideas, notably his attack
on the influence of the moneyed men and his praise of the balanced
constitution. By 1738 he had come to the same conclusion as Bolingbroke:
that the age was so corrupted that it could no longer be expected to reform
itself. After one meeting with the Prince of Wales, in October 1738, he
expressed such views in a letter to Alexander Pope, with whom Bolingbroke was then staying. His sentiments were very much in tune with Bolingbroke's thoughts on how to save the nation's liberties. The age was too
corrupted to reform itself. The work could only be done by the King or
by his closest advisers. They must restore what the nation had sacrificed

by its follies and its vices; they must bring back honesty and honour, which the 'fashion of knavery' had almost destroyed.[40]

A small group of politicians and writers had gathered around Prince Frederick by the time Bolingbroke visited England in 1738. These men had already adopted a 'patriot' programme as the solution to the problem of creating a loyal and effective opposition to Walpole. Most of the 'patriots' can best be described as opposition Whigs, who were ambitious for power, but who were more willing than Pulteney and his supporters to bury the old party labels of Whig and Tory, and who had been converted to some of the policies and aims of Bolingbroke's Country Party. They regarded Walpole as the leader of a corrupt faction, ready to subvert the nation's liberties, and they adopted some of the prejudices of their chief allies, the Country Tories, including the hostility to placemen, large standing armies, and the government's supposed preoccupation with the narrow interests of Hanover. They may have come to the same conclusions as Bolingbroke, quite independently, but it was much more likely that they were directly inspired by Bolingbroke's ideas on patriotism and liberty, which he had expressed so eloquently and so consistently in *The Craftsman* and in his *Letter on the Spirit of Patriotism*. As early as 1735 James Thomson had dedicated to Prince Frederick a poem, entitled *Liberty*. After the Prince's serious breach with his father, in 1737, and after the death of Queen Caroline, there was a positive chorus of praise for the heir to the throne. In 1737 Richard Glover's pseudo-epic poem, *Leonidas*, which expressed the need for a patriotic king to save the nation's liberties, was dedicated to Lord Cobham, the leader of the 'Boy Patriots'. The theme of Henry Brooke's play, *Gustavus Vasa*, was that of a patriotic prince, rallying a disheartened people to the defence of their freedom. Bolingbroke began to play a prominent role in this outburst of political literature. He inspired James Thomson's *Edward and Eleanora*, David Mallet's *Mustapha*, Alexander Pope's poem, *One Thousand Seven Hundred and Forty*, and Gay's *Fables* (especially I, i, and II, vi, xi), all of which could be regarded as appeals to a patriot prince to lead his people. During the summer of 1738 Bolingbroke was advising Aaron Hill on his play, *Caesar*, which was concerned with the problem of liberty. He also contributed three stanzas of an ode in the last scene of David Mallet's *Alfred: A Masque*, which was written to flatter Prince Frederick.[41] This new opposition, which formed around the Prince of Wales, was not led by Bolingbroke, but his ideas had done much to foster it. Once it was in existence the most important statement of its philosophy and aims was Bolingbroke's

The Idea of a Patriot King.[42] He undertook to write this during, or shortly after, his visit to England, in 1738, and a manuscript was soon circulating among Prince Frederick's adherents. This treatise had such an effect that Alexander Pope persuaded Bolingbroke to allow him to have five or six copies printed, for the convenience of his closest political friends.

The Idea of a Patriot King has been more highly praised, and more roundly condemned, than any other of Bolingbroke's works. It has deserved a little of both, but it has not merited the attention lavished upon it. While it was certainly his most philosophical treatise on politics and the most high-flown in style, it does not rank so high as the *Dissertation upon Parties* or *A Letter to Sir William Windham*, either as an answer to contemporary political problems or in its grasp of precisely what those problems were. Bolingbroke claimed that it was only for the amusement of his friends and not for the instruction of mankind,[43] but there can be no doubt that he had in mind both an immediate political objective and a more general concern for the judgement of posterity. Even in his most polemical works Bolingbroke had tried to rise above temporary expedients and to project his political ideas onto a wider canvas. This treatise was his most ambitious attempt to link his immediate political aims to his general philosophical maxims about the nature of government. It was consciously modelled on Machiavelli's *The Prince*, for he was concerned with the same basic problem: the inevitable decay and the constant necessity for the regeneration of the constitution.[44] He likened constitutional forms to a living organism:

> The best instituted governments, like the best constituted animal bodies, carry in them the seeds of their destruction: and, though they grow and improve for a time, they will soon tend visibly to their dissolution. Every hour they live is an hour the less that they have to live. All that can be done, therefore, to prolong the duration of a good government, is to draw it back, on every favourable occasion, to the first good principles on which it was founded.[45]

Bolingbroke stated the problem in the same stark terms as Machiavelli, but he shrank from the latter's revolutionary solution. Machiavelli believed that the prince would have to destroy the decayed constitution and refound the state on a new basis. Bolingbroke was much less of a radical, was more attached to the traditional orders of society, and, even though he wrote of the inevitable decay of all forms of government, he seemed to believe in the existence of an ancient constitution, which might be constantly restored and revitalised. He favoured a return to the purity of the original constitution. This policy might be achieved by a moral, patriotic prince, who would eradicate those corrupt practices which had distorted the original framework of the constitution. A cleansing operation and perhaps a few adjustments were needed, but not a completely new system.

Bolingbroke's views on the nature of monarchical government were rooted in his fundamental philosophical principles. In the first place he had always maintained that natural law was a manifestation of the will of God and that human law should conform as far as possible to this law of nature. The authority and popularity of a king were, therefore, directly linked to his ability to follow these precepts, by the exercise of reason and justice. A good ruler must be a philosopher or have philosophers to guide him. Bolingbroke, however, had always recognised that men did not, in all cases, obey the dictates of reason and so it would never be possible to devise an infallible constitution: 'We must tell ourselves once for all, that perfect schemes are not adapted to our imperfect state.'[46] In a more rational world a republican form of government or an elective monarchy would be sensible solutions to the problem of where to vest supreme authority in the state, but, in an imperfect world, hereditary monarchy was more conducive to political stability. Such an hereditary sovereign could not claim his authority by divine right, for he was always compelled to act according to the law, if the state accepted the principles of natural justice. God Himself did not act in an arbitrary fashion, Bolingbroke claimed, but within the framework He had created. Since no monarch could be trusted never to act in an arbitrary fashion, then his authority should be limited by the constitution. The best arrangement for achieving this was to divide the power of legislating between the several powers in the state. Bolingbroke implied that there was some kind of political contract between the sovereign and the people. The former had a duty to be patriotic, which meant protecting the nation's interests, by governing according to the law of nature. His subjects remained free men and retained their inalienable right to defend their liberties against a tyrannical ruler. Whenever the Patriot King ruled well he obeyed God's law. While his people retained their national spirit, they would insist that he performed his sacred duty. This delicate balance, between the king and his subjects, could best be maintained in a society based on the traditional hierarchy of degree and rank, another recurring element in Bolingbroke's thought. Such a society counterbalanced the monarchical power by aristocratic and democratic forces. If men refused to accept their true station in life, or whenever corruption and faction flourished, then society would be dislocated, the national spirit enervated, and the door opened to a tyrannical king or oppressive ministers.

In so far as Bolingbroke was grappling with the problems of how to prevent the decay of the constitution, and how to base a government upon sound philosophical principles, *The Idea of a Patriot King* was of some significance. In several other respects it was a failure. Despite his long campaign against Walpole, and his willingness to use every political expedient against him, Bolingbroke had not established a working relationship between government and opposition which was accepted by both sides. Nor could he reconcile himself to the view that there might be perpetual tension between the government and the governed, or even between the component bodies, in a balanced constitution. One strand in his philosophy stressed a rational, moral order in the universe, the law of nature, which, when implemented in human society, produced harmony and stability. Another element maintained that man was naturally benevolent and sociable, and so he would desire a civil government which aimed at the greatest good. Thus, the common interest could be rationally perceived by all honest men and this should transcend all private, selfish interests. It was, therefore, the duty of the Patriot King to promote the common good and the general interest, and not to identify himself with one political faction. Though elsewhere he frequently implied that the landed interest could be equated with the national interest, Bolingbroke argued in this treatise that all private, sectional 'interests' were factious and destructive to the nation's liberties. Parties were now anathema to him:

> The true image of a free people, governed by a Patriot King, is that of a patriarchical family, where the head and all the members are united by one common interest, and animated by one common spirit . . . Parties, even before they degenerate into absolute factions, are still numbers of men associated together for certain purposes, and certain interests, which are not, or which are not allowed to be those of the community by others. A more private or personal interest comes but too soon and too often, to be superadded, and to grow predominant in them.[47]

Once the Patriot King had dismissed the 'evil counsellors' and had, of course, brought in the honest patriots, who had been opposing them, then all abuses would be remedied, all differences of principle resolved, and the nation would unite in virtue and patriotic harmony. Opposition would then be unnecessary.

In his search for the 'common good', and in his nostalgia for the idealised harmony of Queen Elizabeth's reign, he failed to recognise that separate 'interests' might together form the public interest. A stable political contest between government and opposition could be based on competing interests provided they did not try to destroy one another. For Bolingbroke there could only be one interest, the public good. He had failed to achieve this through the creation of a patriotic Country Party, so now he turned to the Patriot King. Corruption had gone too far to be resisted successfully by the landed interest or a few superior spirits. He now appeared to regard political degeneration as inevitable and not merely due to a shift in the balance of the constitution as the result of the rise of new financial and moneyed interests. The only solution was the humanist prince. After wrestling for years with the problem of forming an effective opposition, Bolingbroke had produced a superficial answer. Opposition was legitimate but generally unavailing, when a government grew too corrupt and tyrannical. When a patriotic government was in office there was no need for an opposition. He had virtually ignored the problem of creating a political structure, with a constitutional government and a legitimate opposition. Whigs and Tories, 'ins' and 'outs', were rejected as representing sectional interests and competing factions. The people were too corrupt to support a rational Country Party. Bolingbroke turned his back on the question of how to develop political parties, which were based on separate vested interests, but which recognised each other's right to exist and which accepted the general framework of the balanced constitution. This would allow them to compete peacefully for the ear of the king and the support of the people, and to form a government and a loyal opposition, ready to switch roles when circumstances altered. He hankered instead for the medieval notion of an ideal state and a traditional society, based on harmonious interests. *The Idea of a Patriot King* was a confession of his failure to solve contemporary political problems to his own satisfaction, except by turning the clock back to some mythical past.

When he moved from the general to the particular, in order to examine what policies the Patriot King should pursue to restore the nation's liberties, Bolingbroke's suggestions were even more facile and imprecise. A Patriot King, he maintained, would be truly virtuous and, from the moment of his accession, he would be dedicated to the eradication of corruption. Factious ministers would be turned out and replaced by wise and trusty counsellors, who would put their master's principles into effect. Such advisers might usually be found among the opponents of the previous regime, though some of these might have pursued the honest course of action only because they were out of office themselves. This was a direct hit at men such as William Pulteney, but Bolingbroke was sure that the new ruler could find wise ministers (like himself), who would only be concerned with the judgement of posterity and not with the short-term aims of the vulgar herd. With such guides and advisers, the Patriot King would rule in the interests of all and not for the advantage of a particular party: 'To espouse no party, but to govern like the common father of his people, is so essential to the character of a Patriot King, that he who does otherwise forfeits the title . . . party is a political evil, and faction is the worst of all parties.'[48] The Patriot King might come to the throne after a period in which an opposition had legitimately sought the redress of real grievances. In such a case the new ruler might have to turn to this one group for his ministers, but this would only be a temporary solution. With his new government he would soon restore the constitution and revive national unity. He must be on his guard lest his ministers should attempt to brand all their opponents as his enemies, or else he would unwittingly become a party leader. Prudent measures, however, could heal all party divisions. Whigs and Tories had once supported rival claimants to the throne, but genuine parties no longer existed. A stubborn group of Jacobites still remained, but the real threat to the constitution was the corrupt faction which enjoyed royal favour. The Patriot King would have to deal with this menace. Thus, Bolingbroke made it clear that this treatise was a manual for the heir to George II. In many ways it was also the culmination of Bolingbroke's campaign against the distinctions of Whig and Tory. The names might survive to stir up animosity, but the real causes, which had once divided them, no longer subsisted. Party labels had frustrated Bolingbroke's political ambitions, because men believed that they represented serious differences of principle. In Bolingbroke's estimation this was a dangerous misconception: 'A man who has not seen the inside of parties, nor had the opportunities to examine nearly their secret motives, can hardly conceive how little a share principle of any sort, though principle of some sort or other he always pretended, has in the determination of their conduct.'[49]

The more general aims of the Patriot King, Bolingbroke wrote, must be to promote the spiritual welfare of the nation and develop its trade and commerce, though too much wealth and luxury might enervate his subjects. Trade and agriculture should be the special concern of the ruler. Government expenditure should be restricted as far as possible, so that taxation should be light and the national debt repaid. While on this theme, Bolingbroke could not forbear giving vent to his hostility to the existing system of public credit. The Patriot King 'will not continue national debts, by all sorts of political and other profusion; nor, more wickedly still, by a settled purpose of oppressing and impoverishing the people; that he may with greater ease corrupt some, and govern the whole, according to the dictates of his passions and arbitrary will.'[50] In international relations the king would strive to maintain the balance of power. War should be avoided as an expensive and wasteful exercise. If he were forced into war he should place greater trust in the navy. On no account should the army be used to protect the particular interests of other states. In peacetime a large standing army was a constant threat to the nation's liberties. Finally, to ensure that he was properly advised and that the country was justly administered, he should keep his favourites and courtiers out of office and not regard his ministers as his boon companions. This whole programme reflected Bolingbroke's own prejudices and his concern with the existing political situation in Britain. While castigating Walpole, he admitted that the nation was now too corrupt to save itself. The country needed a miracle, 'a Patriot King, the most uncommon of all phenomena in the physical or moral world'.[51] Moreover, the Patriot King's policies were the unrealistic ideals of the Tory country gentlemen, the natural backbenchers. This utopian treatise was also Bolingbroke's confession that he could not create an opposition to defeat Walpole.

The opposition group, gathered around Prince Frederick, was blind to many of the shortcomings of this work, since it could be used to promote its campaign. Its leaders were particularly interested in Bolingbroke's attacks on party divisions, since they, too, were beginning to press for a 'broad-bottomed' administration, which would include the best men, irrespective of the labels Whig and Tory. In order to justify his criticisms and to expand his arguments, Bolingbroke wrote, in about 1739, a short pamphlet entitled *Of the State of Parties at the Accession of King George the First*.[52] His aim was to persuade the new generation of 'patriots' to ignore the labels Whig and Tory. The Tories had been unjustly accused of Jacobite sympathies, but they had never seriously plotted in Anne's reign to frustrate the Hanoverian succession. Unfortunately, the weakness of the Earl of Oxford and the selfish interests of the Whigs had left the Tories divided in 1714. Nevertheless, they had loyally accepted George I, until his Whig ministers had encouraged him to persecute and proscribe their opponents. It was this action which created a Jacobite party. The Whigs had then degenerated into a faction, which placed narrow party advantage above the national interest. Government by faction had divided the nation far more than had the Whigs and Tories, and had produced more mischief. Only a coalition of the two parties and an end to invidious distinctions could retrieve the situation. Bolingbroke claimed that he himself had initiated such a process, but the task had been unaccountably neglected in the last few years. The opponents of Walpole must revive this noble endeavour, 'till it become a union of the head with the members, as well as of the members with one another: and that such a union can never be expected till patriotism fills the throne, and faction be banished from the administration'.[53]

Bolingbroke's appeal to the new patriots and to the supporters of Prince Frederick came just as Walpole was meeting considerable opposition from within the ministry over his conduct of foreign policy, and from a large body of public opinion which insisted on a more bellicose attitude towards the Spanish. It was also timely because, since his retreat in 1735, the opposition to Walpole had steadily disintegrated into its component elements of Whig, Tory, Jacobite and Country. Sir William Wyndham had accepted Bolingbroke's cynical view of the aims of Pulteney and Carteret. He now believed that they were only using the Tories to further their own ambitions for office, and that he should unite his supporters with the patriots around Prince Frederick.[54] In the parliamentary session of 1739 the opposition could not agree on how to react to Walpole's convention with the Spaniards. Wyndham's group was adamant that it must show its strong disapproval of the ministry's settlement with Spain. When it failed to defeat the ministry it decided on the dramatic gesture of leaving the Commons in a body. The opposition Whigs had perforce to follow this lead or remain a ludicrous minority in the Commons. Bolingbroke, though he was accused of instigating Wyndham's secession,[55] deplored what he regarded as the opposition's abdication of responsibility.[56] Once the decision had been taken, however, he urged Wyndham to exploit the situation by appealing to public opinion outside parliament. Constituencies, particularly the City of London, should be persuaded to send up remonstrances in favour of the seceders. When Pulteney opposed the idea of canvassing Whig voters in London, Bolingbroke protested to Wyndham:

But what then does he mean by saying, it would ruin the whig party? The whig faction it might break; and what has he, and you, and every honest man, meant by the opposition you have carried on, and by your coalition, but to break the whig and tory faction both? The whole body of the whigs must be re-united, he says; and this great measure, of the city remonstrance, must be executed by the torys alone. I forbear any remarks on a discourse as wild as a dream. Surely a man of his parts must be fascinated, as you say, to talk in such a stile.[57]

Pulteney frustrated this scheme and so the secession failed to embarrass the ministry.[58] Wyndham's gesture was then generally condemned.[59] Bolingbroke urged him and Lord Polwarth to abandon their partisan allies and to rally around the Prince of Wales.[60]

Before the next session opened Britain had drifted into war with Spain, much against the pacific inclinations of Walpole. Bolingbroke sensed that the minister's days might now be numbered and he urged Wyndham to return to the Commons, in order to expose the government's weakness.[61] To Lord Polwarth, a young Scotsman who had recently joined the patriot opposition, he offered the same advice, but he also warned him to ignore those obsolete party labels which still bedevilled politics: 'We, who were before your time in the public scene, came thither when the vortices of two parties ran so strongly round, that, to be drawn into one or the other, was, I think, inevitable. You have appeared in the world when these parties subsist no longer, neither in appearance nor reality, though knaves and fools amuse and are amused by the names.' The opposition to Walpole, he reminded him, must be founded on the destruction of parties, on the rejection of narrow, selfish interests and on those national principles which promoted the general welfare of the community. Those who would re-place Walpole with their own faction must not be assisted into office. The obstinate Jacobites deserved no consideration and should be ignored.[62] Bolingbroke's advice was certainly hackneyed, but it could still bear repeating. The opposition remained as divided as ever. Pulteney was refusing to cooperate with the Tories and was following an erratic course. During the 1739–40 session he failed to press home the attack on Walpole's foreign policy, because of his fear of an effective alliance between Wyndham's Tories and the patriots around Prince Frederick. His personal ambition, and his support for such measures as a Turnpike bill which could only be regarded as a piece of jobbery, was beginning to arouse considerable hostility among the patriot opposition.[63] Bolingbroke had long suspected that Pulteney's only aim was to fill Walpole's place, but he was just as dissatisfied at the obstinate way in which the Tories clung to outmoded political views and prevented the creation of an effective opposition.[64]

After a disappointing session Sir William Wyndham, whose state of health was now giving cause for concern, and Lord Polwarth, who had in fact just succeeded his father as the Earl of Marchmont, visited Bolingbroke in France to tell him of the state of the opposition. They brought bad news, but worse was to follow. Within days of his return to England Sir William Wyndham died. His death was a disaster for the group of Tories, who had been one of the most stable elements in the Commons since the Hanoverian succession. Numerically quite strong, but with too many natural backbenchers in its ranks, this group had depended on Wyndham's active leadership in the Commons and Bolingbroke's inspiration in the press. Moreover, Wyndham's personal integrity had made him a vital link in the new patriot opposition, for he could not only control most of the Tories, but was acceptable to those opposition politicians, the 'patriots', who regarded themselves as more honest and disinterested than Carteret and Pulteney. George Lyttelton, a young 'patriot', believed that only Wyndham could have created a formidable new opposition by uniting his Tory followers with the supporters of Prince Frederick. His loss was an incalculable blow to the efforts to form an effective patriot party; he was

of the utmost importance to his country in the present conjunction. He was the centre of union of the honest men of all parties. His credit in Parliament was the only check to the corrupt part of the Whig opposition, and his influence with the Tories the only means of keeping that Party in any system of rational measures. Now he is gone, those who look towards the Court will pursue their schemes with little or no difficulty, without any regard to the coalition, or to any material reformation of Government, but rather to build a new fabrick on Sir Robert's narrow and rotten foundations; and it is much to be feared that resentment, despair, and their inability of conducting themselves, may drive the Tories back into their old prejudices, heat, and extravagance.[65]

Bolingbroke grieved over the loss of his closest political friend, and he was only too well aware of the crippling blow which the opposition had suffered. For a time it confirmed him in his decision to remain retired from active politics.[66] A few months later his ambition had returned and his combative spirit had revived. He informed Lyttelton that Wyndham deserved every credit for being one of the first to abandon faction and to support a coalition which was both loyal to the Hanoverian succession and committed to the national interest. More recently Wyndham had agreed that the opposition should be led by the Prince of Wales. Though still fully conscious of the way Wyndham's death had weakened the opposition, Bolingbroke maintained that Wyndham's cause should not die with him. It was as necessary as ever to campaign against Walpole. He urged Lyttelton and his friends to prepare themselves for the next parliamentary session. With the war going very badly, Walpole might at last be defeated. Marchmont was given similar advice, while Alexander Pope began to press Bolingbroke himself to return to England to animate the opposition.[67]

The next session was, in fact, a disaster for the opposition. With Walpole on the defensive, the discontented Whigs and the Tories only succeeded in revealing their own inadequacies. On 13 February 1741 Samuel Sandys, a leading spokesman for the Whig malcontents, introduced a motion to request the King to remove Walpole from office. With the conduct of the war open to severe criticism, and after fifteen years of unavailing opposition, Sandys and his Whig friends believed they were justified in bringing forward this vote of censure. To their surprise and indignation, they found little support from their Tory allies. Some of the Tories were annoyed at not being consulted about this motion to remove Walpole. A few were anxious to show their loyalty to the Hanoverians and reluctant to infringe the royal prerogative. Many other Tories were convinced that Walpole would only be replaced by William Pulteney and his friends, who would continue the same policies with less success. The natural backbenchers among them were not prepared to get embroiled in a mere contest for office. These sentiments conflicted with the natural desire of the Tories to topple Walpole at last. The result was sheer confusion. Some of the Jacobites, including Sir John Hynde Cotton, Sir Watkin Williams Wynn and Lord Noel Somerset, a few of the patriots, notably Lyttelton, Grenville and William Pitt, and a section of the Tories, decided to vote for the motion of censure. Some fifty-five members of the opposition, mainly Tories and Jacobites, including William Shippen and Bolingbroke's friends, William Chetwynd and Sir William Carew, left the House. The majority of the patriots followed their example. A further twenty-eight of the opposition actually voted against the motion. This third group included Lord Cornbury, to whom Bolingbroke had dedicated his *Letter on the Spirit of Patriotism,* Thomas Cartwright, who served the Tories for fifty years, and the sons of Bolingbroke's friends, Lord

Bathurst and Lord Berkeley. Not surprisingly, the censure motion was heavily defeated by 290 to 106 votes.[68]

The incredible disarray of the opposition was a sorry spectacle to Bolingbroke, who had laboured fifteen years to create an effective coalition against Walpole. He was particularly shocked at the conduct of the Tories, whom he had been trying to educate to their political responsibilities. The divisions among them were a sharp reminder of what a valuable ally Bolingbroke had lost when Wyndham died. In his protests he lamented the way so many Tories had followed the lead of William Shippen, whose influence and example he and Wyndham had tried so long to combat. To the Earl of Marchmont he expostulated:

The conduct of the Tories is silly, infamous, and void of any colour of excuse; and yet the truth is, that the behaviour and language of some of those who complain, I dare say very loudly, on this occasion, has prepared it, and given Shippen, who disliked the coalition from the first, as much as Walpole, a pretence to make his fools break it. What shall I say, my dear Lord? Laugh I cannot; and my heart is already so full of indignation and grief, that there is scarce room for more . . . [Wyndham] did not expect, any more than I have long done, to render this generation of Tories of much good use to their country; and, though he came to it late, he came at last to have as bad opinions of Shippen, as you see the man deserves. But still, if he had lived, he would have hindered these strange creatures, – I can hardly call them men, – from doing all the mischief they have lately done, and will perhaps continue to do.[69]

The opposition remained divided throughout this session and could not even unite to attack Walpole's inept conduct of the war. In terms of forming an effective coalition, it was one of the worst displays for more than a decade, yet, ironically, the general election later that same year sounded the deathknell of Walpole's long ministry. His conduct of the war against Spain lost him the support of many independent members and voters, and his own failure, not the opposition's policies, did most to turn the tide against him. Although Walpole continued in royal favour, the general election produced such a marked swing against his administration that his majority was almost wiped out. Even before the final defeat of Walpole the opposition leaders seemed more interested in quarrelling about the composition of the new ministry. Carteret and Pulteney aroused considerable jealousy among their allies, because of their efforts to secure their own political futures at the expense of their colleagues on the opposition benches. Both men had protested for years that they opposed Walpole's government on matters of principle, but both were now showing every sign of being prepared to do a deal with the present ministers. George Bubb Dodington, an important influence on the Prince of Wales, was highly suspicious of Pulteney's declared indifference to the organisation of the opposition and at his expressions of being sick of being at the head of a party. He urged the other opposition leaders to remain united, to end party distinctions and to bring in an entirely new administration, from which even the Tories would not be excluded. Lord Chesterfield, while he was not averse to these aims, urged the need for caution. He warned that Pulteney was not only in contact with the Court, but was still the greatest influence on the opposition Whigs: 'The silly, half-witted, zealous Whigs consider him as the only support of Whiggism, and look upon us as running headlong into Bolingbroke and the Tories.'[70]

The fears of the 'half-witted' Whigs were not entirely without foundation. Chesterfield himself visited Avignon to persuade the Pretender to order the English Jacobites to vote with the opponents of Walpole on every issue in the new parliament.[71] While in France he also ran 'headlong' to Bolingbroke in his retreat. Bolingbroke was aghast at the continued divisions among the opposition, when there was the enticing prospect of ousting Walpole at last. He could barely comprehend the inability of the opposition leaders to concert measures and oppose on sound principles. There were still two major issues on which the opposition could combine: the subordination of Britain's interests to those of Hanover, particularly in the conduct of foreign policy, and the submission of national interests in domestic affairs to the whims and fancies of a degenerate faction. Only Prince Frederick could reverse this foreign policy and extirpate both Jacobite and Whig factions. All the opposition leaders must cease quarrelling and rally to the Prince of Wales. The task of the heir to the throne was equally clear. In this crisis he must seek to lead a united, national party. Bolingbroke reminded Lyttelton that there were some opposition leaders (he clearly had Carteret and Pulteney in mind) 'who look upon you as scaffolding to raise themselves to power'. Lyttelton and other patriots must thwart their selfish designs and bring the opposition back to the principles which Bolingbroke had professed for years. If this were not done then Walpole might succeed in clinging to power, or the only change would be to see Pulteney at the head of the present ministerial faction. In either eventuality he could see no hope for the country.[72]

Bolingbroke's fears for the future welfare of Britain were undoubtedly exaggerated, but his suspicions of Pulteney were entirely justified.

Pulteney was ready to placate George II by offering to restrain the
opposition's attacks on the ministry. His conduct aroused such suspicions
that his influence in the Commons was sensibly reduced. The ill-feeling
among the opposition leaders did not prevent their followers doing well in
the 1741 general election, for the ministry's foreign policy had made it
increasingly unpopular. Walpole's majority was reduced to less than
twenty and he was at last vulnerable to opposition attacks. The opposition
was still not united, but was now in general agreement that Walpole must
go. On this the Tories and the Prince of Wales' group were prepared to
act with Pulteney. In the first few weeks of the new parliament Walpole's
hold on the independent backbenchers was at last broken and even some
of the Treasury party began to abstain, in the expectation that they would
soon have a new leader. Walpole's majority steadily dropped and he
narrowly lost one or two election petitions, though he staved off an
examination of the conduct of the war by a mere three votes. Early in
February 1742 he admitted defeat, before he completely lost control of the
Commons, resigned his posts and retired to the Lords as Earl of Orford.
The support of the King and the loyalty of the pro-government Whigs,
the 'old corps', enabled Walpole's political heirs, the Pelham brothers, to
prevent a wholesale change in the administration. Instead, the remaining
ministers, notably the Duke of Newcastle, his brother Henry Pelham and
his friend the Earl of Hardwicke, who had long served Walpole, though
they had latterly disagreed with his conduct of the war, negotiated with
their leading opponents in order to buy off enough of them to weaken the
opposition and to restore the government's majority. Pulteney wanted to
do a deal, but feared to alienate his old supporters. For the rest of the
session he dithered between timid opposition and partial support for the
government. Carteret had no such inhibitions, for he had never been
the leader of a large faction. Though he would have preferred to go to the
Treasury, rather than serve again as a Secretary of State, he threw his
weight behind Henry Pelham and the Duke of Newcastle. The opposition
managed to pass Place and Pension bills through the Commons (though
these were easily defeated in the Lords), but narrowly failed to secure an
inquiry into the conduct of the ministry over the last twenty years.
The Duke of Argyll, who had just taken office, resigned when the King
and his ministerial colleagues refused to countenance the Jacobite, Sir
John Hynde Cotton, on the Admiralty Board. This was an isolated gesture
to the principle of a broad-bottomed administration after all the talk of
bringing both Whigs and Tories into office. In fact, by the end of the

Profile of Bolingbroke

Bust of Bolingbroke
by Rysbrack

Hugh, 3rd Earl Marchmont

session the opposition's united front, brittle at the best of times, had finally crumbled. Pulteney virtually abandoned his political ambitions, sold out to the Court and moved to the Lords as Earl of Bath. About forty opposition Whigs followed him and Carteret into an uneasy alliance with the old corps, which had readily switched its allegiance from Walpole to Henry Pelham. Further defections followed. Bolingbroke's two Tory friends, Bathurst and Gower, and a leading patriot, Lord Cobham, accepted minor office. Lip-service had been paid to the principle of a broadly based ministry. About 140 Tories remained in opposition, but, since hardly any of these were interested in office, the new ministry had few serious critics in either House. Walpole had gone, but his former colleagues remained in office, and the opposition, which Bolingbroke had assisted for more than fifteen years, had been destroyed.[73]

The fall of Walpole had failed to mark the triumph of a united opposition party, which Bolingbroke had tried so hard to create by every possible expedient. Instead, it witnessed the failure to devise a basis for a legitimate opposition party in the context of early Hanoverian politics and it finally crushed Bolingbroke's chances of a return to power, though neither result was self-evident at the time. Succeeding ministries continued to face opposition, but not of the type Bolingbroke had proposed and fostered. Factious struggles between 'ins' and 'outs' were waged more to gain royal favour than on issues of principle or on questions of national interest. The Tory squires remained in opposition to the Whig ministries, but they had no desire for government office for themselves and no alternative, constructive programme. The limits of their political ambitions were restricted to influence and prestige in their own localities and to support for a negative policy of Place and Pension bills, and the repeal of the Septennial Act. Bolingbroke saw the labels, 'Whig' and 'Tory', disappear as accurate descriptions of the political contest of the mid-eighteenth century, but, paradoxically, his other aim, to see the acceptance of an effective and loyal opposition (though in his mind this need would be temporary), had to await the gradual reappearance of real Whig and Tory distinctions.

After a visit to England, from late April to mid-June 1742, Bolingbroke was bitterly aware that his major political aims, both for himself and for the Tory-Patriot opposition, had suffered a crippling blow. While he lived he would never abandon his political ambitions, but he clearly recognised that these could no longer be so unlimited. His political horizons had been sharply restricted. For this, he blamed the treachery of Pulteney

K

and the short-sighted obstinacy of those Tories who were prepared to accept, though with unavailing expressions of distaste, the new world of the Hanoverian dynasty, Whig factions and the vast system of public credit. He failed to recognise that his political platform was being steadily eroded by social, economic and political developments.[74] The hostility between the landed and the moneyed interests, which had been a vital factor in his propaganda against Walpole, steadily waned. In the late seventeenth and early eighteenth century the landed gentry had seen estates bought up by financiers, who profited from the great wars against France, while the squires had groaned under a land tax of four shillings in the pound. After the 1720s the land market began to dry up and the moneyed men, apart from trying to buy small estates near London or negotiating marriage alliances with the aristocracy, put most of their funds into trade and finance and developed as an urban bourgeoisie. Meanwhile, the landed gentry were gradually freed from their crushing burden of tax and, after a temporary agricultural depression in the 1730s and 1740s, found they could make much larger profits from their estates as demand increased with the growth of population. Some freeholders and lesser squires had gone to the wall in the years after 1688, and the minor gentry had succumbed to the domination of the great Whig aristocrats, but the majority of the more prosperous landowners had weathered the storm and saw their estates rapidly increase in value from the mid-eighteenth century. At the same time their fears about the new financial structure abated. They began to invest in government funds and joint-stock companies, and to exploit the resources of their own estates by loans raised through mortgages. They also learned that the landed men, through parliament, could control the great moneyed corporations, for in 1749–51 Henry Pelham persuaded the financial world to accept a bill which would eventually cut the interest on the National Debt from 4 per cent to 3 per cent. Thus, Bolingbroke had exaggerated the threat to the landed interest posed by the developments since 1688, and had failed to see how well the gentry were weathering the storm.

Bolingbroke's appeal to the economic and social grievances of the landed gentry carried little conviction after the 1740s. Other factors also contributed to his declining influence. With the death of Wyndham and the fall of Walpole, most of the veterans of the Whig-Tory battles of Anne's reign had left the political stage. The new generation of country gentlemen could never raise much hostility to Henry Pelham. With the fall of Carteret in 1744, and the rise of the Elder Pitt, they had little justification for the old charges that Britain's interests were being subordinated to those of Hanover. Moreover, Prince Frederick, and the future George III, appealed to the nation as true, patriotic Englishmen. While Bolingbroke's platform failed to inspire any large parliamentary group after the 1740s, some of his ideas were still attractive to those who had genuinely lost out through the Whig supremacy. The country parsons, the smaller squires, freeholders and traders, the men who were gradually swelling the electorate in the counties and larger towns, shared his reactionary views about the corrupt influence of the recent financial innovations, and his radical denunciations of placemen and managed elections. Without a foothold in parliament, and with no great political issues to unite them, they could never answer Bolingbroke's appeal. Not until the later eighteenth century, with the American, French and Industrial Revolutions, did the radicals and the country freeholders begin to revive some of the objections to the Whig oligarchy which Bolingbroke had expressed in the 1720s and 1730s.

In 1742, however, Bolingbroke could not grasp the extent of the social, economic and political changes which were undermining his appeal to the landed gentlemen in the Commons. He never realised that the root cause of his failure was the impossibility of creating a united, national party in a period lacking the centripetal force of serious questions of principle. While he recognised the gradual disappearance of the former distinctions between Whigs and Tories, and perceived the growth of ministerial influence in the Commons, he failed to see that the first development was indirectly the cause of the second or that the balance between Crown and parliament, which he so desired, required that some close links should be forged between them. Instead of acknowledging the absence of major questions of principle in mid-eighteenth-century politics, he lamented the degeneracy of the age and the decay of the noble spirit of liberty. A national party was no longer possible, Bolingbroke claimed, because there were too few men of virtue left to hold it together. Bolingbroke and his handful of personal friends, all of whom were 'superior spirits', were the remnants and a reminder of a more heroic age. In a trough of despair, following the dismal results of the fall of Walpole, he saw no hope of improvement in the near future. Where he had failed no man could succeed. Such was the burden of a letter to Marchmont:

The principles of the last opposition were the principles of very few of the opposers; and your Lordship, and I, and some few, very few besides, were the bubbles of men, whose advantage lies in having worse hearts; for I am not humble enough to allow them better heads. The effect of another opposition, if you had men to set it on foot, and to carry it successfully on, would be another partial clandestine composition, and another scramble for places.[75]

Bolingbroke's disgust at Pulteney's conduct knew no bounds. He not only attacked him in public,[76] but sent him a long and bitterly ironic letter in November 1742.[77] He protested that, for years, Pulteney had posed as the most strenuous defender of his country's constitutional liberties. This had won him the support of Bolingbroke and all honest men who had the good of their country at heart. In the public press Bolingbroke had pointed out the nature of the constitution and had shown how it had been infringed. Meanwhile, Pulteney had led the campaign in parliament and had suggested much needed remedies. When he had learned of the fall of Walpole, Bolingbroke had expected Pulteney to save the country from a corrupt faction. Instead, Pulteney had suddenly abandoned the idea of a coalition of parties being in the national interest and had sold out to his former opponents:

> Corruption found an advocate, mal-administration a patron, and liberty an enemy when Mr Pulteney had made patriotism a jest, the change of ministry a farce, and the throne the worst of sanctuaries – What! What could I think, what say of him? I pitied him; I scorned him; I condemned him as an hypocritical senator, a false friend, and a concealed enemy of his country.[78]

Bolingbroke claimed that the country had expected a complete change of ministers and a real change of measures. He hoped that the voters would instruct their members to repudiate the reshuffled ministry and to demand Place bills and the repeal of the Septennial Act. If redress were not forthcoming then members should tack such measures to the bills of supply. Bolingbroke's spirits were clearly beginning to revive, yet, now in his mid-sixties, suffering increasingly from ill-health, and after numerous buffetings and several cruel disappointments, he was realistic enough to realise that his day was all but over. While he never gave up his political ambitions, he was prepared in his last years to look for minor victories and to hail them as triumphs.

CHAPTER 14

The Bitter Harvest

IN the last decade of his life Bolingbroke had finally to acknowledge that his political career was over and that many of his cherished ambitions had been frustrated. Ever active and never recognising total failure, he turned most of his attention to those writings of his which he hoped might instruct posterity and revive his name and his cause in future generations. His last years were inextricably linked with the publication of these works and with the name of Alexander Pope. Nevertheless, despite his persistent disclaimers and his assiduous cultivation of the image of the retired sage and the neglected prophet, political events constantly aroused his craving to play a great role once more on the public stage. Even minor successes and minor setbacks still had the power to stir an old, sickly, embittered, but seasoned political campaigner.

From the death of Wyndham in 1740 and particularly after the fall of Walpole, Bolingbroke turned away from political writing and concentrated on revising his philosophical essays. These were based on the research he had undertaken in metaphysics and religion during the 1720s and early 1730s. Under pressure from Alexander Pope, who believed he would be 'more known to posterity as a writer and philosopher than as a statesman',[1] he set about putting his work into some semblance of order. He never completed this task nor did he ever elucidate a coherent philosophy. Four long essays were finished and were prefaced by a dedication to Pope. The rest of his philosophical writings, which made up almost a quarter of his published works, remained unrevised as fragments or minutes of essays. None of Bolingbroke's philosophical works were published during his lifetime. He assured Pope that he had no desire to make a public attack on organised religion, though he acknowledged that his essays were highly critical of orthodox Christianity. The prime reason for his reticence was his reluctance to face the howls of protest with which he knew they would be greeted. 'Prudence forbids me, therefore, to write as I think to the world, whilst friendship forbids me to write otherwise to

277

you,' he wrote in his dedication to Pope. 'I have been a martyr of faction in politics, and have no vocation to be so in philosophy.'[2] He was prepared to let his close friends see these essays and he offered to let Lord Chancellor Hardwicke, with whom he was striving to get on good terms, read them. Their heterodoxy, he explained to Hardwicke, was mainly due to the attack on some of the unwarranted practices of the Christian churches. He was not opposed to 'evangelical religion'.[3] Bolingbroke was also reluctant to see his recent political works circulate too freely. It was only when the manuscripts began to become dog-eared that he agreed to allow Alexander Pope to print about ten private copies of one volume containing *The Idea of a Patriot King*, *A Letter on the Spirit of Patriotism* and *Of the State of Parties at the Accession of George the First*, and of another volume containing the *Letters on the Study and Use of History*. The latter was first printed in 1738 and the former probably in 1739. Since Bolingbroke was in France, Pope arranged the printing and the circulation of these private copies among the author's intimate friends, including Wyndham, Bathurst, Marchmont, Lyttelton, Lord Hyde and William Murray.

Bolingbroke could not return to England until the death of his father, on 8 April 1742, at last eased his precarious financial situation. Early in May he came to England for about two months in order to settle the family estates. It was arranged that he should inherit the family's manor at Battersea, though his father's title and the ancestral seat at Lydiard Tregoze, Wiltshire, passed to his younger half-brother, John St John. Alexander Pope was delighted at the prospect of seeing Bolingbroke again and he hoped to show all his friends the man he regarded as the greatest genius of the age.[4] During his short visit Bolingbroke found little to his liking in the political situation. His disappointment led him to attack Pulteney's reputation and persuaded him to return to his philosophical studies in France, leaving Lord Marchmont as the temporary occupier of Battersea Manor House. In the spring of 1743 and then in October for a longer visit Bolingbroke returned to England. Pressing financial considerations and his concern about whether his agent, John Brinsden, had left any incriminating or embarrassing papers after his death in March 1743 forced him to hurry back. During these visits Bolingbroke spent most of his time at Battersea with the Earl of Marchmont and Alexander Pope. The latter was now very ill and saw as much of Bolingbroke as possible. He was desperately anxious that his more recent friend and guide, William Warburton, should meet Bolingbroke. Warburton, an Anglican clergyman and a future bishop, had entered Pope's circle when he wrote

A Vindication o, Pope's Essay on Man, which laboured to defend the orthodox Christian sentiments of this poem. Pope had become alarmed at criticisms levelled at his orthodoxy and he had been grateful for Warburton's apparently spontaneous defence. In fact, Warburton was most anxious to please, to seek influential friends and to make his reputation. Nevertheless, his defence of Pope's *Essay* was far from convincing and he ignored the implications of the fourth epistle. He was almost certainly aware that tender or scrupulous religious consciences could take exception to some of Pope's ideas, but he attributed these to the baleful influence of Bolingbroke. Pope was shocked at hearing Warburton accuse Bolingbroke of denying the moral attributes of God.[5] Bolingbroke, who was acquainted with Warburton's religious tracts and who recognised the differences between them, was irritated by Warburton's influence on Pope. He was even more indignant when Warburton criticised his works. Pope had apparently shown Warburton one of the private copies of Bolingbroke's *Letters on the Study and Use of History*, which included some sharp criticisms of the clergy and organised religion. Warburton hastily wrote a few pages to refute these opinions and his uncomplimentary remarks were passed on to Bolingbroke by Pope or were discovered by Bolingbroke among Pope's papers after the poet's death.[6] Even before Pope's demise both Bolingbroke and Warburton knew of their differences of opinion and were mutually jealous of each other's influence on the poet. Pope was naively convinced that any clash of opinion or temperament could be easily resolved once his two friends and guides had made each other's acquaintance, and so he laboured in his last months to arrange a meeting between them.[7] It is possible that the two men did meet, though there is no certain evidence of any confrontation. Years later Warburton deliberately put about an account of such a meeting, claiming that he had got the better of his exchanges with Bolingbroke.[8]

Despite Bolingbroke's distaste for Warburton his love for Pope was unaffected. His friend's ill-health persuaded him to extend his stay in England. The dying poet was certainly grateful for Bolingbroke's presence. 'It is a great comfort to me,' he told Hugh Bethel, 'that my old & long experienced friend Lord Bolingbroke is here, in case this should be my last winter.'[9] Pope, as a Roman Catholic, was legally banished from London because of the threat of an invasion by the French or the Jacobites, but Bolingbroke secretly brought him from Twickenham to visit Battersea Manor House. On one such occasion he helped to save Pope's life by the promptness with which he summoned a doctor.[10] During Pope's last, fatal, illness, in May 1744, Bolingbroke was frequently by his bedside, often crying like a child. When Pope died on 30 May Bolingbroke was quite genuinely grief-stricken: 'O Great God! What is Man? (looking on Mr Pope, & repeating it several times, interrupted with sobs) . . . I never knew a man, that had a tenderer heart for his particular friends; or a more general friendship, for mankind . . . I have known him these 30 years: & value myself more, for that man's love & friendship: than -- (sinking his head, & losing his voice in tears).'[11] It was unfortunate for Bolingbroke's reputation and for his peace of mind that his opinion of Pope altered after the poet's death.

Pope had appointed Bolingbroke and Marchmont as the executors of his manuscripts, but left his printed works to Warburton's care. Because he had to leave speedily for France, Bolingbroke did not have time to scrutinise closely all the papers left to his charge. He had been approached at once by the formidable dowager Duchess of Marlborough about the rumoured existence of unpublished poems by Pope, which could be construed as attacking herself or her late husband, the great military commander. The Duchess probably suspected that the verses on Atossa, in *Of the Character of Women,* were aimed at her. Whatever the precise object of her fears she had apparently once paid Pope £1000 to suppress any derogatory verses. Now she was anxious to prevent any posthumous publication. Bolingbroke hastily scanned Pope's papers, but the only damaging poem he could find was the character of Atossa. Pope may well have written this as a description of the Duchess of Buckingham, but Bolingbroke jumped to the conclusion that it referred to Sarah, Duchess of Marlborough. He was most anxious to oblige the Duchess by suppressing these verses, but, since they had already been printed prior to their publication, they came under Warburton's control. Bolingbroke suggested to Marchmont that they should destroy what papers they could and then persuade Warburton to forgo the publication of any others.[12] Though Warburton had no desire to oblige Bolingbroke, he was prepared to safeguard Pope's reputation. The verses were temporarily suppressed.

When, later in 1744, Bolingbroke returned permanently to England he discovered further evidence of Pope's duplicity, this time concerning himself. Pope's printer informed him that the poet had prepared a secret edition of some 1500 copies of *The Idea of a Patriot King* and not merely the ten or so copies authorised by Bolingbroke. Pope's primary motive in printing the edition was to ensure Bolingbroke's undying fame, but Bolingbroke felt that his friend had behaved in an underhand way.

Though justifiably annoyed, his concern for his friend's reputation persuaded him to let the matter rest. He asked Lord Marchmont to destroy
this clandestine edition, though he may have performed the task himself
at Battersea Manor House in October 1744.[13] There was no indication
that Bolingbroke was ready to make his discovery public knowledge until
his hand was forced. In 1745 he learned that Warburton planned a
biography of Pope, which, it was strongly rumoured, would reflect
harshly on Bolingbroke and on his baleful influence on the poet's work.
Never able to exercise restraint or to play a waiting game, Bolingbroke
decided to strike the first blow, to warn Warburton that he was in a position to damage Pope's reputation if provoked into doing so. On 25 July
he wrote to David Mallet, who was later to edit his own works:

> I cannot help mentioning to you what I hear from many different quarters.
> They say that Warburton talks very indecently of your humble servant, and
> threatens him with the terrible things he shall throw out in a life he is writing
> of our poor friend Pope. I value neither the good nor ill will of the man, but if
> he has any regard for the man he flattered living, and thinks himself obliged to
> flatter dead, he ought to let a certain proceeding die away in silence, as I
> endeavour it should.[14]

George Lyttelton, who was concerned for the reputation of both Bolingbroke and Pope, feared a scandal if Warburton brought the controversy
into the open. He at least knew of the large private edition secretly printed
by Pope even if Warburton were not fully apprised of the true situation.
In an appeal to Warburton he urged him to exercise caution:

> The occasion of my troubling you with [this letter], is a report which I
> lately heard very confidently asserted of your designing speedily to publish
> a life of Pope, in which you animadvert by way of a vindication upon the
> affair of Lord Bolingbroke's Papers. Now, as I know more of that affair than
> I believe you do, and am very sure that stirring it more will not turn out to our
> friend's advantage, I earnestly advise you not to publish anything upon that
> delicate subject till you have had some talk with me. You will also consider
> how many friends you have that are also friends to Lord Bolingbroke, par-
> ticularly Lord Chesterfield and Mr Murray; and how disagreeable it would be
> to them to have you two engaged in an angry dispute upon a point of this
> nature.[15]

Warburton was not the man to disoblige men who could further his
career and so he held his hand. Bolingbroke did not. He was not convinced

that Warburton would remain silent until he saw what powerful weapons could be used to assault Pope's reputation. In 1746 Pope's verses on Atossa appeared as a six-page leaflet, entitled *Verses Upon the Late D——ss of M——. By Mr P——*. There was a final note to make Pope's treachery quite explicit: 'These Verses are Part of a Poem, entitled *Characters of Women*. It is generally said, the D——ss gave Mr P. 1000 l. to suppress them. He took the Money, yet the world sees the Verses; but this is not the first Instance where Mr *P*'s practical Virtue has fallen very short of those pompous Professions of it he makes in his Writings.'[16] This disclosure, undoubtedly Bolingbroke's unsavoury handiwork, proved effective. The expected life of Pope did not materialise and Bolingbroke held his fire. He was not prepared to act out of sheer malice. The unpleasant controversy was not renewed until 1749, when again Bolingbroke was provoked into action.[17]

In the midst of his concerns about Pope and the arrangements for his permanent resettlement in England, Bolingbroke could still find time for political intrigue. Since the fall of Walpole the ministry had been torn by dissensions between the Pelhams and the old corps of Whigs on the one hand and their late Whig opponents led by Carteret and Pulteney on the other. In opposition to the ministry were the bulk of the Tories and a group of 'patriots', now often referred to as the 'broad-bottoms', who still pressed for the abolition of all party distinctions, a national ministry and the restoration of the 1688 constitution. These aims were dear to Bolingbroke's heart since he had done more than anyone else to disseminate them. At the same time he was more than willing to intrigue against Carteret and Pulteney because of their desertion of the honest interest. With Walpole gone, Bolingbroke was much less personally hostile to Henry Pelham and Lord Hardwicke. Indeed, for some time he had been on reasonably good terms with the Lord Chancellor.[18] With a divided ministry, distracted by the unsuccessful war the country was now waging not only against Spain at sea, but against France on the Continent, Bolingbroke hoped to exploit the situation to further the construction of a broad-bottom administration. On this occasion he did not seek to inspire the opposition within parliament to put pressure on the ministry, but decided to negotiate secretly with the Pelham-Hardwicke ministerial faction in order to bring in some of the 'broad-bottoms' at the expense of Carteret and his supporters. His aims were much more limited than fifteen years before. Now he hoped that the introduction of a few patriots might postpone the nation's ruin and extricate her from a disastrous war. The restoration of the ancient constitution and the destruction of the moneyed men were too much to hope for in the present juncture.

An opportunity for early negotiations with the Pelhams did not seem likely. Lord Cobham and Lord Gower, patriot and Tory respectively, acted precipitately in declaring their hostility to the ministry's conduct of the war instead of seeking to broaden the base of the ministry by aiding the Pelhams, who were more amenable to the demands of the opposition, against the ambitious diplomatic schemes of Carteret. Gower resigned as Lord Privy Seal and Cobham gave up his regiment. The Earl of Stair also threw up his army post and Lord Chesterfield began writing pamphlets attacking the ministry's preoccupation with Hanoverian interests. Marchmont, Lyttelton and William Pitt supported him, though they were all ready to continue the war in Flanders. Lord Cobham and his nephew, George Grenville, wanted an immediate end to the war.[19] The hasty actions and divided counsels of the opposition made it difficult for the Pelhams to come to terms with the patriots in order to counteract Carteret's influence with George II. Excellent opportunities of reaching some agreement went begging until Bolingbroke took a lead in the negotiations. Throughout 1744 he kept up a constant correspondence with Hardwicke in order to ingratiate himself with the Pelham faction. He made every effort to seek out intelligence about the opinions of the French Court, which he hoped might help to end the war or at least undermine Carteret's influence on foreign affairs. Not surprisingly, in view of his experiences ten years before, he feared that his enemies in England would accuse him of treachery if they learned of his contacts with the French. His information was not in fact particularly valuable.[20] Nevertheless, the Pelhams were anxious to convince Bolingbroke and his patriot friends that Carteret was to blame for the failures abroad.[21] In August 1744 the Solicitor-General, William Murray, asked Bolingbroke to negotiate secretly with the opposition and to urge his friends to tone down their sharp attacks on the ministry since these only served to unite the Pelham-Carteret factions. If Bolingbroke could persuade men like Lord Chesterfield to temper their hostility to the ministry then an agreement might be reached by which Carteret would be isolated and forced to resign. Within days Bolingbroke was advising Chesterfield that the only way to save the country from a disastrous foreign policy was to intrigue against Carteret. Because of George II's great partiality for Carteret, who spoke German and understood the politics of the Holy Roman Empire, he could

only be removed if the leaders of the 'broad-bottoms', particularly Cobham, Gower and Chesterfield himself, combined with the Pelhams in
putting pressure on the King at Court and not on the ministry in parliament. Chesterfield replied that he and his friends were not experienced
in the intrigues of the royal closet, but that they were ready to assist the
Pelhams in view of the dangerous situation abroad.[22]

It appeared that hostility towards Carteret's foreign policy would draw
the Pelhams and the 'broad-bottoms' together. Bolingbroke himself had
long been critical of the way Carteret's diplomacy involved heavy British
commitments in Germany. His own solution was the old Tory policy of
cutting Britain free of continental entanglements and of concentrating
on a naval war against France and Spain. This blue-water policy was
enjoying a new lease of life because of William Pitt's trenchant criticisms
of the Hanover connection. When they saw the enormous cost of Carteret's diplomacy the Pelhams also baulked.[23] On 19 September Hardwicke
was able to draw up a memorial which embodied these criticisms of
the conduct of the war and which suggested an alternative course of
action. The old corps of Whigs agreed to support it. When Bolingbroke
was approached, he replied, 'My Lord, I will seal it with my blood.'[24]
He firmly believed that the reasonable members of the opposition would
come to terms with the Pelhams on the basis of this document, but he soon
found that his friends were having second thoughts. Chesterfield expressed
their common distrust of the Pelhams, who were just anxious to avoid a
difficult parliamentary session. The Pelhams responded by proving their
sincerity. The memorial was presented to George II and the ministers
threatened to resign if Carteret were not dismissed. Despite this clear
declaration of good faith Bolingbroke feared that the discordant leaders of
the opposition would wreck these delicate negotiations. He personally
tackled William Pitt, the most vociferous and dangerous opponent of
Carteret's policies and the conduct of the Pelhams, and advised him that
an accommodation was possible with his opponents without any need to
discard his principles or reverse his opinions. Pitt assailed those ministers
who pretended that they wished to cooperate with the opposition while
refusing to denounce Carteret, as weak and insincere. Union with them
was impossible. Together with Cobham, Grenville and the other patriot
leaders he intended to bring before the Commons motions which almost
amounted to charges of high treason against the ministers. Bolingbroke
begged Pitt not to throw away the game now that the Pelhams were ready
to abandon Carteret. He reminded him that he had done more than any

other patriot to unite all honest men in the national interest. If Pitt and his friends let this opportunity slip the opposition would remain as divided and as ineffective as ever. Pitt, no respecter of persons, was not convinced by Bolingbroke's arguments nor moved by his greater experience of opposition.[25]

Perturbed, but unrepentant, Bolingbroke intensified his efforts, rushing between Chesterfield and Hardwicke and threatening to abandon the opposition leaders if they frustrated his negotiations. Chesterfield finally agreed to a meeting with Henry Pelham, at which he insisted on the expulsion from the ministry of all those who had deserted the patriot opposition with Carteret and Pulteney in 1742. These should be replaced by honest 'broad-bottoms'. Carteret, fully conscious of his crumbling position, tried to make his own agreement with the opposition, but failed.[26] On 24 November 1744 Carteret resigned and in the following weeks the ministry was recast. Some thirteen of the 'deserters' of 1742, those Whigs who had been allied to Carteret and Pulteney and who had followed them into office, were dismissed and fifteen 'broad-bottoms', who accepted the principle of non-party government, came in. Lord Chesterfield was appointed Lord Lieutenant of Ireland and also sent on a special embassy to The Hague. Lord Gower again became Lord Privy Seal and George Lyttelton joined the Treasury Board. William Chetwynd, another close friend of Bolingbroke, was made Master of the Mint. George Grenville, Bedford and Sandwich were included on the Board of Admiralty. Even the Jacobite, Sir John Hynde Cotton, was found a place as Treasurer of the Chamber, while two other Tories, Sir John Philips and John Pitt, were added to the Board of Trade. Of the prominent critics of the ministry only William Pitt was not given office. The King could not easily forget his attacks on the despicable little electorate of Hanover.

Bolingbroke had at last succeeded in fostering the creation of a broad-bottom administration, a 'national' government. Yet it was a superficial achievement and a short-lived triumph. Certainly the new ministry attempted to reverse Carteret's ambitious and expensive foreign policy and to extricate itself from the war, but there was not that complete reversal of policies which Bolingbroke hoped would lead to the restoration of the ancient constitution. Henry Pelham's main concern was to emulate the achievements of Walpole. There was no pledge and no intention of bringing in Place bills, returning to triennial parliaments, weakening the influence of the moneyed interest, ending the system of public credit or restoring the 1688 constitution. The 'broad-bottoms' were not entirely committed to, or had now abandoned, the full programme of the 'patriots' or Bolingbroke's Country Party. They had rejected Carteret's apparent preoccupation with the interests of Hanover, which was costing Britain dear, and they were – largely because they represented a new generation with no personal experience of the events of 1688–1714 – ready to forget the old party labels. While they were prepared to bring some Tories into office, they forgot those fine phrases about safeguarding the nation's liberties which had sounded so convincing to them when they were in opposition. Bolingbroke's policies had always been essentially a 'country' or opposition programme which was continually abandoned by ambitious politicians once they were in office. Thus, his negotiations in 1744 had not effected a change of policy so much as a change of men. Even the extent of this can easily be exaggerated. Most of those given office at the end of 1744 were the 'patriots', that is the leading opposition Whigs. The Pelhams had not incorporated a large body of the opposition, but had simply seduced those opposition leaders who had the prestige and ability to organise effective parliamentary attacks on the ministry. The broad-bottom administration was the product of an intrigue to bring some of the 'outs' into office. Most of these were Whigs and the ministry remained ready to buy off other Whig critics including William Pitt and Carteret himself. The role of the Tories in the administration was negligible. Of the handful who joined the ministry Sir John Hynde Cotton and Sir John Philips could not restrain their ingrained habit of opposing the government of the day and were back in opposition within two years. Those like Lord Gower and John Pitt, who managed the transition into government supporters, were soon indistinguishable from their Whig colleagues. Thus, Bolingbroke had strengthened the Whig ministry of Henry Pelham and had weakened the Tory group in the Commons. He had, however, contributed to the extinction of unreal party divisions, which had long been one of his principal aims. Disconcerted, leaderless and more divided than ever, the Tories lost all semblance of cohesion and discipline. Individual M.P.s could still be labelled 'Tory' for another decade, but they were never again such a recognisable group as when Wyndham had led them and Bolingbroke had inspired them. Their only distinct features were a Tory ancestry, limited political ambition and a studied independence. They only acted together in support of such 'country' measures as Place and Pension bills.

It was soon clear to Bolingbroke that the broad-bottom administration had failed to measure up to his expectations. While he was critical of the recalcitrance of the Tories he also accused the ministry of not doing enough to accommodate them, for the Tories protested that they were still being excluded from the commissions of the peace. As early as 14 January 1745 he was warning Hardwicke: 'I fear a schism even this session, which it is in your power to prevent easily, and cheaply enough, if it be prevented in time; and give me leave to say that the affair of the justices of the peace, made palatable by proper representations to your old corps, is an expedient that would be very effectual.'[27] The Tories had always been more concerned about their local prestige in the counties than about gaining government office, and they insisted on greater representation on the commissions of the peace. By March 1745 the Duke of Beaufort was beginning to rally the Tories against the ministry and won over Sir John Hynde Cotton, who had just accepted office. Lord Chesterfield persuaded Gower, who was anxious to retain his post, to abandon the Tories, but also advised the Pelhams to make some concessions to placate the bulk of the Tories.[28] When this was done the Tories ceased to be a significant threat in the Commons.

While Bolingbroke's projected Whig-Tory coalition was proving an abortive exercise, his own personal ambitions were also being frustrated. He had gained nothing personally from the pact he had helped to negotiate in December 1744, but he still continued to ply Lord Hardwicke with advice on the conduct of the war. He expressed his concern at the way Britain was seeking to impose an Emperor on the Germans and at her increasing involvement in European affairs. Exaggerating the value of his intelligence from France and his knowledge of the disputes at the French Court, he suggested that Silhouette, the French diplomatist, should be brought over to initiate preliminary peace negotiations. The ministry not only refused its sanction, but appeared to pay little heed to Bolingbroke. Fully preoccupied with their problems at home and abroad, the ministers ignored the advice of the 'hermit of Battersea'. Hardwicke feared that any negotiations begun through Silhouette would arouse the suspicions of the Dutch that a separate peace was being contemplated. Though he was too polite to make a direct reference, he was reminding Bolingbroke of the furore caused by the separate peace negotiations of the Tory ministry in Anne's reign. Bolingbroke took the hint and dropped his suggestion, though he continued to send information to Hardwicke.[29] The more his advice was ignored the more he prognosticated ultimate disaster for the country. His tone became increasingly shrill:

You are but too much in the right [he told Sir Charles Wyndham] when you prepare yourself for bad news, instead of expecting good. If we had played a saving game on the continent we might have succeeded; and the opportunity was favourable in '42 and '43, but when we missed that opportunity, and aimed at conquest, without the means of it, nothing would happen better than what has happened, and I fear will happen. I lament these misfortunes with all my heart, and I can only lament them. I lament them the more, because they seem to me on many accounts irretrievable. Would you believe it? There are people who will tell you very coolly at this moment, that you must detach France, and continue the war against Prussia. He must be mad who thinks so wildly, and he must have a strange contempt for the understanding of others who holds such language.[30]

During the crisis of the Jacobite rebellion of 1745–46 Bolingbroke sensibly avoided any outspoken language or public gesture. He told his close friends that neither side was worth fighting for since neither was for the constitution. The suggestion that German troops should be used to quell the rebellion provoked his indignation, but he showed not the slightest desire to see it succeed.[31] The Jacobite menace had not composed domestic quarrels, for the King was adamant that William Pitt would not be brought into the ministry despite considerable pressure from the Pelhams. In February 1746 the leading ministers resigned in a body to force the King's hand. George tried to form a new ministry under Carteret, now Earl of Granville, and William Pulteney, Earl of Bath. These old, but discredited allies were unable to command a majority in parliament and the King had to recall the Pelhams and bring in Pitt. Bolingbroke was pleased to see the defeat of the two men who had betrayed the opposition in 1742, but he regarded the success of the Pelhams as further evidence that the factious spirit bred by Walpole was rendering the King and the constitution contemptible.[32]

Bolingbroke was only a spectator at these events and found himself an isolated and neglected politician: 'I plunge myself therefore deeper and deeper into that retreat from persons, and abstractions from the concerns of the world, which becomes a man, who is destined to pass the remainder of his days out of it, and to live as if he was dead.'[33] This resolution did not prevent him from getting involved in politics whenever the opportunity presented itself. He pricked up his ears at the news that Prince Frederick had gone once more into opposition in 1746 and was looking for allies. A new patriot group, led by Dr George Lee, Lord Egmont and George Bubb Dodington, gathered around the Prince at Leicester House. Whig

malcontents, excluded from power by the Pelhams, attached themselves
to this reversionary interest. Tories, even ex-Jacobites, like Sir John
Hynde Cotton, Sir Watkin Williams Wynn and the Duke of Beaufort,
were enticed by offers from the Prince to abolish party distinctions, to
bring in Place bills and to check corrupt practices when he came to the
throne. With insatiable ambition and indomitable spirit Bolingbroke
embarked on yet another attempt to create a national, patriotic opposition
which would purge the constitution of those dangerous innovations which
had followed the 1688 Revolution. With his habitual pretensions that he
only desired to live quietly in retirement he plunged once more into
political intrigue. He was never, however, at the centre of the new
opposition and his advice was frequently ingored.[34] Marchmont's brother
accused him of creating mischief,[35] while he for his part lamented the decay
of public virtue.[36] The overwhelming success of the Pelham administration
in the general election of 1747 dashed his hopes of any reversal of fortunes
while George II lived. His one success was Chesterfield's decision to
resign from the ministry in February 1748.

In 1749 Bolingbroke wrote his last political tract, *Some Reflections on the
Present State of the Nation*,[37] which expressed his frustration, his fears for
the future of the country if the developments since 1688 were not reversed,
and his lingering hope that a patriot king would restore the balanced
constitution. He complained that for sixty years, ever since the Revolution,
Britain had been waging expensive wars in Europe often for causes, like
the War of the Spanish Succession and the recently concluded War of the
Austrian Succession, which were not vital to the nation's interests. The
real menace, however, was not that the country was being impoverished,
but that she was in danger of being enslaved. It had proved impossible to
pay for these wars out of the taxes levied by parliament. Instead, there had
been a continual expansion of the system of public credit and an enormous
increase in the National Debt. This had enriched the moneyed men, who
profited from their loans to the government, and had plundered the
landed interest, which had to meet the burden of taxation. By this process
stock-jobbers and usurers, men born to serve and to obey, had grown so
powerful that they could command the government itself. It was through
their influence and by following their example that factious ministers had
been able to corrupt parliament and undermine the constitution. The
advance of the moneyed men was ultimately responsible for the degeneration of political life since the Revolution. Private interests and not patriotism or political principles were now the order of the day. Every effort

must be made to raise a disinterested public spirit in order to reduce the nation's debts and to restore her constitutional liberties. Thus, Bolingbroke had defined the same problems which he had confronted all his life and had come up with the same remedies. Real patriotism could only be expected from the leaders of the landed interest and his task was to foster it: 'The landed men are the true owners of our political vessel: the moneyed men, as such, are no more than passengers in it. To the first, therefore, all exhortations to assume this spirit should be addressed. It is their part to set the example: and when they do so, they have a right to expect that the passengers should contribute their proportion to save the vessel.'[38] All his exhortations in the past had not led the patriots to victory against the combined weight of the Whig factions and the moneyed interest. There were, however, enough public-spirited men to carry out the policies of a patriot king: 'Good ministers will never be wanting to a prince who has discernment enough to find them, who chooses them for their superior parts, experience, and integrity; and who resolves to support them . . . against favorite mistresses, the cabals of the court, and the factions of the state.'[39] Bolingbroke was pinning his hopes on Prince Frederick, but these were dashed when the Prince of Wales died early in 1751. The nation could not now be saved during Bolingbroke's lifetime, but he prayed that his works might stimulate a later generation of patriots.

The death of Prince Frederick finally ruined Bolingbroke's ambitions, but his influence had already evaporated in the late 1740s. Embittered and frustrated, his temper was not improved by the constant ill-health suffered by his wife and himself. Lady Bolingbroke had always been delicate and for several years she had been plagued by recurring bouts of sickness. Bolingbroke had always been more vigorous and active, but his heavy drinking, the promiscuous sexual activities of former years, his unceasing labours and his intense, highly-strung temperament had all taxed his strength. Throughout the 1740s he was subject to stomach upsets, fevers, heavy colds and rheumatism. With his wife he had made frequent trips to Bath or to the continental spas seeking relief from incessant pain.[40] Bolingbroke was not of an equable disposition at the best of times and by 1749 bodily sickness and political neglect had not prepared him to face calmly the unauthorised publication of *The Idea of a Patriot King*.[41] Five years before he had tried to destroy all 1500 copies of Alexander Pope's pirated edition of this work, but either he had not succeeded or someone had acquired one of the small number of copies which Bolingbroke had agreed should be printed, for in January 1749

The London Magazine published an extract 'Of the Private Life of a Prince', which was drawn from Pope's text of *The Idea of a Patriot King*. In the following March and April two further extracts were published in the same journal. They had been submitted anonymously, but with the express purpose of inducing Bolingbroke to acknowledge and publish the whole work.[42] It is unlikely that the principal design was to annoy Bolingbroke. The publication of the celebrated treatise did please Prince Frederick,[43] and the aim of the anonymous contributor was probably to revive the flagging spirits of the new patriot opposition. He certainly aroused Bolingbroke's indignation, but he also stampeded him into publishing the full, authorised text.

Bolingbroke had been hurt by the discovery of Pope's double-dealing in 1744, but, after the unsavoury episode of 1746 when the verses on Atossa had been published, he had allowed the matter to rest. Now, he was furious at the reopening of old wounds though it would have been better for his own reputation if he had refused to be provoked on this occasion. Instead, he decided to publish an official version of *The Idea of a Patriot King*, together with his *Letter on the Spirit of Patriotism* and *On the State of Parties at the Accession of King George the First*. He planned to dedicate it to his old friend, George Lyttelton, who had been one of Prince Frederick's first supporters. Lyttelton, who was now trying to play down his past connections with the patriot opposition, was alarmed at this suggestion. He declined the honour since he was now on good terms with many of the friends of the late Robert Walpole and advised Boling-broke not to create a stir by proceeding with the authorised publication. In his reply Bolingbroke agreed to omit any mention of Lyttelton, but refused to forgo publication:

> I have had my uneasiness too, that of being forced to reveal the turpitude of a man with whom I lived long in the intimacy of friendship; and that of being obliged, by your commands, to suppress any marks of my esteem and affection for you. I have obeyed you, and it was reasonable that I should: but I cannot take your advice, nor think it eligible for me to defer the publication of these papers to a more proper time. They should not have been made public at all, if I could have helped it. But since they must be made so, what time can be more proper for me to publish them than the present? I must either suffer them to be sent abroad uncorrected, in such a manner as I would not have published them myself, and with everything in them which you are so desirous to have left out; or I must do what I am doing, let them appear corrected, and less unfit for the public eye.[44]

The mere appearance of an unauthorised serialisation, reviving unpleasant memories of Pope's deceit, was enough to provoke Bolingbroke,
but he was also anxious to publish a somewhat revised version. A great
stylist, Bolingbroke was always reluctant to publish his sometimes hastily
written works until they had undergone revison. His main complaint
about the unauthorised text and his justification for publishing his own
version was that Pope 'had taken upon him further to divide the subject,
and to alter and to omit passages, according to the suggestions of his own
fancy'.[45] It is difficult to decide how far this was a case of special pleading.
There were some changes between Bolingbroke's version and Pope's text,
but no fundamental differences. However, since Bolingbroke's original
manuscript has not survived, Pope may have made some significant
alterations to this which Bolingbroke in fact accepted and incorporated in
his 1749 edition.[46] When Lyttelton refused the dedication Bolingbroke
was not only mortified at this defection of his old friend, but could hardly
claim that he was publishing his version to honour him publicly. Unwilling
to admit that he had been stampeded into hasty publication by *The
London Magazine*'s serialisation, he may have used Pope's alleged tamper-
ings with the text as his excuse for giving his authorised version to the
world. When his volume appeared the dedication to Lyttelton was
replaced by an *Advertisement*, which revealed how Pope had deceived him
and had ordered a secret edition of his work.[47] Although it was unsigned
the *Advertisement* was clearly Bolingbroke's work. The first draft, written
by an amanuensis, was corrected by Bolingbroke's own hand.[48] Without
mentioning Pope by name it disclosed the episode of the clandestine
publication of 1500 copies of the *Patriot King*. When the official version
appeared in May 1749 it caused a sensation, but it was the *Advertisement*
not the *Patriot King* which had the greater impact. By the end of the month
The Gentleman's Magazine had republished the *Advertisement* and the gist
of three pamphlets written in defence of Alexander Pope.[49] In a letter to
Marchmont, Bolingbroke commented wryly on the furore he had caused:
'Chesterfield says, I have made a coalition of Whig, Tory, Trimmer,
and Jacobite against myself. Be it so. I have Truth, that is stronger
than all of them, on my side; and in her company, and avowed by
her, I have more satisfaction, than their applause and their favor could
give me.'[50]

In the controversy which he had aroused Bolingbroke was sometimes
attacked for the ideas expressed in the text of this volume,[51] but most of
the pamphlets which were inspired by the appearance of the official version

of the *Patriot King* were critical of the *Advertisement*. Joseph Spence, who had been a close friend of the poet, wrote *An Apology for the Late Mr Pope*. William Warburton, that old opponent of Bolingbroke and the executor of Pope's printed works, weighed into the controversy.[52] The burden of his defence of Alexander Pope was that the poet could not have been motivated by avarice since he could not have been sure of making a profit out of his edition; that he could have destroyed the evidence himself if he had regarded his action as a betrayal of Bolingbroke; that he was not responsible for the recent serialisation of the *Patriot King;* and that his main aim must have been to preserve Bolingbroke's glory for posterity. Warburton added the ironic comment that if Pope had meant to damage Bolingbroke's reputation he could have published his religious and philosophical works! In answer to Warburton there appeared *A Familiar Epistle to the Most Impudent Man Living*, which was almost certainly written by Bolingbroke himself, though its tone was much more scurrilous than the original *Advertisement* and it added nothing significant to it.[53] A more circumstantial and interesting defence of Bolingbroke appeared in *To the Author of a Libel, entitled, A Letter to the Editor of the Letters on the Spirit of Patriotism*. This pamphlet gave details of how Pope was given permission to print ten copies of the *Patriot King*. The original manuscript was wearing thin and Pope asked to be allowed to print a limited edition. Bolingbroke, who was then in France, had agreed on condition that Pope amended the text as directed. Not only did he fail to make these alterations, but took it upon himself to make his own. Only Bolingbroke himself or one of his close collaborators like David Mallet could have written this criticism of Pope's conduct.

Despite these rejoinders Bolingbroke has failed to survive this unsavoury episode with any credit and yet a case can be made out for him. There remains the unpleasant fact that Pope acted in an unwarranted, deceitful manner and the lingering suspicion that he was interested in making a profit from his clandestine publishing venture.[54] Bolingbroke had always made it crystal clear that he would not publish his works during his lifetime, but he had been provoked into doing so by a serialisation of Pope's text, which probably included some unauthorised alterations from his original manuscript. Moreover, in the whole furore, the actual text of the *Advertisement* has invariably been ignored. It was in fact couched in restrained terms. The original draft, written by an amanuensis, had been more severe, but Bolingbroke had personally toned it down, either because of prudence or good taste. The harshest criticisms levelled at Pope accused him of a breach of trust and of altering the text without permission. The language of the pamphlets attacking Bolingbroke was far more intemperate. Nevertheless, it must be admitted that, for the sake of his own reputation and his peace of mind, Bolingbroke should never have published the *Advertisement*.

By 1749 Bolingbroke was a frustrated, embittered old man of seventy. Most of his friends and contemporaries, Wyndham, Swift, Pope, even Walpole, were dead. His younger protégés and allies, Bathurst, Gower, Lyttelton, Chesterfield and Marchmont, had deserted his cause or had proved incapable of sustaining it. The new generation of politicians, including Henry Pelham, Lord Hardwicke, William Pitt and the Grenvilles, had not experienced the rage of party in the reigns of William III and Anne. To them Bolingbroke's attacks on the system of public credit, on the existence of the National Debt and on the political influence of the moneyed men were both exaggerated and unrealistic. The new political and financial world had struck firm roots and Bolingbroke could not pull them up. The scandalised reaction to his attack on Pope and the physical deterioration of his wife and himself only made his last years more lonely and unhappy. All the infirmities of age rapidly descended upon him. Crippled by rheumatism, he was just able to write his signature in a very tremulous hand. His wife was extremely ill for several months before her death on 18 March 1750, at the age of seventy-four, and he was burdened by her sufferings as well as his own. On 1 February 1750 he wrote to Marchmont of his wife's last illness. It was impossible to describe the torment she had endured for some months and she was now reduced to a pitiful state. All his philosophical resignation was no defence against the blow he would shortly suffer. He was about to lose the comfort of his life just at a time when his misfortunes were growing daily worse.[55] In the past Bolingbroke had frequently claimed a capacity for meeting the blows of an unkind fate with stoical resignation and a desire to control his emotions by the exercise of his reason. He had never lived up to his ideal, but now in these melancholy circumstances even his pretensions were abandoned.

> Resignation my Lord [he confessed to Marchmont] is a principal duty in my system of religion. Reason shews, that it ought to be willing, if not cheerful; but there are passions, and habitudes in human nature, which reason cannot entirely subdue. I should be even ashamed not to feel them in the present case, though I am resigned to the conditions of humanity, and the natural course of things.[56]

After his wife's death Bolingbroke was at once plagued by a law-suit filed in France by her relatives. The case was not settled in his favour until 1752, when he himself was in his grave.[57]

During the last months of his life Bolingbroke was in almost constant physical pain. Retreat and retirement were again forced upon him, though, in a letter to his half-sister, Henrietta, he tried to make the best of it. The world could clearly spare a man as useless as himself and he could as easily renounce the world. He was quite prepared to retreat from it and to exclude its affairs from his concern.[58] In the summer of 1751 he was afflicted by a painful cancer of his cheek-bone, which, in August, was an inch and a half in diameter and three-quarters of an inch thick. Despite the protests of a reputable surgeon he decided to allow a quack doctor to attempt a cure. Though he had examined the mountebank's claims to have effected many cures, the painful remedy only hastened his death. The cancer spread and the pain became intense. Bolingbroke finally lapsed into unconsciousness and died, on 12 December 1751, at the age of seventy-three.[59] He was laid to rest in the same vault as his wife in St Mary's Church, Battersea. A mural monument records the epitaphs of both of them. These were probably Bolingbroke's last compositions. He praised his wife's dignity, grace and 'the superior accomplishments of her mind'. His own epitaph recorded his 'long and severe persecution' for his attachment to Queen Anne and his claim that he had been 'the enemy of no national party; the friend of no faction'.[60] His will, dated 22 November 1751, also reflected the disillusionment of his last years. It began:

> In the name of God, whom I humbly adore, to whom I offer up perpetual thanksgiving, and to the order of whose providence I am cheerfully resigned: This is the Last Will and Testament of me, Henry Saint John, in the reign of Queen Anne, and by her grace and favour Viscount Bolingbroke, after more than thirty years proscription, and after the immense losses I have sustained by unexpected events in the course of it; by the injustice and treachery of persons nearest to me; by the negligence of friends and by the infidelity of servants . . . my fortune is so reduced at this time, that it is impossible for me to make such disposition, and to give such ample legacies as I always intended.[61]

Since he had no children by either of his marriages his title and property went to Frederick St John, the son of his half-brother John. David Mallet was given permission to reprint any of his works or to publish for the first time some of his unpublished works like the *Letters on the Study and Use of History*. He acknowledged a few anonymous pamphlets and some, but not all, of his contributions to *The Craftsman*. No mention was made of his three works published in the *Patriot King* volume of 1749 nor of his philosophical essays. His personal estate went to his executors, JohnTaylor and his old friend William Chetwynd, apart from a diamond ring willed to the Marquis de Matignon and small gifts to his servants. The supreme irony was Bolingbroke's request that for the benefit of his valet-de-chambre, Francis Arboneau, £400 should be invested in those same public funds which he had spent most of his life condemning.[62]

CHAPTER 15

Bolingbroke and His Works

BOLINGBROKE died neglected and almost forgotten by the busy political world, which had always captivated him. Yet he was not done with the world nor it with him. In his last years he had begun to revise his various political and philosophical works and these, edited by David Mallet, began to appear soon after his death. In March 1752 the first volume, containing the *Letters on the Study and Use of History*, *Of the True Use of Retirement and Study* and *Reflections upon Exile*, was published.[1] The first of these contributions produced a considerable critical reaction, because of Bolingbroke's attacks on Old Testament and Church history. Lord Hyde, to whom the *Letters* had originally been dedicated, had predicted a hostile reception for them, if some of the offending passages were not expurgated before publication. He urged Mallet to proceed with caution, for Bolingbroke's ideas would upset the good order of society and men's peace of mind. When he turned to study religion Bolingbroke's strong prejudices dominated his otherwise superior reason. Thus, 'he hurt himself and wounded society by striking at establishments upon which the conduct, at least, of society depends, and by striving to overturn in men's minds the systems which experience, at least, has justified, and which authority, at least, has rendered respectable, as necessary to public order and to private peace, without suggesting to men's minds a better, or indeed, any system'.[2] Mallet replied that he was only obeying Bolingbroke's strict instructions concerning the publication of his works, though Lord Hyde was at liberty to issue a statement denying that he had ever shared Bolingbroke's religious views.[3] Hyde's warning was ignored, but it proved prophetic. Though the work was popular on the Continent, it was severely criticised in Britain. The most formidable attack was launched by John Leland, in *Reflections on the late Lord Bolingbroke's Letters on the Study and Use of History*, which was confined to criticisms of Bolingbroke's observations on religious history.

In the same year, 1752, *Reflections upon Innate Morale Principles*, which has been generally attributed to Bolingbroke, was translated from the French. In 1753 Mallet produced another volume, this time containing *A Letter to Sir William Windham, Some Reflections on the State of the Nation* and the *Letter to Mr Pope*, which was Bolingbroke's introduction to his philosophical essays. Neither of these volumes attracted much critical attention. When, however, Mallet published the collected works of Bolingbroke, in March 1754, the response was a positive flood of hostile pamphlets, which concentrated almost exclusively on Bolingbroke's religious opinions. In the same month that they appeared *The Gentleman's Magazine* published an ode, composed by David Garrick, lamenting that Bolingbroke's attack on religion appeared on the same day that Henry Pelham died:

> The same sad morn to church and state
> (So for our sins 'twas fix'd by fate)
> A double stroke was giv'n;
> Black as the whirlwinds of the north,
> St J—n's fell genius issu'd forth,
> And Pelham's fled to heav'n![4]

Dr Johnson, though he had not in fact read Bolingbroke's works, was roused to fury by the knowledge that they criticised organised religion. He did not hesitate to pronounce sentence: 'Sir, he was a scoundrel, and a coward: a scoundrel for charging a blunderbuss against religion and morality; a coward, because he had not resolution to fire it off himself, but left half a crown to a beggarly Scotchman [David Mallet], to draw the trigger after his death!'[5] Others, who had bothered to read Bolingbroke, were no less critical. William Pitt was very disappointed by the philosophical essays and described them as 'old matter new dressed and often tawdrily enough; trite observations emphatically imposed for most sagacious discoveries, and much fallacious reasoning, or else want of that clearness of conception and luminous discernment to which the author so particularly pretends'.[6] Lady Mary Wortley Montagu expressed small regard for Bolingbroke as an author and the highest contempt for him as a man. His celebrated style she condemned as false eloquence, obscure and trifling. As a staunch Whig, she was prejudiced about all his political writings. On his philosophical works, however, she revealed considerable shrewdness of judgement. 'I am of your opinion,' she told her husband, 'that he has never looked into half the authors he quotes, am much mistaken if he is not obliged to Mr Bayle for the generality of his criticisms, for which reason he affects to despise him, that he may steal from him with less suspicion.'[7]

Bolingbroke's works soon inspired more substantial rejoinders, many of them written by scholarly clergymen. The most prominent of these was Bolingbroke's opponent, William Warburton, who produced *A View of Lord Bolingbroke's Philosophy*, in four parts, 1754-55. He took Bolingbroke to task on nearly all his polemical and unorthodox remarks on religion, but he also laboured to prove that Alexander Pope had never been influenced by such controversial opinions. By revealing his extreme partisanship and evident malice for Bolingbroke personally, Warburton weakened his case and alienated some of Bolingbroke's influential friends.[8] A more temperate and therefore more effective critique was produced by Charles Bulkeley, in *Notes on the Philosophical Writings of Lord Bolingbroke*. Though he justly condemned Bolingbroke's repetitiveness, inconsistency and superficiality, his own work was even more boring and long-winded. The most able rebuttal of Bolingbroke's views was in John Leland's *A View of the principal Deistical Writers*, which carefully analysed his philosophy, reduced it to seven major premises, and then proceeded to demolish each and every one. The most famous reply to Bolingbroke, however, was Edmund Burke's *Vindication of Natural Society*, which argued that the destruction of revealed religion would lead to the end of civil society. He satirised Bolingbroke's philosophy and parodied his style in devastating fashion, but he did not do his victim justice, when he accused Bolingbroke of maintaining that man could and should rely solely on his reason and make it the judge of all things.

Bolingbroke's reputation suffered heavily with the publication of his works, particularly because of his philosophical essays. Not only in England, but in France, his second home, his prestige rapidly declined. Voltaire, who had once been captivated by Bolingbroke and who had been inspired by him to reject the *a priori* reasoning of Descartes, in favour of the empiricism of Locke and Newton, was disenchanted with his posthumous works. He criticised the philosophical essays as long-winded and disorganised; as too many leaves and too little fruit. Nevertheless, he did admit that, if they had been reduced to a single volume, Bolingbroke would have converted Europe. There is also clear evidence that he read the works with great care and noted some of the most useful arguments and examples. He did, of course, welcome Bolingbroke's strictures on organised religion, his praise for the morality of primitive Christianity and his bold attack on superstition; but the actual merit of Bolingbroke's work interested him less than the possibility of using Bolingbroke as a stalking horse for his own more forthright opinions. Voltaire's *Examen Important par milord Bolingbroke* and his *Défense de lord Bolingbroke par le chapelain du comte de Chesterfield* were vehicles for his own trenchant criticisms of organised religion, that conveniently allowed him to transfer obloquy from himself onto Bolingbroke's posthumous reputation. Most other French critics, who did not share the religious opinions of Bolingbroke, were even more outspoken than Voltaire, although they only tended to echo the views expressed in Britain. Thus, Bolingbroke was condemned as superficial and contradictory, pretentious and rhetorical. His French critics invariably accused him of being an enemy of organised religion, who had been too cowardly to publish his opinions during his lifetime.[9] While this was no doubt true, the overwhelmingly hostile reception given to Bolingbroke's philosophical essays explains why he flinched from gaining any further notoriety during his lifetime. Despite the superficial reasonableness of educated opinion in the mid-eighteenth century, attacks on orthodox Christianity or opinions, which smacked of atheism or freethinking, always produced howls of righteous indignation. A man with Bolingbroke's political ambitions, and who had a Jacobite past to live down, should, perhaps, be excused for shrinking from a controversy over his religious views. Nevertheless, Dr Johnson's strictures must carry some weight. Bolingbroke believed that Christianity and the Church were essential bulwarks of the State, but he was prepared to undermine them after his death, when he would not have to face the consequences.

For nearly two centuries Bolingbroke's philosophical essays have been unable to overcome the hurdles of religious prejudice. One reputable scholar wished he had never written on theology; and Leslie Stephen reserved some of his harshest criticisms for Bolingbroke's philosophy. Sir Walter Scott went so far as to describe the publication of Bolingbroke's works as 'an act of wickedness more purely diabolical than any hitherto upon any record in any age or nation'.[10] It is only recently that Bolingbroke's religious views have escaped such partisan treatment.[11] Deism now receives scholarly attention and not just abuse. It is seen as an interesting philosophical and religious movement, linking the bitter religious disputes of the seventeenth century with the more tolerant and rational attitudes of the eighteenth. Though there were more able and thorough-going Deists than Bolingbroke, such a prominent political supporter did add weight and lustre to their cause. Bolingbroke's appeal to empirical reasoning, his criticisms of Old Testament history and revelation, and his hostility to the corrupt practices and political ambitions of the Christian churches, all had a certain validity. In addition, he tackled serious intellectual questions, including the nature of God and of providence, the problem of evil and the difficulty of creating an ethical system, and the existence and immortality of the spirit. His religious opinions were hardly original and were not the product of rigorous scholarship, but they merit serious attention.

In the furore over Bolingbroke's religious views, his general philosophy and, in particular, his discussions on the origins and nature of civil government have usually been ignored. Yet his work illustrates the way in which the scholarship of the Enlightenment could affect the old humanist learning and it reveals both the radical and the conservative, even reactionary, aspects of the Enlightenment. While Bolingbroke accepted Newton's scientific explanation of the universe and leaned heavily on Locke's empirical philosophy, he was also attached to older concepts such as the law of nature and the Great Chain of Being. While he accepted the theory of the ancient constitution as the product of immemorial custom, he still wished to reduce the structure of government to its rational first principles. His empiricism, his secular humanism, his defence of liberty and his praise for those men who tried to control their passions and prejudices, all make him appear one of the more radical *philosophes* of the Enlightenment. This rationalist strand in Bolingbroke's ideas has usually been over-emphasised, for a careful reading of his works reveals the inherent conservatism of his thinking, and the reactionary tendency of his philosophy. His admiration for Locke did not lead him to accept his more liberal interpretation of the origins of civil government. In contrast, he asserted that men had not been free and equal in the state of nature, but had always been subject to some kind of authority. Bolingbroke attacked the abuses of organised religion, but insisted that a state Church was necessary in order to provide men with a moral framework and to control them by moral sanctions. While he urged men to use their reason, he also acknowledged the strength of human passions and never believed that the world could be reshaped on rational principles. His concept of liberty was aristocratic rather than egalitarian. Society was naturally hierarchical and it required the leadership of men of superior birth and virtues, who could procure the benefits of order and stability. In short,

Bolingbroke, throughout his philosophical works, stressed the need to return to original and well-tried concepts: to the law of nature, to the ancient constitution and to primitive Christianity. He was a reactionary, ready to adopt new ideas and new explanations, if they would enable him to refurbish his traditional concepts and assist him to restore a political and social world which was dominated by the landed classes. His rationalism was superficial. It was not rooted in his philosophy, but probably sprang from his desire to impress, to revel in his own learning, to appear *au fait* with the latest ideas and to stand out from the vulgar herd.

As an illustration of the conflict of old and new philosophies among intelligent laymen in the first half of the eighteenth century, Bolingbroke has deserved greater attention and respect than he has usually been given. Nonetheless, it must be acknowledged that he was not a philosopher of distinction. Much of the incidental criticisms expressed in the 1750s retain their validity. A careful scrutiny of his works confirms that he was often illogical and inconsistent. Though he constantly rejected the value of the *a priori* method of reasoning, he was frequently guilty of adopting it when it suited his purpose. In one place he argued that self-love was the only innate principle and that compassion had to be inculcated, but elsewhere he claimed that men were naturally benevolent. He accepted the Gospels, but rejected revelation. In one context Christianity was an exposition of the law of nature, but in another it was an artificial religion inferior to natural religion. He was mainly concerned with metaphysics and theology, yet he was not skilled in either. Though he regularly attacked other philosophers, he relied heavily on his predecessors and he never propounded any important new concept nor advanced any original theory. Despite his desire to systematise his philosophical ideas, Bolingbroke never produced a coherent philosophy. Instead, he made a series of statements, which, with some effort by the reader, can be arranged in a general framework.[12]

As an historian, Bolingbroke has also come in for a great deal of criticism since the publication of his works, though a few scholars have credited him with making some important advances in historiography. When his *Letters on the Study and Use of History* were published the Whigs were incensed by his distorted account of foreign affairs from 1689 to 1710. Old Horatio Walpole eventually published a belated rejoinder, putting forward the Whig interpretation of these events.[13] William Pitt preferred Bolingbroke's *Remarks on the History of England*, which, though they warped the facts, presented the truest constitutional doctrines.[14] Some modern critics have been much more severe. One has boldly asserted that

Bolingbroke had no interest in discovering the truth about the past, only with making his readers better men.[15] In many respects Bolingbroke's utilitarian view of history was both superficial and unscholarly. He was prepared to ignore vast tracts of human history, if their relevance to the contemporary situation could not be proved. Scholars and antiquarians, who restricted themselves to searching diligently for strict accuracy and detailed factual evidence, only earned his contempt. Nevertheless, while not denying the validity of some of these criticisms, Bolingbroke's work did mark some important advances in the development of historical scholarship.[16] There were sound reasons for his rejection of the kind of historical research which consisted solely of identifying minute differences in manuscripts and texts or of tracing obscure references. He realised that history should not be a confused mass of details, but ought to be the product of analysis and interpretation. Thinking about the subject, he maintained, was as important as reading all the sources. Though he was contemptuous of fact-grubbers, he did believe that historians would eventually uncover the truth. Unfortunately, he hoped that this would lead to moral judgements on historical characters.

Bolingbroke not only discussed the correct approach to historical re-search, but reflected on the historical process itself and on man's role in it. Admittedly, his generalisations were sometimes unsound and superficial, but he was trying to appreciate the perspective of history, to understand the reasons for the transformation of one age into another. History, he believed, should be the study of the causes and effects of major events and movements and, therefore, each age should be examined for those domi-nant characteristics which both shaped it and affected the future. To some extent Bolingbroke was moving towards the idea of a single set of laws, which governed the movement of history. The cyclical view of history, the notion of the birth, maturity and decay of civilisations, paralleling that of man himself, always attracted him. While he always tried to draw lessons from history, he was sufficiently perceptive to realise that historical situations did not recur exactly and so generalisations from past experiences must not be applied too rigidly.

Bolingbroke was neither a great philosopher nor a first-rate historian, but there is no doubt that he was a brilliant pamphleteer and he was probably the most perceptive political analyst of the early Hanoverian period. Unfortunately, his personal ambition and his lack of integrity have led too many historians to neglect this aspect of his career.[17] His dubious political actions should not be allowed to invalidate his comments on contemporary politics. Works such as the *Dissertation upon Parties*, *Remarks on the History of England* and *The Idea of a Patriot King* had an impact at the time and for several decades thereafter. If succeeding generations of historians had studied them more there would have been less confusion about parties and politics in the age of Walpole. For, though he was frequently engaged in bitter political campaigns, Bolingbroke's vision was not always obscured by the dust of controversy and he often perceived the general drift of British politics, even if he could not arrest it. He saw, more clearly than any of his contemporaries, the major constitutional and political developments of the age. With great insight, he noted the breakdown of the old party distinctions and the revival of Court and Country as the essential political dichotomy; the important shift in the balance of economic and political power as a consequence of the financial revolution; and the threat to the balanced constitution, to the independence of parliament and to the liberty of the nation posed by the expansion of the central administration, the increase in the number of placemen and the growing power of royal ministers. Others were also aware of these changes, but no one portrayed them so clearly or painted them in such sharp relief. The most serious criticism which can be justifiably levelled at Bolingbroke's political works, is that he diagnosed the disease without providing an effective cure. He could point out those political developments which he abhorred, but his remedies were rarely more than vague generalisations or moral exhortations. Instead of specific medicines for the ills of the body politic, he contented himself with appeals to the ancient constitution, the ideal of balanced government, the spirit of liberty and the patriot king.

It was probably because he spoke in generalities and about the essential principles of government, and did not provide practical remedies to specific political problems, that Bolingbroke's political works had such an impact on other countries and on later generations. It is, perhaps, not surprising that his political ideas had considerable influence in France, his second home for so many years and where he had many friends among the critics of the *ancien régime*. His preoccupation with the problem of establishing a constitution which would balance the interests of Crown, Lords and Commons, and which would secure liberty without the sacrifice of stability, was echoed by many of the French *philosophes*. There was, in fact, considerable rapport between his views and those of the French *parlementaire* class, which was fighting for liberty in the first half of the eighteenth century. The French campaign for a greater degree of representative government, for limitations on the arbitrary power of the king and for the revival of France's ancient 'Gothic liberties', may well have influenced Bolingbroke's campaign against Walpole. Certainly, he, in his turn, was read in France, where his works tended to buttress the arguments of the *parlements*. There was a French translation of *The Craftsman*, in 1737, and a special translation of the *Dissertation upon Parties*, by Etienne de Silhouette, in 1739. Bolingbroke probably influenced French reforming opinion on the advantages of limited monarchy and balanced government, on the danger of corruption and over-powerful ministers. Paradoxically, conservative French theorists, like the Marquis d'Argenson, rejected his praise for the virtues of the mixed constitution, but accepted his fears of a country dominated by financiers and encumbered by a massive national debt, and his portrayal of a despotic minister capable of corrupting a whole nation.[18]

It was on Montesquieu, however, that Bolingbroke's ideas had their greatest impact in France. During his visit to England from 1729 to 1731 Montesquieu regularly read *The Craftsman* and must have become familiar with the *Remarks on the History of England*. Later he obtained the 1735 edition of the *Dissertation upon Parties*. Montesquieu reached some of the same conclusions independently of Bolingbroke. They both stressed the importance of climate and geography on national character, the way laws were adapted to the spirit of the people, the need for a fixed constitution because of the fallibility of human nature, the constant danger of the decay of liberty, and the ability of the government to influence public morality and conduct. On these questions *The Craftsman* probably only served to confirm and corroborate Montesquieu's own theories. In other ways Montesquieu was influenced more directly by Bolingbroke and he certainly extracted a wealth of illustrations and arguments from his works. His sketch of the English character in *L'Esprit des Lois* was strikingly similar to Bolingbroke's conception of the temper of the English. His admiration for the English constitution as established in 1688, his belief in an ancient spirit of patriotism shaping English history, his fear that the corruption of parliament by an over-powerful administration might destroy English liberties, and his analysis of English political disputes in terms of Court and Country, were probably all inspired by reading Bolingbroke's contributions to the campaign against Walpole.[19]

Ironically, Montesquieu's most celebrated and significant theory – the doctrine of the separation of powers – was the result of his *misreading* of Bolingbroke. In defining the separation of powers, Montesquieu laid particular stress on the maintenance of the mutual independence of the legislative and the executive, and distinguished between this separation and the concept of the mixed constitution of Crown, Lords and Commons. In one of his contributions to the *Remarks on the History of England*, Bolingbroke had also written of the balanced constitution resting on the 'mutual independency on one another' of the functions of government.[20] This was at once condemned by a government newspaper, the *London Journal* of 4 July 1730: ' 'Tis plain to common sense and the experience of all the world, that this independency is a mere imagination; there never was really any such thing, nor can any business be carried on or government subsist by several powers absolutely distinct and absolutely independent.' The rival journals indulged in a controversy over this question of the independence of king and parliament. The *London Journal* clearly believed that Bolingbroke was advocating the separation of the executive and legislative powers. Montesquieu was in England during this press debate and it has been shown that he read at least one contribution, in which the separation of powers was shown to be something different and distinct from mixed government.[21] Bolingbroke, however, never stated the theory of the separation of powers as clearly as his opponents claimed nor in that form in which it was made famous by Montesquieu. His references to this doctrine were obscure and often confused with his ideas on the mixed constitution and the balance of powers. He generally stressed that the legislative and executive functions were shared by King, Lords and Commons, but confessed that liberty was threatened whenever the Crown subverted the independence of parliament. The correct and delicate balance of the three estates required that one of them did not try to destroy the power and privileges of the others. In this sense they had to remain mutually independent, so that they would have enough influence to balance each other. He never advocated a strict separation of the legislative and executive powers.[22] Montesquieu could not have lifted his famous doctine directly from Bolingbroke, though he may have believed, with the *London Journal,* that Bolingbroke was advocating the separation of powers. He was probably stimulated by the press debate of 1730, but he almost certainly got his concept from elsewhere.

It was not only in France that Bolingbroke's controversial and, at times, inconsistent political ideas could be adopted and praised by both radicals and conservatives. In America several of the revolutionary leaders of the later eighteenth century admired his works. Jefferson recommended them, while John Adams not only read them thoroughly, but said of the

Dissertation upon Parties: 'This is a jewel, there is nothing so profound, correct, and perfect on the subject of government, in the English or any other language.'[23] In England his ideas provided ammunition for the increasing number of opponents of the Whig oligarchy. The arguments of *The Craftsman*, particularly Bolingbroke's contributions, had been widely disseminated by the rapidly developing provincial press, so that there was a growing body of opinion hostile to corruption, placemen, septennial parliaments and the influence of the Crown.[24] In the reign of George III the demands of Bolingbroke for the restoration of ancient liberties were taken up by the supporters of Wilkes and the county movement. James Burgh's *Political Disquisitions* were full of quotations from Bolingbroke, concentrating particularly on his warnings of the danger to the constitution of a corrupt Court. The Society for Constitutional Information disseminated Bolingbroke's writings and, in the *London Courant* of 6 January 1780, he was described as 'The ablest defender of our liberties and the noblest asserter of the excellence of our constitution as it was established at the Revolution.'[25] Paradoxically, Bolingbroke's influence was held by the old Whigs to be responsible for the policies of George III. As early as 1752 unfounded rumours had suggested that two of Prince George's tutors, Andrew Stone and George Lewis Scott, were educating their young charge in the constitutional doctrines of Bolingbroke's *Patriot King*. The accusations, by two personal rivals in the Prince's educational establishment, claimed that George was being encouraged to abandon the Whigs upon his accession and to rule above party. Though apparently the product of personal jealousies and quarrels, these assertions were accepted without question by many prominent Whigs. Archbishop Herring of York, a staunch Whig, claimed that Scott had been 'brought up in the school of Bolingbroke' and was instilling 'that bad man's principles' into Prince George.[26] The whole affair was blown up by idle gossip and by a mischievous 'anonymous' pamphlet composed by Horace Walpole. The latter's *Memoirs of the Reign of George III* then gave the theory wide currency among generations of historians and undoubtedly exaggerated the influence and importance of the *Patriot King*. Romney Sedgwick's brilliant detective work has exposed this whole episode as Whig propaganda based on a tissue of lies and unconfirmed rumours.[27] Yet he has not proved that George was ignorant of, or opposed to, the ideas of the patriot school. The new King's attacks on the old Whigs in the 1760s and his criticisms of faction and corruption certainly smacked of Bolingbroke's influence.[28]

Bolingbroke's ideas were clearly in the mind of another critic of George III, Edmund Burke, when he wrote *A Vindication of Natural Society* and *Thoughts on the Cause of the Present Discontents*, which sought to combat their pernicious influence. Bolingbroke's principles, he maintained, were a threat to the established constitution and the basis of an ordered society. A patriot king would prove too assertive, while balanced government could only be maintained by the existence, not the extinction, of political parties. These parties must be based on the great landed families and patronage was necessary to further their political principles. Burke thus saw Bolingbroke as a threat to the great Whig families, but he failed to realise that his opponent was just as anxious to preserve the influence of the landed interest and to defend the traditional society hierarchy against dangerous innovations. Though he always remained critical of Bolingbroke's works, Burke had moved closer to some of his ideas by the time he wrote his *Reflections on the Revolution in France*.[29] In this work Burke clearly accepted the idea of the ancient constitution based on immemorial tradition, a notion which Bolingbroke had fostered, but he differed from Bolingbroke, when he denied that there ever was one set of principles upon which this constitution was founded. The ancient constitution, being immemorial, altered from time to time and so it was impossible to restore it to its original principles or re-create the original model.[30]

The conservatism of some of Bolingbroke's political ideas was better appreciated by one of the other great pillars of the Tory tradition, Benjamin Disraeli. In many of his writings, particularly his *Vindication of the English Constitution*, Disraeli revealed his admiration for Bolingbroke's eloquence, style and personality. He commended his foreign and commercial negotiations during his years as Secretary of State, and he echoed his hostility to the moneyed men, who did not have a permanent stake in the country. His greatest praise, however, was reserved for Bolingbroke's attempts to create a new Tory philosophy. He was particularly interested in his rejection of the old Whig and Tory parties and his effort to form a new party, which would embrace the national interest. Bolingbroke, in Disraeli's estimation, had not only sought to rally the landed interest and to defend the ancient institutions of the country, but had infused his party with a new spirit of patriotism. This enabled the gentlemen of England to form a national or 'Country' party, which would also protect popular liberties. Though Bolingbroke failed in his own lifetime, Disraeli gave him the credit of laying the foundations for the eventual re-emergence of the Tory party. In *Sybil*, Disraeli wrote: 'Toryism will yet rise from the tomb over which Bolingbroke shed his last tear, to bring back strength to the crown, liberty to the subject, and to announce, that power has only one duty: to secure the social welfare of the people.' Disraeli obviously felt personal sympathy for Bolingbroke, whose character in some ways resembled his own, and he appreciated his efforts to purge the Tory party of its old guard and its outmoded principles, and to refurbish its national image.[31] Nevertheless, his view of Bolingbroke was distorted and anachronistic, for he saw him in terms of his own political experiences and not those of Bolingbroke himself. He mistakenly envisaged a continually developing Tory political philosophy, leading from the seventeenth to the nineteenth century. In fact, his debt to Bolingbroke was much more imagined than real, for it would be a well-nigh impossible task to trace Disraeli's Toryism back to the doctrines of Bolingbroke. The Tory legacy of Bolingbroke was only of the vaguest kind – a conservative, at times reactionary, attitude of mind, rather than a coherent political philosophy; a desire for a patriotic party embracing the national interest; a nostalgia for a golden past and a plea for constant vigilance to protect the constitution from corruption and unwelcome innovations; a fear of continental entanglements and a conviction that the sea and the colonies were Britain's real interests; and a belief in government by a social élite. All these notions had some tenuous connections with later Toryism, but they were not the sole prerogative of Bolingbroke or of the Tory party. Nevertheless, they help to account for Bolingbroke's place in the Tory pantheon.

Bolingbroke was a second-rate philosopher, but a brilliant political pamphleteer. Too often his critics have concentrated on his philosophy and have ignored or misinterpreted his contribution as a political journalist. Yet, for all this talent, he failed as a practical politician. This was partly because he was supporting a losing cause, but it was also a reflection on his own character and ability. The personal qualities of Bolingbroke have been the subject of as much controversy, both during his life and ever since, as his numerous and varied publications. He has suffered very badly at the hands of those writers who have written of other aspects or concentrated on other personalities of the age in which he lived. In one of his purple passages Winston Churchill, intent on defending his ancestor, the Duke of Marlborough, dismissed Bolingbroke as an 'unpurposed, unprincipled, miscreant adventurer'.[32] John Morley, writing a biography of Walpole, remarked that 'of all the characters in our history, Bolingbroke must be pronounced to be most of a Charlatan'.[33] In his biographers, Bolingbroke

has suffered almost as badly. Walter Sichel, the last writer to attempt a full
biography, fell into the obvious trap of being 'excessively adulatory'.[34] No
modern writer has attempted a re-assessment of his whole career and all
the early biographies have been invalidated by a mass of new evidence
and by new interpretations of eighteenth-century politics. The most
recent studies have concentrated on aspects of his political philosophy
and have not got to grips with the many problems posed by the inconsistencies of his character and of his political career.

A study of all the aspects of Bolingbroke's career makes it possible to
offer some assessment of his ability and his contribution to public life in
the first half of the eighteenth century. His major achievement was in
the realm of the political propagandist and pamphleteer. Intelligent and
capable, energetic and well-informed, a brilliant orator and a distinguished
writer, he was able to draw up and state his case with considerable clarity
and power. His contributions to the debates in parliament, and the press
campaign in *The Craftsman*, rarely went unheard or unheeded. As an
administrator in office or as an organiser in opposition, he was industrious,
decisive, flexible and constantly searching for information and practical
expedients. Moreover, it is even possible to credit him with a greater
degree of political principle and consistency than has usually been granted
to him. Throughout his career he was a lifelong defender of the landed
interest and he strove to restore or maintain its traditional pre-eminence
in political, economic and social life. Though he exaggerated the ability of
the Court and the moneyed interest to corrupt and subvert the natural
leadership of the men of estates, this fear was a constant motivating force
in his political career. Despite his brief flirtation with Jacobitism, he was
always loyal to the constitutional implications of the 1688 Revolution.
The balanced constitution and the limited monarchy, the independence of
parliament and the rule of law, the notion of a political contract between
government and governed, and the liberty of the subject, were always
accepted by Bolingbroke. His claim that power in itself did not attract
him, and that he was interested solely in pursuing certain policies,[35]
cannot go unchallenged, but his attachment to some important 'Tory'
principles throughout half a century of rapid and sometimes bewildering
political changes was at least as consistent as Walpole's loyalty to the
'Whig' cause. Both were prepared to betray some aspects of their party's
philosophy, in order to safeguard the more important elements. Walpole
was dedicated to the Protestant succession, while Bolingbroke was
devoted to the landed interest.

Nonetheless, for all his undoubted ability, his consistent support for the powerful landed interest and his positive relish for political power, his public career was studded with major defeats. A politician with some splendid gifts, he lacked the good sense and sound judgement of Robert Walpole, a man of less spectacular, but more solid accomplishments. He could never manage men, neither his backbenchers nor his intimate colleagues, in the manner of Walpole or Robert Harley. While he was prepared to offer a bold lead, he could not convince, cajole or guide men. Too impatient of restraint, too disdainful of the meaner, but indispensable, political arts, he played too early for the highest stakes. Not until he had been tempered by years of adversity and had witnessed the collapse of the Tory party, did Bolingbroke think out his political philosophy or work out his political strategy. In his early career he was too interested in the rapid acquisition of political power. His policy towards the fundamental problem of the succession to Anne was never clearly stated nor doggedly pursued. His enthusiastic support for the political claims of the Church of England ran counter to his own personal attitudes to religious doctrines and the role of the clergy. He confessed later that he had 'launched into the deep before I had loaded ballast enough' and that his way of acting had not always conformed to his manner of thinking.[36] Most damaging of all to his political pretensions was the impression he gave of being prepared to forgo all loyalty, and to sacrifice his declared principles, in order to further his own career. His disastrous decisions to betray George I and then rapidly to abandon the Pretender ruined his public career before he was forty. The rest of his life was spent vainly trying to live down the events of 1715–16 and to prove his loyalty to his king and his party. Unlike Walpole, he never managed to inspire trust among the uncommitted and independent backbenchers.

To his political failings, Bolingbroke added more personal defects, which compounded this impression of inconsistency and this aura of untrustworthiness. Passionate, loquacious, candid and a heavy drinker, he could be astonishingly indiscreet. In addition to his sexual immorality, he lacked scruples in some of his financial dealings. Bold, even rash, in the conduct of public affairs, he was not renowned for physical courage. His political disloyalty seemed to be matched by his betrayal of his closest friends and political allies, notably Marlborough, Harley and Pope. Nevertheless, as with his political career, there is another side to the coin. Though indiscreet, he was also frank about some of his own mistakes and failings. His financial dishonesty was not in the same class as some of the misdeeds of his contemporaries. He certainly never enriched himself by public office or political malpractices and was always short of money. Not the bravest man nor the coolest head in a crisis, he displayed immense physical and moral stamina. Though at times he quit the field, he never renounced the battle. His affectation, his desire to parade his learning and to dominate a circle of scholars and wits, had another, more creditable, side. He was an active patron, an aristocratic defender of men of letters, and devoted to the proper education of the young.[37] In his personal dealings with his friends, his record stands up to close scrutiny surprisingly well. He himself once made the large claim: 'I was never capricious, nor inconstant in friendship; I can say with truth, that I never broke the terms of it with any man, who had not broken them first with me.'[38] An examination of his major disputes offers some support for this assertion. His dispute with Marlborough has been grossly exaggerated, for they always remained on relatively friendly terms and their major disagreement was over a serious issue of political strategy. With regard to his quarrels with Harley and his attacks on Pope's memory, it could be argued, without straining the evidence unnecessarily, that they both betrayed him first. Bolingbroke's treachery towards George I and his desertion of the Pretender were to some extent in response to attacks first made on him. His ill-treatment of his first wife, whom he had not married for love, can at least be countered by his evident devotion to his second. Of course, all these episodes, whatever the justification for his actions, reveal Bolingbroke in a poor light. He was much too ready to take offence, to bear a grudge and to reply to affronts with excessive animosity. However, in contrast, he could retain the love and affection of men as diverse as Jonathan Swift, Sir William Wyndham, Lord Marchmont, Brook Taylor and Alexander Pope himself.

It is impossible to reconcile the inconsistencies, the merits and the flaws, in Bolingbroke's character. While events occasionally gave his career a push forward and sometimes seemed to conspire against him, and while the main outlines of his career were shaped by the political fortunes of the Tory party, his considerable achievements and his lamentable failures owed much to these contrasting personal qualities. He always attracted the attention, but rarely the loyalty, of the majority of his contemporaries in political life. The stark contrast between his undoubted talent and his defects was obvious to all his contemporaries, and this helps to account for his success as a propagandist and his failure as a politician. Both friends and foes acknowledged that Bolingbroke was an astonishing compound of vices and virtues, and their estimations of his character have not been substantially altered by later historians. Lord Chesterfield, though a favourable witness, could not avoid mentioning Bolingbroke's faults. He described him in the following terms:

> He has been a most mortifying instance of the violence of human passions, and of the weakness of the most improved and exalted human reason. His virtues and his vices, his reason and his passions, did not blend themselves by a gradation of tints, but formed a shining and a sudden contrast. Here the darkest, there the most splendid colours; and both rendered more striking from their proximity.[39]

In contrast, Lord Hervey, who has left historians one of the most savage attacks on Bolingbroke, had to confess that he had good qualities and virtues, too:

> As to Lord Bolingbroke's general character, it was so mixed that he had certainly some qualifications that the greatest men might be proud of, and many which the worst would be ashamed of. He had fine talents, a natural eloquence, great quickness, a happy memory, and very extensive knowledge: but he was vain much beyond the general run of mankind, timid, false, injudicious, and ungrateful; elate and insolent in power, dejected and servile in disgrace . . . Those who were most partial to him could not but allow that he was ambitious without fortitude, and enterprising without resolution; that he was fawning without insinuation, and insincere without art; that he had admirers without friendship, and followers without attachment; parts without probity, knowledge without conduct, and experience without judgement.[40]

References

CHAPTER 1

1. There are a number of biographies of Bolingbroke, but the only ones which have attempted a detailed study of his whole career are G. W. Cooke, *Memoirs of Lord Bolingbroke* (2 vols., 1835); Thomas Macknight, *The Life of Henry St John, Viscount Bolingbroke* (1863); and Walter Sichel, *Bolingbroke and His Times* (2 vols., 1901–2).

2. See, for example, the anonymous review on the front page of *The Times Literary Supplement,* 12 May 1966.

3. The following paragraphs are based on my article, 'Henry St John: a Reappraisal of the Young Bolingbroke', *Journal of British Studies* (1968,) vii, no. 2, 33–55.

4. Lady Mary Hopkinson, *Married to Mercury* (1936), p. 16. This did not prevent Walter Sichel, *op. cit.,* i, 145–6, romanticising about St John's early years with his mother.

5. Lady Mary Hopkinson, *op. cit.,* p. 16; B. M. Egerton MSS. 2378, f. 37; and Frank T. Smallwood, 'Bolingbroke's Birthplace', *The Wiltshire Archaeological and Natural History Magazine* (1965), lx, 96–9. Mr Smallwood has given me invaluable advice on St John's early life and education.

6. B. M. Egerton MSS. 2378, f. 38. These illnesses occurred when St John was about 9 and 15. Sir Walter commissioned elaborate genealogical and heraldic work in the church at Lydiard Tregoze, that all led up to young Henry's birth. In 1694 he added a miniature of his grandson, probably just after his second serious illness.

7. *The Correspondence of Jonathan Swift,* ed. F. Elrington Ball (1910), iii, 92–3, 21 July 1721 (N.S.). Hereafter cited as *Swift's Corr.*

8. *The Dictionary of National Biography* makes the dubious claim that it was his maternal grandmother, the Countess of Warwick, who employed Burgess as young Henry St John's tutor.

9. *Memoirs of the Last Ten Years of the Reign of George the Second* (1822), i, 195.

10. B.M. Add. MSS. 34196, f. 2v. 24 July 1717. It has been wrongly claimed

by other writers that this letter was addressed to St John's half-sister, Henrietta, who was not even married at the time, or to Lord Harcourt. It refers to the education of the two sons of his father's second marriage.

11. *Letters and Correspondence of Henry St John, Viscount Bolingbroke,* ed. Gilbert Parke (1798), iv, 381. Hereafter cited as *Corr.*

12. Although she became an occasional conformist, she appears to have kept her Huguenot faith, for, in his will, her husband left £50 to the poor of the French Church of the Savoy, London.

13. Joshua Toulmin, *An Historical View of the State of the Protestant Dissenters in England* (1814), appendix v, 559; and Dr Williams's Library, London. MSS. 24.59. Robert Harley is also on the same list, but he was not educated at Sheriffhales. See A. J. D. M. McInnes, 'Robert Harley, Secretary of State', Aberystwyth M.A. thesis (1961), pp. 170–2.

14. William Cobbett's *Parliamentary History* (1806–20), vi, 1352. Hereafter cited as *Parl. Hist.*

15. G. W. Cooke, *Memoirs of Bolingbroke,* i, 8; G. M. Trevelyan, *England under Queen Anne* (1934), iii, 282. Friedrich Bonet, the Prussian resident, explained to the Berlin Court, on 11 June 1714, that Lord Wharton had alluded specifically to the education of Robert Harley and Lord Harcourt in Dissenting Academies, but only generally to St John's dissenting ancestors. Prussian Archives, Merseburg, East Germany. Repository xi (England), No. 39a, f. 143.

16. Basil Williams, *Stanhope* (Oxford, 1932), pp. 18–19; M. D. Harris, 'Memoirs of the Right Hon. Edward Hopkins, M.P. for Coventry', *E. H. R.* (1919), xxxiv, 498.

17. H.M.C., *Downshire MSS.,* I, ii, 777 *et seq.*

18. *Ibid,* I, ii, 777. Geneva, 23 May 1798.

19. *Ibid.* 795 and 789. 8 Nov. and 27 Mar. 1699.

20. *Ibid,* 783 and 793. Geneva, 18 Sept. 1698 and Milan, 20 Sept. 1699.

21. It was certainly a marriage of convenience. See *ibid,* 802. To Trumbull, 26 May 1701.

22. *Journal to Stella,* ed. Harold Williams (Oxford, 1948), ii, 495. 23 Feb. 1712.

23. *The Englishman,* ed. Rae Blanchard (Oxford, 1955), p. 288. 8 Aug. 1715.

24. From 1708 to 1710 St John lived on his estates in Berkshire like Xenophon, who had retired for a time to a hunting house in Thrace.

25. *Bolingbroke and His Times,* i, 159.

26. Voltaire started the legend that, when St John was made Secretary of State, the prostitutes of London rejoiced at the money (variously given by Voltaire as 7 or 8 thousand guineas) which would now come their way.

Voltaire's Corr., ed. Theodore Besterman (Geneva, 1953–65), lxxi, 106 (24 Feb. 1769) and xcv, 30 (19 Aug. 1776).

27. H.M.C., *Cowper MSS.,* iii, 49. To Coke, 16 Oct. 1704; Churchill College Library, Cambridge University. Erle papers 2/56. To Erle, 31 July 1706. Cf. the story given by Peter Wentworth to Lord Strafford, 29 June 1714. *The Wentworth Papers,* ed. J. J. Cartwright, p. 395.

28. Cited by Winston S. Churchill, *Marlborough: His Life and Times,* iv, 478. 17 July 1711.

29. *Journal to Stella,* ii, 401. 3 Nov. 1711.

30. Petworth House. Egremont MSS. 26 Dec. 1735.

31. H.M.C., *Portland MSS.,* vii, 193. Stratford to Harley, 1 July 1714. For a study of St John's relations with his first wife, see Lady Mary Hopkinson, *Married to Mercury, passim.*

32. H.M.C., *Downshire MSS.,* I, ii, 782.

33. See their correspondence in the Trumbull Add. MSS. 133, in the Downshire papers, Berkshire Record Office.

34. 'Letters of Henry St John to James Brydges', ed. G. Davies and M. Tinling, *Huntington Library Bulletin,* no. 8, p. 161. 26 June 1709.

35. 'Letters on the Study and Use of History', *The Works of Lord Bolingbroke* (4 volumes, 1967 reprint of the 1844 edition), ii, 295. Hereafter cited as *Works.* In 1728 Bolingbroke composed the inscription for the great pillar at Blenheim Palace, that commemorated Marlborough's victories. David Green, *Sarah, Duchess of Marlborough* (1967), p. 249. Three years later he wrote: 'The Duke of Marlborough was indeed a great man; as great as this or any former age hath produc'd; perhaps I may add, as great as human nature is capable of producing.' *The Craftsman,* no. 252 (1 May 1731).

36. H.M.C., *Bath MSS.,* i, 121. 5 Nov. 1706.

37. Bodleian Library. Eng[lish] MSS. Misc. e. 180, f. 6. To Lord Orrery, 1 Sept. 1709.

38. For St John's early compositions, see G. W. Cooke, *Memoirs of Bolingbroke,* ii, app. 1, 285–99, and G. G. Barber, 'A Bibliography of Henry St John, Viscount Bolingbroke', Oxford B. Litt. thesis, 1963.

39. Churchill College Library, Cambridge. Erle papers 2/56. 25 Feb. 1706–7.

40. *Journal to Stella,* ii, 397, 30 Oct. 1711.

41. *Corr.,* i, 246–7.

42. 'Of the True Use of Retirement and Study', *Works,* ii, 344–5.

43. H.M.C., *Downshire MSS.,* I, ii, 810. To Trumbull, 31 Oct. 1701.

44. Bodleian Library. Eng[lish] MSS. Misc. e. 180, f. 6. To Lord Orrery, 1 Sept. 1709.

45. *Journal to Stella,* ii, 401. 3 Nov. 1711.

46. *The Letters of Philip Dormer Stanhope, Fourth Earl of Chesterfield,* ed. Bonamy Dobrée (1932), iv, 1463. To his son, 12 Dec. 1749. Hereafter cited as *Chesterfield's Letters.*

47. Bodleian Library. Ballard MSS. 31, f. 85. Wm Bishop to A. Charlett, 20 Dec. 1710. Speeches by St John are reported in *Parl. Hist.,* vi, 301–2, 1330 and 1351, and in Alexander Cunningham, *History of Great Britain 1688–1727* (1787), ii, 349–50. The Queen's speeches, which he delivered, are in H.M.C., *House of Lords MSS.,* N.S., x, 269 and 493.

48. *Commons Journals,* xiii, 416, 514, 553, 574, 738, 748, 775.

49. 'An Enquiry into the Behaviour of the Queen's Last Ministry' (1715), *The Prose Works of Jonathan Swift,* ed. Herbert Davis (Oxford, 1939–62), viii, 135. Hereafter cited as *Swift's Works.*

50. Cited by W. S. Churchill, *Marlborough: His Life and Times,* iv, 372. Robethon's report to the Elector of Hanover, 21 Mar. 1711.

51. Cited, *ibid.,* iv, 478. Report to the Emperor, 17 July 1711.

52. B.M. Add. MSS. 34196, f. 136. To Mr Knight, 12 June 1738.

53. H.M.C., *Downshire MSS.,* I, ii, 804–5. 13 Aug. 1701.

54. B.M. Add. MSS. 9100, f.26. Marlborough to Godolphin, 11 July 1707; H.M.C., *Portland MSS.,* v, 379. Bolingbroke to Oxford, 6 Jan. 1714.

55. 'The Earl of Oxford's Account of Public Affairs, 6 June 1710–1 July 1714', H.M.C., *Portland MSS.,* v. 465.

56. Swift, *Journal to Stella,* i, 252. 27 April, 1711.

57. 'Letters from James Brydges to Henry St John', ed. G. Davies and M. Tinling, *Huntington Library Bulletin,* no. 9, pp. 130–1. 20 Oct. 1711.

58. *Parl. Hist.,* vi, 1365.

59. See the report of the Duc d'Aumont to the French Court, 10 Aug. 1712, cited by Felix Salomon, *Geschichte des letzten Ministeriums Königin Annas von England* (Gotha, 1894), p. 356.

60. M. D. Harris, 'Memoirs of the Right Hon. Edward Hopkins, M.P. for Coventry', *E. H. R.* (1919), xxxiv, 498.

61. For a more extended treatment of party politics and, in particular, of the Tory party at this period, see Geoffrey Holmes, *British Politics in the Age of Anne* (1967); *The Divided Society,* ed. Geoffrey Holmes and W. A. Speck (1967); *Britain after the Glorious Revolution, 1689–1714,* ed. Geoffrey Holmes (1969); and my Ph.D. thesis, 'Henry St John and the Struggle for

the Leadership of the Tory Party, 1702–14' (University of Newcastle upon Tyne, 1967–8), chapters 1–4.

62. St John to Marlborough, 12/23 Nov. 1706, cited by Thomas Macknight, *The Life of Henry St John, Viscount Bolingbroke*, p. 106.

63. H.M.C., *Downshire MSS.*, I, ii, 804–5. To Trumbull, 13 Aug. 1701.

64. *Journal to Stella*, ii, 421. 25 Nov. 1711.

65. Berkshire Record Office. Downshire papers. Trumbull Add. MSS. 133, bundle 39/2. 2 June 1710.

66. 'A Letter to Sir William Windham', *Works*, i, 115.

67. *The History of the Tory Party 1640–1714* (Oxford, 1924), p. 386.

CHAPTER 2

1. Among his biographers Sir Charles Petrie, Thomas Macknight and Sir Douglas Harkness all make this error.

2. *Commons Journals*, xiii, 657.

3. *Ibid.*, xiii, 419, 492, 497, 540 and 639.

4. H.M.C., *Downshire MSS.*, I, ii, 803. 22 June 1701.

5. *Ibid.*, p. 805. 13 Aug. 1701.

6. *Ibid.*, p. 806. 24 Aug. 1701.

7. *Ibid.*, pp. 810–11. 12 Nov. 1701.

8. A copy of this blacklist can be seen in the Bodleian Library, pamphlets 242, no. 11.

9. H.M.C., *Bath MSS.*, i, 54, and *Commons Journals*, xiii, 645.

10. *Ibid.*, xiii, 767.

11. *Ibid.*, xiii, 782.

12. *Ibid.*, xiii, 808–9. Bishop Burnet regarded the commissioners as 'the hottest men in the house, who had raised as well as kept up the clamour with the greatest earnestness'. *History of His Own Time* (2nd ed.; Oxford, 1833), v, 6. Hereafter cited as *Burnet's History*.

13. Berkshire Record Office. Downshire papers. Trumbull Add. MSS. 133, letter 1. To Trumbull, 12 June 1702.

14. *Ibid.*, letter 3. 20 June 1702.

15. *Ibid.*, letter 6. 7 Aug. 1702.

16. The division was published on a few later occasions by the Whigs, e.g. in *A Test offered to the Electors of Great Britain* (1710).

17. Richard Chandler, *The History and Proceedings of the House of Commons* (1742), iii, 205. Hereafter cited as *Commons Debates*.

18. National Library of Wales. Penrice and Margam MSS. L 455. E. Lewis to Thomas Mansell, 27 Oct. 1702.

19. *Commons Journals,* xiv, 87; Deutsches Zentralarchiv, Merseburg, East Germany. Rep. xi, England, 25c, f. 181. Spanheim's dispatch to Berlin, 18/29 Dec. 1702. Hereafter cited as Prussian MSS.; and *The Norris Papers,* ed. Thomas Heywood (Chetham Society, 1846), pp. 106–7. J. Johnson to R. Norris, 15 Dec. 1702.

20. Berkshire Record Office. Downshire papers. Trumbull Add. MSS. 133. Letter 9. 21 Aug. 1702.

21. Prussian MSS. 26B, ff. 34v–35. Bonet's dispatch to Berlin, 19/30 Jan. 1703.

22. National Library of Wales. Penrice and Margam MSS. L 462 and 465. E. Lewis to T. Mansell, 8 and 10 July 1703.

23. *The Miscellaneous Works of Bishop Atterbury,* ed. J. Nichols (5 vols., 1789–98) i, 267–9. To Bishop Trelawny, 26 Nov. 1703.

24. H.M.C., *Downshire MSS.,* I, ii, 818. Anon. letter, 23 Dec. 1703.

25. See, for example, H.M.C., *Bath MSS.,* i, 55–6. St John to Harley, 25 Sept. 1703; and H.M.C., *Portland MSS.,* iv, 79. Davenant to Harley, 31 Jan. 1704.

26. Berkshire Record Office. Downshire papers. Trumbull Add. MSS. 133. Letters 3, 6, 13, and 25. To Trumbull, 20 June, 7 Aug., 13 Oct. 1702 and 11 Oct. 1703.

27. *Ibid.,* letter 13, 13 Oct. 1702.

28. B.M. Lansdowne MSS. 773, f. 6, and *Memoirs and Correspondence of Francis Atterbury, Bishop of Rochester,* ed. F. Williams (1869), iii, 140.

29. *Commons Debates,* iii, 387.

30. Narcissus Luttrell, *Brief Historical Relation of State Affairs* (Oxford, 1857), v, 395.

31. *Commons Journals,* xiv, 257, 260, 298 and 320.

32. Berkshire Record Office. Downshire papers. Trumbull Add. MSS. 133, letter 35. 7 June 1706.

33. *Ibid.* Letter 28. 9 May 1704.

34. *Ibid.* Letter 29. 16 May 1704.

35. *Ibid.* Letter 32. 30 May 1704.

36. H.M.C., *Cowper MSS.,* I, iii, 49. To T. Coke, 10 Oct. 1704.

37. H.M.C., *Downshire MSS.,* I, ii, 836. Oct. 1704.

38. H.M.C., *Cowper MSS.,* iii, 49. 16 Oct. 1704.

39. Prussian MSS. 27, f. 130. Spanheim's dispatch, 17/28 Nov. 1704. For the rumour that St John had supported the bill itself, see Mrs Burnet to the

Duchess of Marlborough, c. 14 Nov. 1704. Blenheim Palace. Marlborough papers, E. 30.

40. Longleat House. Portland papers. Misc. volume of Godolphin letters, f. 199. To Harley, 19 [Nov. 1704].

41. *A Numerical Calculation of the Honourable Mem——rs as were elected for the Ensuing Parl——nt,* (London, 1705), B.M. Stowe MSS. 354, ff. 161–2.

42. Blenheim Palace. Marlborough papers, AI–20. 17, 30 April, 18 and 25 May 1705.

43. *Ibid.* 30 April 1705.

44. *Ibid.* 27 July 1705.

45. *Ibid.* 7/18 Aug. 1705.

46. Levens Hall MSS. Box D, file S. 25 Aug. 1705; 'Letters of Bolingbroke to James Grahme', ed. H. T. Dickinson, *Trans. Cumb. and West. Antiq. and Arch. Soc.* (1968), lxviii, 124. Grahme in fact voted for Bromley.

47. H.M.C., *Cowper MSS.,* iii, 63–4. 19 Sept. 1705.

48. Bodleian Library. MSS. Eng. Hist. d. 150, f. 41. To Cardonnel, 1 Oct. 1705.

49. H.M.C., *Cowper MSS.,* iii, 65–6. Granville to Coke, 9 Oct. 1705.

50. W. A. Speck, 'The Choice of a Speaker in 1705', *Bull. Inst. Hist. Res.* (1964), xxxvii, 20–46.

51. W. Coxe, *Memoirs of John Duke of Marlborough* (6 vols., 2nd ed., 1820), ii, 238. Harley to Marlborough, 26 Oct. 1705.

CHAPTER 3

1. The best studies of St John as Secretary at War are in G. A. Dudley, 'The Early Life of Henry St John', University of California Ph.D. (1955–6), pp. 117–278, and Ivor F. Burton, 'The Secretary at War and the Administration of the Army during the War of the Spanish Succession', London University Ph.D. (1960), pp. 254–60. R. E. Scouller, *The Armies of Queen Anne* (Oxford, 1966), pp. 3, 19 and 22, considered the numerous tasks St John performed, but then unaccountably condemned him for lacking application.

2. Berkshire Record Office. Downshire papers. Trumbull Add. MSS. 133, letter 27. 2 May 1704.

3. Blenheim Palace. Marlborough papers. AI–20. 5/16 July 1705.

4. Levens Hall MSS. Box D, file S. 23 June 1705; 'Letters of Bolingbroke to James Grahme', ed. H. T. Dickinson, *Trans. Cumb. and West. Antiq. and Arch. Soc.* (1968), lxviii, 123.

5. Huntington Library, California. Stowe MSS. The letter-books of James

Brydges, 1702–14. ST. 57, vol. ii, ff. 162–3. Brydges to James Stanhope, 12 Feb. 1708/9.

6. B.M. Add. MSS. 9099, f. 62. 9/20 May 1707. See also B.M. Add. MSS. 1900, f. 26, Marlborough to Godolphin, 11 July 1707; B.M. Portland (Harley) papers. Loan 29/64/3. Godolphin to Harley, no date, but July 1707; and *Calendar of Treasury Books* (1707), xxii.

7. *The Private Correspondence of Sarah, Duchess of Marlborough* (1838), ii, 292.

8. P.R.O. State Papers. 41/3. To Hedges, 30 May 1705.

9. H.M.C., *Portland MSS.,* iv, 219. 11 Aug. 1705.

10. P.R.O. State Papers. 41/3 and 44/105, p. 313. To Hedges and reply, 10 Dec. 1705.

11. I. F. Burton's thesis, *op. cit.,* pp. 257–9.

12. H.M.C., *Bath MSS.,* i, 79. 26 Oct. 1705.

13. See his letters to Thomas Fane, Earl of Westmorland, in the latter's letter-book, 1705–8. Huntington Library, California. HM. 774.

14. *Commons Journals,* xiv, 374.

15. Churchill College, Cambridge. Erle MSS. 2/56. 22 Aug. 1706.

16. I. F. Burton, 'The Supply of Infantry for the War in the Peninsula 1703–1707', *Bull. Inst. Hist. Res.* (1955), xxviii, 35–58.

17. H.M.C., *Portland MSS.,* iv, 59. To Harley, 28 Mar. 1703.

18. He congratulated Marlborough on his victories at Oudenarde and Malplaquet, at a time when he himself was not in the Commons. Blenheim Palace. Marlborough papers. BI–28; and B.M. Add. MSS. 9102, f.34. 6/17 July 1708 and 8 Sept. 1709.

19. Berkshire Record Office. Downshire papers. Trumbull Add. MSS. 133, letter 35. 7 June 1706.

20. 'Letters of Henry St John to James Brydges', ed. G. Davies and M. Tinling. *Huntington Library Bulletin* (1935), no. 8, p. 161. 26 June 1709.

21. Churchill College, Cambridge. Erle MSS. 2/56. To Erle, 24 July 1705.

22. H.M.C., *Frankland-Russell-Astley MSS.,* p. 187. 9 Oct. 1705.

23. Churchill College, Cambridge. Erle MSS. 2/56. To Erle, 25 Feb. 1707.

24. *Ibid.* To Erle, 22 Aug. and 24 Dec. 1706; 20 Jan. and 31 Aug. 1707.

25. H.M.C., *Bath MSS.,* i, 74–5. 4 Sept. 1705.

26. Abel Boyer, *The History of Queen Anne digested into Annals* (11 vols., 1703–13), iv, 202; B.M. Add. MSS. 9094, ff. 221–2. Brydges to Marlborough, 4 Dec. 1705; Cambridge University Library. Add. MSS. 7093, ff. 36, 78, 82–3, and 92–3; R. R. Walcott, 'Division Lists of the House of Commons, 1689–1715', *Bull. Inst. Hist. Res.* (1936–37), xiv, 30–3.

27. *Commons Journals*, xv, 65.

28. *Ibid.*, xv, 13. 3 Nov. 1705.

29. Levens Hall MSS. Box D, file S. 16 July and 3 Aug. 1706; 'Letters of Bolingbroke to James Grahme', ed. H. T. Dickinson, *Trans. Cumb. and West. Antiq. and Arch. Soc.* (1968), lxviii, 125–6.

30. H.M.C., *Bath MSS.*, i, 121.

31. B.M. Add. MSS. 9097, ff. 92–3. Godolphin to Marlborough, 18/29 Oct. 1706; *Burnet's History*, v, 340.

32. B.M. Add. MSS. 9100, ff 100–1, 138, and 223. 25 July, 4 Aug., and 12 Oct. 1707.

33. *Commons Journals*, xv. 493, 508, and 512; *The Letters of Addison*, ed. W. Graham (Oxford, 1941), pp. 87–8. Addison to Manchester, 24 Jan. 1708; *Letters . . . to the Duke of Shrewsbury by James Vernon*, ed. G. P. R. James (1841), iii, 318. 20 Jan. 1708.

34. *Ibid.*, iii, 292, 298–9. Vernon to Shrewsbury, 13 and 18 Dec. 1707; P.R.O. W[ar] O[ffice]. 4/6, f. 65. St John to Lord Tyrawley, 9 Dec. 1707.

35. *Ibid.* W.O. 4/6, f. 81.

36. *Commons Journals*, xv, 491.

37. *Ibid.*, 500–1.

38. Carl von Noorden, *Europäische Geschichte im Achtzehnten Jahrhundert* (Leipzig, 1883), iii, 219–20; W. S. Churchill, *Marlborough: His Life and Times,* iii, 351–2; Sir Charles Petrie, *Bolingbroke,* pp. 95–6; G. M. Trevelyan, *England under Queen Anne,* ii, 327.

39. Godfrey Davies, 'The Fall of Harley in 1708', *E.H.R.* (1951), lxvi, 246–54; G. S. Holmes and W. A. Speck, 'The Fall of Harley in 1708 reconsidered', *ibid.* (1965), lxxx, 673–98.

40. *Commons Journals*, xv, 524–5. For his speech, see *Shrewsbury-Vernon Corr.*, ed. James, iii, 335–6. St John's own memorandum is in B.M. Add. MSS. 22264, ff. 16–18.

41. They are accepted by I. F. Burton, 'The Supply of Infantry for the War in the Peninsula, 1703–1707', *Bull. Inst. Hist. Res.* (1955), xxviii, 35–58.

42. *The Letters of Addison,* ed. W. Graham, pp. 91 and 95. To Manchester, 13 and 27 Feb. 1708.

43. 'Memoirs relating to the change . . . in the Queen's Ministry in the Year 1710', *Swift's Works*, viii, 113; *Burnet's History*, v, 351.

44. P.R.O. Shaftesbury papers. 30/24/21/145. To Lord Shaftesbury, 4 Feb. 1708.

45. *Shrewsbury-Vernon Corr.*, ed. James, iii, 345. 10 Feb. 1708.

46. 'Lord Coningsby's account of the state of political parties during the reign of Queen Anne', *Archaelogia* (1860), xxxviii, 7.

47. B.M. Portland (Harley) papers. Loan 29/12/5. Draft of Harley's letter, 28 Jan. 1708.

48. H.M.C., *Bath MSS.*, i, 189–90. Harley to Godolphin, 29 Jan. 1708 and reply, 30 Jan. 1708. See also B.M. Portland (Harley) papers. Loan 29/9/51; 29/12/5–6; and 29/64/1–3; and the article by Holmes and Speck, *E.H.R.* (1965), lxxx, 673–98.

49. *Swift's Corr.*, i, 75. To Archbishop King, 5 Feb. 1708.

50. Letter dated Brussels, 8 Mar. 1707/8. N.S. Cited by Godfrey Davies, 'The Seamy Side of Marlborough's War', *Huntington Library Quarterly* (1951), xv, no. i, 40.

51. *The Wentworth Papers,* ed. J. J. Cartwright (1883), p. 20. To Cadogan, 10 Mar. 1708. N.S.

52. *The Letters and Dispatches of John Churchill, first Duke of Marlborough,* ed. Sir George Murray (1845), iv, 626. To St John, 14 Oct. 1709. N.S.; B.M. Add. MSS. 31143, ff. 586–7. P. Wentworth to Raby, 27 Oct. 1710.

53. *The Private Correspondence of Sarah, Duchess of Marlborough,* ii, 292. 6/17 July 1708.

54. H.M.C., *Bath MSS.*, i, 189.

55. I. F. Burton, 'The Supply of Infantry for the War in the Peninsula, 1703–1707', *Bull. Inst. Hist. Res.* (1955), xxviii, 56–7.

56. Boughton House. Buccleugh MSS. *Vernon-Shrewsbury Corr.* letter 193, 24 Feb. 1708; Prussian MSS. 33B, ff. 82–5. Bonet's dispatch, 27 Feb./9 Mar. 1708; B.M. Add. MSS. 17677 CCC, f. 323. L'Hermitage's dispatch, 27 Feb./9 Mar. 1708; *The Letters of Addison,* ed. W. Graham. To Manchester, 24 Feb. 1708.

57. Huntington Library, California. Stowe MSS. ST. 57, iii, f. 18. 12 Feb. 1708.

CHAPTER 4

1. Huntington Library, California. Stowe MSS. ST. 57, ii, f. 27. 11 April 1708.

2. To James Stanhope, 30 April 1708. Cited by Earl Stanhope, *The Reign of Queen Anne* (4th ed., 1872), ii, 174 note.

3. H.M.C., *Bath MSS.*, i, 190. St John to Harley, 1 May 1708.

4. *Ibid.*

5. H.M.C., *Portland MSS.*, iv, 489. To Harley, 20 May 1708.

6. *Ibid.*, iv, 491. Harcourt to Harley, 28 May 1708; B.M. Portland (Harley) papers. Loan 29/154/1. Harley to Robert Price, 27 May 1708.

7. Levens Hall MSS. Box D, file S. 18 July 1708; 'Letters of Bolingbroke to James Grahme', ed. H. T. Dickinson, *Trans. Cumb. and West. Antiq. and Arch. Soc.* (1968), lxviii, 127-8.

8. For an elaboration of the effect of his defeat in the 1708 election on St John's attitude, see my article 'Henry St John, Wootton Bassett, and the General Election of 1708', in the *Wiltshire Archaeological and Natural History Magazine* (1969), lxiv, 107-11.

9. 'Letters of Henry St John to James Brydges', ed. Godfrey Davies and Marion Tinling, *Huntington Library Bulletin* (1935), no. 8, p. 159. 29 July 1708.

10. H.M.C., *Bath MSS.*, i, 196. 17 Sept. 1709. Lavington was St John's small estate in Sussex.

11. H.M.C., *Portland MSS.*, iv. 515 and 517. To Harcourt, 20 Dec. 1708 and 20 Jan. 1709.

12. Levens Hall MSS. Box D, file S. 16 Sept. 1709; 'Letters of Bolingbroke to James Grahme', ed. H. T. Dickinson, *Trans. Cumb. and West. Antiq. and Arch. Soc.* (1968), lxviii, 129-30.

13. Bodleian Library. Eng[lish] MSS. Misc. e. 180, ff. 6-7. 1 Sept. 1709.

14. H.M.C., *Bath MSS.*, i, 191-2. Oct. 1708.

15. *Ibid.*, i, 193. 6 Nov. 1708.

16. A. H. John, 'War and the English Economy, 1700-63', *Economic History Review* (1955), 2nd series, vii, 334-7; W. S. Churchill, *Marlborough: His Life and Times,* iv, 224 n; and W. A. Speck, 'Conflict in Society', *Britain after the Glorious Revolution, 1689-1714,* ed. Geoffrey Holmes, pp. 148-9.

17. H.M.C., *Bath MSS.*, i, 194.

18. Bodleian Library. Eng[lish] MSS. Misc. e. 180, ff. 4-5. 9 July 1709.

19. *Ibid.*, f. 7. 1 Sept. 1709.

20. 'Letters of Henry St John to James Brydges', ed. Davies and Tinling, *Huntington Library Bulletin* (1935), no. 8, p. 161. 26 June 1709.

21. *Ibid.*, 164-6. 8, 15 Sept. and 18 Nov. 1709.

22. H.M.C., *Portland MSS.*, iv. 535, 8 Mar. 1710.

23. *Ibid.*, iv, 536. To Harley, 9 Mar. 1710.

24. Huntington Library, California. Stowe MSS. ST. 57, iii, ff. 270-1. To Drummond and Cadogan, 20 May 1710.

25. H.M.C., *Portland MSS.*, iv, 536. To Harley, 8 Mar. 1710.

26. Huntington Library, California. Stowe MSS. ST. 57, iv, f. 96. Brydges to Cardonnel, 11 July 1710.

27. Carte's memorandum-book, *Original Papers,* ed. James Macpherson (1775), ii, 531.

28. Huntington Library, California. Stowe MSS. ST. 58, vi, f. 157. 1 Aug. 1710.

29. Berkshire Record Office. Downshire papers. Trumbull Add. MSS. 133, letter 41. 31 Aug. 1710.

30. Bodleian Library. Eng[lish] MSS. Misc. e. 180, ff. 9–10. 22 Aug. 1710.

31. Berkshire Record Office. Downshire papers. Trumbull Add. MSS. 133, letter 39, ff. 1–2. 2 June 1710; 'The Letters of Henry St John to James Brydges', ed. Davies and Tinling, *Huntington Library Bulletin* (1935), no. 8, p. 168. 1 Aug. 1710.

32. Bodleian Library. Eng[lish] MSS. Misc. e. 180, f. 10. 22 Aug. 1710.

33. *A Collection of Scarce and Valuable Tracts . . . of the late Lord Somers,* ed. Walter Scott (2nd ed. 1814), xiii, 72.

34. Christ Church College Library, Oxford. Wake MSS. Lincoln papers, i, f. 256. T. Frank to Bishop Wake, 6 Oct. 1710.

CHAPTER 5

1. 'A Letter to Sir William Windham', *Works,* i, 114–15.

2. I. F. Burton, 'The Committee of Council at the War Office: An experiment in cabinet government under Anne', *Historical Journal* (1961), iv, 84.

3. See St John's letters to Drummond, 10 Nov. 1710/23 Jan. 1711. *Corr.* i, 15–81. St John also wanted to see *The Examiner* treat Marlborough with respect. *Journal to Stella,* i, 195. 17 Feb. 1711. For this leter to Cadogan, see *Corr.* i, 6–7. 24 Oct. 1710.

4. G. M. Trevelyan, 'The "Jersey" period of the negotiations leading to the Peace of Utrecht,' *E.H.R.* (1934), xlx, 101–5.

5. Bodleian Library. Ballard MSS. 31, f. 85. Wm Bishop to Dr Charlett, 20 Dec. 1710.

6. *The Wentworth Papers,* ed. J. J. Cartwright, p. 197. P. Wentworth to Lord Raby, 21 Dec. 1710. The Whig leaders were of course known as the Junto.

7. *Corr.,* i, 40. To Drummond, 12 Dec. 1710.

8. Niedersachsisches Staatsarchiv, Hanover. Calenberg Briefe Archiv, 24 England, 99 ff. 9–10 and 47–8. Kreienberg's dispatches 5/16 Dec. 1710 and 5/16 Jan. 1711. Hereafter cited as Hanover MSS.

9. Berkshire Record Office. Downshire papers. Trumbull MSS. Vol. liv. R. Bridges to Trumbull, 5 Jan. 1710/11.

10. For a detailed study of the October Club, see my article, 'The October Club', *Huntington Library Quarterly* (February 1970), xxxiii, 155–73.

11. *Corr.,* i, 59–60. To Drummond, 5 Jan. 1710/11.

12. H.M.C., *Portland MSS.*, v, 464. Oxford's account of public affairs, 1710–14.

13. For a more detailed account of this incident and its ramifications, see my article, 'The Attempt to Assassinate Harley, 1711', *History Today* (1965), xv, 788–95.

14. H.M.C., *Portland MSS.*, v, 655.

15. Hanover MSS. 99, f. 187. Kreienberg's dispatch, 30 Mar./10 April 1711. Onslow was mistaken in claiming that St John had deliberately engineered the whole affair. *Burnet's History*, vi, 31 note.

16. *The Wentworth Papers*, ed. J. J. Cartwright, pp. 189–90. To Lord Raby, 27 Mar. 1711.

17. Hanover MSS. 99, f. 187. Kreienberg's dispatch, 30 Mar./10 April 1711.

18. *Commons Journals*, xvi, 562, 604, 606 and 611–12. Only £4·3 millions were in fact unaccounted for. The rest was already before the auditors, but not yet passed.

19. Swift, *Journal to Stella*, i, 252–3 and 257; Hanover MSS. 99, ff. 214–15. Kreienberg's dispatch, 1/12 May 1711.

20. *Corr.*, i, 216–7. 18 May 1711.

21. *Ibid.*, i, 245, 12 June 1711.

22. H.M.C., *Portland MSS.*, vii, 39.

23. *Ibid.*, vii, 35. W. Stratford to E. Harley, 25 June 1711.

24. *Corr.*, i, 246–7. To Orrery, 12 June 1711; and *Journal to Stella*, i, 294 and ii, 505–6 note.

25. H.M.C., *Portland MSS.*, iv, 656.

26. *Ibid.*, iv, 676; v, 464; and William Salt Library, Stafford. D1778V, 188. Dartmouth's Cabinet Minutes.

27. H.M.C., *Portland MSS.*, v, 465.

28. The best source for the very complicated peace negotiations leading to the Treaty of Utrecht is A. D. MacLachlan, 'The Great Peace. Negotiations for the Treaty of Utrecht 1710–1713', unpublished Cambridge University Ph.D. thesis (1965), and his article, 'The Road to Peace, 1710–13', in *Britain after the Glorious Revolution, 1689–1714*, ed. Geoffrey Holmes (1969), pp. 197–215.

29. P.R.O., Baschet's transcipts, 31/3/197, f. 349v.

30. MacLachlan's thesis, *op. cit.*, pp. 21–4; and his article in *Britain after the Glorious Revolution, 1689–1714*, ed. Geoffrey Holmes, pp. 207–8.

31. *Journal to Stella*, i, 322; and *Swift's Corr.*, i, 278. 26 Aug. 1711.

32. *Journal to Stella*, i, 346, 27 Aug. 1711.

33. *Ibid.*, ii, 388–90. 20 Oct. 1711; and H.M.C., *Portland MSS.*, vii, 55. Stratford to E. Harley, 8 Sept. 1711.

34. *Corr.*, i, 367–70; and374–81 note; H.M.C., *Bath MSS.*, i, 212; and Staffordshire Record Office. Dartmouth Cabinet Minutes. D/742/VI/2. 21 Sept. 1711.

35. B.M. Add. MSS. 15866, f. 228. St John to Dayrolle, 26 Oct. 1711.

36. D. H. Somerville, 'Shrewsbury and the Peace of Utrecht', *E.H.R.* (1932), xlvii, 646–7; Berkshire Record Office. Downshire papers. Trumbull Add. MSS. 136. J. to R. Bridges, 5 Nov. 1711; Hanover MSS. 107a, f.34. Kreienberg's dispatch, 4/15 Dec. 1711; H.M.C., *Polwarth MSS.*, i, 2; H.M.C., *Portland MSS.*, v, 101; and Northants Record Office. Hatton-Finch MSS. Vol. 281, letter 1. Nottingham to his wife, 16 Dec. 1711.

37. *Journal to Stella*, ii, 394 and 397; *Swift's Corr.*, i, 304. St John to Swift, 16, 17 Nov. 1711.

38. *Corr.*, i, 420. 19 Oct. 1711.

39. Hanover MSS. 107a, ff. 21–3 and 27–8. Kreienberg's dispatches, 12/23 Oct., 30 Oct./10 Nov. 1711.

40. *Ibid.*, ff. 45–7. Kreienberg, 7/18 Dec. 1711; B.M. Add. MSS. 17677, EEE, ff. 391–2. L'Hermitage, 11 Dec. 1711.

41. G. S. Holmes, 'The Commons Division on "No Peace without Spain", 7 December 1711', *Bull. Inst. Hist. Res.* (1960), xxxiii, 223–4.

42. *Journal to Stella*, ii, 433–5.

43. *Corr.*, ii, 53. 8 Dec. 1711.

44. See G. S. Holmes, 'The Hamilton Affair of 1711–12: A crisis in Anglo-Scottish Relations', *E.H.R.* (1962), lxxvii, 257–81.

45. B.M. Portland (Harley) papers. Loan 29/10/16. Harley's memo on new peers; *The Wentworth Papers*, ed. J. J. Cartwright, p. 225; H.M.C., *Seventh Report*, part i, app., *Verney MSS.*, p. 507. R. Palmer to R. Verney, 29 Dec. 1711; and *Journal to Stella*, ii, 451.

CHAPTER 6

1. 'A Letter to Sir William Windham', *Works*, i, 121.

2. Huntington Library, California. Stowe MSS. ST. 57, vi, ff. 152–3. Brydges to Marlborough, 10 Jan. 1712; Hanover MSS. 107a, ff. 96–7. Kreienberg's dispatch, 25 Jan./5 Feb. 1712.

3. *Journal to Stella*, ii, 479.

4. *The Wentworth Papers*, ed. J. J. Cartwright, pp. 226–7; and B.M. Add. MSS. 22227, f. 12. P. Wentworth to Strafford, 15 Feb. 1712; and Hanover MSS. 107a, f. 116. Kreienberg's dispatch, 15/26 Feb. 1712.

5. A. D. MacLachlan, 'The Great Peace. Negotiations for the Treaty of

Utrecht 1710–1713', unpublished Cambridge University Ph.D. thesis (1965), pp. 333–50.

6. *Journal to Stella,* ii, 495. 23 Feb. 1712.

7. *The Wentworth Papers,* pp. 283–4. P. Wentworth to Strafford, 8 April 1712; Hanover MSS. 107a, f. 142. Kreienberg's dispatch, 1/12 April 1712.

8. *Ibid.,* ff. 195–6 and 217–20. Kreienberg's dispatches, 4/15 April and 9/20 May 1712; *Commons Journals,* xvii 168 and 212; and *The Wentworth Papers,* pp. 283–4.

9. *Corr.,* ii, 303. 2 May 1712.

10. Pierpont Morgan Library, New York. To Lord Orrery, 8 May 1712.

11. A. D. MacLachlan's thesis, *op. cit.,* p. 360, citing French source. The following paragraph follows MacLachlan's account, pp. 410–36.

12. B.M. Portland (Harley) papers. Loan 29/10/15. Memo., 25 April 1712.

13. *Corr.,* ii, 324. To Strafford, 10 May 1712. See also, *ibid.,* ii, 312–13. 6 May 1712.

14. *Ibid.,* ii, 320; H.M.C., *Dartmouth MSS.,* iii, 75. 10 May 1712.

15. 'Letters on the Study and Use of History', *Works,* ii, 321; *Burnet's History,* vi, 128 note.

16. Letter of Gaultier to Torcy, 21 May 1712, cited by W. S. Churchill, *Marlborough: His Life and Times,* iv, 542.

17. *Commons Debates,* iv, 310; Hanover MSS. 107a, f. 241. Kreienberg's dispatch, 30 May/11 June 1712.

18. *Ibid.,* ff. 256 and 262. Kreienberg's dispatches, 10/21 and 13/24 June 1712.

19. *Corr.,* ii, 369–84. To Ormonde, 7, 11, 14 and 20 June 1712; Huntington Library, California. HM21548. To Ormonde, 22 July 1712; and Berkshire Record Office. Lord Barybrooke's MSS. D/EN. F16/2. G. Neville to H. Grey, 21 June 1712.

20. *Ibid.* Downshire papers. Trumbull Add. MSS. 1346. R. Bridges to Trumbull, 27 June 1712; *Journal to Stella,* ii, 545.

21. H.M.C., *Portland MSS.,* v, 198. St John to Oxford, 3 July 1712.

22. *Ibid.,* v, 466.

23. *Corr.,* ii, 484–5. 23 July 1711.

24. In 'A Letter to Sir William Windham', *Works,* i, 117, he wrote: 'I was dragged into the house of lords in such a manner; as to make my promotion a punishment, not a reward.'

25. H.M.C., *Portland MSS.,* v, 465; B.M. Portland (Harley) papers. Loan 29/194/4. Draft of a letter from Oxford to his brother. For the Secretary's long-standing interest in Savoy, see H. N. Fieldhouse, 'St John and Savoy in the War of Spanish Succession', *E.H.R.* (1935), l, 278–91.

26. *Corr.*, iii, 2–6 note.

27. *Ibid.*, iii, 1–23. To Dartmouth, 21 Aug. 1712. N.S.

28. H.M.C., *Various Collections (Wood MSS.)*, viii, 89. Cf. Conti's report, cited by Arthur Hassall, *Bolingbroke*, p. 63.

29. *Corr.*, iii, 45–6, 53–61, 63, 71–3, 82, 91–2, 125–7. 10 Sept.–30 Sept. 1712.

30. For this Cabinet meeting, see Hanover MSS. 107a, ff. 320, 326–29. Kreienberg's dispatches, 26 Sept./7 Oct., 3/14 Oct., and 7/18 Oct. 1712; B.M. Add. MSS. 17677, FFF, ff. 361, 371 and 374. L'Hermitage's dispatches, 7, 14 and 18 Oct. 1712. N.S.; Lincoln Record Office. Monson MSS. 7/12/197. P. Lamb to Sir J. Newton, 13 Oct. 1712; and *The Correspondence of Sarah, Duchess of Marlborough*, pp. 82–3. A. Maynwaring to the Duchess, 29 Sept. 1712.

31. *Corr.*, iii, 130–4. 30 Sept. 1712.

32. *Ibid.*, iii, 125–30. 30 Sept. 1712.

33. H.M.C., *Portland MSS.*, v, 285 and 466; James Macpherson's *Original Papers,* ii, 358–9; and Hanover MSS. 107a, ff. 330–1. Kreienberg's dispatch, 10/23 Oct. 1712.

34. H.M.C., *Portland MSS.*, v, 234–5. 13 and 14 Oct. 1712.

35. A. D. MacLachlan, 'The Great Peace. Negotiations for the Treaty of Utrecht 1710–1713', Cambridge University Ph.D. thesis (1965), pp. 604–14.

36. H.M.C., *Portland MSS.*, v, 134. Bolingbroke to Oxford, Nov. 1712 not Dec. 1711 as printed; *ibid., Bath MSS.,* i, 223. Queen to Oxford, 13 Nov. 1712.

37. H. T. Dickinson, 'The Mohun–Hamilton Duel: Personal Feud or Whig Plot?', *Durham University Journal* (June 1965), lvii, no. 3, 159–65.

38. *Corr.*, iii, 304, 417–39, 449 and 497–9. To Prior (19 Jan. 1713), Shrewsbury (17 Feb. 1713) and Torcy (17 Feb.), and from Torcy (8 Mar. 1713); *Matthew Prior's History of His Own Time,* ed. Adrian Drift (1740), p. 380. Bolingbroke to Prior, 22 Jan. 1713.

39. B.M. Add. MSS. 34493, f. 82. Gaultier to Torcy, 29 Oct. 1712.

40. H. N. Fieldhouse, 'Oxford, Bolingbroke, and the Pretender's place of residence, 1711–14', *E.H.R.* (1937), lii, 289–96.

41. H.M.C., *House of Lords MSS.*, x, 258–63; *Lords Debates,* ii, 411–12. 2 and 5 April 1712.

42. *Bolingbroke's Defence of the Treaty of Utrecht,* ed. G. M. Trevelyan (Cambridge, 1932). See also A. D. MacLachlan, 'The Road to Peace, 1710–13', *Britain after the Glorious Revolution, 1689–1714,* ed. Geoffrey Holmes, pp. 212–13.

43. Swift, *Journal to Stella,* ii, 656.

44. *Corr.*, 488–9.

45. B.M. Add. MSS. 37273, f. 178. Bolingbroke to the Lords Plenipotentiary, 7 April 1713.

46. *Corr.*, iv, 165–6. To Strafford, 20 June 1713.

47. *The Wentworth Papers*, ed. J. J. Cartwright, p. 338; Bodleian Library. Ballard MSS. 31, f. 104. Wm. Bishop to Dr Charlett, 20 June 1713.

48. H.M.C., *Portland MSS.*, vii, 144–7. To Lord Harley, 18–25 June 1713.

CHAPTER 7

1. P.R.O. Baschet transcripts. 31/3/201, ff. 71–2 and 79. Duc d'Aumont's dispatches, 30 July and 7 Aug. 1713; H.M.C., *Portland MSS.*, v, 660.

2. *Corr.*, iv, 180–1. 4 July 1713.

3. H.M.C., *Portland MSS.*, v, 468.

4. *Ibid.*, v, 311–2.

5. *Corr.*, iv, 233. 7 Aug. 1713.

6. *Ibid.*, iv, 201. 25 July 1713.

7. H.M.C., *Portland MSS.*, vii, 161.

8. P. W. J. Riley, *The English Ministers and Scotland, 1707–1727* (1964), pp. 244–8.

9. *Corr.*, iv, 254. 1 Sept. 1713.

10. H.M.C., *Portland MSS.*, v, 466.

11. For the emergence of these two groups, see Geoffrey Holmes, *British Politics in the Age of Anne* (1967), pp. 279–83.

12. *Ibid.*, pp. 270–80.

13. Essex Record Office. D/DKW. 01/31/3. List of deputy-lieutenants, Jan. 1712/13.

14. H.M.C., *Portland MSS.*, v, 369. 3 Dec. 1713.

15. *Ibid.*, v, 373. 17 Dec. 1713.

16. *Ibid.*, v, 377. 31 Dec. 1713.

17. B.M. Egerton MSS. 2618, f. 213. 19 Dec. 1713.

18. H.M.C., *Portland MSS.*, v, 661.

19. *Ibid.*, vii, 174. 26 Nov. 1713.

20. Levens Hall MSS. Box B, file A. [Dec. 1713]; B.M. Stowe MSS. 225, f. 322. To Robethon, 4/13 Dec. 1713.

21. H.M.C., *Portland MSS.*, v, 374. From Bolingbroke, 24 and 25 Dec. and Erasmus Lewis, 25 Dec. 1713.

22. *Corr.,* iv, 443. 25 Jan. 1714.

23. *Ibid.,* iv, 470. To Lord Strafford, 13 Feb. 1714.

24. See, L. G. Wickham Legg, 'Extracts from Jacobite Correspondence, 1712–14', *E.H.R.* (1915), xxx, 501–18; and H. N. Fieldhouse, 'Bolingbroke's Share in the Jacobite Intrigue of 1710–14', *ibid.* (1937), lii, 443–59.

25. *Ibid.,* lii, 454.

26. Geoffrey Holmes, 'Harley, St John and the Death of the Tory Party', in *Britain after the Glorious Revolution 1689–1714,* ed. Geoffrey Holmes (1969), p. 227.

27. B.M. Add. MSS. 47087.

28. George Lockhart, *The Lockhart Papers* (1817), i, 412–13, 441–2.

29. *Corr.,* iv, 494. 23 Mar. 1714.

30. B.M. Add. MSS. 34495, ff. 31–3. D'Iberville to Torcy, 3/14 April 1714.

31. *The Lockhart Papers,* i, 444, 460.

32. H.M.C., *Portland MSS.,* v, 404.

33. *The Byng Papers,* ed. Brian Tunstall *(Navy Records Society, 1931),* iii, 71.

34. Abel Boyer, *Quadriennium Annae Postremum; or the Political State of Great Britain* (8 vols., 1718–19), vii, 263–4; B.M. Add. MSS. 31139. f. 78. Bromley to Strafford, 2 April 1714; Scottish Record Office. Montrose MSS. Box vi. List of commissions signed by the Earl of Mar; *Hardwicke State Papers* (1778), ii, 522. Stair's memorial; *An Apology for the Army, written by an Officer* (1715); Captain Robert Parker, *Memoirs of the most remarkable military transactions 1683–1718* (1747), pp. 247–9; Charles Hamilton, *Transactions during the reign of Queen Anne* (Edinburgh, 1790), p. 324.

35. B.M. Egerton MSS. 2618, f. 215. Bolingbroke to George Clarke, 20 May 1714.

36. 'Proceedings in the House of Commons, March–June 1714 (from the diary of Sir Edward Knatchbull),' ed. A. N. Newman, *Bull. Inst. Hist. Res.* (1961), xxxiv, 213.

37. B.M. Add. MSS. 47027, ff. 175–8. John Perceval to his brother, 8 April 1714.

38. 'Proceedings in the House of Commons, March–June 1714 (from the diary of Sir Edward Knatchbull)', ed. A. N. Newman, *Bull. Inst. Hist. Res.* (1961), xxxiv, 214.

39. B.M. Add. MSS. 47027, ff. 192–3. Perceval to his brother, 16 April 1714; B.M. Add. MSS. 17677, HHH, f. 187v. L'Hermitage's dispatch, 15/26 April 1714.

40. *The Life and History of the Right Honourable Henry St John, Lord Viscount Bolingbroke* (1754), p. 60. Cf. *Swift's Corr.,* ii, 137. To Peterborough,

18 May 1714; and Berkshire Record Office. Downshire papers. Trumbull Add. MSS. 134a. T. Bateman to Trumbull, 21 May 1714.

41. H.M.C., *Portland MSS.,* v, 425.

42. *Corr.,* iv, 524. 27 April 1714.

43. L. G. Wickham Legg, 'Extracts from Jacobite Correspondence, 1712–1714', *E.H.R.* (1915), xxx, 517. Gaultier to Torcy, 29 Mar. 1714.

44. B.M. Stowe MSS. 227, f. 220. Bothmer's dispatch, 13/24 July 1714.

45. *The Lockhart Papers,* i, 467.

46. For the debates, see B.M. Add. MSS. 17677, HHH, f. 221. L'Hermitage's dispatch, 14/25 May 1714; B.M. Add. MSS 47027, f. 222. John Perceval to D. Deering, 15 May 1714; P.R.O. Baschet transcripts. 31/3/202, f. 217. D'Iberville to Torcy, 16/27 May 1714; H.M.C., *Portland MSS.,* vii, 185. Stratford to Lord Harley, 3 June 1714.

47. Prussian MSS. 39A, f. 143. Bonet's dispatch, 11/22 June 1714.

48. B.M. Add. MSS. 17677, HHH, f. 238. L'Hermitage's dispatch, 1/12 June 1714; *Debates and Speeches . . . concerning the Schism Bill* (1715), p. 6.

49. *Ibid.,* p. 6.

50. *Lords Debates,* ii, 424–8; H.M.C., *Portland MSS.,* vii, 186–8. Stratford to Lord Harley, 5, 12 June 1714.

51. B.M. Add. MSS. 22202, f. 98. Newsletter, 25 June 1714; *Lords Debates,* ii, 430–33.

52. 'Proceedings in the House of Commons, March–June 1714 (from the diary of Sir Edward Knatchbull)', ed. A. N. Newman, *Bull. Inst. Hist. Res.* (1961), xxxiv, 217.

53. *The Wentworth Papers,* ed. J. J. Cartwright, p. 388. Peter Wentworth to Lord Strafford, 14 June 1714.

54. *The Lockhart Papers,* i 476–7.

55. B.M. Add. MSS. 47027, ff. 237–8. Sir John Perceval to D. Deering, 14 June 1714.

56. B.M. Portland (Harley) papers. Loan 29/10/6. July 1714.

57. James Macpherson's *Original Papers,* ii, 630. Galke to Robethon, 8/19 June 1714; *The Wentworth Papers,* p. 395. Wentworth to Strafford, 29 June 1714.

58. H.M.C., *Portland MSS.,* vii, 193. Stratford to Lord Harley, 1 July 1714. For evidence of Bolingbroke's dissolute life in 1714 see *The Wentworth Papers,* p. 395.

59. B.M. Stowe MSS. 227, f. 162. Kreienberg's dispatch, 18 June 1714.

60. B.M. Add. MSS. 25495, ff. 166–83. Minutes of the Court of the South Sea

Company, 16–29 June 1714; *Swift's Corr.*, ii, 176. From Charles Ford, 10 July 1714.

61. D'Iberville to Torcy, 28 June/9 July 1714. Cited by Felix Salomon, *Geschichte des letzten Ministeriums Königin Annas von England,* p. 298.

62. *Lords Debates,* ii, 433–7 for this debate.

63. *The Wentworth Papers,* p. 404.

64. *The Works and Life of . . . Charles, late Earl of Halifax* (1715), p. 256.

65. *Lords Debates,* ii, 437; B.M. Stowe MSS. 227, f. 220. Bothmer's dispatch, 13/24 July 1714; Prussian MSS. 39A, f. 193. Bonet's dispatch, 13/24 July 1714.

66. H.M.C., *Portland MSS.,* vii, 189, 191–2. To Lord Harley, 17, 27 June and 1 July 1714; *Swift's Corr.,* ii, 170. From Charles Ford, 6 July 1714; B.M. Add. MSS. 22202, f. 97. Newsletter to Strafford, 25 June 1714.

67. *Corr.,* iv, 567–8. 14 July 1714.

68. B.M. Add. MSS. 22202, f. 135. Newsletter, 23 July; *Swift's Corr.,* ii, 171, 193–4. From Ford, 6, 24 July; B.M. Add. MSS. 17677, HHH, f. 294. L'Hermitage's dispatch, 17 July; Cambridge University Library. Cholmondeley (Houghton) MSS. No. 680a. Anon, 29 July 1714.

69. *Swift's Corr.,* ii, 193. From Charles Ford, 24 July 1714.

70. *Ibid.,* ii, 199. From Erasmus Lewis, 27 July 1714.

71. B.M. Portland (Harley) papers. Loan 29/154/6. 18/29 July 1714.

72. Cited by Wolfgang Michael, *The Beginnings of the Hanoverian Dynasty,* i, 49. See also *Swift's Corr.,* ii, 202. From Lewis, 29 July 1714; and Basil Williams, *Stanhope* (Oxford, 1932), pp. 145–6.

73. Michael, *op. cit.,* i, 54; *Swift's Corr.,* ii, 208. From Charles Ford, 31 July 1714; *The Wentworth Papers,* p. 408. Wentworth to Strafford, 30 July 1714.

74. *Swift's Corr.,* ii, 207, 215. From Ford, 31 July, 5 Aug. 1714.

75. *Ibid.,* ii, 214. 3 Aug. 1714.

76. H.M.C., *Townshend MSS.,* p. 220. Bolingbroke to Northampton, 30 July 1714; B.M. Add MSS. 37361, f. 28. Bolingbroke to Whitworth, 3 Aug. 1714; *The Wentworth Papers,* p. 409. Wentworth to Strafford, 3 Aug. 1714.

77. *Ibid.,* p. 411. Bathurst to Strafford, 10 Aug. 1714; *Swift's Corr.,* ii, 235–6. From Ford, 14 Aug. 1714; *The Correspondence of Sir James Clavering,* ed. H. T. Dickinson *(Surtees Society, 1967),* clxxviii, 128. Ann Liddell to Clavering, 14 Aug. 1714.

78. For these developments, see Prussian MSS. 39A, f. 286. Bonet's dispatch, 31 Aug./11 Sept. 1714; B.M. Add. MSS. 47027, f. 300. Perceval to Deering, 7 Aug. 1714; Berkshire Record Office. Downshire papers. Trumbull Add. MSS. 134a. Bateman to Trumbull, 16 Aug. 1714; R. Pauli, 'Aktenstücke

zur Thronbesteigung des Welfenhaus in England', *Zeitschrift des historischen Vereins für Niedersachsen* (Hanover, 1883), pp. 61–2. Bothmer to George I, 31 Aug./11 Sept. 1714; and entries in his diary, 1,12 and 3/14 Sept. 1714.

79. *Memoirs and Correspondence of Francis Atterbury, Bishop of Rochester,* ed. F. Williams, i, 279. Sept. 1714; *Swift's Corr.,* ii, 229. 11 Aug. 1714 (before his actual dismissal); Hertfordshire Record Office. Cowper/Panshanger MSS.

80. *The Diary of Mary, Countess Cowper,* ed. Spencer Cowper (2nd ed., 1865), p.5.

81. H.M.C., *Tenth Report (Bagot MSS.),* app. pt. iv, p. 343. H. Todd to James Grahme, 23 Oct. 1714.

82. *Swift's Corr.,* ii, 214, 225, 227–8. From Bolingbroke, 3 Aug.; To Bolingbroke, 7 Aug.; From Lewis, 10 Aug. 1714.

83. *Memoirs and Correspondence of Francis Atterbury, Bishop of Rochester,* ed. F. Williams, i, 279–80. Sept. 1714.

84. B.M. Add. MSS. 47027, ff. 342–8; Bodleian Library. Ballard MSS. 31, f. 129. Bishop to Charlett, 28 Sept. 1714; Leicester Museum. Braye MSS. 23D57, 2890. Beaumont to Cave, Oct. 1714.

85. H. N. Fieldhouse, 'Bolingbroke and the d'Iberville Correspondence, August 1714–June 1715', *E.H.R.* (1937), lii, 674. D'Iberville to Louis XIV, 11 Oct. 1714 and 6 May 1715.

86. When Daniel Defoe defended Oxford in *The Secret History of the White Staff* (1714), Bolingbroke replied with *Considerations upon the Secret History of the White Staff* (1714).

CHAPTER 8

1. Huntington Library, California. Stowe MSS. ST. 57, xi, f. 250. 7 Feb. 1715.

2. H.M.C., *Portland MSS.,* v, 508. Drummond to Oxford, Mar. 1715.

3. Cobbett's *Parl. Hist.,* vi, 45.

4. H. N. Fieldhouse, 'Bolingbroke and the d'Iberville Correspondence, August 1714–June 1715', *E.H.R.* (1937), lii, 678–9. D'Iberville to Torcy, 14, 21 Mar., 4, 5 April and 3 May 1715.

5. B.M. Stowe MSS. 242, f. 179. Bolingbroke to Stanhope, 15 Mar. 1715.

6. B.M. Add. MSS. 36243, ff. 1–2, and 17; 'Letters from James Brydges to Henry St John', ed. G. Davies and M. Tinling, *Huntington Library Bulletin* (1936), no. 9, pp. 144, 150, 152. 14 April, 22 May, 11 July 1715. These arrangements were later to cause Bolingbroke considerable problems.

Parts of his estates were subsequently sold to pay off his debts, but his wife left the rest to her godson and nephew. It was not until 1733 that Bolingbroke gave up his struggle to recover his estate at Bucklebury, though he did receive some £2025 compensation. B.M. Add. MSS. 36243, ff. 3–16, 19–20v. See also H.M.C., *Portland MSS.*, vii, 244–5, 410–11. Stratford to Lord Harley, 27, 29 Oct. 1718, and 23 Dec. 1725.

7. *London Gazette,* 29 Mar./2 April 1715.

8. Scottish Record Office. Stair MSS. GD135, vol. 145. C. Cathcart to Stair, 24 and 28 Mar. 1715.

9. H. N. Fieldhouse, 'Bolingbroke and the d'Iberville Correspondence, August 1714–June 1715', *E.H.R.* (1937), lii, 674. D'Iberville to Torcy, 7 Nov. 1714.

10. Scottish Record Office. Stair MSS. GD135, vol. 145. Cathcart to Stair, 31 Mar. 1715. See also Carlisle Record Office. Lonsdale MSS. D/Lons., bundle 27a. To James Lowther, 31 Mar. 1715; and Studley Royal. Vyner MSS. 13498. M. Robinson to his mother [Mar. 1715].

11. Hertfordshire Record Office. Cowper/Panshanger MSS. [Feb. 1715]. Published in *The Diary of Mary, Countess Cowper,* ed. Spencer Cowper, pp. 178–9. See also, *ibid.,* pp. 48–9.

12. *Somers Tracts,* ed. Sir Walter Scott, xiii, 627. Lansdowne was Bolingbroke's old friend George Granville.

13. *Swift's Corr.,* ii, 278. From John Barber, 3 May 1715.

14. Huntington Library, California. LO 12553. Paris, 17 April 1715, N.S.

15. B.M. Egerton MSS. 2618, f. 217. 27 June 1715. See also 'Letters from James Brydges to Henry St John', ed. G. Davies and M. Tinling, *Huntington Library Bulletin* (1936), no. 9, pp. 141–3, 145. 14, 17 April 1715; and H.M.C., *Stuart MSS.,* i, 359.

16. H.M.C., *Stuart MSS.,* i, 361–2; Bodleian Library. MSS. French d. 18, ff. 5–5v. Bolingbroke to Madame de Ferriol, 26 June 1715; *Lettres Historiques Politiques, Philosophiques . . . de Bolingbroke,* ed. P. H. Grimoard (3 vols., Paris, 1808), ii, 429. To Madame de Ferriol, 3 June 1715. Hereafter cited as Grimoard, *Lettres Historiques.*

17. 'Letters of James Brydges to Henry St John', ed. G. Davies and M. Tinling, *Huntington Library Bulletin* (1936), no. 9, pp. 146–81. 29 April, 22 May, 9 June 1715; Cobbett's *Parl. Hist.,* vii, 66; B.M. Add. MSS. 47087. Lord Perceval to his brother, 11 June 1715.

18. Bolingbroke's Jacobite correspondence, on which the following sections are based, has been published in the appendices of Lord Mahon's first three volumes of *History of England from the Peace of Utrecht* (1836) and H.M.C., *Stuart MSS.,* i, *passim.*

19. 'Letter to Sir William Windham', *Works,* i, 141.

20. H.M.C., *Stuart MSS.,* i, 447. 24 Oct. 1715. N.S.

21. Lord Mahon, *op. cit.,* i, app., pp. xxix–xxx. 2 Nov. 1715. N.S.

22. These charges, dated 16 March 1716, can be seen in Bodleian Library. Rawlinson MSS. A311, f. 15; H.M.C., *Tenth Report,* app. i, pp. 181–2; B.M. Add. MSS. 38851, ff. 94–5v; and Nicholas Tindal, *Continuation of Rapin's History of England* (1746 ed.), xxvi, 245–7 n. A further attack, dated 27 April 1716, can be seen in H.M.C., Fourth Report *(Erskine Murray MSS.),* p. 526a.

23. Bodleian Library. Rawlinson MSS. A311, ff. 15–17v; H.M.C., *Tenth Report,* pp. 182–3; and Nicholas Tindal, *op. cit.,* xxvi, 247–63 n. His defence was elaborated in his famous *Letter to Sir William Windham,* written in 1717.

24. Cited by Lord Mahon, *op. cit.,* i, 288–9.

25. George Hilton Jones, *The Mainstream of Jacobitism* (Cambridge, Mass., 1954), pp. 116–21. The renewed Jacobite charges can be seen in Bodleian Library. Rawlinson MSS. A311, ff. 18–21v; and Nicholas Tindal, *op. cit.,* xxvi, 263–84 n.

26. *Hardwicke's State Papers,* ii, 533–6 and 551–2. Stair's journal.

27. H.M.C., *Stuart MSS.,* ii, 85 and 91.

28. P.R.O. State Papers, Foreign (France). 78/160, f. 256; *Lettres Inédites de Bolingbroke à Lord Stair 1716–1720,* ed. Paul Baratier (Trévoux, 1939), p. 14. Hereafter cited as Baratier, *Lettres Inédites.*

29. Scottish Record Office. Stair MSS. GD135, vol. 147, letters 6, 8 and 10. From Stanhope, 7 June; from Craggs, 15 Nov. and 6 Dec. 1716.

30. *Ibid.* Vol. 141/29, letter 4. Bolingbroke to Stair [No date]; Bolingbroke's *Works,* i, 179–80. Stair to Craggs [No date].

31. Blenheim Palace. Marlborough MSS. BII–27. 7 June 1716. See also H.M.C., *Eighth Report,* part i, p. 41a, where this letter is inaccurately transcribed and wrongly dated 16 June.

32. William Coxe, *Memoirs of the Life and Administration of Sir Robert Walpole, Earl of Orford* (3 vols., 1798), ii, 308–9. Hereafter cited as Coxe, *R. Walpole's Memoirs.*

33. Scottish Record Office. Stair MSS. GD135, vol. 147, letter 10. Craggs to Stair, 6 Dec. 1716.

34. For these developments, see H.M.C., *Stuart MSS.,* ii, 105–6, 125, 218, 406 and 488, and *ibid.,* v, 309.

35. *Swift's Corr.,* ii, 348. To Archbishop King, 16 Dec. 1716.

36. *Ibid.,* ii, 334. 12/23 Oct. 1716. See also, H.M.C., *Stuart MSS.,* iii, 69 and 389.

M

37. *Works,* i, 135.

38. *Ibid.,* i, 167 and 174.

39. *Ibid.,* i, 116.

40. Scottish Record Office. Stair MSS. GD135, vol. 141/3. To [Stanhope?] c. 1717.

41. H.M.C., *Stuart MSS.,* v, 310. Mar to Menzies, 23 Dec. 1717. See also, *ibid.,* v, 311, 341, and vi, 90, 129, 258, and 529–30; and H.M.C., *Portland MSS.,* vii, 228. Stratford to Lord Harley, 29 Oct. 1717.

42. Baratier, *Lettres Inédites,* pp. 47–8. To Stair, 19 Dec. 1717.

43. *Ibid.,* pp. 49, 56 and 74–5.

44. *Ibid.,* pp. 46 and 57. To Stair, 17 Dec. 1717 and 19 Jan. 1718.

45. *Ibid.,* pp. 57, 62 and 99. To Stair, 19 Jan., 12 Feb. 1718 and c. Dec.–Jan. 1719/20.

46. *Ibid.,* pp. 18 and 77 note.

47. *Ibid.,* pp. 65–6 note. Craggs to Bolingbroke, 27 March 1718; 'Letters of James Brydges to Henry St John', ed. G. Davies and M. Tinling, *Huntington Library Bulletin* (1936), no. 9, p. 153. 5 Oct. 1717.

48. Scottish Record Office. Stair MSS. GD135. Vol. 141/13B. Craggs to Stair, 20 Oct. 1718; vol. 141/18. Bolingbroke to Stair, 4 Dec. 1718; vol. 141/19A and 19B. Craggs to Stair, 10 Mar. and 27 May 1719. Baratier, *Lettres Inédites,* pp. 87–91. Bolingbroke to Stair, 26 Feb., 3, 18 Mar. 1719.

49. Cited by Lord Mahon, *History of England from the Peace of Utrecht,* ii, 76–7.

50. Scottish Record Office. Stair MSS. GD135, vol. 141/19B. 18 Dec. 1719.

51. B.M. Add. MSS. 34196, f. 12. To his father, 12 Aug. 1720.

52. B.M. Add. MSS. 34518, f. 66. Harcourt to Sunderland, 25 Mar. 1721; *The Harcourt Papers,* ed. E. W. Harcourt (Oxford, 1880), ii, 110–12. Harcourt to Bolingbroke, c. Mar.–April 1721.

53. Baratier, *Lettres Inédites,* p. 40.

54. *Ibid.,* pp. 46 and 49. 17 and 19 Dec. 1717.

55. East Sussex Record Office. Danny MSS. 394. To Stair, 18 Aug. 1718 (copy).

56. Baratier, *Lettres Inédites,* pp. 84–5. 10 Jan. 1719.

57. *Swift's Corr.,* iii, 171. Aug. 1723.

CHAPTER 9

 1. *Swift's Corr.,* iii, 26. 6/17 Mar. 1719. See also *ibid.,* iii, 172 and 184. Aug. and Dec. 1723; and *The Letters of Jonathan Swift to Charles Ford,* ed. David Nichol Smith (Oxford, 1935), pp. 231–2 and 239. Bolingbroke to Ford, 21 Feb. 1717 and 10 Oct. 1724.

2. *Works*, i, 181–200. The work is dated 1716, though he told Swift on 21 Dec./1 Jan. 1721/22 that he had just finished a treatise on exile. *Swift's Corr.*, iii, 111.

3. *Works*, i, 182–3.

4. *Ibid.*, i, 199–200.

5. Paul Baratier, *Lord Bolingbroke. Ses Ecrits Politiques* (Paris, 1939), p. 194; Dennis James Fletcher, 'The Intellectual Relations of Lord Bolingbroke with France', University of Wales M.A. thesis (1953), pp. 33–8.

6. Sheila Radice, 'Bolingbroke in France', *Notes and Queries* (1939), clxxvii, 309.

7. See the Bolingbroke-Alary correspondence in Grimoard, *Lettres Historiques*, ii, 439 *et seq.* and iii, *passim;* Harvard University Library. Houghton MSS. 51M–176(6–8); and National Library of Scotland. MSS. 3419, ff. 40–1 and 3420, ff. 212–12v.

8. Brook Taylor's *Contemplatio Philosophica,* ed. Sir William Young (1793), pp. 126–7 and 135–6. 28 Nov. 1721 and 26 Dec. 1723.

9. *The Correspondence of Alexander Pope,* ed. George Sherburn (5 vols., Oxford, 1956), ii, 249–52. Bolingbroke to Pope, 18 Aug. 1724. Hereafter cited as *Pope's Corr.*

10. 'The Substance of Some Letters to M. de Pouilly', written c. 1720. *Works*, ii, 473. See *ibid.,* ii, 467–9, 474–8 and 489–90.

11. 'A Letter occasioned by one of Archbishop Tillotson's Sermons', written in the early 1720s, *Works,* iii, 17.

12. Grimoard, *Lettres Historiques,* iii, 163. To Alary, 2 April 1722; National Library of Scotland. MSS. 3419, ff. 40–41. To Alary, 27 April 1722.

13. 'The Substance of Some Letters to M. de Pouilly', *Works,* ii, 467.

14. Grimoard, *Lettres Historiques,* iii, 236. To Alary, June 1724.

15. 'The Substance of Some Letters to M. de Pouilly', *Works,* ii, 463, 496–7 and 503–4.

16. Dennis J. Fletcher, 'Bolingbroke and the diffusion of Newtonianism in France', *Studies on Voltaire and the Eighteenth Century* (1967), liii, 29–46.

17. *Pope's Corr.,* i, 220. 18 Feb. 1723/24.

18. *Works,* ii, 464. See also ii, 462, 465, 493 and 504.

19. *Ibid.,* ii, 495, 508.

20. *Ibid.,* ii, 478–9, 491; iii, 15–25, 32.

21. *Ibid.,* iii, 32–3. See also iii, 25–8 and 38.

22. *Swift's Corr.,* ii, 208–9. 1/12 Sept. 1724.

23. This was not published in England until 1752, but it had originally been composed in French, probably in the early 1720s. It is the essay which

some historians have referred to as 'The Short Treatise on Compassion', which they mistakenly believed had been lost. See George H. Nadel, 'New Light on Bolingbroke's Letters on History', *Journal of the History of Ideas* (1962), xxiii, 550–1 note.

24. *Op. cit.,* pp. 35–7.

25. *Works,* vi, 111; *Swift's Corr.,* iv, 289, v, 67, 92, 102. Letters of 1732 and 1734; George Sherburn, 'Two Notes on the *Essay on Man', Philological Quarterly* (1933), xii, 402.

26. *Swift's Corr.,* iv, 253. 2 Aug. 1731.

27. Alfred O. Aldridge, 'Shaftesbury and Bolingbroke', *Philological Quarterly* (1952), xxxi, 1–16; Walter McIntosh Merrill, *From Statesman to Philosopher: A Study in Bolingbroke's Deism* (New York, 1949), pp. 249–68; and Dennis James Fletcher, 'The Intellectual Relations of Lord Bolingbroke with France', University of Wales M.A. thesis (1953), pp. 115–31.

28. Isaac Kramnick, 'An Augustan Reply to Locke: Bolingbroke on Natural Law and the Origin of Government', *Political Science Quarterly* (1967), lxxxii, 571–94.

29. The connection between his philosophy and his political theories is discussed in chapter 11, section iv. The following section on his religious and ethical views is based on W. M. Merrill, *From Statesman to Philosopher: A Study in Bolingbroke's Deism, passim;* D. J. Fletcher's M.A. thesis, *op. cit.,* pp. 127–62; Arthur O. Lovejoy, *The Great Chain of Being* (Cambridge, Mass., 1936), pp. 183–207; Sydney Wayne Jackman, *Man of Mercury* (1965), pp. 71–85; D. G. James, *The Life of Reason* (1949), pp. 237–62; Harvey C. Mansfield, *Statesmanship and Party Government* (Chicago, 1965), pp. 50–64; Kurt Kluxen, *Das Problem der Politischen Opposition* (Freiburg, 1956), pp. 233–47; John Hunt, 'Henry St John, Lord Bolingbroke', *The Contemporary Review* (1869), x, 405–21; Isaac Kramnick, *Bolingbroke and his Circle* (Cambridge, Mass., 1968), pp. 84–110; and, of course, *Bolingbroke's Works.*

30. *Works,* iv, 25. See also *ibid.,* iii, 55–64, 107, 139–41, 390–1, 401–4, 409–15, 485–97, 518–23, 526–8; iv, 5–75, 92–105, 243, 271–3, 416, 484.

31. *Ibid.,* iii, 148, 218–19, 226–30, 421–31; iv, 283.

32. *Ibid.,* iii, 396. When he returned to England, Bolingbroke kept a domestic chaplain, Mark Hildesley, at Dawley, perhaps to placate his Tory critics.

33. *Ibid.,* iv, 105, 108. See also iii, 223–4, 485–7.

34. *Ibid.,* iii, 485–97.

35. e.g. *ibid.,* iii, 71–82, 100–117, 143–4, 282–3; iv, 318–23, 357–8, 415, 465.

36. *Ibid.,* iii, 300–9, 434–57.

37. H.M.C., *Hastings MSS.*, iii, 65–6. 24 Oct. 1748.

38. *Works,* iv, 212, 332. See also *ibid,* ii, 339–42, 352; iii, 104; and iv, 214, 246, 263–4, 291, 332, 372–3, 434.

39. Petworth House. Egremont MSS. 12 Jan. 1736.

40. *Works,* iii, 380–1. See also *ibid.*, iii, 331–47, 370, 377, 392–4, 399, 401; and iv, 171–7, 214, 251.

41. H.M.C., *Hastings MSS.*, iii, 68. 10 Nov. 1748.

42. *Works,* iv, 323. For Bolingbroke's ideas on the nature of God, see also, *ibid.*, iv, 152–5, 170, 318–19, 350–3, 388–92, 395–401, 442, 453, 462–5, 472–3.

43. *Ibid.*, iii, 138; and iv, 327, 330–1, 338–9, 364–7, 374, 435.

44. *Ibid.*, iii, 396–401; and iv, 146–7, 165, 215, 231, 251, 270, 297, 327, 344–9, 355, 376, 432, 446, 456–7, 474, 482.

45. For a fuller discussion of this question, see Isaac Kramnick, 'An Augustan Reply to Locke: Bolingbroke on Natural Law and the Origin of Government', *Political Science Quarterly* (1967), lxxxii, 571–94, and his book, *Bolingbroke and His Circle,* pp. 84–110; Alfred Owen Aldridge, 'Shaftesbury and Bolingbroke', *Philological Quarterly* (1952), xxxi, 1–16; Kurt Kluxen, *Das Problem der Politischen Opposition* (Freiburg/München, 1956), esp. pp. 233–49; Sydney W. Jackman, *Man of Mercury,* pp. 86–102; and Harvey C. Mansfield, *Statesmanship and Party Government,* pp. 50–64.

46. *Works,* iv, 211–12, 246.

47. *Ibid.*, iv, 149–64, 167, 181–8, 297, 368–9.

48. *Ibid.*, iv, 145–51.

49. *Ibid.*, iv, 146, 150, 181, 185, 194–8, 228.

50. See the discussion of these two concepts, in J. A. W. Gunn, *Politics and the Public Interest in the Seventeenth Century* (1969).

51. *Works,* iv, 194–9.

CHAPTER 10

1. H.M.C., *Polwarth MSS.*, iii, 86. Polwarth to Carteret, 4/15 Mar. 1722; *The Harcourt Papers,* ed. E. W. Harcourt, iii, 94. Pope to Harcourt, 21 June 1723.

2. B.M. Add. MSS. 36243, f. 103; William L. Clements Library, University of Michigan, Sydney MSS. Copy of Bolingbroke's pardon.

3. Coxe, *R. Walpole's Memoirs,* iii, 311–12. Bolingbroke's letter, 28 June 1723 and Townshend's reply, 9/20 July 1723.

4. *The Harcourt Papers,* ii, 107–8. Bolingbroke to Harcourt, 26 July 1723.

5. H.M.C., *Polwarth MSS.,* iii, 285. George Baillie to Lord Polwarth, 10 July 1723.

6. Coxe, *R. Walpole's Memoirs,* ii, 264–5; and B.M. Stowe MSS. 251, ff. 13v–14v. Walpole to Townshend, 23 July 1723.

7. B.M. Add. MSS. 32686, f. 301. To Newcastle, 10 Aug. 1723.

8. B.M. Stowe MSS. 251, ff. 21v–26v. To Walpole, 6, 11, 31 Aug. 1723 N.S.

9. *Ibid.,* 242, f. 213. To Townshend, Aix la Chapelle, 17 Sept. 1723 N.S. He did not visit Hanover though he did write directly to the King from Paris in January 1724. P.R.O. State Papers, Foreign (France) 78/180, ff. 2–2v.

10. Coxe, *R. Walpole's Memoirs,* i, 182–92, and ii, 313–29. Bolingbroke to Harcourt and Townshend, Dec. 1723–Jan. 1724; William Coxe, *Memoirs of Horatio, Lord Walpole* (3rd ed., 1820), i, 108–24. Horatio to Robert Walpole, 15, 16 and 29 Dec. 1723. Hereafter cited as Coxe, *Horatio Walpole's Memoirs.*

11. Coxe, *R. Walpole's Memoirs,* ii, 326. Bolingbroke to Townshend, c. Jan. 1724.

12. *Ibid.,* ii, 328–31. Townshend to H. Walpole, 2 April 1724; Lady Bolingbroke to Townshend, n.d.; Bolingbroke to Wyndham, 22 May 1724.

13. Lord Mahon, *History of England from the Peace of Utrecht,* ii, app. pp. xx–xxi. Lord Lansdowne to the Pretender, 10 July 1724.

14. Coxe, *R. Walpole's Memoirs,* ii, 345. Rev. Etough's minutes; B.M. Stowe MSS. 242, f. 218. Etough to Dr Birch, 14 Jan. 1743/44; *Some Materials Towards Memoirs of the Reign of King George II, by John, Lord Hervey,* ed. Romney Sedgwick (3 vols., 1931), i, 11–13. Hereafter cited as *Lord Hervey's Memoirs.*

15. Coxe at first claimed that Walpole had not opposed Bolingbroke's full restoration, but he later changed his mind. *R. Walpole's Memoirs,* i, 210–11 and *Horatio Walpole's Memoirs,* i, 125. For confirmation of the second opinion, see H.M.C. *Fourteenth Report,* app. ix, *Onslow MSS.,* p. 515; John, Lord Campbell, *Lives of the Lord Chancellors* (1846), iv, 490; *Lord Hervey's Memoirs,* i, 183; and Lord Mahon, *History of England from the Peace of Utrecht,* ii, 108 and note. Walpole's fears were at least partially confirmed by the opposition to the emasculated bill.

16. Coxe, *R. Walpole's Memoirs,* ii, 329. To Newcastle, 24 Oct. 1724.

17. e.g. *ibid.,* ii, 333. Bolingbroke to Wyndham, 29 Nov. 1735; *Lord Hervey's Memoirs,* i. 11.

18. Coxe, *R. Walpole's Memoirs,* ii, 332. Bolingbroke to Wyndham, 30 Jan. and 6 Feb. 1725.

19. The best account of this debate is in *The Parliamentary Diary of Sir Edward Knatchbull, 1722–1730*, ed. A. N. Newman (*Camden Society*, 3rd series, 1963), xciv, 46–8.

20. Lord Mahon, *History of England from the Peace of Utrecht*, ii, app., pp. xxii–xxiii. Duke of Wharton to the Pretender, 1 May 1725; MSS. Journal of Mrs Charles Caesar, Book iv (unfoliated).

21. Lord Mahon, *op. cit.*, ii, app. p. xxiv. Wharton to the Pretender, 29 May 1725; Cobbett's *Parl. Hist.*, viii, 460–81; *Commons Journals*, xx, 507–8; and *Lords Journals*, xxii, 549, 552–3.

22. H.M.C., *Portland MSS.*, vii, 409–11. Wm. Stratford to the 2nd Earl of Oxford, 14, 23 Dec. 1725.

23. *Ibid.*, vii, 411. 23 Dec. 1725. See also Coxe, *R. Walpole's Memoirs*, iii, 343–4. Bolingbroke to Hardwicke, 12 Nov. 1744.

24. *Ibid.*, ii, 332. To Wyndham, 6 Feb. 1725.

25. Lord Mahon, *History of England from the Treaty of Utrecht*, iii, app., pp. xlvi–xlvii; *The Harcourt Papers*, ed. E. W. Harcourt, ii, 109–10. Dawley, 22 Mar. 1725/26. Harcourt was disappointed at Bolingbroke's decision to join the opposition. MSS. Journal of Mrs Charles Caesar, Book ii.

CHAPTER 11

1. The dedication to the 'Dissertation upon Parties', *Works,* ii, 15. J. H. Plumb has also claimed that Bolingbroke's works must be seen in their political context, but he voiced precisely the opposite view when he maintained that Bolingbroke's ideas were shallow when seen in context and acquired an illusory depth when abstracted from it. 'Who now reads Bolingbroke?', *The Spectator* (24 Jan. 1969), p. 108.

2. The best discussion of Bolingbroke's contributions to *The Craftsman* is by Giles G. Barber, 'A Bibliography of Henry St John, Viscount Bolingbroke', Oxford University B.Litt. thesis (1963), pp. 121–51. Mr Barber lists them as the *Remarks,* the *Dissertation* and nos. 16, 25, 29, 30, 35, 52, 54, 60–2, 65, 68, 71, 91, 93, 96, 105, 111, 114, 123, 130, 131, 133, 134, 142, 147, 149, 154, 161, 167, 182, 185, 186, 199, 252, 264, 319, 324–6, 346, 350, 351, 353, 371, 377, 406, 430, 507, 508, 510 and 511. Isaac Kramnick, *Bolingbroke and His Circle,* pp. 273–4, note 43, has argued that all the essays in *The Craftsman* reflect Bolingbroke's ideas and could well have been written by him. Kramnick was analysing the opposition to Walpole. The biographer needs to consider Bolingbroke's specific contribution, and only those essays cited by Barber have been used for this chapter.

3. *Remarks,* nos. 218 (5 Sept. 1730) to 255 (22 May 1731), *Works,* i, 292–455; *Dissertation,* nos. 382–96 (27 Oct. 1733/2 Feb. 1734) and 436–43 (9 Sept./28 Dec. 1734), *Works,* ii, 5–172.

4. 'Dissertation', *Works,* ii, 25, 37.

5. For an elaboration of this following section, see Geoffrey Holmes, *British Politics in the Age of Anne,* pp. 150–64, 175–80; P. G. M. Dickson, *The Financial Revolution in England* (1967), pp. 15–35; G. E. Mingay, *English Landed Society in the Eighteenth Century* (1963); Isaac Kramnick, *Bolingbroke and His Circle,* pp. 39–55; H. J. Habakkuk, 'English Landownership 1680–1740', *Econ. Hist. Rev.* (1940), x, 2–17; W. A. Speck, 'Conflict in Society', *Britain after the Glorious Revolution, 1689–1714,* ed. Geoffrey Holmes, pp. 135–54; and my Ph.D. thesis, 'Henry St John and the Struggle for the Leadership of the Tory Party, 1720–1714', University of Newcastle upon Tyne (1967–8), pp. 53–65.

6. *Works,* i, 116.

7. H.M.C., *Portland MSS.,* vii, 449. To the second Earl of Oxford, 15 July, 1727.

8. *The Craftsman,* no. 114 (Sept. 1728). See also nos. 65, 68, 71, 91, 93 and 96, all contributed by Bolingbroke.

9. 'Dissertation', *Works,* ii, 163–4.

10. Alfred James Henderson, *London and the National Government, 1721–1742* (Durham, N. Carolina, 1945), *passim.*

11. *The Craftsman,* no. 130 (28 Dec. 1728).

12. Both quotes from *ibid.,* no. 114 (7 Sept. 1728).

13. *Ibid.,* nos. 35 (7 April 1727); 61 (2 Sept. 1727); 130 (28 Dec. 1728); 131 (4 Jan. 1729); and 133 (18 Jan. 1729).

14. *Ibid.,* nos. 91 and 93 (30 Mar. and 13 April 1728).

15. *Ibid.,* no. 350 (17 Mar. 1733). See also no. 346 (17 Feb. 1733).

16. See J. G. A. Pocock, 'Machiavelli, Harrington, and English Political Ideologies in the Eighteenth Century', *William and Mary Quarterly* (Oct. 1965), xxii, 549–83.

17. 'Dissertation', *Works,* ii, 163–5; *The Craftsman,* nos. 29 (17 Mar. 1727); 147 (26 April 1729); 161 (2 Aug. 1729); and 'On Luxury', *Works,* i, 474–7.

18. For these practices, see 'Remarks', *Works,* i, 306, 331, 416–18; 'Dissertation', *ibid.,* ii, 93, 146, 151–72; *The Craftsman,* nos. 16 (27 Jan. 1727), 62 (9 Sept. 1727), 111 (17 Aug. 1728), 123 (9 Nov. 1728), 161 (2 Aug. 1729).

19. *Ibid.,* no. 114 (7 Sept. 1728). See also nos. 111 (17 Aug. 1728) and 123 (9 Nov. 1728).

20. *Ibid.,* nos. 161 (2 Aug. 1729), 324–6 (16, 22, 30 Sept. 1732), 377 (22 Sept.

1733), 406 (13 April 1734); *The Craftsman Extraordinary* (c. Jan. 1734); 'Dissertation', *Works*, ii, 100–6, 151; and *The Freeholder's Political Catechism* (1733).

21. In 1736 Bolingbroke admitted that some form of corruption might be necessary 'to maintain subordination and to carry on even good government, and, therefore, necessary to be preserved in the crown, notwithstanding the abuse that is sometimes made of them; for no human institution can arrive at perfection, and the most that human wisdom can do, is to procure the same or greater good, at the expense of less evil'. 'A Letter on the Spirit of Patriotism', *Works*, ii, 365.

22. See H. N. Fieldhouse, 'Bolingbroke and the Idea of Non-Party Government', *History* (1938–9), xxiii, 41–56.

23. 'Remarks,' *Works*, i, 341; *The Craftsman*, no. 123 (9 Nov. 1728); and *The Freeholder's Political Catechism*, p. 22.

24. *The Craftsman*, no. 185 (17 Jan. 1730). See also no. 186 (24 Jan. 1730).

25. 'Remarks', *Works*, i, 308; 'Dissertation', *ibid.*, ii, 19; and *The Craftsman*, no. 25 (3 Mar. 1727).

26. 'Dissertation', *Works*, ii, 126. See also *ibid.*, ii, 70–1, 81; *The Craftsman*, no. 430 (28 Sept. 1734); and *The Freeholder's Political Catechism*, pp. 7–9.

27. 'Dissertation', *Works*, ii, 25 *et seq.*

28. *Ibid.*, ii, 54.

29. *Ibid.*, ii, 67. The differences between Churchmen and Dissenters could now, of course, be composed, according to Bolingbroke.

30. *Ibid.*, ii, 24.

31. The dedication to the 'Dissertation', *Works*, ii, 11.

32. 'Remarks', *Works*, i, 295. See also, 'Dissertation', *ibid.*, ii, 25; *The Craftsman*, no. 264 (24 July 1731); Harvey C. Mansfield, *Statesmanship and Party Government*, pp. 10–18; and H. N. Fieldhouse, 'Bolingbroke and the Idea of Non-Party Government', *History* (1938–39), xxiii, 41–56.

33. For Bolingbroke's lavish praise of Elizabeth, see 'Remarks', *Works*, i, 363–98.

34. See also his 'Dissertation', *Works*, ii, 109–15

35. Isaac Kramnick, 'Augustan Politics and English Historiography: The Debate on the English Past, 1730–35', *History and Theory* (1967), vi, 33–56; and the same writer's *Bolingbroke and His Circle*, pp. 127–36, 177–81. For the whole concept of the ancient constitution, see J. G. A. Pocock's seminal work, *The Ancient Constitution and the Feudal Law* (Cambridge, 1957); Caroline Robbins, *The Eighteenth Century Commonwealthman* (Cambridge, Mass., U.S.A., 1959); and Christopher Hill, 'The Norman Yoke', in *Puritanism and Revolution* (1958), pp. 50–122.

M*

36. See the discussion in J. G. A. Pocock, 'Burke and the Ancient Constitution – a Problem in the History of Ideas', *Historical Journal* (1960), iii, 125–43.

37. Bolingbroke accepted the constitutional notion that the king could do no wrong and that the royal ministers were answerable for the government's policies. The dedication to the 'Dissertation', *Works,* ii, 7.

38. *Ibid.,* ii, 88–9.

39. *Ibid.,* ii, 14, 85, 87, 107, 112, 117–18, 150–1; J. H. Burns, 'Bolingbroke and the Concept of Constitutional Government', *Political Studies* (1962), x, 264–76; Caroline Robbins, '"Discordant Parties." A Study of the Acceptance of Party by Englishmen', *Political Science Quarterly* (1958), lxxiii, 505–29; and Archibald S. Foord, *His Majesty's Opposition, 1714–1832* (Oxford, 1964), esp. pp. 37–40 and 149–50.

40. 'Remarks', *Works,* i, 296–7.

41. Robert Shackleton, 'Montesquieu, Bolingbroke, and the Separation of Powers', *French Studies* (1949), iii, 25–38; and the same author's *Montesquieu. A Critical Biography* (Oxford, 1961), pp. 126–9, 297–301, has argued that Bolingbroke advocated the separation of powers. In the following section I have relied more on the arguments of J. H. Burns, 'Bolingbroke and the Concept of Constitutional Government', *Political Studies* (1962), x, 264–76; W. B. Gwynn, *The Meaning of the Separation of Powers* (New Orleans, 1965), pp. 91–9; and Isaac Kramnick, *Bolingbroke and His Circle,* pp. 137–87.

42. 'Remarks', *Works,* i, 306. See also 'Dissertation', *ibid.,* ii, 114–20.

43. 'Remarks', *ibid.,* i, 332.

44. *Ibid.*; and the *London Journal,* 4 July, 19 Sept. 1730.

45. 'Remarks', *Works,* i, 333.

46. *The Freeholder's Political Catechism,* p. 5; *The Craftsman,* no. 430 (28 Sept. 1734); and 'Dissertation', *Works,* ii, 114–19.

47. 'Dissertation', *Works,* ii, 85. Bolingbroke always saw the political system as a machine rather than as an organism.

48. 'Remarks', *Works,* i, 427. See also *The Freeholder's Political Catechism,* p. 9.

49. 'Dissertation', *Works,* ii, 85, 91, 107 and 117.

50. *Ibid.,* ii, 85.

51. For a discussion of Bolingbroke's philosophy, see *supra,* chapter 9, section ii.

52. *Swift's Corr.,* v. 77–8. 27 June–6 July 1734.

53. *The Craftsman,* no. 264 (24 July 1731).

54. *The Letters of Horace Walpole,* ed. Mrs Paget Toynbee (16 vols., Oxford, 1904), xi, 102. To Sir Horace Mann, 13 Jan. 1780.

CHAPTER 12

1. *Swift's Corr.*, iv, 35–6. Pope to Swift, 28 June 1728. See also *ibid., iv*, 8. Bolingbroke to Swift, 15 Feb. 1728; and *Pope's Corr., ii*, 525. Pope to Bathurst, 7 Nov. 1728.

2. *Swift's Corr.*, iii, 280–1. Pope to Swift, 15 Oct. 1725; Lord Orrery's remarks are cited in *The Gentleman's Magazine* (1751), p. 572; Bolingbroke's comment was to Bathurst, 19 Nov. 1728. P.R.O. Bathurst Papers. 30/62/74. Letter 18.

3. *Swift's Corr.*, iv, 277. Pope to Swift, 1 Dec. 1731; *ibid., iv*, 19. Swift to Mrs Caesar, 30 July 1733; and *Pope's Corr., iii*, 276. Pope to Swift [Mar. 1732].

4. For an extended treatment of their views, see Isaac Kramnick, *Bolingbroke and His Circle*, pp. 205–35.

5. Bolingbroke asked Swift to contribute to the opposition campaign, but his pamphlets were not published at the time. *Swift's Corr., iii*, 392–4. Swift had planned to publish his *History of the Four Last Years of Queen Anne* in about 1727, but Bolingbroke had dissuaded him, pointing out that such a partisan work would only stir up the old Whig-Tory rivalry which he was attempting to suppress. Yale University Library. Osborn Collection. Bolingbroke to Lord Orrery, 28 Dec. 1744.

6. Arthur E. Case, *Four Essays on Gulliver's Travels* (Princeton, 1945), pp. 69–74; Irvin Ehrenpreis, 'The Origins of *Gulliver's Travels*', in *Fair Liberty was all his Cry,* ed. Norman Jeffares (1967), pp. 201–7; *Gulliver's Travels* (Penguin ed., 1967), pp. 73–5, 89–90, 95–6, 103–11, 168–73, 214–15, 232–7, 241, 244–5, 247, 299, 302–3 and 310; and *Swift's Corr., iii*, 392–4, iv, 77, 136, 193. From Bolingbroke, 18 May, 6 June 1727; to Bolingbroke, 5 April 1729, 21 Mar. 1730; From Bolingbroke, 17 Jan. 1731.

7. Bolingbroke was sensitive to Swift's objections to his religious views and tried to convince him that he was not an atheist nor the type of free-thinker who dabbled in metaphysics to undermine religion. He claimed that he was using his reason to understand Christianity. *Swift's Corr., iii*, 209. 12 Sept. 1724; and George Sherburn, 'Errors concerning the Houyhnhnms', *Modern Philology* (1958), lvi, 95–6.

8. Irvin Ehrenpreis, 'The Origins of *Gulliver's Travels*', in *Fair Liberty was all his Cry,* ed. Norman Jeffares, pp. 215–18; and Kathleen Williams, *Jonathan Swift and the Age of Compromise* (Kansas, 1959), pp. 65–87, 187–90, have argued that Swift deliberately rejected Bolingbroke's rationalism. Their views were based on a faulty reading of Bolingbroke's

philosophy since they regarded him as an optimistic rationalist. Their interpretation of Swift's philosophy has been rejected by George Sherburn, 'Errors concerning the Houyhnhnms', *Modern Philology* (1958), lvi, 92–7; W. B. Carnochan, 'The Complexity of Swift: Gulliver's Fourth Voyage', *Studies in Philology* (1963), lx, 23–44; and R. S. Crane, 'The Houyhnhnms, the Yahoos, and the History of Ideas', in *Reason and the Imagination*, ed. J. A. Mazzeo (New York, 1962), pp. 231–53. Ehrenpreis repudiated his earlier views in 'The Meaning of Gulliver's Last Voyage', *Review of English Literature* (1962), iii, 18–38.

9. For Bolingbroke's exaggerated claims, Swift's scepticism and his desire to emulate him, see *Swift's Corr.*, iii, 25–7, 170–2, 207 and 209. From Bolingbroke, 6/17 Mar. 1719, Aug. 1723, 1/12 Sept. 1724, 14 Dec. 1725; *ibid.*, iv, 105. To Bolingbroke, 31 Oct. 1729; and, *ibid.*, iii, 42. To Bolingbroke, 19 Dec. 1719.

10. *Ibid.*, iii, 359. From Pope, 17 Nov. 1726.

11. *Pope's Corr.*, ii, 218–20. From Bolingbroke, 18 Feb. 1723/4; *Swift's Corr.*, iv, 253–4, 289. From Bolingbroke, 2 Aug. 1731, Mar. or April 1732; P.R.O. Bathurst Papers. 30/62/74. Letter 19. Bolingbroke to Lord Bathurst, 8 Oct. 1730; and Bolingbroke's *Works*, iii, 40 and iv, 111.

12. William Warburton, who hated Bolingbroke's influence on Pope, started the tradition of denying that Bolingbroke's philosophy influenced his friend's poetry. Warburton directly inspired Owen Ruffhead's *Life of Alexander Pope* (1769), which first refuted Bolingbroke's influence. This has been supported, though to different degrees, by Dr Samuel Johnson's *Lives of the English Poets*, ed. G. B. Gill (Oxford, 1905), p. 163; *The Works of Alexander Pope*, ed. W. Elwin and W. J. Courthope (10 vols., 1871–89), ii, 263–4 and note; George Sherburn, 'Pope at Work', in *Essays on the Eighteenth Century presented to David Nichol Smith* (Oxford, 1945), pp. 45–69; and *The Twickenham Edition of the Poems of Alexander Pope*, vol. III, i, ed. Maynard Mack (1950), pp. xi–lxxii and 69. For the evidence in support of the view that Bolingbroke did influence the *Essay on Man*, see *Swift's Corr.*, iv, 253–4. From Bolingbroke, 2 Aug. 1731; Lord Bathurst's letter of 1769 cited by George Sherburn, 'Two Notes on the *Essay on Man*', *Philological Quarterly* (1933), xii, 402; and *Anecdotes, Observations and Characters of Books and Men collected from the conversation of Mr Pope and other eminent persons of his time by the Reverend Joseph Spence*, ed. S. W. Singer (new ed., 1964), pp. 103–4, 177–8. Hereafter cited as *Spence's Anecdotes*.

13. William H. Irving, *John Gay. Favorite of the Wits* (Durham, N. Carolina, 1940), *passim*; Lewis Melville, *Life and Letters of John Gay* (1921), pp. 24–9; William E. Schultz, *Gay's Beggar's Opera. Its Contents, History, and Influence*

(1923), pp. 209–25; and Sven M. Armens, *John Gay. Social Critic* (New York, 1954), esp. pp. 57–62, 190–207.

14. *Voltaire's Correspondence,* ed. Theodore Besterman (Geneva, 1953–65), i, 177–8. To Thieriot, two letters, Dec. 1722. Hereafter cited as *Voltaire's Corr.* See also Grimoard, *Lettres Historiques,* iii, 7. Bolingbroke to Madame de Ferriol, 4 Feb. 1719.

15. Charles Dedeyan, *Voltaire et la pensée anglaise* (Paris, n. d.), p. 17.

16. *Voltaire's Corr.,* i, 178 note, 199, 246–7. Bolingbroke to Madame de Ferriol, 4 Dec. 1722, Voltaire to the Marquise de Bernières, 7 June 1723, Bolingbroke to Voltaire, 27 June 1724; and *Pope's Corr.,* ii, 222, 228–9. From Bolingbroke, 18 Feb. 1724 and Pope's reply, 9 April 1724.

17. Grimoard, *Lettres Historiques,* iii, 268–9, 274. Bolingbroke to Madame de Ferriol, 5, 28 Dec. 1725; and *Voltaire's Corr.,* ii, 37, 40–2. To Thieriot, 26 Oct. 1726, to Pope, 28 Oct. 1726.

18. A. Ballantyne, *Voltaire's Visit to England 1726–1729* (1893), p. 136.

19. The accusation was first made in Owen Ruffhead's unreliable *Life of Alexander Pope,* p. 213 note. It was repeated by John Churton Collins, *Voltaire in England* (1886), pp. 249–51, who misunderstood Bolingbroke's letter to Swift, 18 May 1727 (*Swift's Corr.,* iii, 392) and Voltaire's to Thieriot, 27 May 1727 (*Voltaire's Corr.,* ii, 52). For a detailed refutation of the charge, see Lucien Foulet, *Correspondance de Voltaire (1726–1729)* (Paris, 1913), appendix vi, pp. 258–69.

20. For the government's attacks on *The Craftsman,* see Laurence Hanson, *Government and the Press, 1695–1763* (Oxford, 1963), pp. 67–9; P. C. Yorke, *The Life and Correspondence of Philip Yorke, Earl of Hardwicke* (3 vols., Cambridge, 1913), i, 82–7; and *The Wentworth Papers,* ed. J. J. Cartwright, pp. 465–72. Peter Wentworth to Strafford, 15, 26 July, 3 Aug. 1731.

21. *Swift's Corr.,* iii, 388. To Thomas Sheridan, 13 May 1727.

22. *Lord Hervey's Memoirs,* i, 263.

23. Archibald S. Foord, *His Majesty's Opposition 1714–1830* (Oxford, 1964), pp. 142–6, 166, 198; and H.M.C., *Egmont Diary,* i, 221, 263.

24. Cited by Laurence Hanson, *Government and the Press, 1695–1763,* p. 69.

25. Cited by W. T. Laprade, *Public Opinion and Politics in Eighteenth Century England* (New York, 1936), p. 351. The provincial newspapers rarely added their own criticisms to those of the Whig press in London, but one exception was the *Northampton Mercury*'s bitter attack on Bolingbroke on 20 Sept. 1731. Cited by G. A. Cranfield, *The Development of the Provincial Newspaper 1700–1760* (Oxford, 1962), p. 129.

26. Hervey, *Remarks on the Craftsman's Vindication of his Two Hon*^{ble} *Patrons in his paper of May 22, 1731* (1731); Yonge, *Sedition and Defamation*

Display'd: In a Letter to the Author of the Craftsman (1731). In a more moderate tone Lord Hervey also criticised Bolingbroke for distorting history in his 'Remarks on the History of England' in order to malign Walpole. See *Observations on the Writings of the Craftsman, Sequel of a pamphlet intitled Observations on the Writings of the Craftsman,* and *Farther Observations on the Writings of the Craftsman,* all published in 1730.

27. *A Final Answer to the Remarks on the Craftsman's Vindication* (1731), in *Works,* i, 456–73. Bolingbroke made no effort to defend his conduct in Anne's reign, perhaps to avoid reopening old Tory wounds. See *Swift's Corr.,* iv, 255–6. Bolingbroke to Swift, 2 Aug. 1731.

28. Anon: *A Letter to the Person last mentioned in the Craftsman of the 22d of May* (1731).

29. Rev. Etough's minutes, 13 Sept. 1737 *(sic),* in Coxe, *R. Walpole's Memoirs,* ii, 344–5; and *Lord Hervey's Memoirs,* i, 15–16.

30. Speaker Onslow claimed that Henry Pelham feared that Walpole would be dismissed in 1727. H.M.C., *Fourteenth Report,* app. ix, *Onslow MSS.,* p. 516. Horace Walpole convincingly showed that Pelham only came to this conclusion years later, when he accepted the account of one of Bolingbroke's friends. *The Yale Edition of Horace Walpole's Correspondence,* ed. W. S. Lewis *et al.* (1937–), xx, 452–5. From Horace Mann, 8 Nov. 1754, and Walpole's reply, 1 Dec. 1754. In his letter to Wyndham, 20 Feb. 1736, Bolingbroke reduced his claim to maintaining that, while the King did not dare support him openly, he *could* nevertheless have plotted with Bolingbroke to overthrow Walpole. Coxe, *R. Walpole's Memoirs,* ii, 340.

31. *The Works of Horace Walpole, Earl of Orford* (5 vols., 1798), iv, 279 note.

32. H.M.C., *Townshend MSS.,* p. 242. Lady Compton to Lady Northampton, 21 Nov. 1734.

33. *Yale Edition of Horace Walpole's Correspondence,* xxxi, app. 2, p. 420 and note 10.

34. Coxe, *R. Walpole's Memoirs,* ii, 508. To the Emperor, 17 Dec. 1726.

35. H.M.C., *Fourteenth Report,* app. part ix, *Onslow MSS.,* p. 467.

36. Les Archives du Ministère des Affaires Étrangères, Paris. Correspondance Politique: Angleterre. Vol. 379, ff. 38v–39, and 380, ff. 213–213v. To the French Foreign Minister, 8 Jan. and 22 May 1733. Hereafter cited as Aff. Étr. Corr. Pol. Angl.

37. *Lord Hervey's Memoirs,* i, 21.

38. *Works,* i, 201–35.

39. *The Parliamentary Diary of Sir Edward Knatchbull, 1722–1730,* ed. A. N. Newman, *Camden Society,* 3rd series (1963), xciv, 67.

40. Coxe, *R. Walpole's Memoirs,* i, 305; and *The Craftsman,* no. 35 (7 April 1727).

41. Scottish Record Office. Clerk of Penicuik MSS. GD18. No. 3207. R. Arbuthnot to Baron Clerk, 17 June 1727.

42. *The Craftsman,* nos. 60, 61. 26 Aug., 2 Sept. 1727.

43. *Ibid.,* nos. 62, 111, 114, 123, 147 and 161 (9 Sept. 1727; 17 Aug., 7 Sept., 9 Nov., 1728; 26 April and 2 Aug. 1729).

44. H.M.C., *Egmont Diary,* i, 32. 6 Feb. 1730.

45. *The Craftsman,* nos. 91, 93, 105 (30 Mar., 13 April, 6 July 1728).

46. *Ibid.,* nos. 65, 68, 71, 93, 96, 114, 130, 131, 133 (30 Sept., 21 Oct., 11 Nov. 1727; 13 April, 4 May, 7 Sept., 28 Dec. 1728; 4 and 18 Jan. 1729).

47. Aff. Étr. Corr. Pol. Angl. 365, ff. 87–88v. Broglie to French Foreign Minister, 7 Feb. 1729; and Pointz to Tilson, 28 Aug. 1728, N.S., cited by J. H. Plumb, *Sir Robert Walpole,* ii, 190.

48. *An Answer to the London Journal* (c. Jan. 1729); *An Answer to the Defence of the Inquiry into the Reasons of the Conduct of Great Britain* (1729); *Remarks on a late pamphlet, entitled, Observations on the Conduct of Great Britain* (1729), *Works,* i, 240–60, 261–91 and 478–91.

49. J. H. Plumb, *Sir Robert Walpole,* ii, 203–7; and *Lord Hervey's Memoirs,* i, 114–15.

50. *The Craftsman,* nos. 185, 186, 199 (17, 24 Jan. and 25 April 1730).

51. Coxe, *R. Walpole's Memoirs,* i, 323; *Swift's Corr.,* iv, 97–101. Bolingbroke to Swift, 19 Aug.–5 Oct. 1729; *Spence's Anecdotes,* p. 187 note; and B.M. Add. MSS. 34196, f. 78. Bolingbroke to his half-sister, Henrietta St John, 12 Sept. 1730.

52. H.M.C., *Egmont Diary,* i, 44. 13 Feb. 1730.

53. *Ibid.,* i, 35. 10 Feb. 1730.

54. *Ibid.,* i, 39. 12 Feb. 1730.

55. *Ibid.,* i, 37, 50. 10, 16 Feb. 1730.

56. *Ibid.,* i, 72. 27 Feb. 1730.

57. *Ibid.,* i, 74; *The Parliamentary Diary of Sir Edward Knatchbull, 1722–1730,* ed. A. N. Newman, *Camden Society,* 3rd series (1963), xciv, 110; and Montesquieu's *Notes sur l'Angleterre,* cited by Paul Baratier, *Lord Bolingbroke. See Écrits Politiques* (Paris, 1939), p. 236.

58. H.M.C., *Egmont Diary,* i, 74.

59. Coxe, *R. Walpole's Memoirs,* ii, 669. To Lord Harrington, 2 Mar. 1730.

60. H.M.C., *Egmont Diary,* i, 83–8. 20–30 Mar. 1730.

61. *The Craftsman,* no. 264 (14 July 1731). His only other separate contribution

to *The Craftsman* during this period was a panegyric on the late Duke of Marlborough. No. 252 (1 May 1731).

62. *The Daily Courant,* cited in *The Gentleman's Magazine* (1932), ii, 559; and P. C. Yorke, *The Life and Correspondence of Philip Yorke, Earl of Hardwicke,* i, 84.

63. H.M.C., *Egmont Diary,* i, 126.

64. *Ibid.,* i, 134. 17 Feb. 1731; and H.M.C., *Carlisle MSS.,* pp. 81–2. C. Howard to Carlisle, 23 Feb. 1731.

65. *Ibid.,* pp. 88–90. Howard to Carlisle, 12 and 22 Feb. 1732; and H.M.C. *Egmont Diary,* i, 220, 240 and 244. 10 Feb., 16 and 23 Mar. 1732.

66. Aff. Étr. Corr. Pol. Angl. 376, f. 229v. Chavigny's dispatch, 18 Feb. 1732.

67. *Ibid.,* 376, f. 322; and 377, ff. 22v–23, 52–5 and 125. Chavigny's dispatches, 17 Mar., 7, 13 and 24 April 1732.

68. *Ibid.,* 376, ff. 299–301v; 379, ff. 162–4; and 380, ff. 204v–205v. Chavigny's dispatches, 12 Mar. 1732, 16 Feb. and 22 May 1733.

69. *Ibid.,* 377, ff. 35–35v, 51v–52; and 380, f. 205. Chavigny's dispatches, 10, 13 April 1732 and 22 May 1733.

70. Coxe, *R. Walpole's Memoirs,* iii, 138–9. To Baron Gedda, c. April 1733.

71. Aff. Étr. Corr. Pol. Angl. 377, ff. 64v–65, 110v, 147; and 379, f. 41v. Chavigny's dispatches, 13, 24 April, 5 May 1732 and 8 Jan. 1733.

72. *Ibid.,* 376, ff. 264–6; 377, ff. 129v–130; 379, f. 164; and 380, ff. 205v–207v. Chavigny's dispatches, 3 Mar., 24 April 1732, 16 Feb. and 22 May 1733.

73. *Ibid.,* 378, ff. 390v–392 and 400–400v. Chavigny, 11 Dec. 1732 and Chauvelin, 22 Dec. 1732.

74. *Ibid.,* 380, ff. 229v–230. Chavigny's dispatch, 22 May 1733.

75. Alfred James Henderson, *London and the National Government, 1721–1742,* pp. 138–63.

76. H.M.C., *Egmont Diary,* i, 312. 31 Jan. 1733.

77. *The Craftsman,* no. 346 (17 Feb. 1733).

78. *Ibid.,* no. 350 (17 Mar. 1733). Bolingbroke was probably encouraged by the way the landed and trading interests among the opposition members had cooperated in opposing Walpole's plan to raid the sinking-fund of £500,000 in order to reduce the land tax by one shilling in the pound. This was achieved despite the skilful efforts of Walpole and his friends to detach the country gentlemen from the opposition on this issue. See *Parl. Hist.,* viii, 1200–14, and *The Gentleman's Magazine* (1733), p., 450 for the speech of Joseph Danvers, one of Walpole's supporters.

79. *The Craftsman,* nos. 351 and 353 (24 Mar., 7 April 1733). In *The Freeholder's Political Catechism,* pp. 20–1, which he wrote with the 1734

general election in mind, he again attacked the excise scheme and urged his readers not to support any venture of this kind merely because it might allow a reduction of the land tax.

80. The list can be seen in H.M.C., *Carlisle MSS.*, pp. 112–13. It included Wyndham, Pulteney, Sandys, Sir John Barnard and Sir John Hynde Cotton, the Jacobite.

81. H.M.C., *Egmont Diary*, i, 367. 25 April 1733.

82. *Ibid.*, i, 365–6. 23 April 1733.

83. *Lord Hervey's Memoirs*, i, 183–4.

84. *Parl. Hist.*, ix, 49–68; *Commons Journals*, xxii, 10, 133, 201.

85. H.M.C., *Egmont Diary*, i, 372. 9 May 1733.

86. H.M.C., *Carlisle MSS.*, pp. 115–18. Thos. Robinson to Carlisle, 24 and 26 May 1733.

87. H.M.C., *Egmont Diary*, ii, 14. 25 Jan. 1734.

88. Aff. Étr. Corr. Pol. Angl. 380, ff. 318–34.

89. *Works*, ii, 24.

90. *Ibid.*, ii, 25.

91. *The Craftsman*, nos. 371 and 406 (11 Aug. 1733 and 13 April 1734).

92. Aff.Étr.Corr.Pol.Angl. 381, ff. 35–40v.

93. *Ibid.*, ff. 81–3. 20 July 1733.

94. *Ibid.*, ff. 123–4, 172–5 and 225v–228. Chavigny's dispatches, 17 July, 5 and 28 Aug. 1733; and *ibid.*, ff. 163–4. Chauvelin to Chavigny, 14 Aug. 1733.

95. e.g. *ibid.*, ff. 114–24. Chavigny's dispatch, 17 July 1733.

96. *Ibid.*, 389, ff. 65v–68v. Chavigny's dispatch, 5 Nov. 1734; and *ibid.*, 390, f. 188. An anonymous report, probably from Bolingbroke, 15 Feb. 1735.

97. *Ibid.*, 388, ff. 178–9 and 389, ff. 78–80 and 155v–158v. Chauvelin to Chavigny, with advice on the conduct of the opposition, 17 Oct., 11 Nov. and 9 Dec. 1734; and *ibid.*, 389, ff. 14–22v and 125v–131v. Chavigny's reports, that the opposition had been advised as Chauvelin required, 5 and 19 Nov. 1734.

98. *Ibid.*, 390, f. 21. Chavigny's dispatch, 8 Jan. 1735.

99. Chavigny reported his meetings with Horatio Walpole, who protested at his intimacy with Bolingbroke. *Ibid.*, 384, ff. 198v–199 and 386, ff. 28v–29v. 16 April and 4 July 1734. Lord Hervey mentioned that the ministry intercepted some of Chavigny's later dispatches to France, but he did not link this with Bolingbroke's decision to retire from active political opposition to Walpole. *Lord Hervey's Memoirs*, i, 522.

100. e.g. H.M.C., *Egmont Diary*, ii, 15–18. 28 Jan. 1734.

101. H.M.C., *Mar and Kellie MSS.*, pp. 531–2. Pulteney to Lord Grange, 24, Feb. 1734; and J. H. Plumb, *Sir Robert Walpole*, ii, 308–9.

102. Scottish Record Office. Stair MSS. GD135, vol. 138, ff. 28–30. To James Erskine, 2 Mar. 1734.

103. This can be seen in the collected edition of *The Craftsman* (1737), xii, 112–27.

104. H.M.C., *Carlisle MSS.*, p. 133. C. Howard to Carlisle, 14 Mar. 1734; H.M.C., *Mar and Kellie MSS.*, p. 536. Pulteney to Lord Grange, 22 Mar. 1734; Coxe. *R. Walpole's Memoirs*, i, 412; and *Parl. Hist.*, ix, 394–5 note. For the debate as a whole, see *ibid.*, ix, 396–472.

105. *Ibid.*, ix, 471–2. See also Chavigny's dispatch, 4 April 1734. Aff. Étr. Corr. Pol. Angl. 385, f. 38.

106. Coxe, *R. Walpole's Memoirs*, iii, 552. To Wyndham, 18 Nov. 1739.

107. Yale University Library. Osborn Collection. Bolingbroke's papers, no date, but 1734.

108. *The Craftsman*, no. 430 (28 Sept. 1734).

109. W. T. Laprade, *Public Opinion and Politics in Eighteenth Century England*, p. 361.

110. e.g. *The Free Briton*, 6 and 13 Mar. 1735; and *The London Journal*, 15 Mar. 1735.

111. *Pope's Corr.*, v, 17. Swift to Pope, 3 Sept. 1735; and *Swift's Corr.*, v, 282. Pulteney to Swift, 22 Nov. 1735.

112. Aff. Étr. Corr. Pol. Angl. 390, ff. 58–58v and 93. Chavigny's dispatches, 14 and 28 Jan. 1735. See also *ibid.*, 389, ff. 14–22v; 390, f. 265v; and 391, ff. 16–16v. Dispatches of 1 Nov. 1734, 28 Feb. 1735 and 1 April 1735. Bolingbroke later admitted that Pulteney had regarded him as a liability to the opposition. Coxe, *R. Walpole's Memoirs*, iii, 523. To Wyndham, 23 July 1739; and *A Selection from the papers of the Earls of Marchmont*, ed. G. H. Rose (3 vols., 1831), ii, 179. To Lord Polwarth [No date. Mar.– July 1739?]. Hereafter cited as *Marchmont Papers*. Pulteney had never liked Bolingbroke personally. Their hostility was apparently not only political, but stemmed from Pulteney's knowledge that his wife, the former Anna Maria Gumley, had been Bolingbroke's mistress in Anne's reign. *Catalogue of Prints and Drawings in the British Museum*. Division I. *Political and Personal Satires*, ed. F. G. Stephens (1873), ii, 389–91.

113. Petworth House. Egremont MSS. No date, but about April 1735.

114. Coxe, *R. Walpole's Memoirs*, ii, 333. To Wyndham, 29 Nov. 1735.

CHAPTER 13

1. B.M. Add. MSS. 27733, ff. 186–186v; and 27734, ff. 27–8, 144 and 162. To Lord Essex, 25 June, 23 Aug., 18 Sept. and 2 Oct. 1735, N.S. All the dates of Bolingbroke's letters from France are dated according to the new style.

2. Petworth House. Egremont MSS. To Sir William Wyndham, 1 May 1736–19 Jan. 1738.

3. *Pope's Corr.*, iv, 110–73; and *Swift's Corr.*, vi, 129. Pope to Swift, 17 May 1739.

4. *Ibid.*, vi, 129. Pope to Swift, 17 May 1739; Coxe, *R. Walpole's Memoirs,* iii, 319. Bolingbroke to Wyndham, 18 Mar. 1736; and Petworth House. Egremont MSS. Bolingbroke to Charles Wyndham, Chantelou[p], 19 Feb. 1736; and to Sir William Wyndham, 22 Mar. 1736, 22 April 1737 and Argeville, 5 May 1737.

5. *Ibid.* To Charles Wyndham, 26 Dec. 1735; 5, 13 Jan., 14 Mar. 1736; 7 July 1740; To Sir William Wyndham, 12 Jan. 1736; Pierpont Morgan Library, New York. Bolingbroke to Cotton junior, 9 June, 3 Dec. 1739; 26 Jan., 14 May, 25 Oct. 1740; and H.M.C., *Denbigh MSS.,* pp. 116–21. Lady Bolingbroke to Lady Denbigh, 29 Nov. 1735, 25 Oct., 11, 25 Dec. 1736.

6. *Marchmont Papers,* ii, 213–14 and 228–30. To Marchmont, 13 June, 8 Aug. 1740; Coxe, *R. Walpole's Memoirs,* ii, 337 and 342. To Sir William Wyndham, 5 Jan., 20 Feb. 1736; *Swift's Corr.*, vi, 26. Barber to Swift, 23 June 1737.

7. B.M. Add. MSS. 27735, f. 59. To Lord Essex, 29 Jan. 1736.

8. Petworth House. Egremont MSS. 5 May 1737.

9. *Works,* ii, 339–51.

10. *Ibid.,* ii, 345.

11. *Ibid.,* ii, 350.

12. *Ibid.,* ii, 343.

13. *Swift's Corr.*, vi, 26, 37–8, 41, 130; *Marchmont Papers,* ii, 224–5 and 254. Bolingbroke to Marchmont, 17 Mar. and c. June 1741; and Petworth House. Egremont MSS. Bolingbroke to Sir William Wyndham, 16 Mar. 1738.

14. G. H. Nadel, 'New Light on Bolingbroke's Letters on History', *Journal of the History of Ideas* (1962), xxiii, 557.

15. *Works,* ii, 173–334. Bolingbroke also wrote a short essay, 'A Plan for a General History of Europe', *ibid.,* ii, 335–8.

16. B.M. Add. MSS. 4948A, ff. 438–438v. Lord Hyde to David Mallet, Paris, 7 Mar. 1752, N.S.

17. *Works,* ii, 213. See also pp. 200–15 and 230–4.

18. *Ibid.,* ii, 174–94.

19. *Ibid.,* ii, 229–30.

20. *Ibid.,* ii, 281.

21. *Ibid.,* ii, 333.

22. *Ibid.,* ii, 285.

23. See *Bolingbroke's Defence of the Treaty of Utrecht,* ed. G. M. Trevelyan (Cambridge, 1932).

24. *Works,* ii, 187–8.

25. B.M. Add. MSS. 34196, f. 93.

26. *The Craftsman,* nos. 507–8 and 510–11. 20, 27 Mar., 10, 17 April 1736.

27. Coxe, *R. Walpole's Memoirs,* ii, 335, 341. To Wyndham, 5 Jan., 20 Feb. 1736; *ibid.,* iii, 312. Lord Hervey to Horace Walpole, 3 Jan. 1736.

28. See *ibid.,* ii, 340 and iii, 318–19, 478. To Wyndham, 20 Feb., 18 Mar. 1736 and 9 June 1737.

29. P.R.O. Bathurst papers. 30/62/vol. 74. Letter 20. 14 Sept. 1736.

30. *Works,* ii, 352–71.

31. *Ibid.,* ii, 352–4.

32. *Ibid.,* ii, 370–1.

33. See, for example, Lady Bolingbroke's letters to Lady Denbigh, 15 Feb. 1737 to 18 June 1738, in H.M.C., *Denbigh MSS.,* pp. 122–32.

34. B.M. Add. MSS. 34196, f. 95. To Robert Knight, 5 Jan. 1736. Knight, the son of the South Sea Company cashier who had absconded after the Bubble had burst, married Bolingbroke's half-sister, Henrietta St John.

35. H.M.C., *Egmont Diary,* ii, 360; and *Memoirs and Correspondence of George, Lord Lyttelton, from 1734 to 1773,* ed. Robert Phillimore (2 vols., 1845), i, 73, 81. Hereafter cited as *Lyttelton's Corr.*

36. Coxe, *R. Walpole's Memoirs,* iii, 494–5. To Wyndham, 13 Oct. 1737. See also *ibid.,* iii, 479–80. To Wyndham, 9 June 1737; and Petworth House. Egremont MSS. To Wyndham, 11 May 1737.

37. H.M.C., *Denbigh MSS.,* p. 231. Dawley, 20 Nov. 1738. See also Bolingbroke's contribution to the letter of Lady Bolingbroke to Lady Denbigh, 8 April 1738. H.M.C., *Eighth Report,* app., pt. i, pp. 566b–567a.

38. Coxe, *R. Walpole's Memoirs,* iii, 505–7. Bolingbroke to Wyndham, 3 Feb. 1738.

39. Blenheim MSS. Marlborough papers. E. 36. Lord Stair's letters to Sarah, Duchess of Marlborough, from 18 Oct. 1737 through to 1739.

40. *Pope's Corr.*, iv, 139.

41. *Ibid.*, iv, 126–9. Pope to Hill, 12 Sept. 1738 and Hill's reply, 23 Sept. 1738. Bolingbroke's contribution to *Alfred: A Masque* is mentioned in *The Works of Horatio Walpole, Earl of Orford* (5 vols., 1798), i, 449. The stanzas are in *The Works of David Mallet* (1759), iii, 68–9. For Pope's poem, see *The Twickenham Edition of the Poems of Alexander Pope,* ed. John Butt, iv (1953), 329–37. See also Mabel Hessler Cable, 'The Idea of a Patriot King in the Propaganda of the Opposition to Walpole, 1735–1739', *Philological Quarterly* (1939), xviii, 119–30.

42. *Works,* ii, 372–429.

43. *Lyttelton's Corr.,* i, 144–5. To Lyttelton, 6 May 1740.

44. Herbert Butterfield, *The Statecraft of Machiavelli* (1940), pp. 135–65; Jeffrey Hart, *Viscount Bolingbroke: Tory Humanist,* pp. 83–163; and Isaac Kramnick, *Bolingbroke and His Circle,* pp. 163–8. For Bolingbroke's criticisms of Machiavelli, see *Works,* ii, 389–90. Butterfield and Hart tend to exaggerate these criticisms.

45. *Works,* ii, 397.

46. *Ibid.,* ii, 381.

47. *Ibid.,* ii, 401–2.

48. *Ibid.,* ii, 401.

49. *Ibid.,* ii, 410.

50. *Ibid.,* ii, 416.

51. *Ibid.,* ii, 375.

52. *Ibid.,* ii, 430–8.

53. *Ibid.,* ii, 438.

54. *Pope's Corr.,* iv, 142–3. Pope to Lyttelton, c. 1 Nov. 1738.

55. H.M.C., *Fourteenth Report.,* app., pt. ix, *Trevor MSS.,* p. 25. Horatio Walpole to Robert Trevor, 16 Mar. 1739.

56. *Marchmont Papers,* ii, 180. To Lord Polwarth [c. Mar.–July 1739].

57. Coxe, *R. Walpole's Memoirs,* iii, 523. 23 July 1739.

58. Scottish Record Office. Stair MSS. GD135, vol. 141/26. Chesterfield to Stair, 27 May 1739 and James Erskine to Stair, 6 Sept. 1739; *Marchmont Papers,* ii, 142–7. Polwarth to Marchmont, 17 Aug. 1739.

59. Scottish Record Office. Clerk of Penicuik MSS. GD18, bundle 3225. P. Lindsey to Sir John Clerk, 12 April 1739; H.M.C., *Egmont Diary,* iii, 32–3. 12 Mar. 1739; and H.M.C., *Fourteenth Report.,* app., pt. ix, *Hare MSS.,* pp. 243–8. F. Hare to F. Naylor, 14 Mar., 31 May, 14 June 1739.

60. Coxe, *R. Walpole's Memoirs,* iii, 524–5. To Wyndham, 23 July 1739; *Marchmont Papers,* iii, 184–91. To Polwarth, 22 July 1739.

61. Coxe, *R. Walpole's Memoirs,* iii, 549–52 and 554–6. 1, 18 Nov. 1739 and 25 Jan. 1740.

62. *Marchmont Papers,* ii, 195–205. 15 Oct. 1739, 1 Jan. 1740.

63. Chatsworth House. Devonshire MSS. 249/5, 245/8 and 257/13. H. Pelham, Edw. Walpole and H. Legge to the Duke of Devonshire, 17, 24 Nov. 1739 and 13 Mar. 1740.

64. *Lyttelton's Corr.,* i, 143. To Lyttelton, 6 May 1740.

65. B.M. Add. MSS. 35586, ff. 273–4. Lyttelton to Bolingbroke, 30 July 1740. See also Marchmont's letter to Bolingbroke, 24 Sept, 1740. *Ibid.,* ff. 298–298v.

66. Petworth House. Egremont MSS. To Charles Wyndham, 7 July 1740; and *Marchmont Papers,* ii, 226–7. To Marchmont, 8 Aug. 1740.

67. *Lyttelton's Corr.,* i, 153–6. Nov. 1740; *Marchmont Papers,* ii, 240–4. To Marchmont, 30 Nov. 1740; and *Pope's Corr.,* iv, 260–1, 271–3. Pope to Bolingbroke, 3 Sept. 1740 and to Marchmont, Oct. 1740.

68. Coxe, *R. Walpole's Memoirs,* iii, 563–5; H.M.C., *Egmont Diary,* iii, 192–3; Yale University Library. Osborn Collection. Stair MSS. Dowager Duchess of Marlborough to Lord Stair, 21 Feb. 1741; *Lyttelton's Corr.,* i, 158–9. Thomas Carte to the Pretender, 17 April 1741; and John B. Owen, *The Rise of the Pelhams* (1957), p. 3.

69. *Marchmont Papers,* ii, 245–7. 26 Mar. 1741. See also his letter to Charles Wyndham, 14 April 1741. Petworth House. Egremont MSS.

70. Coxe, *R. Walpole's Memoirs,* iii, 566–77, 579–81. Dodington to Argyll, 18 June 1741; Chesterfield to Dodington, 8 Sept. 1741.

71. Yale ed. of *Horace Walpole's Corr.,* xvii, 231. To H. Mann, 10 Dec. 1741.

72. *Lyttelton's Corr.,* i, 194–200. Letter dated 4 Nov. 1741.

73. H.M.C., *Egmont Diary,* iii, 254, 260; Yale ed. of *Horace Walpole's Corr.,* xvii, 336–7, 363. To H. Mann, 18 Feb., 10 Mar. 1742; Scottish Record Office. Clerk of Penicuik MSS. GD18, bundle 3228. John Drummond to Sir J. Clerk, 11 Mar. 1742; and John B. Owen, *The Rise of the Pelhams,* pp. 3–35, 87–98.

74. The conclusions of the rest of this paragraph are based on G. E. Mingay, *English Landed Society in the Eighteenth Century;* G. E. Mingay, 'The Agricultural Depression, 1730–1750', *Econ. Hist. Rev.* (1956), second series, viii, 323–38; H. J. Habakkuk, 'English Landownership, 1680–1740', *ibid.,* (1939–40), x, 2–17; H. J. Habakkuk, 'The English Land Market in the Eighteenth Century', in *Britain and the Netherlands,* ed. J. S. Bromley and

E. H. Kossmann (1960), pp. 154–73; and P. G. M. Dickson, *The Financial Revolution in England*, pp. 239–41.

75. *Marchmont Papers*, ii, 283–4. 30 Oct. 1742.

76. [Bolingbroke], *A congratulatory Letter to a certain Right Hon. Person upon his late Disappointment* (1742). Pulteney returned the fire with *A Proper Reply to a late infamous and scurrilous libel intitled: A congratulatory Letter . . .* (1743).

77. B.M. Egerton MSS. 1717, ff. 83–87v. (Copy.)

78. *Ibid.*, f. 85v.

CHAPTER 14

1. *Spence's Anecdotes*, p. 103.

2. *Works*, iii, 53.

3. P. C. Yorke, *The Life and Correspondence of Philip Yorke, Earl of Hardwicke*, i, 367–8. 12 Nov. 1714.

4. *Pope's Corr.*, iv, 393–401. Letters 23 April–10 June 1742.

5. *Ibid.*, iv, 402. Pope to Warburton, 18 June 1742; *Spence's Anecdotes*, p. 213; and *The Works of Alexander Pope*, ed. W. Elwin and W. J. Courthope, ii, 279–89.

6. *A View of Lord Bolingbroke's Philosophy* (1755), in *The Works of the Right Reverend William Warburton* (1778), vii, 841; Owen Ruffhead, *The Life of Alexander Pope* (1769), pp. 410 *et seq.*; B.M. Add. MSS. 4948A, ff. 456–62; and George H. Nadel, 'New Light on Bolingbroke's *Letters on History*', *Journal of the History of Ideas* (1962), xxiii, 551–3.

7. *Pope's Corr.*, iv, 488–520.

8. Owen Ruffhead, *The Life of Alexander Pope*, p. 219. This biography was directly inspired by Warburton.

9. *Pope's Corr.*, iv, 499. 20 Feb. 1744. Cf. *ibid.*, iv, 501. To Warburton, 21 Feb. 1744.

10. *Ibid.*, iv, 498. Bolingbroke to Marchmont, 14 Feb. 1744; *ibid.*, iv, 501. Pope to Warburton, 21 Feb. 1744.

11. *Spence's Anecdotes*, pp. 188–9; *Pope's Corr.*, iv, 525–6.

12. *Marchmont Papers*, ii, 332–5. May–June 1744; *The Works of Alexander Pope*, ed. Elwin and Courthope, iii, 78–93; and Giles Barber, 'Bolingbroke, Pope, and the *Patriot King*', *The Library* (1964), xix, 77–8.

13. *Marchmont Papers*, ii, 338–9. 22 Oct. 1744. In the first draft of the *Advertisement* to the 1749 edition of *Patriot King* Bolingbroke said that he had burned Pope's copies, but he did not repeat this remark in the printed version. B.M. Add. MSS. 4948A, f. 449.

14. B.M. Add. MSS. 4948A, f. 419. This letter was wrongly dated as 1749 in Giles Barber, 'Bolingbroke, Pope, and the *Patriot King*', *The Library* (1964), xix, 79.

15. *A Selection from the unpublished papers of the right reverend William Warburton*, ed. F. Kilvert (1841), pp. 207–8.

16. *The Works of Alexander Pope,* ed. Elwin and Courthope, ii, 289.

17. See my paper, 'Bolingbroke's attack on Alexander Pope in 1746', *Notes and Queries* (Sept. 1969), ccxiv, new series xvi, 342–4.

18. B.M. Add. MSS. 35585, f. 173. Bolingbroke to Philip Yorke (later Lord Hardwicke), 23 May 1733; Petworth House. Egremont MSS. To Wyndham, 5 May 1737; and Coxe, *R. Walpole's Memoirs,* iii, 507 and ii, 343. To Wyndham, 3 Feb. 1738 and to Hardwicke, 30 Oct. 1742.

19. *Marchmont Papers,* ii, 295–6. Bolingbroke to Marchmont, 5 July 1743; and P.R.O. Granville MSS. 30/29/1/11, f. 285. Chesterfield to Gower, 2 Oct. 1743. For a detailed study of the political intrigues of 1742–51 see John B. Owen, *The Rise of the Pelhams* (1957), *passim,* and Archibald Foord, *His Majesty's Opposition, 1714–1830,* pp. 226–79.

20. B.M. Add. MSS. 35587, ff. 271–318. To Hardwicke, 28 July to 12 Nov. 1744; and George Harris, *The Life of Lord Chancellor Hardwicke* (3 vols., 1847), ii, 99–112.

21. *Marchmont Papers,* i, 38–57. Marchmont's diary, Aug–Oct. 1744.

22. *Ibid.,* i, 9–12, 18–20. 7 and 11 Aug. 1744.

23. *Ibid.,* i, 31, 54–66, and ii, 313–20. Bolingbroke to Marchmont, Sept. 1743.

24. *Parl. Hist.,* xiii, 977.

25. *Marchmont Papers,* i, 67–70. 22 Oct. to 6 Nov. 1744.

26. *Ibid.,* i, 75–88. 8–24 Nov. 1744.

27. B.M. Add. MSS. 35588, f. 7.

28. P.R.O. Granville MSS. 30/29/1/11, ff. 290–1. Chesterfield to Gower, The Hague, 13 April 1745, N.S.; *Chesterfield's Letters,* ii, 594–6. To Newcastle, The Hague, 13 April 1745, N.S., and Dr William King, *Political and Literary Anecdotes of His Own Time* (2nd ed., 1819), pp. 45–7.

29. B.M. Add. MSS. 35588, ff. 9–162 and George Harris, *The Life of Lord Chancellor Hardwicke,* ii, 113–213. Bolingbroke to Hardwicke, Jan. to Nov. 1745.

30. Petworth House. Egremont MSS. 30 July 1745.

31. *Marchmont Papers,* i, 101–59.

32. *Ibid.,* i, 173.

33. *Ibid.,* ii, 357. To Marchmont, 25 Nov. 1746.

34. *Ibid.,* i, 178, 273; and ii, 361–78. Letters to Marchmont, 1747–8.

35. H.M.C., *Polwarth MSS.*, v, 185, 188, 236. Hume Campbell to Marchmont, 11, 24 Nov. 1746 and 16 April 1747. See also B.M. Add. MSS. 37994, f. 52. Bolingbroke to Marchmont (c. April 1747).

36. *Lyttelton's Corr.*, i, 294–5. To Lyttelton, 20 Aug. 1747.

37. *Works*, ii, 439–61.

38. *Ibid.*, ii, 458.

39. *Ibid.*, ii, 450.

40. H.M.C., *Denbigh MSS.*, pp. 134–68. Lady Bolingbroke to Lady Denbigh, July 1742 to Nov. 1749.

41. The best account of this episode is in Giles Barber, 'Bolingbroke, Pope, and the *Patriot King*', *The Library* (1964 though not published until 1968), xix, 67–89. I am also indebted to Frank T. Smallwood for helpful suggestions.

42. *The London Magazine* (1749), xviii, 3.

43. *The Private Journal and Literary Remains of John Byrom*, ed. Richard Parkinson (Chetham Society, 1857), ii, pt. 2, 492. Byrom to Mrs Byrom, 27 May 1749.

44. B.M. Add. MSS. 4948A, ff. 442–442v and 420–21. Lyttelton to Bolingbroke, 14 April 1749 and Bolingbroke's reply, 15 April. These letters are also printed in *Lyttelton's Corr.*, ii, 428–30, where they are both misdated 1748.

45. The *Advertisement* to the 1749 edition.

46. Fannie E. Ratchford, 'Pope and the *Patriot King*', *University of Texas, Studies in English* (1926), vi, 157–77; and Giles Barber, 'Bolingbroke, Pope, and the *Patriot King*', *The Library* (1964), xix, 70–3, 80–3.

47. *Marchmont Papers*, ii, 379. Bolingbroke to Marchmont, 7 June 1749.

48. B.M. Add. MSS. 4948A, ff. 449–50v.

49. *The Gentleman's Magazine* (May 1749), xix, 195–6. See also Horace Walpole to Horace Mann, 17 May 1749. *The Yale Edition of Horace Walpole's Corr.*, xx, 59–62.

50. *Marchmont Papers*, ii, 380. 7 June 1749.

51. e.g. *The Imposter Detected and Convicted: Or, The Principles and Practices of the Author of a Pamphlet Lately Published, On the Spirit of Patriotism, etc. Set forth in a clear Light. In a Letter to a Member of Parliament in Town, From his Friend in the Country* (1749). Old Horatio Walpole also planned an assault on Bolingbroke's political principles. *The Yale Edition of Horace Walpole's Corr.*, xx, 62. To Horace Mann, 17 May 1749.

52. *A Letter to the Editor of the Letter on the Spirit of Patriotism, The Idea of a*

Patriot King, and The State of Parties, &c., occasioned by the Editor's Advertisement (1749).

53. There is a manuscript draft of this pamphlet among David Mallet's collection of papers about Bolingbroke in B.M. Add. MSS. 4948A, ff. 443–445v. Warburton accused Mallet of writing it, but Mallet expressly denied this. *Ibid.*, f. 446, and in a letter to Aaron Hill in July 1749, now in the Widener Library, Harvard University and cited by Giles Barber, 'Bolingbroke, Pope, and the *Patriot King*', *The Library* (1964), xix, 79.

54. *Ibid.*, pp. 80–1; *Letters written by . . . Lady Luxborough to William Shenstone,* ed. John Hodgetts (1775), p. 105. 24 June 1749, and *The Yale Edition of Horace Walpole's Corr.,* xx, 65–66. To Horace Mann, 4 June 1749.

55. *Marchmont Papers,* ii, 384.

56. *Ibid.,* ii, 386. 1 Mar. 1750.

57. H.M.C., *Denbigh MSS.,* pp. 272, 275 and 279. Letters to Lady Denbigh from France, 1751–52; H.M.C., *Eighth Report,* app., pt. i, p. 567b. Bolingbroke to Lady Denbigh, 8 Aug. 1751.

58. B.M. Add. MSS. 34196, f. 151. To Henrietta, Lady Luxborough, 11 April 1751.

59. *Ibid.,* f. 155. Bolingbroke to Lady Luxborough, 16 Aug. 1751; *Letters written by . . . Lady Luxborough to William Shenstone,* ed. John Hodgetts, pp. 287–9. 21, 25 Aug. 1751; *Chesterfield's Letters,* iv, 1777, and v, 1802. To the Marquise de Monconseil, 1 Aug., 30 Dec. 1751. In his last, pain-racked days Bolingbroke was still able to dictate a letter to Lord Orrery, congratulating him on his work on Swift and thanking him for the kind comments he had made about himself. Yale University Library. Osborn Collection. 16 Nov. 1751.

60. There are several inaccurate versions of these inscriptions as with so many of the incidents of Bolingbroke's life. See Frank T. Smallwood, 'The Bolingbroke Inscriptions at Battersea', *Notes and Queries* (1968), ccxiii, new series, xv, 211–12.

61. *Works,* i, 85–6.

62. *Ibid.,* i, 86–7. Thomas Hearne made the strange, unconfirmed claim that Bolingbroke had two daughters by his first marriage. *Remarks and Collections of Thomas Hearne,* ed. C. E. Doble and D. W. Rannie (4 vols., Oxford, 1885–98), vi, 252. 19 Nov. 1718.

CHAPTER 15

1. There have been several inaccurate lists of Bolingbroke's works. The best account of the early editions is Giles Barber's 'Some Uncollected Authors

XLI: Henry St John, Viscount Bolingbroke, 1678–1751', *The Book Collector* (1965), xiv, 528–37.

2. B.M. Add. MSS. 4948A, ff. 438–439v. Paris, 7 Mar. 1752, N.S.

3. B.M. Add. MSS. 4254, ff. 124v–125. No date.

4. *Op. cit.*, (1754), xxiv, 145.

5. James Boswell, *The Life of Samuel Johnson* (4 vols, 1816), i, 246–7.

6. *The Grenville Papers,* ed. W. J. Smith (4 vols., 1852), i, 118. To George Grenville, 24 Mar. 1754.

7. *The Complete Letters of Lady Mary Wortley Montagu,* ed. Robert Halsband (3 vols., Oxford, 1965–67), iii, 61–5, 76–7. July, Dec. 1754.

8. See the anonymous criticism of Warburton, perhaps by Lord Chancellor Mansfield, who as plain William Murray had been on good terms with Bolingbroke. B.M. Egerton MSS. 1959, ff. 31–33v.

9. *Voltaire's Corr.,* xxiv, 201, 212, 222, 228; xxxv, 4, 22; lvi, 24–5; and D. J. Fletcher, 'The Fortunes of Bolingbroke in France in the eighteenth century', *Studies on Voltaire and the eighteenth century* (1966), xlvii, 207–32. Several authorities have detected a similarity between the ideas of Bolingbroke and Voltaire, and have suggested that the former influenced the latter. See, for example, Arthur Sydney Hurn, *Voltaire et Bolingbroke* (Paris, 1915); Eduard Sonet, *Voltaire et l'influence anglaise* (Paris, 1926); and D. J. Fletcher, 'The Intellectual Relations of Lord Bolingbroke with France', University of Wales M.A. thesis (1953), pp. 82–91. This suggestion was rejected by Norman L. Torrey, 'Bolingbroke and Voltaire – A Fictitious Influence', *Publications of the Modern Language Association of America* (1927), xlii, 788–97. Later, in *Voltaire and the English Deists* (New Haven, 1930), especially chapter 6, Professor Torrey amended this to an 'exaggerated influence'. While Voltaire was the greater genius and ultimately went much further than Bolingbroke, the latter's influence on him was probably somewhat greater than Professor Torrey would allow.

10. John Hunt, 'Henry St John, Lord Bolingbroke', *The Contemporary Review* (1869), x, 405–21; Leslie Stephen, *English Thought in the Eighteenth Century* (1876), i, 170–83; and *The Works of Jonathan Swift,* ed. Sir Walter Scott (Edinburgh, 1824), xvi, 478.

11. See particularly Walter McIntosh Merrill, *From Statesman to Philosopher: A Study in Bolingbroke's Deism* (New York, 1949); Sydney W. Jackman, *Man of Mercury: An Appreciation of the Mind of Henry St John, Viscount Bolingbroke* (1965), chapter three; and Alfred Owen Aldridge, 'Shaftesbury and Bolingbroke', *Philological Quarterly* (1952), xxxi, 1–16.

12. For an attempt to arrange Bolingbroke's philosophy into a general framework, see Walter McIntosh Merrill, *From Statesman to Philosopher:*

A Study in Bolingbroke's Deism. The most devastating modern attack on Bolingbroke as a philosopher is in D. G. James, *The Life of Reason* (1949), pp. 174–267.

13. *An Answer to the latter part of Lord Bolingbroke's Letters on the Study of History* (1763). For his preparation of this and Whig support for it, see Coxe, *Horatio Walpole's Memoirs,* ii, 387–403.

14. *Correspondence of William Pitt, Earl of Chatham* (4 vols., 1838–40), i, 107–9. To Thomas Pitt, 4 May 1754.

15. D. G. James, *The Life of Reason,* p. 200. There are more considered and impartial assessments in Sydney Wayne Jackman, *Man of Mercury,* pp. 44–68, and J. G. A. Pocock, *The Ancient Constitution and the Feudal Law* (Cambridge, 1957), pp. 246–8.

16. It has been suggested that he influenced Voltaire's development as an historian. Voltaire could have seen one of the private copies of Bolingbroke's *Letters on the Study and Use of History* at any time from 1738, but, while he followed Bolingbroke in ignoring ancient history because of the lack of accurate information and in concentrating on recent European history, he had a much wider concept of history and was by far the greater historian. See George H. Nadel, 'New Light on Bolingbroke's Letters on History', *Journal of the History of Ideas* (1962), xxiii, 555–6; and J. H. Brumfitt, *Voltaire: Historian* (Oxford, 1958), pp. 40–5.

17. See, for example, the comments of Charles Grant Robertson, *Bolingbroke* (Historical Association pamphlet, General Series, G5, 1947).

18. Dennis James Fletcher, 'The Intellectual Relations of Lord Bolingbroke with France', unpublished University of Wales M.A. thesis (1953), pp. 101–205, 248–60, 267–74; and Isaac Kramnick, *Bolingbroke and His Circle,* pp. 150–2.

19. Fletcher's M.A., *op. cit.,* pp. 205–44; and Robert Shackleton, *Montesquieu: A Critical Biography* (Oxford, 1961), pp. 126–9.

20. *The Craftsman,* no. 208. 27 June 1730.

21. Robert Shackleton, 'Montesquieu, Bolingbroke, and the Separation of Powers', *French Studies* (1949), iii, 25–38.

22. W. B. Gwynn, *The Meaning of the Separation of Powers* (New Orleans, 1965), pp. 91–9; and Isaac Kramnick, *Bolingbroke and His Circle,* pp. 144–50.

23. Cited by Kramnick, *op. cit.,* p. 262.

24. G. A. Cranfield, *The Development of the Provincial Press 1700–1760* (Oxford, 1962), pp. 123–32, 166–7, 271–3.

25. Herbert Butterfield, *George III, Lord North, and the People* (1949), p. 14 and note.

26. B.M. Add. MSS. 35599, f. 63. To Hardwicke, 14 Sept. 1752. See also the 'Memorial concerning the Prince of Wales, Dec. 1752', H.M.C., *Eyre Matcham MSS., Various Collections*, iv, 22–3.

27. *Letters from George III to Lord Bute, 1756–66* (1939), ed. Romney Sedgwick, pp. xxi–xlii.

28. Harvey C. Mansfield, 'Sir Lewis Namier Considered', *Journal of British Studies* (1962), ii, 28–37. The political aims of George III in the early years of his reign are still a subject of controversy, despite the major reappraisal by Sir Lewis Namier and his disciples. It is difficult to portray the King as totally devoid of political ideas and principles.

29. Harvey C. Mansfield, *Statesmanship and Party Government. A Study of Burke and Bolingbroke* (Chicago, 1965), *passim*. Burke dismissed Bolingbroke's works, but only after he had carefully studied them and, to some extent, had reacted against him. *Reflections on the Revolution in France* (World Classics edition, Oxford, 1950), pp. 98, 138.

30. J. G. A. Pocock, 'Burke and the Ancient Constitution – a Problem in the History of Ideas', *Historical Journal* (1960), iii, 125–43.

31. See Anneliese Dahle, *Disraelis Beziehungen zu Bolingbroke* (Freiburg, 1931); and Richard Faber, *Beaconsfield and Bolingbroke* (1961),

32. *Marlborough: His Life and Times* (1938), iv, 619.

33. *Walpole* (1893), pp. 79–80.

34. J. H. Plumb's comment, *Sir Robert Walpole* (1956), i, 130 note.

35. e.g. B.M. Add. MSS. 34196, f. 136. To Mr Knight, 12 June 1738.

36. *Swift's Corr.*, iv, 253. 2 Aug. 1731.

37. For Bolingbroke's interest in the education of the young, see his letters to his half-sister, Henrietta, in B.M. Add. MSS. 34196; to Wyndham's son in Petworth House. Egremont MSS.; to Sir John Hynde Cotton's son, June 1739–Oct. 1740, in Pierpont Morgan Library, New York; to Francis, Earl of Huntingdon, Oct.–Dec. 1748, in H.M.C., *Hastings MSS.*, iii, 65–9 (the originals are in the Huntington Library, California); and his concern for the education of his half-brother, George St John, in his letter to Henry Watkins, 2 Nov. 1711. Huntington Library, California. HM21547.

38. *Marchmont Papers*, ii, 371. To Marchmont, 14 Sept. 1747.

39. *Chesterfield's Letters*, iv, 1462. To his son, 12 Dec. 1749.

40. *Lord Hervey's Memoirs*, i, 16.

Bibliography

Only those sources which have a direct bearing on Bolingbroke's life and career have been listed. Some of the many other sources which have illuminated either the general period or particular topics are cited in the references.

I. MANUSCRIPT SOURCES

British Museum:

Additional MSS. 4948A (Bolingbroke's Works); 9092–121 (Coxe transcripts); 15866; 15916; 17677XX–YYY (L'Hermitage's dispatches); 22227; 22264; 22628; 25495; 27732–5 (Essex MSS); 29549; 32686; 34196 (Bolingbroke MSS); 34493–521 (Mackintosh transcripts); 35584–8 and 35913 (Hardwicke MSS); 36243 (Bolingbroke's estate papers); 37272–3 (Utrecht papers); 37354–61 (Whitworth MSS); 37994 (Bolingbroke-Marchmont Corr.); 38851; 40621; 40787 (Egmont MSS); and 49970–71 (Bolingbroke MSS).

Stowe MSS. 222–7 (Hanover MSS); 241–2 (Astle papers); and 251.

Egerton MSS. 1717; 1959; and 2618.

Lansdowne MSS. 773.

Portland (Harley) papers. Loan 29.

Public Record Office:

State papers, Foreign and Domestic.

War Office papers.

Baschet transcripts, 31/3.

Shaftesbury papers, 30/24.

Bathurst papers, 30/62/74.

Scottish Record Office:

Stair MSS. GD. 135, vols. 138–47.

Montrose MSS. from Auchmar House.

Niedersachsisches Staatsarchir, Hanover:

Calenberg Briefe Archiv, 24 (England) 99, 107a and 113a (Kreienberg's dispatches).

Deutsches Zentralarchiv, Merseburg (East Germany):
Rep. XI (England) Nos. 25B–39A (Bonet's dispatches).

Les Archives du Ministère des Affaires Étrangères, Quai d'Orsay, Paris:
Correspondance Politique, Angleterre, vols. 358–91.

Bibliothèque Nationale, Paris:
MS. 15176.

National Library of Scotland:
MSS. 3419–20.

Bodleian Library, Oxford:
Add. MSS. A269, D23; Ballard MSS. 6, 7, 8, 10, 18, 21, 31, 38; Rawlinson
MSS. A286, 92; Eng[lish] MSS. e. 4, e. 180; French MSS. d. 18; Carte MSS.
211; and North MSS. c. 9.

Cambridge University Library:
Add. MSS. 6570; 7093; and Cholmondeley-Houghton MSS. (Walpole
papers).

Churchill College Library, Cambridge:
Erle MSS. 2/56 My edition of the St John-Erle Corr. will appear in the
Journal of the Soc. of Army Hist. Research in 1970.

Birmingham Public Library:
Cobham MSS. from Hagley (Bolingbroke-Lyttelton Correspondence).

William Salt Library, Stafford:
Dartmouth correspondence and Cabinet minutes.

Trinity College Library, Dublin:
MSS. S.3.11. Bolingbroke-Shrewsbury Correspondence.

Henry E. Huntington Library, California:
Stowe MSS. ST. 57–8 (Brydges MSS); HM774 Letter Book of Thomas Fane,
Earl of Westmorland; and miscellaneous Bolingbroke letters in HA 10646–48;
HM 20298, 21547–8, 22329; and LO 9379, 12552–3.

New York Public Library:
Montague Collection (Bolingbroke's official papers 1710–14).

Boston Public Library:
Two Bolingbroke letters in the Rare Book Department.

Yale University Library:
Osborn Collection, Miscellaneous Bolingbroke letters.

Harvard University Library:
Houghton MSS. 51M–176 (6–8). Letters of Bolingbroke to Alary.

Pierpont Morgan Library, New York:
Miscellaneous Bolingbroke letters to Cotton, Orrery and Ford.

William Clements Library, Ann Arbor, Michigan:
Miscellaneous Bolingbroke material in Shelburne and Sydney collections.

Folger Shakespeare Library, Washington D.C.:
One Bolingbroke letter, published by Gilbert Parke.

Blenheim Palace:
Marlborough (Churchill) MSS.
Spencer (Sunderland) MSS.

Petworth House:
Egremont MSS. (Bolingbroke–Wyndham family Correspondence). This collection was consulted at West Sussex Record Office.

Levens Hall, Westmorland:
Bagot (Grahme) MSS. I have edited the Bolingbroke letters in this collection, 'Letters of Bolingbroke to James Grahme', for the *Transactions of the Cumberland and Westmorland Antiquarian and Archaeological Society* (1968), New Series, lxviii.

Boughton House:
Buccleugh MSS. (Vernon-Shrewsbury Correspondence).

Berkshire Record Office:
Downshire papers (St John-Trumbull Correspondence); Hartley Russell MSS. D/E.Hy and Baxendale MSS. D/EBx (Bolingbroke estate papers); and Braybrooke MSS. D/EN.

East Sussex Record Office:
Danny MSS. 394.

Hertfordshire Record Office:
Cowper-Panshanger MSS.

Norwich and Norfolk Record Office:
Hare MSS. 6160 and 6164.

Staffordshire Record Office:
Dartmouth MSS; Lord Gower MSS; and Chetwynd diplomatic papers.

2. ORIGINAL SOURCES IN PRINT

The Letters of Addison, ed. W. Graham. Oxford, 1941.

The Letters and Diplomatic Instructions of Queen Anne, ed. Beatrice Curtis Brown. London, 1935.

The epistolary correspondence of Francis Atterbury, Bishop of Rochester, ed. J. Nichols. 5 vols. London, 1799.

N

The Works of Lord Bolingbroke, 4 vols. 1967 reprint of the London, 1844 edition.

Bolingbroke's Defence of the Treaty of Utrecht, ed. G. M. Trevelyan. Cambridge, 1932.

Henry St John, Viscount Bolingbroke, *Reflections concerning Innate Moral Principles.* London, 1752.

——, *A Letter to the Examiner,* in *Lord Somers' Tracts,* ed. Walter Scott. 2nd ed., London, 1814, vol. xiii.

——, *Considerations upon the Secret History of the White Staff.* London, 1714.

——, *The Case of Dunkirk.* London, 1730.

——, *A Final Answer to the Remarks on the Craftsman's Vindication.* London, 1731.

——, *The Freeholder's Political Catechism.* London, 1733.

The Letters and Correspondence of Henry St John, Lord Viscount Bolingbroke, ed. Gilbert Parke. 4 vols., London, 1798.

Lettres Historiques, Politiques, Philosophiques . . . de Bolingbroke, ed. P. H. Grimoard. 3 vols., Paris, 1808.

Lettres Inédites de Bolingbroke à Lord Stair 1716–1720, ed. Paul Baratier. Trévoux, 1939.

'Letters of Henry St John to James Brydges', ed. Godfrey Davies and Marion Tinling. *Huntington Library Bulletin,* No. 8 (Oct. 1935).

'Letters from James Brydges . . . to Henry St John', ed. Davies and Tinling, *ibid.,* No. 9 (April 1936).

'Letters from Bolingbroke to James Grahme', ed. H. T. Dickinson, *Transactions Cumberland and Westmorland Antiquarian and Archaeological Society* (1968), New Series, lxviii.

The Case of the Right Honourable the Lord Viscount Bolingbroke. London, 1715.

A Letter to the Right Honourable the Lord Viscount B—ke. London, 1715.

Memoirs of the Life and Ministerial Conduct . . . of the late Lord Viscount Bolingbroke. London, 1752.

Authentick Memoirs of the Conduct and Adventures of Henry St John, late Viscount Bolingbroke. London, 1754.

The Life and History of the Right Honourable Henry St John, Lord Viscount Bolingbroke. London, 1754.

Bulkeley, Charles: *Notes on the Philosophical Writings of Lord Bolingbroke.* London, 1755.

Boyer, Abel: *The History of the Reign of Queen Anne digested into Annals.* 11 vols., London, 1703–12.

——, *Quadriennium Annae Postremum; or the Political State of Great Britain.* 8 vols., 2nd ed., London, 1718–19.

Bishop Burnet's *History of His Own Time.* 6 vols., 2nd ed., Oxford, 1833.

Letters of Philip Dormer Stanhope, Fourth Earl of Chesterfield, ed. Bonamy Dobrée. 6 vols., London, 1932.

Cobbett, William: *Parliamentary History of England.* 36 vols., London, 1806–20.

The History and Proceedings of the House of Commons (Commons Debates), ed. Richard Chandler. London, 1742.

Diary of Mary, Countess Cowper, 1714–1720, ed. S. Cowper. 2nd ed., London, 1865.

Coxe, William: *Memoirs of John, Duke of Marlborough, with his original correspondence.* 6 vols., 2nd ed., London, 1820.

——, *Memoirs of Horatio, Lord Walpole.* 2 vols., with original correspondence, 3rd ed., London, 1820.

——, *Memoirs of the Life and Administration of Sir Robert Walpole, Earl of Orford.* 3 vols., two volumes of original correspondence, London, 1789.

The Craftsman. 14 vols., collected edition, London, 1731 and 1737.

[Lord Hervey], *Remarks on the Craftsman's Vindication of his Two Honourable Patrons in his paper of May 22, 1731.* London, 1731.

An Answer to one part of a late Infamous Libel intitled Remarks on the Craftsman's Vindication of his two Honourable Patrons. London, 1731.

[Sir William Yonge], *Sedition and Defamation Display'd: In a Letter to the Author of the Craftsman.* London, 1731.

The Letters of John Gay, ed. C. F. Burgess. Oxford, 1966.

The Gentleman's Magazine.

Letters from George III to Lord Bute 1756–1766, ed. Romney Sedgwick. London, 1939.

The Correspondence of Sir Thomas Hanmer, ed. Sir Henry Bunbury. London, 1838.

The Harcourt Papers, ed. E. W. Harcourt. 2 vols., Oxford, 1880.

Hardwicke's State Papers. 2 vols., London, 1778.

Some Materials Towards Memoirs of the Reign of King George II, by John Lord Hervey, ed. Romney Sedgwick. 3 vols., London, 1831.

The Works of Aaron Hill. 4 vols., London, 1753.

Historical Manuscripts Commission (H.M.C.) *Fourth Report, Erskine Murray MSS.*

——, *Eighth Report,* part one, app. *Denbigh MSS.* and *Marlborough MSS.*

——, *Tenth Report,* part one. app. *Stirling, &c. MSS;* part four, app. *Bagot MSS.*

——, *Fourteenth Report,* part nine, app. *Onslow MSS* and *Trevor MSS.*

——, *Bath MSS,* i–ii.

——, *Carlisle MSS.*

——, *Cowper MSS.,* iii.

Historical Manuscripts Commission (H.M.C.), *Dartmouth MSS.*, i and iii.

——, *Denbigh MSS.*

——, *Downshire MSS.*, I, ii.

——, *Egmont Diary*, 3 vols.

——, *Egmont MSS.*, ii.

——, *Fortescue MSS.*, i.

——, *Frankland–Russell–Astley MSS.*

——, *Hastings MSS.*, iii.

——, *House of Lords MSS.*, v–x.

——, *Mar and Kellie MSS.*, i.

——, *Onslow MSS.*

——, *Polwarth MSS.*, i, iii, and v.

——, *Portland MSS.*, ii–x.

——, *Stuart MSS.*, i–vii.

——, *Townshend MSS.*

'Memoirs of the Right Hon. Edward Hopkins, M.P. for Coventry', ed. Mary Dormer Harris, *English Historical Review* (1919), xxxiv.

The Parliamentary Diary of Sir Edward Knatchbull, 1722–1730, ed. A. N. Newman, *Camden Society* (1963), 3rd series, xciv.

'Proceedings in the House of Commons, March–June 1714 (Diary of Sir Edward Knatchbull),' ed. A. N. Newman, *Bulletin of the Institute of Historical Research* (1961), xxxiv.

George Lockhart, *The Lockhart Papers*. 2 vols., London, 1817.

The History and Proceedings of the House of Lords (Lords Debates), ed. Ebenezer Timberland. London, 1742.

Letters written by . . . Lady Luxborough to William Shenstone, ed. John Hodgetts. London 1775.

Memoirs and Correspondence of George, Lord Lyttelton, from 1734 to 1773, ed. Robert Phillimore. 2 vols., London. 1845.

Macpherson, James (ed.), *Original Papers; containing the secret history of Great Britain from the Restoration to the accession of the House of Hanover*. 2 vols., London, 1775.

A Selection from the papers of the Earls of Marchmont, ed. G. H. Rose. 3 vols., London, 1831.

The Letters and Dispatches of John Churchill, first Duke of Marlborough, ed. Sir George Murray. 5 vols., London, 1845.

The Private Correspondence of Sarah, Duchess of Marlborough. 2 vols., London, 1838.

Minutes of the negotiations of Mons. Mesnager at the Court of England. London, 1717.

The Complete Letters of Lady Wortley Montagu, ed. Robert Halsband. 3 vols., Oxford, 1965–67.

Catalogue of the collection of autograph letters and historical documents formed by Alfred Morrison, ed. A. W. Thibaudeau. 6 vols., London, 1883–92.

Pauli, R. (ed.), 'Aktenstücke zur Thronbesteigung des Welfenhaus in England', *Zeitschrift des Historischen Vereins für Niedersachsen.* Hanover, 1883.

The Correspondence of Alexander Pope, ed. George Sherburn, 5 vols., Oxford, 1956.

The Twickenham Edition of the Poems of Alexander Pope, ed. John Butt, *et al.* 10 vols., London, 1939–67.

Prior, Matthew: *The History of His Own Time,* ed. Adrian Drift. London, 1740.

Debates and Speeches in both Houses of Parliament concerning the Schism Bill. London, 1715.

Letters illustrative of the reign of William III from 1696 to 1708 addressed to the Duke of Shrewsbury by James Vernon, ed. G. P. R. James. 3 vols., London, 1841.

Anecdotes, Observations and Characters of Books and Men collected from the conversation of Mr Pope and other eminent persons of his time by the Reverend Joseph Spence, ed. S. W. Singer. London, 1964.

Annals and Correspondence of the Viscount and the first and second Earls of Stair, ed. J. M. Graham. 2 vols., Edinburgh, 1875.

Letters to and from Henrietta, Countess of Suffolk . . . from 1712 to 1767, ed. John Wilson Croker, 2 vols., London, 1824.

The Prose Works of Jonathan Swift, ed. Herbert Davis. 13 vols., Oxford, 1939–64.

The Correspondence of Jonathan Swift, ed. F. Elrington Ball. 6 vols., London, 1910–14.

The Letters of Jonathan Swift to Charles Ford, ed. David Nichol Smith. Oxford, 1935.

Swift, Jonathan: *Journal to Stella,* ed. Harold Williams. 2 vols., Oxford, 1948.

Taylor, Brook: *Contemplatio Philosophica,* ed. Sir William Young. London, 1793.

Tindal, Nicholas: *The Continuation of Rapin de Thoyras's History of England.* London, 1746.

Memoirs of the Marquis of Torcy. 2 vols., London, 1757.

Voltaire's Correspondence, ed. Theodore Besterman. 107 vols., Geneva, 1953–65.

Correspondance de Voltaire 1726–1729, ed. Lucien Foulet. Paris, 1913.

Walpole, Horace: *Memoirs of the Reign of King George the Second,* ed. Lord Holland. 3 vols., London, 1846.

The Yale Edition of Horace Walpole's Correspondence, ed. W. S. Lewis, *et al.* London, 1937–.

Walpole, Horatio: *An Answer to the latter part of Lord Bolingbroke's Letters on the Study of History*. London, 1763.

The Works of the Right Reverend William Warburton, ed. Richard Hurd. 10 vols., London, 1811.

Warner, Rebecca (ed.), *Original Letters from Richard Baxter, Matthew Prior, Lord Bolingbroke, Alexander Pope, &c.* (Bath, 1817).

A Catalogue of letters and other historical documents exhibited in the library at Welbeck, ed. S. A. Strong. London, 1903.

The Wentworth Papers, 1705–1739, ed. James J. Cartwright. London, 1883.

Wickham-Legg, L. G.: 'Torcy's Account of Matthew Prior's Negotiations at Fontainebleau in July 1711', *English Historical Review* (1914), xxix.

——, 'Extracts from Jacobite Correspondence, 1711–14', *ibid.* (1915), xxx.

Wyndham, Maud (ed.): *Chronicles of the Eighteenth Century.* 2 vols., London, 1924.

Yorke, Philip C.: *Life and Correspondence of Philip Yorke, Earl of Hardwicke.* 3 vols., Cambridge, 1913.

3. SECONDARY SOURCES

Aldridge, Alfred Owen: 'Shaftesbury and Bolingbroke', *Philological Quarterly* (1952), xxxi.

Bagehot, Walter: 'Bolingbroke as a Statesman'. *The Works and Life of Walter Bagehot,* ed. Mrs Russell Barrington. London, 1915, vol. iv.

Ballantyne, Archibald: *Voltaire's Visit to England 1726–1729.* London, 1893.

Baratier, Paul: *Lord Bolingbroke: Ses Écrits Politiques.* Paris, 1939.

Barber, Giles: 'A Bibliography of Henry St John, Viscount Bolingbroke'. Unpublished Oxford University B.Litt thesis, 1963.

——, 'Some Uncollected Authors. Henry Saint John, Viscount Bolingbroke, 1678–1751', *The Book Collector* (1965), xiv.

——, 'Bolingbroke, Pope, and the *Patriot King*', *The Library* (1964), xix.

Brosch, Moritz: *Lord Bolingbroke und die Whigs und Tories seiner Zeit.* Frankfurt, 1883.

Brumfitt, J. H.: *Voltaire: Historian.* Oxford, 1958.

Burns, J. H.: 'Bolingbroke and the Concept of Constitutional Government', *Political Studies* (1962), x.

Burton, Ivor F.: 'The Secretary at War and the Administration of the Army during the War of the Spanish Succession'. Unpublished London University Ph.D. thesis, 1960.

——, 'The Supply of Infantry for the War in the Peninsula 1703–1707', *Bulletin of the Institute of Historical Research* (1955), xxxiv.

——, 'The Committee of Council at the War-Office: An experiment in Cabinet Government under Anne', *Historical Journal* (1961), iv.

Butler, G. G.: *The Tory Tradition*. London, 1914.

Butterfield, Herbert: *The Statecraft of Machiavelli*. London, 1940.

Cable, Marion Hessler: '*The Idea of a Patriot King* in the Propaganda of the Opposition to Walpole, 1735–1739', *Philological Quarterly* (1939), xviii.

Churchill, Winston S.: *Marlborough: His Life and Times*. 4 vols., London, 1934–38.

Collins, John Churton: *Bolingbroke: A Historical Study, and Voltaire in England*. London, 1886.

——, 'Lord Bolingbroke', 'Lord Bolingbroke in Exile', and 'Literary Life of Lord Bolingbroke', *Quarterly Review* (1880–81), vols. 149 and 151.

Cooke, G. W.: *Memoirs of Lord Bolingbroke*. 2 vols., London, 1835.

Coxe, William: See original sources.

Cranfield, G. A.: *The Development of the Provincial Press 1700–1760*. Oxford, 1962.

Dahle, Anneliese: *Disraelis Beziehungen zu Bolingbroke*. Freiburg, 1931.

Davies, Godfrey: 'The Fall of Harley in 1708', *English Historical Review* (1951), lxvi.

——, 'The Seamy Side of Marlborough's War', *Huntington Library Quarterly* (1951), xv.

Dickinson, H. T.: 'Henry St John and the Struggle for the Leadership of the Tory Party, 1702–1714'. Unpublished Newcastle University Ph.D. thesis, 1967–68.

——, 'The Attempt to Assassinate Harley, 1711', *History Today* (1965), xv.

——, 'Henry St John: a Reappraisal of the Young Bolingbroke', *Journal of British Studies* (1968), vii, no. 2.

——, 'Bolingbroke's attack on Pope in 1746', *Notes and Queries* (1969), vol. ccxiv, New Series, xvi.

——, 'Henry St John, Wootton Bassett and the General Election of 1708,' *Wiltshire Archaeological and Natural History Magazine* (1969), lxiv.

Dickson, P. G. M.: *The Financial Revolution in England*. London, 1967.

Dudley, G. A.: 'The Early Life of Henry St John'. Unpublished University of California Ph.D. thesis, 1955–6.

Egremont, Lord: 'Bolingbroke on Dalliance', *The Spectator* (17 June 1966).

Evans, A. W.: *Warburton and the Warburtonians.* London, 1951.

Faber, Richard: *Beaconsfield and Bolingbroke.* London, 1961.

Feiling, Keith: *A History of the Tory Party 1640-1714.* Oxford, 1924.

——, *The Second Tory Party 1714–1832.* London, 1938.

Fieldhouse, H. N.: 'A note on the Negotiations for the Treaty of Utrecht', *American Historical Review* (1935), xl, no. 2.

——, 'St John and Savoy in the War of the Spanish Succession', *English Historical Review* (1935), l.

——, 'Bolingbroke's Share in the Jacobite Intrigue of 1710–14', *ibid.* (1937), lii.

——, 'Oxford, Bolingbroke, and the Pretender's Place of Residence, 1711–14', *ibid.*

——, 'Bolingbroke and the d'Iberville Correspondence, August 1714–June 1715', *ibid.*

——, 'Bolingbroke and the Idea of Non-Party Government', *History* (1938–39), xxiii.

Fletcher, Dennis James: 'The Intellectual Relations of Lord Bolingbroke with France'. Unpublished University of Wales M.A. thesis, 1953.

——, 'The Fortunes of Bolingbroke in France in the Eighteenth Century', *Studies on Voltaire and the Eighteenth Century* (1966), xlvii.

——, 'Bolingbroke and the diffusion of Newtonianism in France', *ibid.* (1967), liii.

Foord, Archibald S.: *His Majesty's Opposition, 1714–1830.* Oxford, 1964.

Gwyn, W. B.: *The Meaning of the Separation of Powers.* New Orleans, 1965.

Hamilton, Elizabeth: *The Backstairs Dragon. A Life of Robert Harley, Earl of Oxford.* London. 1969.

Hanson, Laurence: *Government and the Press 1695–1763.* Oxford, 1936.

Harkness, Douglas: *Bolingbroke. The Man and His Career.* London, 1957.

Harris, George: *The Life of Lord Chancellor Hardwicke.* 3 vols., London, 1847.

Harrop, Robert: *Bolingbroke: A Political Study and Criticism.* London, 1884.

Hart, Jeffrey: *Viscount Bolingbroke. Tory Humanist.* London, 1965.

Hassall, Arthur: *Bolingbroke.* Revised ed., Oxford, 1915.

Hearnshaw, F. J. C. (ed.): *The Social and Political Ideas of some English Thinkers of the Augustan Age.* London, 1928.

Holmes, Geoffrey S.: 'The Commons' Division on "No Peace without Spain", 7 December 1711', *Bulletin of the Institute of Historical Research* (1960), xxxiii.

——, *British Politics in the Age of Anne.* London, 1967.

——, (ed.): *Britain after the Glorious Revolution, 1689–1714.* London, 1969.

——, and Speck, W. A.: 'The Fall of Harley in 1708 reconsidered', *English Historical Review* (1965), lxxx.

Hopkinson, M. R.: *Married to Mercury*. London, 1936.

Hunt, John: 'Henry St John, Lord Bolingbroke', *The Contemporary Review* (1869), x.

Hurn, Arthur Sydney: *Voltaire et Bolingbroke*. Paris, 1915.

Jackman, Sydney Wayne, *Man of Mercury, An Appreciation of the Mind of Henry, Viscount Bolingbroke*. London, 1965.

James, D. G.: *The Life of Reason*. London, 1949.

Jones, George Hilton: *The Mainstream of Jacobitism*. Cambridge, Massachusetts, 1954.

Kluxen, Kurt: *Das Problem der Politischen Opposition*. Freiburg/München, 1956.

Kramnick, Isaac: 'An Augustan Reply to Locke: Bolingbroke on Natural Law and the Origin of Government', *Political Science Quarterly* (1967), lxxxii.

——, 'Augustan Politics and English Historiography: The Debate on the English Past, 1730–35', *History and Theory* (1967), vi.

——, *Bolingbroke and His Circle*. Cambridge, Massachusetts, 1968.

Kronenberger, Louis: *Kings and Desperate Men*. London, 1942.

Laprade, William T.: *Public Opinion and Politics in Eighteenth Century England*. New York, 1936.

Leland, John: *A View of the Principal Deistical Writers*. 2 vols., London, 1808.

Lovejoy, Arthur O.: *The Great Chain of Being*. Cambridge, Massachusetts, 1936.

Ludwig, Walter: *Lord Bolingbroke und die Aufklärung*. Heidelberg, 1928.

Macdonald, W. L.: *Pope and His Critics*. London, 1951.

Macknight, Thomas: *The Life of Henry St John, Viscount Bolingbroke*. London, 1863.

Mahon, Lord: *History of England from the Peace of Utrecht*. London, 1836.

Mansfield, Harvey C.: *Statesmanship and Party Government*. Chicago, 1965.

Merrill, Walter McIntosh: *From Statesman to Philosopher, A Study in Bolingbroke's Deism*, New York, 1949.

Michael, Wolfgang: *England under George I*. 2 vols., London, 1936–39.

Morgan, W. T.: 'Queen Anne's Canadian Expedition of 1711', *Bulletin of the Departments of History . . . in Queen's University, Kingston, Ontario* (1928), lvi.

Nadel, George H.: 'New Light on Bolingbroke's *Letters on History*', *Journal of the History of Ideas* (1962), xxiii.

Oliver, F. S.: *The Endless Adventure*. 3 vols., London, 1930–35.

Owen, John B.: *The Rise of the Pelhams*. London, 1957.

Petrie, Charles, *Bolingbroke*. London, 1937.

——, 'Bolingbroke and his influence on English Politics', *Quarterly Review* (1951), 289.

Plumb, J. H.: *Sir Robert Walpole*. 2 vols., London, 1956–60.

——, *The Growth of Political Stability in England*. London, 1967.

Pocock, J. G. A.: *The Ancient Constitution and the Feudal Law*. Cambridge, 1957.

——, 'Machiavelli, Harrington, and English Political Ideologies in the Eighteenth Century', *William and Mary Quarterly* (1965), xxii.

Radice, Sheila: 'Bolingbroke in France', *Notes and Queries* (1939), clxxvii.

Ratchford, Fannie E.: 'Pope and the *Patriot King*', *Texas Studies in English* (1926), vi.

Realey, Charles B.: *The Early Opposition to Sir Robert Walpole 1720–1727*. Philadelphia, 1931.

Rémusat, Charles de: *L'Angleterre au dix-huitième siècle*. 3 vols., Paris, 1856.

Robertson, Charles Grant: *Bolingbroke*. Historical Association pamphlet, G.5, 1947.

Robertson, J. M.: *Bolingbroke and Walpole*. London, 1919.

Salomon, Felix: *Geschichte des letzten Ministeriums Königin Annas von England*. Gotha, 1894.

Shackleton, Robert: 'Montesquieu, Bolingbroke, and the Separation of Powers', *French Studies* (1949), iii.

——, *Montesquieu, A Critical Biography*. Oxford, 1961.

Sichel, Walter: *Bolingbroke and His Times*. London, 1901–2.

Skelton, John: *The Great Lord Bolingbroke*. Edinburgh 1868.

Smallwood, Frank T.: 'Bolingbroke's Birthplace', *The Wiltshire Archaeological and Natural History Magazine* (1965), lx.

——, 'The Bolingbroke Inscriptions at Battersea', *Notes and Queries* (1968), ccxiii, New Series, xv.

Stephen, Leslie: *English Thought in the Eighteenth Century*. 2 vols., London, 1876.

Stevens, David H.: *Party Politics and English Journalism 1702–1742*. Menasha, Wisconsin, 1916.

Taylor, John George: *Our Lady of Batersey*. London, 1925.

Torrey, Norman L.: 'Bolingbroke and Voltaire – A Fictitious Influence', *Publications of the Modern Language Association of America* (1927), xlii.

——, *Voltaire and the English Deists*. New Haven, Connecticut, 1930.

Trevelyan, G. M.: 'The "Jersey" period of the negotiations leading to the Peace of Utrecht', *English Historical Review* (1934), xlix.

——, *England under Queen Anne*. 3 vols., London, 1930–34.

Turberville, A. S.: *The House of Lords in the XVIIIth Century*. Oxford, 1927.

Turner, Raymond: 'The Excise Scheme of 1733', *English Historical Review* (1927), xlii.

Vaucher, Paul: *La Crise du Ministère Walpole en 1733–1734*. Paris, 1924.

——, *Robert Walpole et la Politique de Fleury (1731–1742)*. Paris, 1924.

Ward, A. W.: 'Bolingbroke', in *Cambridge History of English Literature*, vol. ix. Cambridge, 1912.

Webb, M. I.: 'Portraits of Bolingbroke', *Country Life* (24 May 1956).

Williams, Basil: *Stanhope*. Oxford, 1932.

Williams, Kathleen: *Jonathan Swift and the Age of Compromise*. Kansas, 1959.

Addenda
The following studies, bearing directly on Bolingbroke's life and work, appeared after this book was in the press.

Dickinson, H. T.: 'Bolingbroke and *The Idea of a Patriot King*, 1749', *History Today* (Jan. 1970), xx.

Fletcher, Dennis James: '*Le Legislateur* and the Patriot King: A Case of Intellectual Kinship', *Comparative Literature Studies* (1969), vi.

Grainger, J. H.: 'The Deviations of Lord Bolingbroke', *Australian Journal of Politics and History* (1969), xv.

McInnes, Angus: *Robert Harley, Puritan Politician* (1970).

Rogers, Pat: 'Swift and Bolingbroke on Faction', *Journal of British Studies* (May 1970), ix.

Notes on Dates, Quotations and Abbreviations

During Bolingbroke's lifetime Britain used the Old Style of the Julian Calendar, while France used the New Style. In the text and notes it is assumed that the new year began on 1 January and not, as with the Old Style, on 25 March, but the Old Style is used for the years when Bolingbroke lived in England and the New Style for the years of his residence in France. Where there is likely to be any confusion dates are given in both styles.

In passages quoted from manuscripts the original spelling has been retained, though abbreviations have been extended and, very occasionally, the punctuation has been modernised where the sense would remain obscure. All the printed sources cited in the notes were published in London unless otherwise stated.

The following abbreviations have been used in the notes.

Add. MSS.	Additional Manuscripts
Aff. Étr. Corr. Pol. Angl.	Correspondance Politique: Angleterre, in Les Archives du Ministère des Affaires Étrangères, Paris
B.M.	British Museum
Baratier, *Lettres Inédites*	*Lettres Inédites de Bolingbroke à Lord Stair 1716–1720*, ed. Paul Baratier. Trévoux, 1939
Bull. Inst. Hist. Res.	*Bulletin of the Institute of Historical Research*
Burnet's History	*Bishop Burnet's History of His Own Time*. 2nd ed., Oxford, 1833
Chesterfield's Letters	*The Letters of Philip Dormer Stanhope, Fourth Earl of Chesterfield*, ed. Bonamy Dobrée. 6 vols., London, 1932
Commons Debates	Richard Chandler, *The History and Proceedings of the House of Commons*. London, 1742
Corr.	*The Letters and Correspondence of Henry St John, Lord Viscount Bolingbroke*, ed. Gilbert Parke. 4 vols., London, 1798

Coxe, *Horatio Walpole's Memoirs*	William Coxe, *Memoirs of Horatio, Lord Walpole.* 2 vols., 3rd ed., London, 1820
Coxe, *R. Walpole's Memoirs*	William Coxe, *Memoirs of the Life and Administration of Sir Robert Walpole, Earl of Orford.* 3 vols., London, 1798
E.H.R.	*English Historical Review*
Econ. Hist. Rev.	*Economic History Review*
Grimoard, *Lettres Historiques*	*Lettres Historiques, Politiques, Philosophiques . . . de Bolingbroke,* ed. P. H. Grimoard. 3 vols., Paris, 1808
Hanover MSS.	Niedersachsisches Staatsarchiv, Hanover. Calenberg Briefe Archiv, 24 England
H.M.C.	Historical Manuscripts Commission
Journal to Stella	Jonathan Swift's *Journal to Stella,* ed. Harold Williams. 2 vols., Oxford, 1948
Lord Hervey's Memoirs	*Some Materials Towards Memoirs of the Reign of King George II, by John, Lord Hervey,* ed. Romney Sedgwick. 3 vols., London, 1931
Lords Debates	Ebenezer Timberland, *The History and Proceedings of the House of Lords.* London, 1742
Lyttelton's Corr.	*Memoirs and Correspondence of George, Lord Lyttelton, from 1734 to 1773,* ed. Robert Phillimore. 2 vols., London, 1845
Marchmont Papers	*A Selection from the Papers of the Earls of Marchmont,* ed. G. H. Rose. 3 vols., London, 1831
Parl. Hist.	William Cobbett's *The Parliamentary History of England.* London, 1806–20
Pope's Corr.	*The Correspondence of Alexander Pope,* ed. George Sherburn. 5 vols., Oxford, 1956
P.R.O.	Public Record Office, London
Prussian MSS.	Deutsches Zentralarchiv, Merseburg, East Germany. Rep. XI, England. Dispatches of Bonet and Spanheim
Spence's Anecdotes	*Anecdotes, Observations and Characters of Books and Men collected from the conversation of Mr Pope and other eminent persons of his time by the Reverend Joseph Spence,* ed. S. W. Singer. New ed., London, 1964

Swift's Corr.   *The Correspondence of Jonathan Swift,* ed. F. Elrington
                                   Ball. 6 vols., London, 1910–14

Voltaire's Corr.   *Voltaire's Correspondence,* ed. Theodore Besterman.
                                   107 vols., Geneva, 1953–65

Works   *The Works of Lord Bolingbroke.* 4 vols., 1967
                                   reprint of the London 1844 edition

Index

In this index B = Bolingbroke